W0259579

India Emerging

About the Author

Veena Jha is the Director, Maguru Consultants Limited, U.K., and is currently engaged in working on issues related to trade, climate change, food security, effects of fiscal stimulus packages on employment at the global level and on inclusive growth issues. She was a visiting professorial fellow at Warwick University, U.K., and a Research Fellow at IDRC. She wrote this book during this period. She worked for the United Nations and its specialised organisations for over 20 years. She has published twelve books and served as an expert on several advisory boards in India and abroad.

India Emerging

The Reality Checks

VEENA JHA

ACADEMIC FOUNDATION
NEW DELHI

International Development Research Centre
Ottawa • Cairo • Montevideo • Nairobi • New Delhi

First published in 2012
by

ACADEMIC FOUNDATION
4772-73 / 23 Bharat Ram Road, (23 Ansari Road),
Darya Ganj, New Delhi - 110 002 (India).
Phones : 23245001 / 02 / 03 / 04.
Fax : +91-11-23245005.
E-mail : books@academicfoundation.com
www.academicfoundation.com

Co-published with the

INTERNATIONAL DEVELOPMENT RESEARCH CENTRE
PO Box 8500, Ottawa, ON K1G 3H9
Canada
E-mail: info@idrc.ca
www.idrc.ca

Cataloging in Publication Data--DK
Courtesy: D.K. Agencies (P) Ltd. <Docinfo@dkagencies.com>

Jha, Veena, 1959-
India emerging : the reality checks / Veena Jha.
p. cm.
Includes bibliographical references.
ISBN 9788171889525
ISBN 9781552505489 (e-book)

1. Economic development--India. 2. Informal sector (Economics)--India. 3. India.--Economic policy--1991- I. Title.

DDC 338.954 23

Typeset by Italics India, New Delhi.
Printed and bound in India.

Contents

Part II

Part III

List of Tables and Figures

TABLES

FIGURES

Preface

Three decades ago, if asked to draw lessons from the Indian development experience for some of the great development debates—democracy *versus* development, states *versus* markets, opportunities *versus* guarantees—the answer would have been straightforward: never do as India does. With the exception of a stubbornly persistent democracy, Indian economic performance had been unremarkable, and India remained the poster child for development policy choices gone wrong.[1]

Today, though, these questions have acquired a new relevance because India has something to offer after all. After nearly three decades of disappointing but not disastrous growth, famously dubbed the 'Hindu growth', it has in the following three decades posted solid growth of 6.5 per cent per year, and nearly 8 per cent in the last decade or so. As a result, poverty has declined measurably and nearly all indicators of social outcomes have improved substantially. And although it is struggling to get out of China's shadow, and despite Lord Meghnad Desai's dashing of Indian hopes and perhaps pretensions in his pronouncement that 'China will be a Great Power but India will just be a Great Democracy,' the buzz is that India is now becoming impossible to ignore. In fact, in the aftermath (if indeed the crisis is behind us) of the global financial crisis, with the prospects of the industrial countries heading south rapidly, India with its strong performance will attract even more attention.

With success and transformation, however, have come a new set of challenges, which Veena Jha in this book summarises correctly as the problem of making growth inclusive. Inequality—across states and regions, skill levels and sectors—has been rising, the writ of the state does not run

1. It is telling that in a famous paper authored by the Nobel Prize winner, Robert Lucas, as recently as 1988, India was chosen as the archetypal 'poor' country, the exemplar of underdevelopment.

in about 25 per cent of Maoist insurrection-afflicted India, the quality of essential public services has been deteriorating, and above all corruption seems to have crossed some *lakshman rekha* of tolerability. Analysing and making sense of these inter-related pathologies and coming up with some sensible solutions are the tasks that Veena Jha has set for herself in this ambitious, comprehensive and timely book.

It is commendable that instead of going down the well-trodden path of clichéd dichotomies—agriculture *versus* manufacturing or manufacturing *versus* services—Veena has identified a few sectors and issues that answer the question of inclusive growth but in a non-obvious manner. Each of the chapters provides a useful review of the academic literature to ground the subsequent discussion.

For example, there is an important chapter on inter-state migration and how it affects inter-state inequality. What is the effect of migration on inequality, on poverty reduction, and informal wage growth? In theory, migration should be an important channel that exercises a restraining influence on inequality and divergence. If one state does very well, labour should move to that state from other parts of the country in search of better opportunities, exerting an equalising effect on labour market outcomes. Veena sheds interesting empirical light on these questions.

The author has also been careful in illuminating the role and importance of gender issues. Amartya Sen famously and starkly characterised the gender problem as one of 'missing women'. Veena Jha examines whether economic growth has been good for women, noting the improvement in female labour force participation and declining fertility, and also the effect on poverty of having households headed by women. A section on the plight of widows in India is particularly intriguing.

Perhaps my favourite chapter in the book is on philanthropy in India. Here Veena Jha surveys the history of philanthropic giving in India going back to the *Rig Veda* down to Mahatma Gandhi; provides a taxonomy of charities, and presents some very interesting data on them. For example, it might come as a surprise to know that India has about 2 million to 3 million charities; that the Indian Government may be the largest source of funding for charities in India; that the percentage of registered charities is highest in Maharashtra (74%) and lowest in Tamil Nadu (47%); and that the number of employees in the charity sector almost equal (82%) of all Central government employees.

One clear theme that recurs through this book is the need for India to sustain high levels of economic growth to facilitate the famous trickle-down effect to the poor and vulnerable. The book also illustrates that the growth-equity debate is founded on a false dichotomy. As this book neatly shows, India needs sustained and high growth and a set of actions by the public, private and non-profit sectors to ensure trickle down and inclusiveness. Growth will prove to be politically unsustainable unless there is a widely shared perception that a wide cross-section has a reasonable shot at participating in it; it will also prove unsustainable if growth is seen as the result of a rigged system of rules. On the other hand, equity without growth has rarely in history proved to be a successful formula for economic advancement.

Veena Jha's well-researched and important book will serve to enrich the quality of debate on these difficult and pressing issues.

— Arvind Subramanian

Senior Fellow
Peterson Institute for International Economics
and Centre for Global Development

Introduction

The major challenge for India's development is inclusive growth. Growth has reduced poverty and improved the human condition in India. But economic gains of the middle and richer classes have been greater than those that went to the poorer sections of society. This is evident from the fact that reforms in areas such as telecommunications, banks, stock markets, airlines, trade and industrial policy have not been matched by agricultural and human development. India's industrialisation continues to be capital and knowledge intensive at a time when over 250 million people survive on less than a dollar a day. If India grows in this way, it will take a long time to eradicate poverty, illiteracy and malnutrition. Moreover, slow progress in human development in areas such as education and health will make it tougher for India to grow in the long run. Increased inequality in the initial phases of growth has been noted in both theoretical and empirical economic literature. In this sense, India's experience is no different from those of other countries. The big challenge for India is that being a democratic state, tolerance for inequality and poverty is rapidly diminishing as is shown by the increase in crime, naxalism and other socioeconomic problems. Nevertheless, it is instructive to briefly review economic literature before analysing India's growth experience.

Theoretical and Empirical Literature

The much discussed Kuznets hypothesis (1955) stated that economic growth and equality were related in a 'Converse U Curve'. At the early stages of economic growth, inequality increases; in the middle stages, inequality becomes stable and in the final stages, inequality decreases along with economic growth. This means, inequality rises until countries reach 'middle income status'.

Kaldor (1956) also thought that inequality in income distribution transfers wealth from the poor to the rich. Because the marginal savings rate of the rich is higher than that of the poor, wide gaps in income distribution would boost economic growth when growth and savings rates were positively correlated.

Adelman and Morris (1973) and Chenery and Syrquin (1975) mostly supported Kuznets' and Kaldor's hypothesis. However, Persson and Tabellini (1994) showed that there was a significantly negative correlation between inequality and growth in democratic countries. Atkinson (1995) had also shown that many European countries which had experienced increases in income inequality had also seen an increasing number of people suffering from poverty and social exclusion.

Sen (1983) cited such examples as Brazil, Mexico and South Korea, whose per capita GDPs are much higher than those of Sri Lanka and China. However, in terms of social development indicators, Sri Lanka and China are much further ahead than the other three countries. In fact, after the reforms of 1978 in China, the growth in life expectancy and the reduction of infant mortality rates have slowed down. Studies by Chen and Ravallion (2000), Deaton and Drèze (2002), Wade (2004) and Biswas and Sindzingre (2006) found that economic growth is not always related to reduced poverty or inequality. Rather, it can impoverish more people and widen gaps of inequality. Even Nobel Laureate Michael Spence (2009) stated that inequality often rises in the presence of growth.

However, Bruno *et al.* (1997) examine evidence concerning the relation between growth and distribution (equity), the effect of pro-growth policies on distribution and distribution on growth. They review a large volume of empirical research, including some of their own analyses. The results did not support Kuznets that growth is initially associated with inequality. Their study showed that many countries that are recovering from economic crisis have experienced rapid economic growth as well as equitable distribution, and some transitory economies have experienced decline in economic growth and worsening inequality. Solimano *et al.* (2000) said that countries which have been most successful in reducing poverty are those that have grown fastest. During the 1990s it was estimated that growth elasticity of poverty was between -2.0 to -3.0 (Adams, 2004; Chen and Ravaillon, 2000). However, estimates by Bhalla (2002) suggest that the earlier correct growth elasticity of poverty was around -5.0.

How does India's Experience Relate to these Theoretical and Empirical Evidence

How do these theories apply to India's growth experience. The size of India's middle class has quadrupled to almost 250 million people over the past 15-20 years.[1] If one looks at the economy as a whole, the consumer sector of the economy continues to prosper, spending power and modern consumer behaviour look set to 'trickle down' through the economy for decades.[2] Personal consumption accounts for just over 60 per cent of Indian GDP, making it increasingly comparable with a fully-developed Western economy. Thus it has been argued (for example Das, 2006) that India's 'boom' is intrinsically more durable than China's, noting that China's population is likely to peak around 2030, whereas India's will continue to grow, on current projections, till about 2065.

The miracle growth period of India, i.e., 2004-2009 has been broad-based and the laggard states which are also the most populous states such as Bihar and Uttar Pradesh have enjoyed high rates of growth (Aiyar, 2010). (See Table 1).

Four of the poorest states—Bihar (11.03%), Orissa (8.74%), Jharkhand (8.45%) and Chhattisgarh (7.35%)—now qualify as miracle economies, going by the international norm of 7 per cent growth. Uttar Pradesh grew at 6.29 per cent quite close to the miracle growth norm of 7 per cent.[3]

1. "An Increasingly Affluent Middle India Is Harder to Ignore", Knowledge@Wharton — *www.mynews.in*. Published on July 16, 2008.

2. Ibid.

3. Central Statistical Office, Government of India. *http://mospi.gov.in*

Table 1

Annual Growth (%) of Gross State Domestic Product

State	*2004-05*	*2005-06*	*2006-07*	*2007-08*	*2008-09*	*5-Year Average*
Gujarat	8.88	13.44	9.09	12.79	N.A.	11.05
Bihar	12.17	1.49	22.00	8.04	11.44	11.03
Kerala	9.97	9.17	11.10	10.42	N.A.	10.14
Haryana	8.64	9.37	14.20	9.35	8.02	9.92
Karnataka	9.85	13.53	7.33	12.92	5.08	9.74
Maharashtra	8.71	9.67	9.82	9.18	N.A.	9.34
Uttarakhand	12.99	5.66	9.84	9.37	8.67	9.31
Andhra Pradesh	8.15	10.24	11.16	10.62	5.53	9.14
Orissa	12.61	6.37	12.12	5.85	6.74	8.74
Tamil Nadu	11.45	11.89	11.29	4.41	4.55	8.72
Himachal Pradesh	7.56	8.54	9.20	8.59	N.A.	8.47
Jharkhand	15.21	2.79	12.53	6.18	5.52	8.45
Chhattisgarh	5.49	6.94	7.99	8.63	7.69	7.35
West Bengal	6.89	5.72	8.77	7.74	N.A.	7.28
Uttar Pradesh	5.40	5.25	7.18	7.16	6.46	6.29
Rajasthan	-1.85	6.89	11.81	7.33	7.12	6.25
Jammu & Kashmir	5.23	6.17	6.25	6.28	N.A.	5.98
Punjab	4.95	4.50	7.32	6.54	6.26	5.91
Assam	3.74	4.94	6.97	6.06	6.04	5.55
Madhya Pradesh	3.08	6.48	4.75	5.25	N.A.	4.89
All-India	7.47	9.52	9.75	9.01	6.70	8.49

Note: N.A.: Not Available.

Source: Central Statistical Organisation (CSO), Delhi, India.

This is not a case of a few sectors, or services driving growth, but rather of widespread growth, especially in poor states with large populations. Once these high growth rates had been achieved, government revenues also increased dramatically. Though fiscal deficits remain high, government spending on social sectors and welfare increased significantly. Thus programmes such as National Rural Employment Guarantee Scheme (NREGS), Bharat Nirman (infrastructure development programmes), Sarva Shiksha Abhiyan (SSA) (education for all), the farm loan waiver and enormous oil subsidies could be sustained (Aiyar, 2010). These were part of the trickle down policies of the government.

The widespread participation in the growth process is confirmed by the rapid rise in rural sales of motorcycles and branded consumer goods. Even stronger confirmation comes from the spread of the cellphone revolution. The rate of new cellphone connections has risen steadily to touch 12-18 million per month reaching 51.05 per cent of the population in terms of teledensity.[4] Hundreds of millions earlier excluded from telecom are now getting included.

As of September 2009, urban teledensity in Rajasthan (104.4%) and Orissa (101.59%) exceeded the national level (101.38%). Bihar and Jharkhand (99.41%) were almost on par, with Uttar Pradesh and Uttarakhand (88.13%) not far behind (Aiyar, 2010).

Analysing the Agents of Trickle Down: The Purpose of the Book

While rapid growth was substantially inclusive, India still has a burden of poverty to the extent of one-quarter to one-third of its population. Much more needs to be done and these growth miracle patches need to be sustained. India's high growth trajectory, which is essential for development, has become reasonably stable. The debate is not about whether India will grow at 6 per cent or at 4 per cent per annum. The debate is whether India will grow at 10 per cent or 8 per cent per annum. As *Economic Survey 2009-10* reveals, the Indian economy has been in recent times, to a large extent, affected by the happenings in developed economies because of its growing integration with a globalised world. The annual growth rate had reached 9.7 per cent in 2006-07, began sliding down to 9.2 per cent in 2007-08 and 6.7 per cent in 2008-09 and in (2009-2010) it was about 7.2 per cent.[5] This is a substantial achievement. However, poverty has not reduced especially in terms of absolute numbers.

There are certain factors which are instrinsic to the Indian economy's growth process which is inherently inimical to reducing poverty. These include the growth of its informal or unorganised sector, the huge

---

4. Statement by Telecom Regulatory Authority of India, (TRAI), *http://www.siliconindia.com/shownews/Teledensity_in_India_touches_5105_percent-nid-66647-cid—sid-.html*

5. *Economic Survey, 2009-10.*

differences in the rates of growth of different states, the increasing dependence on services, especially ITES and telecommunications for sustaining high growth rates. Additionally, development literature has thrown up gender disparity as a major cause of poverty in countries. These issues are examined in the book. Additionally, the book examines the measures adopted by both the private sector philanthropies and the government in the field of social development.

The book is divided into three parts. The first examines the sources of growth in the Indian economy and whether they can be effective agents of trickle down. The major thrust of growth in the Indian economy has been the IT, ITES sector and telecommunications. The two account for over 10-15 per cent of the GDP and if their output multipliers are correct (see Chapter 1), their share of the GDP is almost double. This sector has been growing at an average rate of well over 30 per cent over the last 15 years. A back of the envelope calculation shows that this sector therefore accounts for roughly half to two-thirds of the growth rate of India. Hence, this sector is an intrinsic part of India's growth miracle. Given that its share of growth is so high, it must also be an important agent of trickle down to alleviate poverty. However, while its share of GDP is very high, its share in overall employment, even using the employment multiplier is no more than 1-2 per cent of the total labour force.

Services, particularly computer software and hardware industries together accounted for 35.49 per cent of the total FDI in India between 2000 and 2007 (Sarker, 2009). Even in this period of economic recession (2007-onwards), India's services sector expanded at a faster pace in the first seven months of the fiscal year (2009-10) compared to (2008-09).[6] This is despite the fact that India was hit by the worldwide recession in this sector.[7] It is argued that high technology industries, especially IT and ITES have not yet been able to generate significant linkages with the rest of the Indian economy. Hence, services and particularly IT and telecommunications led growth process has little potential to be an agent of

6. Confederation of Indian Industry, Survey of 33 Service Sectors, December 2009, *http://www.calcuttanews.net/story/579570*

7. Ibid.

transmission of growth to the poorest section of society. In other words these sectors can see little trickle down. Chapter 1 analyses in detail the multiplier growth and employment effects of the miracle growth sectors (i.e., IT and telecommunications) of the Indian economy. It also identifies the poverty alleviation aspects of these two miracle sectors and policies to strengthen their interlinkages with the rest of the economy. These interlinkages would in turn improve the play of agents which are critical to poverty alleviation. In fact the direct contribution of IT and ITES as well as telecommunication to poverty alleviation may be low, but the indirect contribution when these technologies start becoming general purpose technologies (GPTs) can be quite large. Thus, for example if these technologies are used in providing better governance and reducing corruption, their contribution to poverty alleviation will indeed be significant. Further if the surplus generated from this sector is used in philanthropic institutions for social development purposes, or the tax raised by the government is used for social development purposes, its contribution to poverty alleviation will not be insignificant. The rise of IT philanthropies and their new *modus operandi* is examined in Chapter 5.

The period of high growth in India especially between 1991-2001 was associated with a high level of inter-state income inequalities (Dhindsa and Bhatia, 2007). As the Central government's role in funding the state governments became less, the states needed to attract private investment for furthering their development. Well governed states attracted more funds while the laggards stayed behind. However, the laggard states have also seen some 'trickle up' in the last four or five years largely because of better governance (Aiyar, 2010). While the rapid growth in the poorer states may have decreased interstate inequality, it has to be noted that the poorer states started from less than a quarter of the per capita income of the richer states. Interstate inequality was also to some extent been compensated by interstate migration. Chapter 2 explores how interstate variations in growth promoted interstate migration and at the same time trickled down the benefits of growth to poorer states. However, it also makes a plea for the development of middle-sized towns or Tier-II towns which will relieve the infrastructural pressures in large metros and also spread the benefits of economic growth. This phenomenon is already happening in India.

The development of Tier-II cities in India is presaged on industrial growth. India's industrialisation is beginning to demand more and more land (Euro RSCG, 2007; Ernst & Young, 2008). Industrial land acquisition needs to be based on the consent of the local people. Acquisition needs to be preceded by compensation and welfare measures that render the acquisition of land for industrial purposes a developmental endeavour. Fertile double cropped land needs to be largely left for cultivation. The current laws give the government substantial powers to acquire land.[8] Forced land acquisition by the government has led to violent unrest in some parts of India.[9] Land acquisition has been successful in areas where developers have worked with state governments and the local people for gaining consent by attempting to uplift their human condition. States like Tamil Nadu, Andhra Pradesh, Gujarat and Maharashtra have tried to streamline some of these procedures at the sub-national level (Mukherji, 2005). Investment-friendly states are able to craft developmental bureaucracies that work more effectively for the local people and investors (Bhide *et al.*, 2005). The processes need to be streamlined in the poorer states too. This will undoubtedly lead to the development of Tier-II towns which will also relieve the infrastructural pressures of inter-state migration. The emerging middle class is also to be found in Tier-II towns rather than metro cities of India. Thus, the policy prescriptions of Chapter 2 are presaged on how middle-sized towns should be developed.

The second part of the book focusses on the sectors that have largely been bypassed by the growth process. While these sectors and sections of society are not the epicentre of India's growth process, nevertheless growth dynamics and interlinkages have not left them untouched.

An examination of India's economic growth process shows that it has more or less bypassed the agriculture sector in the 1990s.[10] According to most estimates, 50-70 per cent of India's population is dependent on

8. The Land Acquisition (Amendment) Bill, 2007, *http://www.dolr.nic.in/LABill2007.pdf*

9. "Recent Unrest in Andal, West Bengal: Site of Aerotropolis", April 18, 2010, *http://sanhati.com/excerpted/2277/*

10. Dholakia (2007). Also Arjun Sengupta Report on the Unorganised Sector, 2007.

agriculture either directly or indirectly. Most of the labour in this sector works informally (Bhalla, 2010). Hence, the plight of the informal sector would be of critical importance in determining whether this sector has been an agent for trickling up growth. Furthermore even in the industrial sector, India's trade union laws increase the propensity of Indian industry to remain capital intensive, resulting in unemployment and increased employment in the unorganised sector. The textile industry, which is the largest industry after agriculture, has managed to create some such linkages, but the availability of local inputs makes it almost entirely self-sufficient, so these linkages are not dynamic, rendering them largely inefficient. Furthermore, 80 per cent of the jobs in the textile industry have been outsourced to the informal sector.[11] In the services sector too, a large proportion of the employment is informal. This implies that one of the important indicators of social development of the Indian economy would be the state of the informal sector. Equally, economic growth should be reflected in improvements in income and asset formation in the informal sector. It is also important to analyse the triggers which result in the maximum gains for the informal sector. Policy could thus be oriented to improve the play of these factors to improve the lot of the informal sector. These issues are analysed in detail in Chapter 3. It is hoped that the policies identified in Chapter 3 would be an integral part of a strategy of inclusive growth and would help achieve poverty alleviation more rapidly. In other words, the trickle up story should come from the informal sector.

It is also important in a growing economy to examine the plight of women who constitute one half of India's population. It is argued that a reduction of gender disparity leads to an increase in the rate of economic growth, which, in turn, is poverty reducing. This is because greater gender equality enables women to take up income-earning opportunities, and participate in the growth process (Klasen, 1999). Furthermore, gender inequality in access to education may hinder a reduction in fertility and infant mortality (Balatchandirane, 2007). This issue is examined in detail in Chapter 4. This chapter also evaluates various policy options zeroing in

11. "Economic Growth and Social Inequality: Does the Trickle Down Effect Really Take Place?". *www.ojs.library.ubc.ca*

on those that would result in the maximum social benefit, given the cultural context of the Indian economy. The gender dimensions of the Indian economy would also reflect how growth has trickled up from the grassroots. These issues are examined in Chapter 4.

The third section of the book deals with an examination of the schemes and policies for 'trickling down' the benefits of economic growth to the poor. The so-called growth elasticity of poverty reduction is much higher in China than in India because the same one per cent growth rate reduces poverty in India by much less than it does in China (Bardhan, 2010). A 2002 study of Dutt and Ravallion that compared the Indian provinces has pointed out that the growth elasticity of poverty depends on the initial distribution of land and human capital. This elasticity is low in high-growth states such as Maharashtra and Karnataka, and high in states such as Kerala and West Bengal (Dutt and Ravallion, 2002). A recent World Bank study shows that land distribution inequalities play a relatively insignificant role in development in comparison to inequalities in human capital (Do and Levchenko, 2009). It is these inequalities, i.e., primarily education, health and income-earning opportunities, that private philanthropy or social development schemes of the government seek to correct.

Recognising the unequal growth which India has seen, where a very small number of high net worth individuals account more than one-fourth of India's GDP, it is incumbent on them and the government to help the process of poverty alleviation. India has a long established tradition of philanthropy. The number of wealthy Indians has been rising fast over the last decade, by 11 per cent every year since 2000, possibly the fastest pace in the world, to more than 115,000 now. However, philanthropy in India probably totalled about $7.5 billion in 2009, according to the study by Bain & Co., equivalent to about 0.6 per cent of the country's GDP.[12] While this is higher than Brazil's 0.3 per cent and rival China's 0.1 per cent, but it falls way short of the 2.2 per cent in the United States and 1.3 per cent in Britain.[13] Most Indians have no qualms about giving cash to family, friends,

12. Asian Philanthropy News Digest 03/18/10. *http://www.asianphilanthropyforum.org/india/index.html*

13. Ibid.

household staff and religious institutions, but this form of giving needs to be channelled to the most needy households. The wealthiest social class has the lowest level of giving, just 1.6 per cent of household income, which palls when compared to billionaire investor Warren Buffett, who has given away some 82 per cent of his net worth.[14] This could be for a variety of reasons including onerous processes for obtaining tax breaks for charitable donations and a deep-seated suspicion of what charitable organisations really do with the money. Further, accumulation of wealth is a fairly recent phenomenon in India and many fear that this phenomenon may be reversible. However, educated professionals turned businessmen such as Azim Premji of WIPRO (a famous IT firm) and telecom tycoons such as Sunil Mittal (Bharati Telecommunications) have set up new forms of philanthropy. Such high-profile private foundations have led to greater organisation in the NGO landscape.[15] Philanthropy and the NGO sector as agents of social development is analysed in Chapter 5.

The Indian government also acknowledges the critical role of philanthropies and the non-governmental sector in India's development. To quote from the Budget Speech 2010 of the Finance Minister, Mr Pranab Mukherjee: 'With development and economic reforms, the focus of economic activity has shifted towards the non-government actors, bringing into sharper focus the role of government as an enabler. "An enabling government does not try to deliver directly to the citizens everything that they need. Instead it creates an enabling ethos so that individual enterprise and creativity can flourish. Government concentrates on supporting and delivering services to the disadvantaged sections of the society".'[16] There are an estimated 2.5 million non-profit organisations in India, and about half of all donations in the country go to religious, sports and cultural organisations.[17] A huge 65 per cent of donations comes from the Central and state governments, with a focus on disaster relief. A large amount also comes from foreign organisations. Only 10 per cent comes from individuals and corporates, in sharp contrast to the United States, where 75 per cent of

14. Ibid.

15. Ibid.

16. Budget Speech presented to the Parliament by the Finance Minister, Mr Pranab Mukherjee on 28th February 2010.

17. *Asian Philanthropy News Digest op.cit.*

charitable giving is from individuals and corporates.[18] Models of interaction between philanthropy, NGO and the government in delivering social services is studied in detail in Chapter 5. This chapter also examines how the NGO sector can be made more effective in delivering social services.

While philanthropy may be important, it is the government that can provide its citizens with basic needs through employment generation programmes, land reforms, extending credit to the poor, crop insurance, rural roads, rural housing, rural water supply, rural electrification, universalising primary education, comprehensive health care system, labour welfare etc. Without government intervention, it is impossible to have egalitarian growth. It is natural for market-driven growth to only occur in certain areas, which may be determined either by geography or sector. The increase in products and/or services in those areas either create a demand for domestic consumption or for export. Ever since recession has set in, prices of consumer items have been increasing at an accelerated rate and it means a substantial portion of the incomes of the poor at large is taken away to meet basic needs and this makes the ultimate distribution of national income more skewed. The incidence of unemployment has been increasing because of severe recession in the countries that have been buyers of India's goods and services. Many of the BPOs and call centres have closed down or shifted elsewhere. Moreover, the rate of growth of employment opportunities has plummeted to just one per cent. The emphasis has been on increasing labour productivity or getting a smaller number of workers produce more and more surplus value. While manufacturing sector seems to have recovered and its rate of growth that declined from 14.9 per cent in 2006-07 to 10.3 per cent in 2007-08 and 3.2 per cent in 2008-09, it had gone up to 8.9 per cent in 2010; the agricultural sector on which almost 60 per cent of the population depends for its livelihood has grown very little. The rate of growth of agricultural production has declined from 4.7 per cent in 2007-08 to 1.6 per cent in 2008-09 and during 2010 it is was negative, i.e., -0.2 per cent.[19]

---

18. Ibid.

19. *Economic Survey 2009-10*, Planning Commission, Government of India.

A recent study from the UN says that in 2008-09 alone as many as 34 million people were pushed below the poverty line. According to the figures of the last Census, between 1991 and 2001, 8 million farmers were forced to quit agricultural sector and seek sources of livelihood elsewhere. In 2008, in spite all the efforts of the government to lessen the incidence of indebtedness, the major factor behind the suicides, 16,196 farmers ended their lives. Thus, between 1997 and 2008, 199,132 farmers took their lives (Sarker, 2009). In this situation the major programmes of the government such as National Rural Employment Guarantee Act (NREGA), Sarva Siksha Abhiyan (SSA) (education for all), the National Rural Health Mission (NRHM), Nutrition for All, assume special significance. An examination of the government programmes and how they have helped alleviate poverty is the subject of Chapter 6.

Finally, the book sums up the policy recommendations from the earlier chapters pointing to the future growth scenario of the Indian economy. On the basis of confirmed high growth rates, the book points to a prioritisation of issues and policies which can accelerate trickle down. The policies suggested by each of the individual chapters which are self-standing in their own way are however interlinked in the conclusions.

References

Adams, Richard H. (2004). "Economic Growth, Inequality and Poverty: Estimating the Growth Elasticity of Poverty", *World Development* 32(12): 1989-2014.

Adelman, I.G. and C.T. Morris (1973). *Economic Growth and Social Equity in Developing Countries*. Stanford, USA: Stanford University Press.

Aiyar, Swaminathan S. Anklesaria (2010). "Fast Growth Trickles up from the States". *Economic Times Bureau Report*, January 6. India.

Atkinson, Anthony B. (1995). "Income Distribution in OECD Countries: Evidence from Luxemburg Income Study", *OECD Social Policy Studies* No. 18. Paris.

Balatchandirane, G. (2002). *Gender Discrimination in Education and Economic Development*, Institute of Developing Economies, Japan External Trade Organisation, *http://www.ide.go.jp/English/Publish/Download/Vrf/pdf/426.pdf*

Bardhan, P. (2010). *Awakening Giants, Feet of Clay: Assessing the Economic Rise of China and India*. Princeton University Press.

Bhalla, Surjit S. (2002). *Imagine there is No Country: Poverty, Inequality and Growth in the Era of Globalization*. Washington DC: Institute for International Economics.

———. (2010). "India's Economy: Performances and Challenges, Essays in Honour of Montek Singh Ahluwalia", *Indian Economic Growth: Three Puzzles*. February 10. New Delhi: O[X]US Research & Investments.

Bhide, Shashanka, Rajesh Chadha and Kaliappa Kalirajan (2005). "Growth Interdependence among Indian States: An Exploration", *Asia-Pacific Development Journal* 12(2), December.

Biswas, Rongili and Alice Sindzingre (2006). "Trade Openness, Poverty and Inequality in India: Literature and Empirics at the Sub-National Level", Paper presented at the International Conference on the *Indian Economy in the Era of Financial Globalization.* Paris, September 28-29.

Bruno, Michael, Martin Ravallion and Lyn Squire (1997). "Equity and Growth in Developing Countries: Old and New Perspectives on the Policy Issues", in Vito Tanzi and Ke-Young Chu (eds), *Income Distribution and High Quality Growth*. pp.117-50. Cambridge: MIT Press.

Chen, S. and M. Ravallion (2000). *How did the World's Poor Fare in the 1990s*. Development Research Group. Washington: World Bank.

Chenery, H. and M. Syrquin (1975). *Patterns of Development 1950-1970*. London: Oxford University Press.

Das, G. (2006). "The Indian Model (Economic Development)", *Foreign Affairs* 85(4), July–August 2006.

Deaton, Angus and Jean Drèze (2002). "Poverty and Inequality in India: A Reexamination", *Economic and Political Weekly*: 3729-48. (September 7th).

Dhindsa, Paramjeet Kaur and Seozy Bhatia (2007). "Growth and Poverty in India: An Analysis of Interstate Differences". *https://editorialexpress.com/cgi-bin/conference, India.*

Dholakia, Bakul H. (2007). "Sources of India's Accelerated Growth and the Vision of Indian Economy in 2020", *Indian Economic Journal* 49(4).

Do, Quy-Toan and Andrei Levchenko (2009). "Trade, Inequality, and the Political Economy of Institutions", *Journal of Economic Theory* 114(4): 1489–520.

Dutt, G. and M. Ravallion. (2002). "Has India's Post–Reform Economic Growth Left the Poor Behind", *Journal of Economic Perspectives* (Summer): 80-108. Nashville.

Ernst & Young (2008). "The Dhoni Effect: Rise of Small Town India", *Ernst & Young,* March.

Euro RSCG (2007). "The Bunty Syndrome", *Euro RSCG India*. October.

Kaldor, N. (1956). "Alternative Theories of Distribution", *Review of Economic Studies* XXIII: 83-100.

Klasen, Stephan (1999). "Does Gender Inequality Reduce Growth and Development? Evidence from Cross-Country Regressions", *Policy Research Report on Gender and Development Working Paper Series*, No. 7, November 1999, The World Bank Development Research Group/Poverty Reduction and Economic Management Network.

Kuznets, S. (1955). "Economic Growth and Economic Inequality", in Mitchell A. Seligson and John T. Passé-Smith (eds.), *Development and Underdevelopment*. Colorado: Lynne Rienner Publishers. 1998. pp.43-55.

Mukherji, Rahul (2005). "The State, Economic Growth, and Development in India", *India Review* 4(5), April.

Persson, T. and G. Tabellini (1994). "Is Inequality Harmful for Growth? Theory and Evidence", *American Economic Review* 84: 600-21, *Journal of Economic Literature*. New York. F22, F40.

Sarker, Kanchan (2009). "Economic Growth and Social Inequality: Does The Trickle Down Effect Really Take Place", *Journal of Marxism and Interdisciplinary Inquiry* 3(1): 42-60. (October). Grant MacEwan College.

Sen, A. (1983). "Economics and the Family", *Asian Development Review* 1.

Solimano, Andres, Eduardo Aninat and Nancy Birdsall (2000). *Distributive Justice and Economic Development: The Case of Chile and Developing Countries*. Ann Arbor: University of Michigan Press.

Spence, M. (2009). *Report of the Growth Commission*. Jointly hosted by DFID, World Bank.

Wade, R. (2004). "Is Globalization Reducing Poverty and Inequality?", *World Development* 32(4): 567-89.

Part I

1 Role of ICTs and its Trickle-Down Effects on India's Economic Emergence

Introduction

Two technologies which have dominated India's economic emergence and made it a global player are information technology (IT) and mobile telephony. In fact both may be described as general purpose technologies (GPTs) which affect an economy and its global interaction profoundly. Wikipedia describes GPTs as great leaps of innovation that can affect an entire economy (usually at a national or global level). Unlike traditional technologies, which economists view as a smooth advancement, GPTs are drastic advancements that redefine society. Examples are the steam engine, railroad, electricity, electronics, the automobile, the computer and the internet and mobile telephony.

India has the cheapest internet and mobile access at the global level. Among its 500 million mobile users in 2010 which was growing at the rate of over 10 million a month, roughly a quarter use mobiles for their internet connection. As 3G technology spreads in India and is used in large numbers, internet penetration which stood at only 3 per cent *versus* 50 per cent mobile penetration in 2010 is likely to increase dramatically. Along with an almost unlimited supply of workers and the huge potential for widespread use, ICT has the potential to work like a GPT in the Indian context.

The information technology and information technology enabled sector (IT/ITES) accounted for over 6.4 per cent of India's GDP (2010) up from about 1.2 per cent a decade ago. Another estimate of computer-related services and communication services shows that these together account for nearly 9 per cent of GDP (DIT and NCAER, 2010). It earned the country about US $59 billion of foreign exchange in 2010—a crucial commodity for India—and directly employed about 2 million people. In the composition of India's exports of goods and services, it grossed by far the largest export revenue. According to the Ministry of Labour and Employment, India's IT/ ITES sector employs 12 per cent of the private sector workforce, making it the sector's biggest employer (NASSCOM, 2010). The dominant share of the ICT sector in the Indian economy is borne out by its size, which is about 60 per cent that of all registered manufacturing activities and exceeds the combined size of the banking and insurance sectors (DIT and NCAER, 2010). The output multiplier for computer-related services is 2.1 (DIT and NCAER, 2010).

The telecom sector in 2009 grossed about US $25 billion in terms of revenue of which 90 per cent was accounted for by the mobile telephony sector. Indian telecom service sector contributed approximately 2 per cent of the GDP in FY 2008-09 and its contribution was expected to rise further. Teledensity grew from a mere 1.3 per cent in 1995 to over 50 per cent as of April 2010. Despite the significant volumes and growth story, India still had over 500 million addressable population. This provides a huge opportunity as well as challenge for the operators and telecom sector as a whole. Due to hyper competition (approximately 8-9 operators in each circle) and the dynamics of the market, India has one of the lowest tariffs globally (PricewaterhouseCoopers, 2010).

The Indian IT and mobile telephony sector is recognised as a global phenomenon for its economic contribution to both India and the global economy. While the role of IT and mobiles on the Indian economy may be profound, a related issue that is addressed by this chapter is whether it trickled down to the poor in such a way that it increased their capacity to generate incomes and reduce poverty. The real trickle down of the IT sector is not simply through software and hi-tech services, but it is through socially relevant products and services, community initiatives, human resource development, education, health and women's empowerment.

This chapter examines the role of both IT/ITES and mobile telephony services in promoting the trickle down of India's high growth rates. The first section of the chapter focusses on how IT/ITES could act as a GPT to fuel India's growth process. The second section analyses the effects of e-readiness, a proxy of ICT usage on poverty in different states of India. The third section looks at secondary studies for an analysis of multiplier effects of ICT. The fourth section analyses the trickle-down effects of mobile telephony. The last section concludes with the potential and real socioeconomic effects of the two technologies on India.

I

Is IT a GPT in India

The Theoretical Basis of a GPT

GPTs are radical new ideas or techniques that have the potential to impact many industries in an economy. Bresnahan and Trajtenberg (1995) identified three key characteristics of GPTs: commonness (they are used as inputs by many downstream industries); technological dynamism (inherent potential for technical improvements); and innovational complementarities with other forms of advancement (meaning that the productivity of R&D in downstream industries increases as a consequence of innovation in the GPT) (Laursen *et al.*, 2002).

India's recent ICT 'revolution' can be seen to be one such GPT, since today, computers and related equipment are used in several industries and in a number of services of the economy. ICTs have also displayed a substantial level of technological dynamism spurring not only radical improvement in computational capacity, but also a successive wave of new technologies (ranging from the semiconductor to the internet). Moreover, ICTs have seriously facilitated new ways of organising firms, including the decentralisation of decision-making and team production (Milgrom and Roberts, 1990; Brynjolfsson and Hitt, 2000; Bresnahan *et al.*, 2002). Thereby, ICTs have clearly exhibited innovational complementarities with other forms of advancement. As India was starting from a much lower level of IT-adoption, the potential gains would be expected to be very high. In fact, countries such as India have leapfrogged over older, more expensive approaches such as Electronic Data Interchange, which represent significant legacy investments in countries such as the US (Laursen *et al.*, 2002).

Bresnahan and Trajtenberg (1995) point to the importance of the match between GPTs and specific institutions that facilitate or hinder GPTs in playing out their roles as engines of growth. If institutions show a disinterest in new technologies, an economy with the 'wrong' institutions may prove inadequate for supporting GPTs, including the application industries. This sector has been marked by an absence of regulation in the Indian economy, even being exempted from corporate taxes. Critics claim that this absence of regulation could have had a beneficial facilitating effect on the ICT sector (NASSCOM, 2010).

To analyse the contribution of information and communication technology (ICT) to economic growth, Schreyer (2000) used a well-established growth accounting framework and considered three ways in which ICT can influence economic growth:

1. ICT production: The role of ICT producers on the economy's total value added or GDP. Using this parameter, the contribution of ICT to the Indian GDP has increased from less than 1 per cent in 2000 to over 6 per cent in 2010. The growth rate of this sector has been over 30 per cent and this growth has contributed about 2 percentage points to GDP growth (Nasscom, 2010).

2. ICT as capital input: This approach focusses on the importance of computers and information technology as an input in other industries. This approach treats ICT capital goods as all other types of capital goods. In India too, there are strong complementarities between the IT sector and other sectors. Examples of areas where increased efficiency have been observed include: accounting, procurement, inventory management and production operations (Bhatnagar and Schware, 2000). In the context of complementarities, it is also important to recognise that these effects are not just in terms of cost savings. IT implementation may enhance the quality of service beyond anything that is feasible through other methods (Desai, 2000). Furthermore, depending on who the 'customers' are, the benefits may accrue to a broad cross-section of the population. Improved

efficiency in the stock market as a result of automated trading and settlement may benefit a small section of the population (though the indirect benefits of greater capital market efficiency may be broader). The use of IT in banking may impact only the middle classes. However, the computerisation of the Indian Railways' reservation system has had tremendous benefits for the masses who use this mode of transportation (Singh, 2002).

Information processing may enhance efficiency in agriculture as well as in manufacturing. While individual farmers cannot make IT investments, agricultural cooperatives can provide the institutional framework that allows farmers to benefit. For example, Chakravarty (2000) gives the example of IT use at milk collection centres in cooperative dairies. This permits faster and safer testing, better quality control, quicker and more accurate payments to farmers and time savings for farmers in their deliveries. The falling cost of information processing means that such success stories can potentially be widely replicated. The second impact is in the communication of information. Here there are a number of successful case studies. Farmers and fishermen can receive weather forecasts, market price quotes, advice on farming practices and specific training. Offers to buy or sell livestock, or other two-way communications are also possible. Some of this information dissemination and exchange is best done through voice media, while other types require the capabilities of the internet. Some evidence suggests, not surprisingly, that richer farmers and fishermen, as well as middlemen, are faster adopters of such technologies, but falling access costs has helped to broaden the base of these benefits (The Economist, 2001).

3. ICT as a catalyser: Part of the discussion about the new economy is based on the claim that ICTs produced benefits go beyond those pertaining to investors and owners. In fact, in addition to their direct (and remunerated) contribution to output growth, ICTs generate spillovers or free benefits that exceed the direct returns to ICT capital. Such positive externalities are always characterised by a discrepancy between a private investor's rate of return and the

rate of return for society as a whole. In other words, ICT equipment generates benefits above and beyond those reflected in its measured income share. Thus, as GPTs improve they spread throughout the economy, bringing about general productivity gains. The use of IT in rural banking and microfinance, through pilot schemes such as the InfoTech Smart Card project is encouraging. Handheld computers and smart cards can substantially reduce the costs of making loans, as well as monitoring them. Reducing these transactions costs may turn out to be critical for the scalability and sustainability of microfinance schemes. These benefits could be classified as indirect spillover effects (Singh, 2002).

Anecdotal Evidence on the Widespread Use of ICT in India

In a country like India, which has huge governance deficits, IT also offers a way of changing the way business can be done by governments. E-governance is at its initial stages in terms of governance but there are numerous examples of successful pilot e-governance programmes (Singh, 2003). These include:

- Computer-aided registration of land deeds and stamp duties in Andhra Pradesh, reducing reliance on brokers and possibilities for corruption.
- Computerisation of rural local government offices in Andhra Pradesh for delivery of statutory certificates of identity and landholdings, substantially reducing delays.
- Computerised checkpoints for local entry taxes in Gujarat, with data automatically sent to a central database, reducing opportunities for local corruption.
- Consolidated bill payment sites in Kerala, allowing citizens to pay bills under 17 different categories in one place, from electricity to university fees.
- E-mail requests for repairs to basic rural infrastructure such as hand pumps, reducing reliance on erratic visits of government functionaries.

In addition to using internet directly, franchises of low-cost rural internet kiosks for accessing government services have been organised by Drishtee in Madhya Pradesh. It is important to note that once internet access is available, its benefits are not restricted to e-governance. Individuals can obtain market information, training, job information, advice on farming techniques, and so on, as discussed earlier in this section (Singh, 2003).

Another useful purpose served by IT has been the facilitation of collection of direct taxes in India. Direct tax collection has increased by over 50 per cent from 2006-2009 in India (World Bank, 2010). Part of the reason is the high rates of growth experienced by the Indian economy, but the Department of Direct Taxation also claims that in part the convenience of e-filing and e-payment of direct taxation has facilitated a higher tax collection.

Leveraging ICT for Online Taxes and Levies

Direct taxes are made up of income taxes and corporate taxes, which together contribute about 34 per cent of total government revenues (and a mere 2.9 per cent of the GDP) (Rupanagunta, 2004). Traditionally, India has had an extremely poor collection of direct taxes, not least due to the complicated and time-consuming process of tax collection. Indirect taxes including excise taxes and customs, together make up about 66 per cent of the total government revenue (and 5.7 per cent of the GDP) (Rupanagunta, 2004).

A total savings of about 10 per cent of the cost of tax collection was envisaged through online tax payment. Similarly, in corporate taxes, it was envisaged to save about 30 per cent of the total cost, whereas for excise and customs duties savings were to be in the range of 20 per cent (Rupanagunta, 2004). Apart from cost savings, income tax collection through online services has become much higher accounting for nearly 40 per cent of total taxes in 2008 in comparison to 34 per cent in 2000 (World Bank, 2010).

Box 1.1

E-Governance

Issuance of Unique Identification Numbers (UIN) to all the citizens: A Unique Identification Authority of India has been established recently with statutory powers for creating a database of all the citizens and for issuance of UIN to them. This would help, *inter alia*, (a) in avoiding duplication of identification and will help in weeding out illegal immigrants; (b) in issuing a multi-purpose national ID card, and (c) in targetting and monitoring of inclusion programmes of the government through issuance of smart cards to intended beneficiaries.

National e-Governance Programme (NeGP): Ambitious programme of Government of India with three pillars: state data centres (SDCs) as a central repository of state-level data; state-wide area networks (SWANs) for integration of different layers of state government and common services centres (CSCs) as one-stop front-end delivery points for a variety of citizen-centric services (Application forms, payment of utility bills etc.). Apart from this there are many Central and state mission mode programmes (MMPs) which are sought to be implemented in a time-bound, mission-mode manner.

National Knowledge Network/Grid (Garuda Project): Interlinking of educational and research institutes across India electronically for sharing of intellectual resources on one common platform.

Smart Card for Inclusion of Disadvantaged Sections: For e.g., Bhamashah Financial Inclusion Project of Government of Rajasthan which aims at opening no-frills bank account for 5 million below poverty line (BPL) families through biometric ID cards.

Source: Department of Information Technology and National Council of Applied Economic Research (2010).

All these add up to a savings potential of around US $10 billion on an annual basis. To put this in perspective, let's assume that this would release US $1 billion (10 per cent of the savings realised every year, after accounting for the infrastructure and operating costs of such a system) (Author's calculations). This could provide health care to a million people in India according to a World Bank survey (World Bank, 2010).

While anecdotal evidence on the use of ICT in various aspects of the Indian economy are several, it is important to model ICT as a GPT for the Indian economy.

II

Modelling ICT as a GPT

One central feature of a GPT (such as ICT) is that its impact on productivity and hence performance is 'indirect' rather than direct. More specifically ICT increases the productivity of direct knowledge accumulation (e.g. investment in R&D), which would otherwise exhibit decreasing returns. Thus for example, in India, the impact of ICT should be felt on total factor productivity in states which have a higher exposure to ICT. This implies that with given levels of capital and labour inputs, it is to be expected that better networked states are likely to see higher impacts on per capita output. Thus, ICT enters as an input into the production process. The regression analysis below shows this relation clearly. While correlation cannot be chosen as a measure of causality, in terms of highlighting the policy variable, this analysis provides adequate results.

Impact of Network Development upon Output

The objective of this regression is to look upon the possible impact of ICTs on gross output. The policy variable is network development, the dummy variable. An index of network development can be gauged from the e-readiness of states. The e-readiness index of a state is a composite index which includes several variables besides ICT penetration and expenditure. For a comprehensive discussion of the e-readiness index see Appendix A-1.1. All states with average and above e-readiness have a dummy of 1, while those below that level have a dummy of 0 (See Appendix A-1.1). It can be seen from the regression result that, given the growth of labour and productive capital, a state with better network development should be better off in terms of growth of gross output. For every 0.18 per cent increase in e-readiness across states, the increase in output per capita is 1 per cent. This shows that a small improvement in e-readiness results in a large improvement in output. However, e-readiness is a composite index and states with a higher level of e-readiness are also those with a higher level of development (see section below on poverty and e-readiness). However, some of the backward states such as Bihar and Uttar Pradesh have improved their e-readiness significantly over the period 2004-2008 and have also seen an improvement in their growth rates (DIT and NCAER, 2010). A surprising outlier is Rajasthan which has remained nearly stagnant in its position in the e-readiness index but has seen high rates of growth.

Table 1.1

Definitions

'Pop'	Population of the state
'GrOp'	Gross output
'PrCap'	Productive capital
'Lab'	Number of workers
'Dum'	Dummy variable = 1 if the state falls in the category of network developed as E-readiness; otherwise = 0
Lit	Literacy rate

Table 1.2

Regressing Growth in Output Per Capita with Dummy of E-Readiness

Dependent Variable: Log of (GrOp/Pop)

Explanatory Variables:	
Log(PrCap/Pop)	0.74*** (0.051)
Log(Lab/Pop)	0.39*** (0.06)
Dum	0.18** (0.08)
Lit	-0.69 (0.42)
R-sqr	0.98
F-stat (4, 26)	583.93***
Observations	31

Table 1.3

Summary of Variables

Var: 'GrOp/Pop'	*No. of States*	*Mean*	*Std.*
Aggregate	31	1.04	3.41
Network developed states	15	0.32	0.32
Network less-developed states	16	1.7	4.7
Var: 'Lab/ Pop'	*No. of States*	*Mean*	*Std*
Aggregate	31	0.03	0.08
Network developed states	15	0.01	0.009
Network less-developed states	16	0.04	0.12
Var: 'PrCap/Pop'	*No. of States*	*Mean*	*Std*
Aggregate	31	0.36	1.10
Network developed states	15	0.12	0.12
Network less-developed states	16	0.58	1.51
Var: 'Lit'	*No. of States*	*Mean*	*Std*
Aggregate	31	0.69	0.09
Network developed states	15	0.72	0.09
Network less-developed states	16	0.66	0.09

The relationship between ICT and the structure of the economy is crucial to understand the channels through which such an indirect effect takes place as well as how strong such an impact will be. As the use of ICT takes different intensities according to the sectors in which it is applied, a given increase in ICT investment will generate a different impact according to the presence in the economy of sectors in which ICT can be better combined with other factors and/or in which organisational improvements can be more easily introduced. For example business services are intensive ICT users, therefore, a widespread presence of such services in the economy enhances the impact of ICT on performance. Thus again in the Indian case, it is to be expected that higher the exposure to ITES in a state, the higher would be the overall productivity of both agriculture and manufacturing as well as services. At the same time, in these states the share of services in the state domestic product (SDP) would be expected to be high.

While conjectures on the efficiency introduced by ICT in the operating environment are high, a concrete example which illustrates the role of ICT is that of Reliance Industries. Reliance Industries, a firm mostly engaged in chemical production and distribution, is a company actively involved in building a fiberoptic network linking major Indian cities. This company, in addition, expects that the internet will become a primary mechanism to improve operations, and it already has in place an internet-ready communications and control system. But, much of the system today uses leased telephone lines, not yet the internet. For example, of the company's 20,000-odd customers around India, 3,000-4,000 are major buyers, accounting for perhaps 75 per cent or more of total sales. These major customers for chemicals are now linked electronically to an internet-based market exchange introduced by Reliance, one of several now existing in the country. In addition, through leased-line facilities, customers can process orders, and Reliance can deliver despatching details, better manage inventory, carry out invoicing, and provide technical service, all done electronically. This customer network will be transferred to the internet at the earliest possible moment, since the internet should provide substantially lower operational costs (Aisbett *et al.*, 2008).

To provide some measure of the benefits already apparent from this system, Reliance has been able to reduce receivables from 310 days to 90 days, only one area of savings. Cost improvements come primarily from a general tightening and acceleration of processing within the company and between the firm and its customers. Savings do not occur as a result of reducing manpower. In addition, the speed of order delivery has been improved greatly and inventories reduced in a system that is now integrated into the firm's overall management control function that links not only important customers but also over 50 of the company's own operations. These results for Reliance are similar in nature to cost reductions experienced by companies in industrial parts of the world, even though, thus far, the internet has not been much utilised. One might anticipate even greater savings in India, as compared with more industrialised countries, since operational efficiency prior to the introduction of electronic controls is likely to have been far lower than comparable figures for companies in the developed world (Aisbett *et al.*, 2008).

'As an efficiency and productivity enhancer, the IT/ITES sector also stimulates many other sectors,' said Kiran Karnik, the past president of NASSCOM. 'Besides nurturing and encouraging start-up companies and small and medium-scale enterprises, the sector has collectively taken some very useful steps in areas of data security, certification, and promotion of new locations, creation of angel funds, mentoring for start-ups, as well as identifying and promoting new areas for the industry's growth and stimulating the domestic market' (Basu, 2008).

ICT and Poverty

Modelling ICT and Poverty

The effects of ICT on poverty alleviation can be examined on a macro basis by examining the e-readiness of a state and its poverty rate. Using a multivariate regression analysis and the e-readiness, the significance of network development of states (e-readiness) upon their poverty level can be assessed. The information used is from 2000/2008. Thirty data points on Indian states have been identified. The dependent variable is proportion of people below poverty level in that particular state. On the other hand, the explanatory variables are growth of gross state domestic product, growth of informal sector assets and a dummy variable on the basis of network development situation of the state. The policy variable is the dummy variable on network development. Following the *E-readiness Report 2008*, the dummy is 1 if network development of the state is either 'leaders', 'aspiring leaders', 'expectants'. Otherwise 0, if the state is in the category of 'average achievers', 'below average achievers' or 'least achievers'.

The equation therefore used is:

Poverty of ith state= F(e-readiness of state i, GSDP of state i, asset structure of state i)

The result indicates that irrespective of growth of GSDP and even growth of assets, a state, with better network development (when dummy is equal to 1), should have a lower proportion of poor people.

Both variables, i.e., dummy variable and asset-growth is significant at 1 per cent level. The explanatory variables explain around 40 per cent of total variation. The root MSE reflects the presence of small residuals in this regression.

Table 1.4

Impact of E-Development upon Poverty

Summary of Data	*Pov*	*Gsdp*	*Ias*	*Number of State*
Developed IT sector	36.4 (10.7)	0.10 (0.05)	63.8 (36.6)	17
Underdeveloped IT sector	26.7 (9.32)	0.12 (0.06)	54.2 (53.2)	13

Table 1.5

Regression Result of the Impact of E-Impact on Poverty

Dependent Variable Log of Poverty	
Explanatory Variables:	
Gsdp	1.79 (1.28)
Ias	-0.005*** (0.001)
Dev	-0.32*** (0.12)
R-square	0.38
Root MSE	0.33
Number of Obs	30
Pov	Number of people below poverty level
Gsdp	Growth of SDP
Ias	Growth of asset
Dev	Dummy variable =1 if the state is E-developed, otherwise=0

While the R-square is low indicating several missing explanatory variables, nevertheless the effect of e-readiness on poverty is significant at the 1 per cent level. The results indicate that approximately poverty reduces by 1 per cent when the e-readiness of a state increases by 0.32 per cent.

Leveraging ICT for the Informal Sector

Hernando De Soto (1996), an economist from the Institute of Liberty and Democracy in Peru argued that most of the poor already possess the assets that could be used to raise capital for their enterprises. However, these resources, according to him, are in 'defective forms': houses built on land whose ownership rights are inadequately recorded, unincorporated businesses (e.g. street vendors) with undefined liability and industries located where financiers and investors cannot see them (e.g. hundreds and thousands of village enterprises). Because the rights to these possessions are not adequately documented, they cannot be traded outside of the narrow local circles (where all transactions are based on trust), cannot be used as collateral for a loan and cannot be used as a share against investment.

Can IT Help Capitalise these Assets?

Needless to say, creating a system to record these assets presents an enormous challenge in a country like India. This is where the power of IT can be leveraged to organise information. For instance, capturing property ownership in an urban area in a database would be the first step to generating house ownership deeds. Once this is in place, a shopkeeper, armed with asset ownership documents for their house as well as the shop, can raise capital to expand their business. Likewise, in principle, in the rural areas, a small farmer, with their ownership documents, can apply for loans at the local bank instead of having to resort to the local moneylenders.

Here, it is important to recognise that capital formation is not just restricted to supply of funds (as is normally thought). It is just as important to provide the businesses the ways and means to absorb the funds. In today's India, small businesses obtain capital—but that is primarily through local lenders—at prohibitively high interest rates, which is in turn, a reflection of the risk level of the investment. By contrast, a loan backed by a properly documented asset as collateral, would significantly reduce risk and consequently, prove to be less of a burden on the borrower.

The following example shows an estimate of the level of capital 'locked' in India. The rural areas used for productive purposes (croplands and grasslands) in India total up to about 30 per cent of the total area (a conservative estimate, given that 60 per cent of India lives in rural areas). Assuming that 40 per cent of this land is used on an 'informal' basis—i.e., no formal ownership deeds exist—(with 75 per cent being used for crop cultivation and 25 per cent for grasslands), approximately 30,000 hectares are used for agriculture and 10,000 hectares are used as grasslands. Putting a notional price of US $ 3/sq ft for croplands and US $1/sq ft for grasslands (in reality, the value would be much higher); there would be US $15 billion informal assets in rural India (Rupanagunta, 2004).

In case of urban areas, the results are even starker. In India, around 400 million people live in urban areas. Assuming an average occupancy rate of five people per house, there are around 80 million urban dwellings. Of these, around 85 per cent are 'informal' dwellings (built in an 'extra-legal' framework—i.e., in violation of land laws; without proper ownership documents; in violation of legal requirements—which usually means that the dwelling is improperly valued). This is obvious to anyone who has been to any Indian town or city. Assuming an average urban dwelling size of 200 sq ft, and putting a notional value of US $5/sq ft (it should be noted that both the dwelling size and the value would be higher than what has been used here); there are US $68 billion informal sector assets in urban India.[1]

> Formalising a mere 20 per cent of the informal assets would create the potential of injecting over US $17 billion into the Indian economy.

Thus, this adds up to a whopping figure of US $83 billion of informal assets in India—assets which cannot be put to productive use because the Government of India does not have the necessary systems in place to formally capture this information. To put this in perspective, the total FDI to India in 2008 was a mere $15 billion.

However, it is necessary to sound a word of caution on the ICT euphoria especially for grassroot project in India. The propositions listed below (Keniston, 2002) derive from an ongoing study of grassroot ICT projects in India:

a) Projects may be more hyped up than is warranted and may often be late.

b) Unexpected difficulties may arise. For example the computerisation of land records may be difficult because half of the records may be legally contested or in the names of dead people or be otherwise ineligible.

c) The goal of financial sustainability may be difficult to achieve.

d) IT should not be simply identified with computers and internet. Some of the most inventive uses of IT involve radio, television, and embedded chips, potentially useful satellite inventories, etc.

1. Calculations of the author.

The classic example is the use of automated butterfat assessment equipment in Gujarat, which has radically simplified the process of evaluating milk and paying dairy farmers.

e) Top-down projects simply do not work as they may involve comprehensible level of technical detail and terminology, or in a literary language that local people do not understand. Providing information in local languages has proved a challenge so far. Also, development of locally relevant content is essential.

f) E-governance has proved difficult and costly to implement and has faced resistance from middlemen.

g) E-commerce in terms of customer-to-business online buying within India, is probably many years away for a majority of Indians.

h) Commercially funded ICT networks have considerable promise. Several examples were cited above.

i) While there are several grassroot projects in India, the agents are not usually in touch with each other, rarely publish or write anything about what they are doing, and—if they are public officials—are constantly transferred. There is little accumulation of knowledge, not even the most preliminary kinds of on-the-site evaluation. So, there is little possibility of learning from the successes or failures of other projects.

Finally, there is the question of whether the IT and ITES sector offers the most productive deployment of skilled human resources at the national level. Many of the call centre and back office workers in India are overqualified for their jobs. College graduates, chartered accountants, MBAs and engineers are at work answering customer questions during odd hours—the same jobs are held by high school graduates in the West. Although these jobs pay relatively high wages and provide employment opportunities for new graduates, the opportunity costs of such employment from a societal viewpoint may be high. There is evidence that the annual churn rate is reaching 40-50 per cent for call centre jobs (Konana *et al.*, 2004). There is increased dissatisfaction with the type of work and there is no clear path for personal development that matches the qualifications of the workers. These skilled employees may contribute more strongly to economic development in a broad sense if they were encouraged to be entrepreneurs or focussed their energies on the infrastructure and core manufacturing sectors.

The IT industry growth has shown an overwhelmingly urban bias. Much of the rural and small town India has been bypassed by this boom. Even within the urban centres, the growth has been largely restricted to the small segment of the population with college degrees, which itself comes from the middle and upper middle classes. To be sure, the very nature of the IT industry demands an urban concentration and job creation for college graduates.

At least in the short run, IT may not play a pivotal role in promoting an equitable development process. But it is indeed possible to harness the power of technology to release resources, which can then be channelled into financing public welfare projects. IT is essentially an enabler of knowledge management, i.e., effective capture and efficient dissemination of information. While it might sound a little presumptuous to talk of information organisation in a society which is still unable to provide basic public services to the population, there is growing awareness that IT can be leveraged to harness the 'knowledge capital' that abounds across the country. This in turn can play an important catalytic role in the development process.

III

Multiplier Effects of IT and ITES

Apart from directly contributing to the growth of the economy, the IT-ITES sector also generates 'derived' demand for a wide variety of goods and services such as transport for ferrying employees from their workforce, onsite catering, security and health care services in a 24x7 business environment through backward linkages. Further, it can also be argued that, to the extent that the IT-ITES sector is generating employment for a large number at wages that they could not aspire to earn in any other employment avenue, it is adding significantly to aggregate disposable income. This, in turn, stimulates consumer demand for a wide range of goods and services, which could not otherwise manifest (Gokarn *et al.*, 2007).

Findings on Output and Employment Multipliers

In 2005-06, of the total turnover of US $30 billion, the IT-ITES sector spent 46 per cent on salaries and wages, 28 per cent on non-wage operating expenses and had an operating margin of 26 per cent. A part of this turnover got spent in the domestic economy, and through forward and backward linkages affected other sectors as well. A study estimates that of the total turnover roughly half was spent in the domestic economy *via* non-wage operating expenses, capital expenditure and consumption spending by professionals. This spending, in turn, generated an additional output of US $15 billion *via* its direct and indirect backward linkages with other sectors and induced effect of wages and salaries. In 2005-06, IT-ITES employees spent US $6 billion on domestic consumption. Of the total, the maximum spending was housing related (26 per cent of gross income) followed by food items, durable goods and holidays. Consumption spending generated an additional output of US $7 billion. Thus, the output multiplier works out to about 2 (Gokarn *et al.*, 2007).

IT-ITES spending on other sectors and its multiplier effect generated additional employment. While the IT-ITES sector provided direct employment to 1.3 million people, it created additional employment for 5.2 million people. Thus, for each person employed in the IT-ITES sector, around four people were employed in rest of the economy. Among the various consumption categories, spending on housing/construction, food items, clothing, outdoor eating/holidays induce maximum employment. The above approach to the computation of output and employment effects of IT-ITES activity would be perfectly valid in a scenario of unlimited supply of human capital. In the current scenario, this may not be a reasonable assumption. It can be argued that large scale hiring by the IT-ITES sector is drawing people away from other employment opportunities by offering higher salaries. In other words, in the absence of the IT/ITES sector, these people would have still found employment given their skill sets, but perhaps not at the high salaries offered by the IT-ITES sector. Thus, the kick to the economy arises essentially from the differential between the salary of an IT-ITES professional, and his salary in other avenues of employment.

The average salary of an IT-ITES professional was over US $15,000 per annum in 2005-06. Based on this, two scenarios were created in a CRISIL-NASSCOM study (NASSCOM-CRISIL, 2007): in the first scenario, the difference between the wage rates of an IT-ITES professional and his salary in other job avenues was estimated at US $5,000; in the second scenario, this difference was US $2,500. Under these assumptions, the additional employment generated was found to be 3.2-3.6 million. With reference to these simulations, it needs to be emphasised that, if the supply of human capital to the sector were, in fact, unlimited, the aggregate indirect impact would be larger, because it would not be coming at the expense of activity in some other sector. Expanding the capacity of the educational system, to provide the necessary skills, clearly has a role to play here.

A survey by CRISIL of some of the service providers to the IT-ITES sector revealed that services such as catering, transport and housekeeping, security and technology had received a boost from the IT-ITES sector. IT-ITES was increasing its share in the turnover of these service providers. Further, all these services, require low skilled/educated workforce. Of the total workforce that provided these services to the IT-ITES sector, the share of unskilled workers was 72-78 per cent. Thus, the IT-ITES sector provides employment to low skilled/educated workers as well.

Much of the success achieved by the sector has been attributed to the meteoric growth in exports. Obviously, the backward and forward linkages would be much higher if the IT sector had a significant domestic component. While the domestic IT sector is not as large as exports, it is nevertheless becoming important.

Domestic IT Services Market Opportunity

Domestic demand for IT in India is witnessing a gradual transformation from being predominantly hardware driven towards a solutions oriented approach—resulting in a growing emphasis on services. In fact, revenue growth in the services segment alone has reported faster growth than that for the overall domestic IT market (including hardware, software and services) over the past few years. As depicted in Figure 1.1, this trend is expected to continue over the forecast period.

Figure 1.1

Growth of IT Spending in India

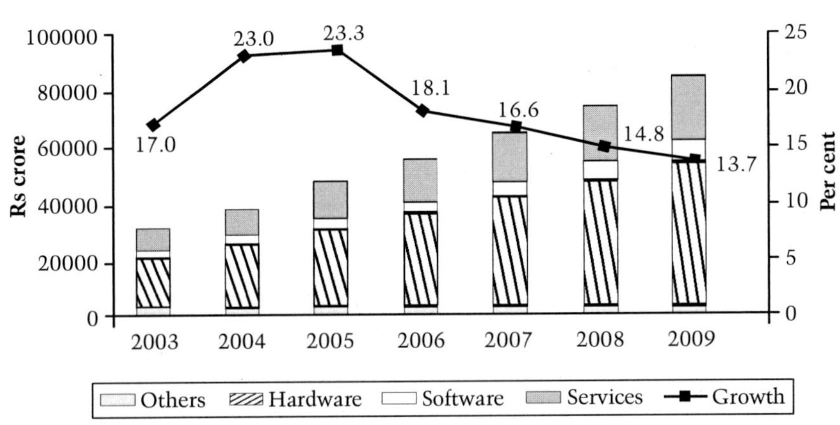

Source: NASSCOM-IDC (2006).

The liberalisation of Indian economic policy, deregulation of key sectors and progressive moves towards further integrating India with the global economy has been a key driver of increased IT adoption in the country. This is best reflected in the fact that most indigeneous players in telecom and banking, two key sectors with significant multinational corporation (MNC) participation, have significantly upgraded their levels of IT adoption to offer best-in-class services comparable to those offered by the global competition and these two sectors together account for approximately 35-40 per cent of the domestic spend on IT services.

Table 1.6

Five-Year Revenue Forecasts for Key Service Lines in the Domestic Market

(INR million)

Breakups	*2004*	*2005*	*2006*	*2007*	*2008*	*2009*	*CAGR (%)*
IT consulting	4,784	5,669	6,775	7,774	9,109	10,674	17.4
System integration	34,011	42,979	51,900	62,065	72,960	85,399	20.2
Application development	13,997	17,115	19,852	22,586	25,113	27,924	14.8
End-to-end outsourcing	6,328	8,221	10,247	12,343	14,344	16,850	21.6
Discrete outsourcing	16,731	21,055	25,819	31,401	36,262	41,509	19.9
Deploy and support	23,631	28,321	32,907	37,651	42,510	48,186	15.3
IT education and training	4,126	4,879	5,609	6,534	7,260	8,067	14.3
Grand total	103,606	128,239	153,109	180,354	207,559	238,607	18.2

Source: NASSCOM-IDC (2006).

Similar competitive pressures in other more recently deregulated service sectors such as airlines and insurance, and the uptake in the manufacturing and industrial sectors; and the several large e-governance initiatives launched by the government under the National E-Governance Plan (NEGP) are expected to provide sustained growth in domestic demand for IT services over the next few years.

Box 1.2

According to Gartner's Senior Research Analyst 'India's domestic IT services market is expected to see a CAGR of 16 per cent by 2014, which would make that market worth $13.6 billion.'

Further large government spending in areas such as e-governance is expected to drive IT services market in the country. Higher consumer spending would boost economic growth, which in turn is expected to increase the demand for IT services.

Source: "Domestic IT Spending to Drive IT Services Biz"; *http://www.deccanherald.com/content/107218/domestic-spending-drive-services-biz.html*

Systems integration and network integration make up a high growth-large size category within the IT services engagements. These services will continue to be prime drivers of the domestic IT services market in the enterprise segment due to the increasing growth in the enterprise application implementation and increased demand for network integration from telecom & banking verticals.

Figure 1.2

Domestic IT Services Revenues by Key Vertical Markets (2004)

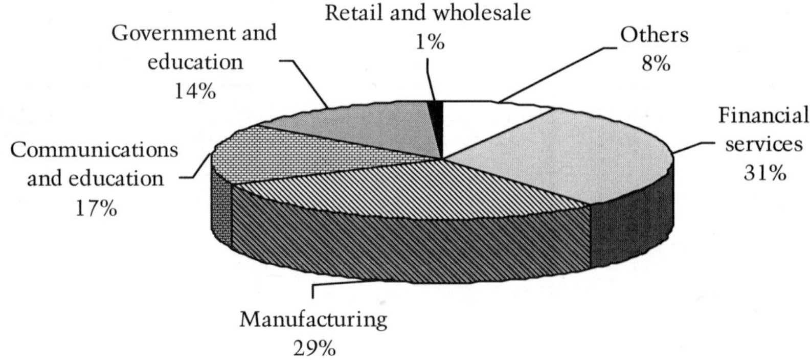

Source: NASSCOM-IDC (2006).

The financial services, communications and media and manufacturing verticals accounted for over 3/4th of the revenues earned by service providers in the domestic IT services market in 2004.

It is estimated that in-house spending on IT services (including training costs, salaries of in-house IT staff and associated overheads) still accounts for more than half of the corporate IT spend in India, while the outsourced/vendor addressed spends account for just 45 per cent of the total.

Domestic ITES-BPO Market Opportunity

ITES-BPO is a very nascent segment of the domestic market, driven by voice-based services with customer care and sales and marketing activity accounting for approximately 70 per cent of the total.

Table 1.7

Comparison of the Vendor Addressed Market and the In-House Spend by Key Services

(INR million)

Breakups	*2004: Vendor Addressed Market*	*2005: In-House Team Addressed Market*	*Total Market*	*Vendor Addressed Market as % of Total Market*
IT consulting	4,784	11,163	15,947	30
System integration	34,011	34,011	68,022	50
Application development	13,997	20,995	34,992	40
End-to-end outsourcing	6,328	N.A.	6,328	100
Discrete outsourcing	16,731	25,096	41,827	40
Deploy and support	23,631	23,631	47,262	50
IT education and training	4,126	9,628	13,754	30
Grand total	103,608	124,524	228,132	45

Source: NASSCOM-IDC (2006).

Table 1.8

Domestic ITES-BPO Revenues

(INR million)

	2004	*2005*	*2006*
HR	2,428.9	4,412.5	8,019.5
F&A	2,563.9	2,975.4	3,454.1
Customer care	7,696.1	16,161.8	33,939.7
Sales & marketing	8,465.2	12,019.6	17,756.4
Other	2,059.2	2,449.4	2,914.6
Total	23,213.3	38,018.6	66,084.4

Source: NASSCOM-IDC (2006).

Currently, banking and financial services and telecom verticals account for over 70 per cent of the demand for ITES-BPO services in the domestic market (See Table 1.9).

While cost savings have been the primary driver of offshore outsourcing, vendors do not have comparable differences in labour costs to leverage while serving the domestic market. As a result, the primary motivation for the domestic market, in its early years of evolution were not cost savings but access to specialist skills and freeing client resources to focus on the core business. Scalability and process efficiency is expected to return some degree of cost savings in the domestic market as well. However, this may not compare with the levels achieved by overseas (e.g. US/UK) clients.

Table 1.9

Domestic ITES-BPO Revenues by Vertical Market (2004)

Verticals	*% Share (2004)*	*Typical Processes Outsourced*
Banking and financial services	47.4	Customer support, marketing and sales, collections, billing, transaction processing, market analytics, HR
Telecom	24.1	Customer support, cross-selling, loan processing, claim processing, market analytics, data validation, HR
Manufacturing (customer durables/automoblies)	12.2	Customer support, sales and marketing, transportation, supply chain management, accounts payable/receiveable
Others (IT-ITES, aviation, hospitality, retail)	16.4	HR, customer support, marketing and sales, billing, transaction processing, analytics, etc.

Source: NASSCOM-IDC (2006).

Effects of the Global Meltdown on India's IT Sector

Given the large role of IT and ITES in the Indian economy including in poverty alleviation, there is justifiable concern about the effects of global meltdown on the Indian economy. Much is being assumed on the possible effects of slowdown in the US economy on the IT and BPO industry.

The annual growth of the IT and ITES industry plunged to 6 per cent in 2009 10, after recording a cumulative growth of 25 30 per cent during the previous four years. The industry returned to double-digit growth in

2010-11 due to renewed investments by global firms across verticals in IT infrastructure, software and back office services.[2]

NASSCOM has projected $56-57 billion or 13-15 per cent year-on-year (YoY) growth from exports and 15-17 per cent YoY growth in domestic market in the fiscal year 2010-11.[3] Sustaining growth in 2011 would depend on Europe's recovery. Sovereign debt fallout in any country, as happened in the case of Greece would have a domino effect on the global economy, which in turn would impact the IT industry.[4] The global financial crisis and tech meltdown however changed the strategy of the Indian IT industry.

To sustain the growth momentum and make optimal use of their resources, even export-oriented firms like TCS, Infosys, Wipro and HCL turned to domestic market. As shown above, state-run organisations and governments across the country have decided to enhance their investments in IT infrastructure, products and services for the benefit of its people.

Buoyed by increased tech spending in the private and public sectors, the industry has been gearing up to offer its services in new areas such as engineering services and product development. The industry is thus using its global presence to service the domestic market effectively. While domestic market still accounts for only one-fourth of the total market, its growth rate is higher than that of international markets.

With 450 delivery centres in 60 countries worldwide, the Indian IT industry has an unparalleled global value chain. The industry has resumed enhancing its global workforce, hiring specialised talent in developed markets and building a truly global delivery model.[5]

However, hiring by the IT sector moved to fourth place in 2009 from first place in 2005 in the Indian economy. Additional hiring by the IT sector was only 33,000 in 2009 compared to 60,000 in 2005.[6] For raising

2. "Buoyant Indian IT Industry Rebounds but Remains Cautious", 30 December 2010. *http://economictimes.indiatimes.com/infotech/ites/buoyant-indian-it-industry-rebounds-but-remains-cautious/articleshow/7190235.cms*
3. Ibid.
4. Ibid.
5. Ibid.
6. "IT/ITes is no hot sector for job seekers post meltdown", September 15, 2010, *http://www.hindustantimes.com/tabloid-news/sectorsbpos/IT-ITes-is-no-hot-sector-for-job-seekers-post-meltdown/Article1-600521.aspx*

human capital, besides the big firms jointly offering about 100,000 jobs in 2010/11 to build capacity in anticipation of better growth in (2011-12), small and medium business too have resumed hiring to meet the demand for ICT services and products.[7]

As a top outsourcing destination and back office operations hub, India dominates the global IT services market with 51 per cent share (Nasscom, 2010).

IV

Mobile Telephony and its Trickle Down

Earlier studies on economic growth and the increase in mobile telephony (Waverman *et al.*, 2005a) show that mobile telephony has a positive and significant impact on economic growth, and this impact may be twice as large in developing countries compared to developed countries. This result is largely attributed to the fact that in developing countries the growth dividend is far larger because mobile phones provide, by and large, the main communications networks; hence they supplant the information-gathering role of fixed-line systems. It has been estimated that a mobile network costs 50 per cent less per connection than fixed lines and can be rolled out appreciably faster.[8] The cost advantages of mobile phones as a development tool consist not only of the lower costs per subscriber but also the smaller scale economies and greater modularity of mobile systems. A study by the London Business School has also found that, in a typical developing country, an increase of 10 mobile phones per 100 people would boost GDP growth by 0.6 percentage points (Waverman, 2005).

A study by Waverman *et al.* (2005b) shows that:

- Differences in the penetration and diffusion of mobile telephony explains some of the differences in growth rates between developing countries. If gaps in mobile telecoms penetration

7. Ibid.

8. "Africa: The Impact of Mobile Phones, Moving the Debate Forward", *The Vodafone Policy Paper Series* 3, March 2005. *http://mobileactive.org/files/file_uploads/AfricaImpactOfMobilePhones.pdf*

between countries persist, then their results suggest that this gap will feed into a significant difference in their growth rates in future.

- As Romer (1986) and Barro (1991) hypothesised for human capital stocks, there are also increasing returns to the endowment of telecoms capital (as measured by the telecoms penetration rate).
- Given the speed with which mobile telecoms have spread in developing nations, it is unlikely that large gaps in penetration will persist forever. However, differences in the speed of adoption will affect the speed with which poor countries converge to rich countries' level.

The main contribution of mobile telephony in alleviating poverty in India has been to extend connectivity to rural areas and for the urban poor. Focussing on extending telecommunications services to rural areas and urban slums should in principle help alleviate poverty, encourage economic and social growth and overcome a perceived 'digital divide'. However, relatively little is known about how the poor benefit from modern telecommunications services and what impact it is having on their lives and livelihoods.

To answer this question it is essential to ascertain the importance of information in the livelihood opportunities for the poor. The next question that needs to be asked is whether mobile telephony is the most appropriate and effective delivery mechanism for that information? Indian telecom market has been growing at approximately 30 per cent since 1995 and still growing strong. The high growth of the Indian telecom market can mainly be attributed to mobile services which have grown by more than 117 per cent during the period 1995-2009. With additions of more than 14 million subscribers per month in the year 2009, the telecom subscriber base had grown to 601 million in April 2010, second only to China (PricewaterhouseCoopers, 2010).

An examination of the perceived correlation between GDP per capita and mobile penetration across Indian states would help to assess the output effects of mobiles and its operation as a GPT.

Mobiles as a GPT

Table 1.10

Analysis of the Impact of Density of Mobile Users upon Gross Output

Name of Variables:	
Short name	Variables
Prc	Productive capital
Lab	Number of employees
GOp	Gross output
Mous	Density of mobile users, per 100
***	Significant at 1 per cent level

The test design is to understand the impact of density of mobile users upon gross output in the respective state. The policy variable here is the density of mobile users per 100 (Mous in the regression below). The methodology used for examining the effects of mobile density on gross output is the use of panel data analysis (Table 1.14). Both fixed effects and random effects have been ascertained. The fixed effect model incorporates state-specific constants such as labour and productive capital. The random effect model assumes state-specific characters are random, rather than fixed. In both models, the impact of 'Mous' on gross output in the state is positive and significant at 1 per cent. However, following Hausman specification test, the fixed effect result is accepted, which is consistent with the random effects. The other variables are also significant at 1 per cent level. The F-test and Chi2 test indicate that the model is significant at 1 per cent level, for fixed and as well as random effect, respectively.

Table 1.11

Summary of Variables

Variables	*Mean*	*Std Dev*
Prc	2941174	2995702
Lab	416258	359985
GOp	6400852	6918613
Mous	3.53	6.20

In addition, Table 1.9 presents the picture of states regarding base and growth of density of mobile users. It can be seen that density of mobile users in different states is quite diversified. From the table, we can differentiate states, according to high-base—low-growth (e.g. Delhi), low-base—low-growth (Uttar Pradesh), and low-base—high-growth states (Assam, J&K).

Table 1.10 presents the differences between the states having higher and lower density mobile users. In each group there are nine states. It can be seen that states having higher density in mobile users also have higher level of gross output, employees and productive capital and vice-versa.

Table 1.12

List of Average of Density of Mobile Users (per 100) in Major States during 2001 to 2004

States	*Average Density of Mobile Users, per 100*	*Average Growth of Density of Mobile Users*
Andhra Pradesh	2.81	0.978
Assam	0.25	33
Bihar	0.56	1.24
Delhi	22.5	0.744
Gujarat	4.05	1.09
Haryana	2.50	34
Himachal Pradesh	2.42	1.51
Jammu & Kashmir	0.50	66.3
Karnataka	3.47	1.16
Kerala	4.25	1.1
Madhya Pradesh	1.13	0.97
Maharashtra	4.25	1.11
Orrisa	0.75	33.3
Punjab	7.62	1.19
Rajasthan	1.50	33.5
Tamil Nadu	3.49	1.14
Uttar Pradesh	0.01	0.0
West Bengal	1.46	1.13

Source: LIRNE*asia* (2006).

Table 1.13

Average Difference between States Having Higher and Lower Density of Mobile Users: 't' Test

Variables	*Lower Density States*	*No. of States*	*Higher Density States*	*No. of States*	*'t' Test*
Prc	1527059 (199148.1)	9	4355289 (593094.4)	9	-4.52***
Lab	211757 (32108)	9	620758 (62302)	9	-5.83***
GOp	3012378 (458809)	9	9789326 (135302)	9	-4.74***

Source: LIRNE*asia* (2006).

Table 1.14

Panel-Regression Results

Dependent Variable: Log of GOp

Explanatory Variables	*Fixed Effect Model*	*Random Effect Model*
Log of (Prc)	0.78***	0.65***
(0.11)	(0.07)	
Log of (Lab)	0.72***	0.35***
(0.25)	(0.08)	
Log of (Mous)	0.04***	0.05***
(0.01)	(0.009)	
R-sq within	0.84	0.83
F(3,51)	89.6***	-
Wald Chi2 (3)	-	885.22***
Number of states	18	18
Hausman specification test	13.65***	

Figures 1.3 and 1.4 present the picture that emerges from the above regression, i.e., as the linear predictive rate of mobile penetration increases, the gross output also increases, for that state.

Figure 1.3

Log of Gross Output versus Linear Prediction: For Year 2001

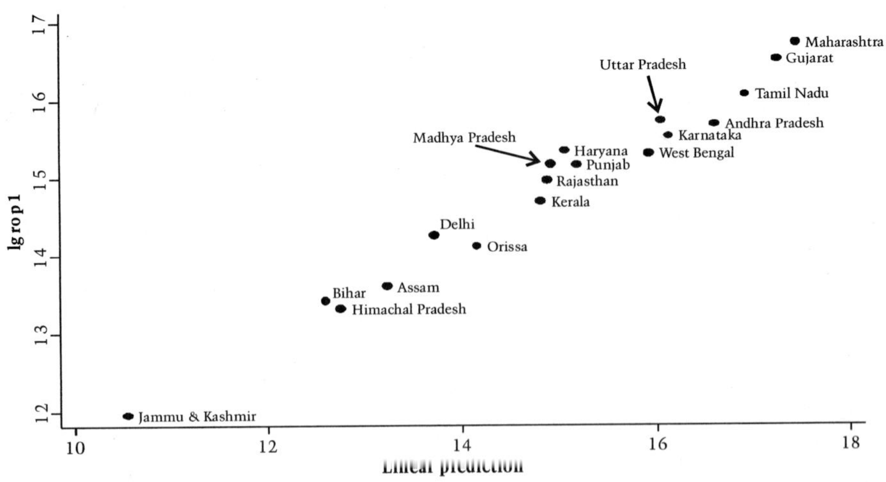

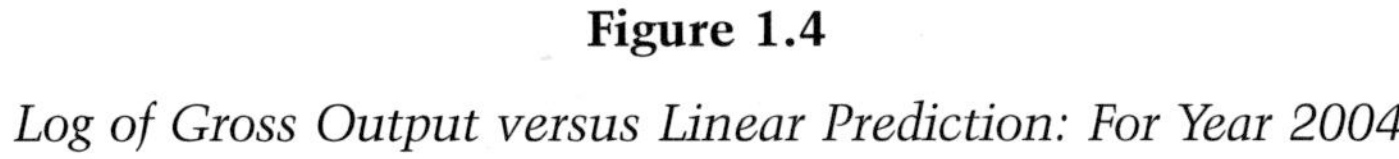

Figure 1.4

Log of Gross Output versus Linear Prediction: For Year 2004

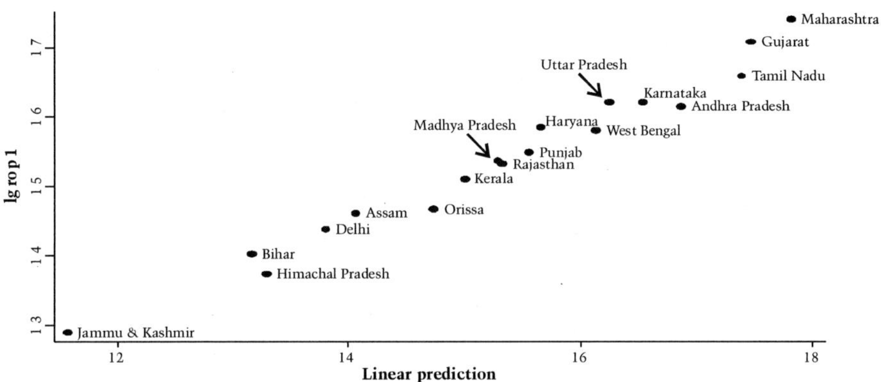

The effects of mobile penetration in high growth states is to be expected, as all other factors go in their favour. Thus the effects of mobile growth rates on Maharashtra, Tamil Nadu, Karnataka or Andhra Pradesh are not surprising. However, the fact that Uttar Pradesh, Madhya Pradesh and Rajasthan show greater effects of mobile penetration on gross output than Delhi is an indication of the effects of mobile on gross output growth. Moreover, the effects of mobiles on gross output in Assam and Orissa, two of the poorer states in India, are higher than that in Delhi in 2004. This is a reaffirmation of the impact that mobile penetration can have in low usage high mobile growth states. It also indicates that the potential of mobiles to contribute to growth probably reaches a plateaux with a penetration of 97 per cent as is the case with Delhi. It is possible that a major technological leap may be required at this level for mobile telephony to yield higher gross output benefits. It is also possible that at such high levels of mobile density, the quality of services start falling and service provision deteriorates. This could in part account for the plateaux in the contribution of mobile penetration to gross output growth in Delhi.

Another important observation from the above figure is that at lower levels of teledensity, the contribution of improved teledensity to output increases more than proportionately. The lowest levels of teledensity are those of Bihar, Uttar Pradesh, Orissa and Assam and these states show greater sensitivity of economic growth to teledensity growth. Thus, the poverty alleviating effects of mobiles are likely to be higher in poorer states.

Table 1.15

Mobile Teledensity per 100 Persons

	2000	*2004*	*2005*	*2006*	*2007*	*2008*
Andhra Pradesh	0.14	3.73	5.37	9.58	16.21	25.31
Assam	0.00	0.00	1.00	3.00	8.00	13.00
Bihar	0.02	0.66	1.16	2.77	5.32	9.19
Delhi	3.00	30.00	39.00	56.00	74.00	97.00
Gujarat	0.30	5.17	7.89	12.35	19.97	29.82
Haryana	0.00	3.00	6.00	10.00	19.00	27.00
Himachal Pradesh	0.08	2.80	5.44	11.01	21.76	33.78
J&K	-	0.00	2.00	7.00	13.00	19.00
Karnataka	0.25	4.49	7.06	12.28	20.03	29.63
Kerala	0.00	5.00	9.00	15.00	23.00	35.00
Madhya Pradesh	0.05	1.35	2.28	4.12	8.28	14.39
Maharashtra	0.00	6.00	8.00	12.00	19.00	27.00
North East	0.01	0.37	1.16	3.39	9.33	15.74
Orissa	0.00	1.00	2.00	4.00	8.00	13.00
Punjab	0.40	9.99	15.01	21.15	32.12	44.42
Rajasthan	0.00	2.00	3.00	7.00	13.00	21.00
Tamil Nadu	0.24	4.36	7.02	11.72	19.32	29.01
Uttar Pradesh	0.00	0.00	0.00	1.00	2.00	4.00
West Bengal and Andaman and Nicobar	0.08	1.93	2.95	4.78	8.03	12.41

Source: Telecom Regulatory Authority of India (TRAI), Quarterly Bulletins.

Socioeconomic Effects of Mobiles

Arguably, the value of mobile phone services and the associated benefits are higher in remote rural areas, or in urban slums which is poorly served by public transport. One tangible benefit which studies, especially surveys show is that mobiles substitute for physical transport. Although the poor are not a homogeneous group—consisting of artisans, farmers, fishermen, herders, migrant workers and tribals—one common element is their lack of affordable access to relevant information and knowledge services and affordable transportation. This lack of access can lead to other contributors to poverty (e.g., ignorance of income earning or market opportunities and inability to make their voices heard).

The important effects of mobiles on poverty in India are intermediated through the following factors:

a) Affordability (demand side): The Telecom Regulatory Authority of India (TRAI) formulated policies which introduced competition in the markets. These pricing models offer affordability and choice, even for very low-income customers (cheap handsets, micro prepayments, top-up cards).

b) Affordability (supply side): Establishing mobile masts is a relatively inexpensive way of serving large and remote rural areas. The number of mobile towers established in the remotest locations has shown an exponential growth in India.

c) Flexibility: It is not pricing models that are flexible—usages are also. Mobiles can be used in the most remote areas. They can be charged at train and bus stations and car batteries can also be used to charge them.

d) Low barriers to entry: Anyone can own a mobile. It has become the most easily accessible and ubiquitous communications device in rural areas. Easy availability of low priced new handsets with basic features and emergence of secondary markets for used devices, whose prices are even lower, make them within reach for even the poorest of the poor.

The growth of wireless phones from 2000-2008 has been phenomenal in India with the poorest states showing some of the highest growth (Table 1.16). Prices declined sharply after 2004 because of the regulatory framework and competition. The effective coverage of the network had also reached a state of maturity which could cover several more circles. Thus after 2004, there has been a huge increase in most circles upwards of 500 per cent.[9] The highest increases were to be found in low mobile density, poor and most populous states. Thus Eastern and Western Uttar Pradesh, Bihar and Orissa saw the highest increases in mobile density over this period. The effects on gross output growth in the case of Eastern and Western Uttar Pradesh and Orissa have been higher than that of Bihar. This shows that while mobiles may increase productivity, other factors such as income-earning opportunities need to improve too. The increase in Bihar probably is due to the high numbers of migrant labour who need to communicate with their hometowns and districts. While anecdotal

9. TRAI quarterly bulletins. Published by TRAI, New Delhi, India.

evidence on the productivity enhancing effects of mobiles can be found from Kerala, Gujarat, Uttar Pradesh and Delhi, there is little anecdotal evidence from Bihar which indicates that income-earning opportunities may not improve on account of access to mobile telephony. However, there is a good body of anecdotal evidence which suggests that improvement in mobile networks has had a distinct impact on migration from Bihar to the service sectors of the high growth states in India. For instance, the chauffeur networks in Delhi have benefitted from immediate access to information through mobiles and the numbers of *Bihari* chauffeurs have increased exponentially between 2004 and 2008.[10]

Table 1.16

Wireless Subscriber Base

Circle	*Mar-2008*	*Mar-2004*	*Mar-2000*
Andhra Pradesh	20,577,632	2,911,760	105,469
Gujarat	16,968,200	2,731,856	146,175
Karnataka	17,043,556	2,455,317	127,967
Maharashtra	21,079,326	3,008,144	115,086
Tamil Nadu	18,284,050	2,103,772	90,956
Haryana	6,401,457	701,785	25,047
Kerala	11,698,216	1,681,648	106,560
Madhya Pradesh	13,192,338	1,154,014	40,544
Punjab	11,715,504	2,506,150	94,403
Rajasthan	13,586,738	917,867	20,025
Uttar Pradesh (E)	16,165,268	1,205,235	113,587
Uttar Pradesh (W)	12,887,001	1,283,705	55,950
West Bengal and Andaman & Nicobar	9,438,941	371,120	3,978
Assam	3,913,099	102,490	5,823
Bihar	11,509,688	763,048	21,901
Himachal Pradesh	2,299,811	178,835	5,048
J&K	2,201,912	47,219	-
North East	2,118,532	46,523	722
Orissa	5,180,156	398,296	9,139
Chennai	7,061,200	1,521,161	54,256
Delhi	16,280,448	4,438,309	332,330
Kolkata	7,844,469	1,286,034	90,036
Mumbai	13,631,670	3,805,705	319,309

Source: Telecom Regulatory Authority of India (TRAI), Quarterly Bulletins.

10. Author's survey on the informal sector. See Annexure to Chapter 3.

One of the most important indicators of increased mobile usage among the poor is reflected through increased rural teledensity. In September 2008, rural teledensity in India was approximately 13 per cent, while urban was 73 per cent (PricewaterhouseCoopers, 2010). This compares very favourably to less than 1 per cent rural teledensity in 2005. There is the myth that the rural poor are not able or not willing to pay for mobile telecommunication services. Initially, this led to a tendency to invest in the more affluent urban areas rather than poor rural areas but now there are also growing rural networks. Second, there is the myth that natural barriers, such as lack of education or electricity, would prevent mobile take-up. Strong growth in India, in spite of still prevalent difficulties with low education, low access to electricity and low income levels has also gone some way to refuting this theory.

Evidence from India through the increased rural teledensity indicates that the benefits outweigh the constraints. Yet what are these benefits? Benefits of mobile telephony have been divided into three categories in a paper by the World Bank (July 2008) (Bhavnani *et al.*, 2008): (a) direct benefits, (b) indirect benefits, and (c) intangible benefits (e.g., disaster relief, local content, low education, social capital and cohesion).

Direct Benefits

Mobile telephony has a positive impact on the economic welfare in the following direct ways: (a) by generating GDP, (b) by job generation (both in the mobile industry and the wider economy), (c) productivity increases, and (d) taxation revenue (mobile operators are usually a sizeable contributor).

Vodafone (2005) reported that, in a typical developing country, an increase of 10 mobile phones per 100 people boosts GDP growth by 0.6 per cent.[11] Ovum (2006) reported that the mobile services industry contributed $7.8 billion towards GDP in India in 2004. Obviously its phenomenal growth since 2004 by nearly 500 per cent would imply that its GDP contribution would be in the range of 35-40 billion dollars in 2008. This compares very favourably with the revenue generation of the IT and ITES

11. *http://www.telecomcircle.com/2009/01/impact-of-mobility-on-economic-growth-in-developing-countries/*

sectors. Another economic impact is the employment generation of the mobile telephony sector. Ovum (2006) found that the mobile telephony industry created about 3.6 million jobs in India, directly and indirectly. This figure is expected to increase by 30 per cent per year. This implies that its employment in 2008 was likely to be in the range of about 6.2 million (PricewaterhouseCoopers, 2010). Again this compares very favourably with the IT and ITES sector. Although the mobile operators themselves only create limited employment, jobs they do create are highly paid and sought after, and there is a major knock-on effect in retail (through the sale of airtime, handsets and SIM cards). Various measures and estimates of productivity gains are available in India. However, the nature of this evidence is mostly anecdotal. Ovum (2006) reported that the mobile telephony sector contributed Rs 145 billion ($3.6 billion) per year in import duties, licence fees, spectrum fees and taxation revenues in India. Deloitte (2007) estimated the overall taxation revenue, by segmenting the benefit into taxation revenue from the mobile operators themselves, their supplier chain and other industry retailers. They found that in six countries analysed, the direct tax contributions from the mobile operators outweighed those from indirect players, as government directly captured revenue from the operations of those companies (Deloitte, 2007). On average, mobile operators contributed 26 per cent of total revenues in taxes. This rose to 29 per cent when regulatory fees were included though this varied considerably (Deloitte, 2007).

Indirect Benefits

In addition to revenue generation, the use of a mobile phone can itself produce follow-on economic and social benefit, e.g., enhance entrepreneurship, reduce information asymmetries and market inefficiencies and substitute transportation (resulting in another knock-on effect).

A recent economic study carried out by World Resources Institute (WRI) and the International Finance Corporation (IFC) (WRI/IFC, 2007) found that even very poor families were buying cell phones and airtime, usually in the form of prepaid cards. Another finding was that as their family's income grew—from $1 per day to $4, for example—their spending on ICT increased faster than spending in any other category, including education, health and housing (WRI/IFC, 2007).

Due to the intangible nature of some of the benefits, these factors are difficult to monetise. Deloitte (2007) used the consumer's willingness to pay and 'consumer surplus' as proxies to estimate the market value placed on such factors.[12] Mobiles reduce the cost of running a business—and may even enable a user to start one. Overall, there is a body of anecdotal evidence to support the theory that the use of a mobile phone is an invaluable enabler of entrepreneurship and job search—not to mention the social benefits on the side. Over several years, research teams have spoken to: day labourers, farmers, prostitutes, rickshaw drivers, shopkeepers and all of them say more or less the same thing: 'their income gets a big boost when they have access to a mobile'. Ownership of a mobile phone can itself be leveraged as a form of entrepreneurship: there are many examples of end users using the mobile phone: (a) for m-banking applications, (b) to make payments, and (c) transfer resources to family back home by migrant labour (Bhavanani *et al.*, 2008).

The use of mobile phones may reduce information asymmetries, enabling users to access arbitrage, market or trade opportunities that they otherwise would have missed out on. Jensen (2007) in a study of fishermen in the Kerala state in India has shown that the use of mobile phones by fishermen in Kerala to arbitrage over price information from potential buyers and coordinate sales has helped them to increase incomes and reduce wastage. Since the use of mobile phones in 1997, there has been noticeable impact on reduction in price variation (mean coefficient of variation declined from 60-70 per cent to 15 per cent), which ensured price stability for the consumer and a nearly perfect spatial arbitrage replaced a collection of autarkic fishing markets (Jensen, 2007).

Surveys have found that phones were bought by the largest boats first as they could get the largest possible arbitrage gains and could afford the $100 phones. This study concluded that the use of mobile phones: (a) increased consumer surplus (by an average of 6 per cent); (b) increased the fishermen's profits (by an average of 8 per cent); (c) reduced price dispersion (by a decline of 4 per cent), and (d) reduced waste (which was averaging 5-8 per cent of daily catch, before the use of mobile phones).[13]

---

12. *http://www.deloitte.com/assets/Dcom-UnitedStates/Local%20Assets/Documents/us_chs_OpportunitiesforHealthPlansinConsumerDrivenMarket.pdf*

13. "India Second-Largest Wireless Market in the World", 8th August 2008, *http://www.siliconindia.com/shownews/India_secondlargest_wireless_market_in_the_world-nid-45326.html*

One interesting side-effect of the use of mobiles is the reduction of transportation costs: household expenditure dropped and consumer surplus increased. Improvements in the information flows between buyers and sellers allow for the efficient trading of information without travelling. This is particularly significant in rural areas, where traders would have needed to travel to urban areas to check for demand and negotiate on price, this business is now conducted on the mobile. Traders are able to ensure demand exists for their products, before setting out on a journey. Moreover, in certain circumstances, mobile phones can allow the 'middle man' to be cut out (Bhavanani *et al.*, 2008).

The theory of consumer surplus takes the average revenue per user (ARPU)—at the time the mobile phone is purchased)—and assumes that it does not change over time, i.e., it is used as fixed proxy for the value the end user places on his/her mobile phone. By subtracting contemporary ARPU figures from historical ARPU figures (because, as subscriber levels increase, ARPU falls), the value 'returned' to the end user and presumably reinjected into the economy as a whole, represents a so-called 'consumer surplus'. The value of this consumer surplus can be considerable: in 2005, it was $37 billion for China and $4 billion for both India and the Philippines. (These figures are approximate and conservative, because they do not take into account advances in the coverage and quality of the network.) (Enriquez *et al.*, (2007).

Intangible Benefits

Mobile phones can also be a tool for: (a) aiding disaster relief, (b) enabling the dissemination of locally-generated and locally-relevant educational and health information, and (c) promoting social capital and social cohesion. Mobiles were used by rescue teams in 2008 in Bihar to locate flood victims and to guide them to safer locations. There are examples of the use of mobiles to deliver health services in India.[14]

Mobile computing and wireless communication technologies provide an essential element of a comprehensive solution by expanding the size of the population that can be reached, by improving the quality of the information transfer and data accuracy, and by creating a mode for timely communication for medical interventions and enhanced patient monitoring.

14. *http://www.karmayog.org/biharfloods/biharfloods_18191.htm*

A prominent NGO in India used hand-held mobile devices in the detection and prevention of chronic kidney disease. Through mobiles they have created a flexible data collection solution with the potential to scale and include other co-morbid diseases. Second, they have reduced the transaction costs and time required for field data to be communicated to specialists at tertiary referral centres. Third, health care workers were able to cover larger populations than would otherwise be possible. Finally, timely communication between specialist nephrologists and health care workers in the field allowed intensive management of chronic kidney disease (CKD) and related conditions.[15]

Mobile services are being used to disseminate locally-generated and locally-relevant educational and health information, in order to target rural communities, whose populations typically have low levels of education and income and would not otherwise benefit from such information. There is evidence to suggest that this type of benefit could save lives in rural communities (Sundar and Garg, 2005).

The formation of social capital or social cohesion could be one of the most important forms of intangible benefit of using mobile telephones. It provides an informal platform for cooperation between individuals through the exchange of information. Mobiles enable the sharing of information, development of trust and promote norms of reciprocity inherent in social networks. Either way, economists are interested in social capital for its contribution to productivity and spillover from the individual to the group: a network effect or social externality, and it is clearly an impact that mobile phones can provide. Studies from Gujarat indicate the importance of this form of cohesion (Souter *et al.*, 2005).

V

Conclusions and Recommendations

The ICT and mobile telephony sector account for roughly 10 to 15 per cent of the GDP directly. Using output and employment multipliers their share to GDP nearly doubles. The ICT sector also accounts for over 25 per

15. *Globalization, Crisis & Health Systems: Confronting Regional Pespectives, 2010. http://www.ghf10.org/ghf10/files/ghf10_final_programme.pdf*

cent of export revenue and is an important earner of revenue. Its capitalisation is also high and has thus resulted in an inflow of foreign equity in the sector. It is very competitive globally occupying about 51 per cent of the global market share. However, its employment potential is limited. Directly it employs less than 0.33 per cent of the labour force, though indirectly it employs over 1 per cent of the labour force. Most of the employment is, however, in the formal private sector. Mobile telephony employs a slightly higher number over 2 per cent, but all in all employment in this sector is miniscule in comparison to its share of GDP or exports (authors' calculations based on NASSCOM data). Given the limited employment both directly and indirectly of the sector, the trickle-down effects of necessity would be somewhat limited looking at the numbers.

Few ordinary Indians can be said to have been affected one way or another by the software sector's astronomical growth and increasing international prominence. However, the common man has been affected by the introduction of mobile telephony in India. Even in the case of ICT, a broader view of the sector in terms of its potential effects on the larger economy should be taken. Some of these impacts are apparent already; others may take longer to come to fruition.

Aside from India's very large informal sector, software development is probably the only sector to have grown largely free of inhibiting governmental regulation or interference. In fact, Central and state governments have provided such incentives as tax exemptions, investment concessions and setting aside areas for technology parks, among other steps, to encourage the sector's growth. Nurtured by these incentives, the sector has provided the primary example in India of the growth potentialities that can occur by allowing relatively unfettered entrepreneurialism to flourish. One consequence has been a commensurate growth in venture capital availability, as investors see the chance of multiplying their investments by a hopefully propitious selection of opportunities.

The example set by the software sector has not been lost in government circles, where a similar growth pattern in a number of other high technology areas is a fervent hope, if not quite yet an expectation. Plans that are afoot include the creation through private companies of a fiberoptic 'backbone' linking the nation's cities and towns, a rapid expansion in the availability of fast internet connections, the building of a system of 'info-kiosks' to bring internet availability even to rural areas, and an overall improvement in telephone service nationwide.

The hope is for India to become an international leader not only in software development, by now an accomplished fact, but to leapfrog many other developing countries by establishing a world-class telecommunications infrastructure and associated technology capabilities.

The fact that India is demonstrably competitive internationally in the production of sophisticated software brings other advantages to the country. Indian technological sophistication, though still narrowly defined, has begun to alter international perceptions of the country. Instead of viewing India as a country burdened by decades of heavy-handed government regulation of the economy, foreigners now view the country somewhat more favourably, though not yet as a country where future growth will approximate that of China and several of the Southeast Asian countries.

Deficits of Indian infrastructure would cripple a country whose development hinges on manufacturing, it is less debilitating for one whose future is being driven by information and communication. The fact that Bangalore's airport is antiquated and that it is hard to drive to its office parks has not stopped Indian engineers telecommuting to the US inside space-age buildings powered by privately run generators.

India does not even need to build telephone landlines to feed its software habit. The wireless industry, powered by software, is doing the job at warp speed. There are about 40 million Indian landline-phone subscribers; the number of cellphone subscribers is already over 600 million—and increasing at more than 10 million a month.

As the Indian economy further opens up, other ICT applications including manufacturing, travel and tourism, health care, entertainment will increasingly look towards IT to increase competitiveness. For both new and existing verticals, the small and medium business (SMB) segment will represent an important source of growth for the domestic IT services market. More focus should be given to the domestic market.

The convergence of mobile telephony and internet usage through new technologies is likely to lead to greater gains for India. However, a lot will depend on the prices at which these technologies are available in the Indian market. Economies of scale may generate great gains only if they are affordable.

IT and mobile telephony have not yet started acting as a GPT, however, there are signs that their widespread usage has begun. While IT is export oriented though with a growing share directed to domestic usage, mobiles are almost exclusively domestically oriented. The multiplier effects of both are high as they employ young people with a high marginal propensity to consume. When both start being used widely for improving the productivity of the economy its trickle down will accelerate. Thus while trickle down at this point of time has been limited, there is a high potential for improving its widespread usage and hence its trickle down.

To fully realise the potential of ICT and mobile telephony, educational improvements to support not only this sector but also other related sectors (telecom, internet, data processing, etc.) will be required. The immediate impact can be seen in the expansion of technical colleges and universities as well as more attention to lower-level training institutes. While not helping directly with the more basic problems of illiteracy and inadequate primary and secondary education, such moves certainly do support not only software producers but also other technology-based sectors that have been receiving attention as sources of more general economic growth in India. It is also necessary to introduce computers at the primary level along with language training. In a country like India where numeracy comes more easily than literacy, it would be of material interest to tap this advantage.

References

Aisbett, Janet, Greg Gibbon, Anthony J. Rodrigues, Joseph Kizza Migga, Ravi Nath, Gerald R. Renardel (2008). *Strengthening the Role of ICT in Development*. Volume IV. Kampala, Uganda: Fountain Publishers.

Barro, R.J. (1991). "Economic Growth in a Cross Section of Countries", *Quarterly Journal of Economics* 106(2): 407-43.

Basu, Inderjit (2008). *India's IT Industry is Changing Lives*. UPI correspondent. June 17. *http://www.upiasia.com/Society_Culture/2008/06/17/indias_it_industry_is_changing_lives/5374/*

Bhatnagar, Subhash and Robert Schware (2000). *Information and Communication Technology in Development: Cases from India*. New Delhi: Sage Publications.

Bhavnani, Asheeta, Rowena Won-Wai Chiu, Subramaniam Janakiram, Peter Silarszky (TTL), Practice Leader: Deepak Bhatia (2008). *The Role of Mobile Phones in Sustainable Rural Poverty Reduction*. ICT Policy Division, Global Information and Communications Department, World Bank, *http://siteresources.worldbank.org/EXTINFORMATIONANDCOMMUNICATIONANDTECHNOLOGIES/Resources/The_Role_of_Mobile_Phones_in_Sustainable_Rural_Poverty_Reduction_June_2008.pdf*

Bresnahan, T.F. and M. Trajtenberg (1995). "General Purpose Technologies: Engines of Growth", *Journal of Econometrics* 65: 83-108.

Bresnahan, T.F., E. Brynjolfsson and L.M. Hitt (2002). "Information Technology, Workplace Organization, and the Demand for Skilled Labor: Firm-Level Evidence", *Quarterly Journal of Economics* 117: 339-76.

Brynjolfsson, E. and L.M. Hitt (2000). "Beyond Computation: Information Technology, Organizational Transformation and Business Performance", *Journal of Economic Perspectives* 14: 23-48.

Chakravarty, Rupak (2000). *IT at Milk Collection Centers in Cooperative Dairies: The National Dairy Development Board Experience. http://unpan1.un.org/intradoc/groups/public/documents/APCITY/UNPAN019011.pdf*

Deloitte & Touche LLP (2007). *Economic Impact of Mobile in Bangladesh, Malaysia, Pakistan, Serbia, Thailand & Ukraine*.

De Soto, Hernando (1996). "Securing Property Rights: The Foundation of Markets", (an interview). CIPE. *Economic Reform Today* 1.

Department of Information Technology (DIT) and National Council of Applied Economic Research (NCAER) (2010). *India e-Readiness: Assessment Report 2008 for States and Union Territories*. Released in January. *http://www.mit.gov.in*

Desai, Ashok V. (2000). "The Peril and the Promise: Broader Implications of the Indian Presence in Information Technologies", *Working Paper*. August. CREDPR. Stanford University.

Economist Intelligence Unit (2005). "The 2005 E-Readiness Rankings", A White Paper from the Economist Intelligence Unit, written in Cooperation with the IBM Institute for Business Value. *http://graphics.eiu.com/files/ad_pdfs/2005Ereadiness_Ranking_WP.pdf*

Enriquez, Luis, Stefan Schmitgen and George Sun (2007). *The True Value of Mobile Phones to Developing Markets*. February. *http://www.mckinseyquarterly.com*

Gokarn, Subir, Dharmakirti Joshi, Vidya Mahambare, Pooja Mirchandani, Manoj Mohta, Kumar Subramaniam (2007). *The Rising Tide: Employment and Output Linkages of IT-ITES*. February. *http://www.nasscom.in/upload/51269/NASSCOM_CRISIL.pdf*

Jensen, Robert (2007). "The Digital Provide: Information Technology, Market Performance and Welfare in the South Indian Fisheries Sector", *The Quarterly Journal of Economics* CXXII(3): 879 to 924.

Kapur, Devesh and Ravi Ramamurti (2001). "India's Emerging Competitive Advantage in Services", *Academy of Management Executive* 15(2): 20-31.

Keniston, Kenneth (2002). "Grassroots ICT Projects in India: Some Preliminary Hypotheses", *ASCI Journal of Management* 31(1&2). *http://web.mit.edu/~kken/Public/PDF/ASCI_Journal_Intro__ASCI_version_.pdf*

Konana, Prabhudev, John. N. Dogett and Sridhar Balasubramanian (2004). *Comparing India and China Growth Strategies: Chaotic Or Planned?. http://www.mccombs.utexas.edu/faculty/prabhudev.konana/indiachina.pdf; http://www.hinduonnet.com/thehindu/thscrip/print.pl?file=20050325003600400.htm&date=fl2206/&prd=fline&*

Laursen, Keld, Valentina Meliciani and Ammon Salter (2002). *The New Economy Meets the Old: The Importance of International ICT Knowledge-Flows for Market Share Dynamics. http://www.druid.dk/laursen/papers/gron.pdf*

LIRNE*asia* (2006). *Report on Workshop on ICT Indicators for Benchmarking Performance in Network and Services Development*. March 1-3. Available at *www.lirneasia.net*

Milgrom, P. and J. Roberts (1990). "The Economics of Modern Manufacturing Technology, Strategy and Organization", *American Economic Review* 80: 511-28.

NASSCOM (2010). *IT-BPO Sector in India: Strategic Review 2010: Section-wise Report. http://www.nasscom.in*

NASSCOM-CRISIL (2007). *The Rising Tide: Employment and Output Linkages of IT-ITES*. Mumbai: NASSCOM-CRISIL. *http://www.nasscom.in/upload/51269/NASSCOM_CRISIL.pdf*

NASSCOM-IDC (2006). *Study on Domestic Services Market Opportunity.* Published by NASSCOM, New Delhi, India. *www.nasscom.in.*

Ovum (2006). *The Economic Benefit of Mobile Services in India.* GSM Association Asia Pacific, January.

PricewaterhouseCoopers (2010). "Mobile-Broadband Outlook 2015", Paper presented at ICRIER seminar on *Socio-Economic Impact of Mobile Phones on Indian Agriculture,* February. *http://www.pwc.com/in/en/publications/Mobile-Broadband-Outlook-2015.jhtml*

Romer P.M. (1986). "Increasing Returns and Long-Run Growth", *Journal of Political Economy* 94(5).

Rupanagunta, Krishna (2004). *Infotech and Creating Resources. http://www.indiatogether.org/2004/feb/gov-itunlock.htm*

Schreyer, Paul (2000). "Recent Developments in Information and Communication Technologies and their Impact on the Brazilian Economy", Paper Presented at the *Eastern Economic Association Conference*. March. Boston, USA.

Singh, Nirvikar (2003). "India's Information Technology Sector: What Contribution to Broader Economic Development", *OECD Technical Paper* 207. *http://www.oecd.org/dataoecd/59/12/2503442.pdf*

————. (2002). *Information Technology as an Engine of Broad-Based Growth in India. http://129.3.20.41/eps/dev/papers/0412/0412012.pdf*

Souter, David, Nigel Scott, Christopher Garforth, Rekha Jain, Ophelia Mascarenhas and Kevin McKemey (2005). "The Economic Impact of Elecommunications on Rural Livelihoods and Poverty Reduction: A Study of Rural Communities in India (Gujarat),

Mozambique and Tanzania", *Report of DFID KaR Project 8347*. DFID. *http://www.telafrica.org/R8347/files/pdfs/FinalReport.pdf*

Sundar, Diatha Krishna and Shashank Garg (2005). *M-Governance: A Framework for Indian Urban Local Bodies. http://www.m4life.org/proceedings/2005/PDF/41_R359SK.pdf*

The Economist (2001). "Another Kind of Net Work: Mobile Phones in India", *The Economist* 59, March 3.

Waverman, Leonard (2005). *The Impact of Telecoms on Economic Growth in Developing Countries.* London Business School. Available at: *http://web.si.umich.edu/tprc/*

Waverman, Leonard, Meloria Meschi and Melvin Fuss (2005a). "The Impact of Telecoms on Economic Growth in Developing Countries", *Working Paper: The Vodafone Policy Paper Series* 3, March 10-23.

———. (2005b). *The Impact of Telecoms on Economic Growth in Developing Countries. http://web.si.umich.edu/tprc/papers/2005*

World Bank (2010). *India Economic Update.* Economic Policy and Poverty Team: South Asia Region. *http://siteresources.worldbank.org/INDIAEXTN/Resources/295583-268190137195/India_Economic_Update_June_23_2010.pdf*

WRI/IFC (2007). *The Next Four Billion*, 2007. *http://archive.wri.org/archive.cfm*

Annexure A-1.1

e-Readiness Index

The framework used to determine e-Readiness is based on the following premise:

There are three important stakeholders to consider in the development and use of ICT: individuals, business and governments. The degree of usage of ICT by (and hence the impact of ICT on) the three stakeholders is linked to their degrees of readiness (or capability) to use and benefit from ICT. There is a general macroeconomic and regulatory environment for ICT in which the stakeholders play out their respective roles. The environment for ICT offered by the concerned state governments, the readiness of the key stakeholders (individuals, businesses and government) to use ICT and finally the actual usage of ICT by these various stakeholders comprises this index.

Identification of the levels of e-Readiness at the state level requires a three-step procedure.

1. Identification of appropriate measures of those characteristics.
2. Identification of the most important characteristics that represent e-Readiness.
3. A rating of states based on the Composite Index, which reflects the position of a particular state, as indicated by the comparative position of important characteristics identified in Step 2.

Box 1

e-Readiness of States

Using ICTs is not just a matter of installing hardware and buying relevant software. In order to reap its benefits, its users—government, businesses and citizens—must be e-ready i.e., be able to skillfully exploit the opportunities provided by ICTs. Over the past decade or so, islands of e-governance initiatives in India at the national, state, district and even block level have emerged. These initiatives have helped these states gain a headstart in e-Readiness. Objective assessment of e-Readiness helps states evolve proactive policy and robust ICT infrastructure.

The Department of Information Technology (DIT), Government of India, through National Council of Applied Economic Research (NCAER) conducts e-Readiness Assessment and publishes the findings as e-Readiness Assessment Report. The value of the e-Readiness Index at the state level reflects the capacity of a state to participate in the networked economy in relation to the country at large. The e-Readiness Index developed by DIT/NCAER is composed of variables that fall into three broad categories: 'environment', 'readiness' and 'usage' as shown in Figure 1.

Figure 1

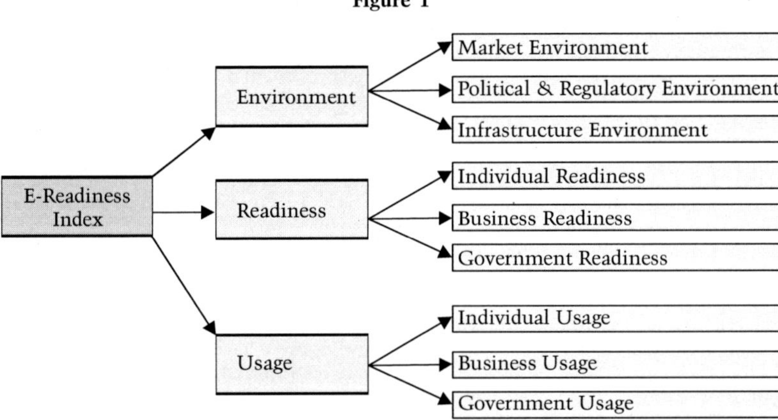

The final report of the survey on 'E-Readiness Assessment of States in India' submitted by NCAER to DIT slotted states in five categories: leaders, aspiring leaders, expectants, average achievers, under achievers and laggards.

Andhra Pradesh, Karnataka, Maharashtra and Tamil Nadu are the four Indian states that have emerged as leaders in terms of e-Readiness.

The states at the bottom of the list have been termed as 'laggards' and include Arunachal Pradesh, Assam, Bihar, Dadra & Nagar Haveli, Jammu & Kashmir, Jharkhand, Lakshadweep, Manipur, Nagaland and Sikkim.

Delhi, Chandigarh, Goa and Gujarat are 'aspiring leaders' and have been ranked at level two. The level three of 'expectants' include West Bengal, Uttar Pradesh and Kerala while 'average achievers' (level 4) are Rajasthan, Punjab, Pondicherry, Madhya Pradesh and Haryana. The rest of the states: Chhattisgarh, Daman & Diu, Himachal Pradesh, Meghalaya, Mizoram, Orissa, Tripura and Uttaranchal have been termed 'under achievers' by the report.

The states have also been rated on seven parameters: network access, network learning, network society, e-governance and network economy.

Delhi has been rated the best in terms of network access that includes indicators like teledensity, percentage of households with phones and cable TV, cellular phones, personal computer population, internet connections, length of optical fibre in operation and number of villages covered by village public telephones (VPTs).

Five states: Chandigarh, Maharashtra, Delhi, Karnataka and Tamil Nadu are on the top in terms of network learning. Network learning is monitored in terms of percentage of colleges and schools with internet access, computer labs, universities offering infotech courses, number of websites of schools and colleges, etc.

Karnataka and Chandigarh are also ahead of others in maintaining the network society, which is measured on number of online companies, local language websites and interfaces, number of government websites and number of households accessing internet as percentage of households with computers and phones. The best network policy is in place in Maharashtra, Chandigarh, Tamil Nadu, Karnataka, Goa and Gujarat. Network policy is evaluated on government's efforts to address issues related to telecom, e-commerce taxation, intellectual property and presence of an IT policy and cyber laws.

The state of e-governance depends on the rural IT applications in agriculture, education, medicines, trade, initiative and success related to e-governance projects like e-procurement, land registration, utility billing, etc. Karnataka, Andhra Pradesh, Tamil Nadu and Gujarat are on the top in terms of e-governance. Interestingly, Maharashtra is alone on top in terms of network economy. The states are rated on the basis of number of IT parks, floor area of IT parks, sales turnover of IT companies in states and number of jobs that require infotech skills.

The e-Readiness report shows the state of ICT penetration and how ICT could be used to reduce poverty in a state. While this is the picture for India as a whole, at the global level India's ranking is still relatively low. This is because all the components of a digital economy-infrastructure, security, transparency, innovation and skills—must be properly interlaced to ensure adequate e-readiness. These are still in deficit in most emerging markets, but a few are world-class or near to it in selected areas, the best examples being Estonia (26th), Slovenia (27th) and the Czech Republic (29th) with their strong development of e-government services. India (49th) and China (54th) remain on the lower rungs of the e-Readiness ladder, but are making growing contributions to the global digital economy on the strength of a strong ICT skills base (India) and a prodigious ICT manufacturing sector (China).

Table 1

E-Readiness at a Global Level

2005 e-Readiness Rank (of 65)	*2004 Rank*	*Country*	*2005 e-Readiness Score (of 10)**	*2004 Score*
1	1	Denmark	8.74	8.28
2	6	US	8.73	8.04
3	3	Sweden	8.64	8.25
4	10	Switzerland	8.62	7.96
5	2	UK	8.54	8.27
6 (tie)	9	Hong Kong	8.32	7.97
6 (tie)	5	Finland	8.32	8.08
8	8	Netherlands	8.28	8.00
9	4	Norway	8.27	8.11
10	12	Australia	8.22	7.88
11	7	Singapore	8.18	8.02
12 (tie)	11	Canada	8.03	7.92
12 (tie)	13	Germany	8.03	7.83
14	12	Austria	8.01	7.68
15	16	Ireland	7.98	7.45
16	19	New Zealand	7.82	7.33
17	17	Belgium	7.71	7.41
18	14	S. Korea	7.66	7.73
19	18	France	7.61	7.34
20	22	Israel	7.45	7.06

contd...

...contd...

2005 e-Readiness Rank (of 65)	*2004 Rank*	*Country*	*2005 e-Readiness Score (of 10)**	*2004 Score*
21	25	Japan	7.42	6.86
22	20	Taiwan	7.13	7.32
23	21	Spain	7.08	7.20
24	23	Italy	6.95	7.05
25	24	Portugal	6.90	7.01
26	26	Estonia	6.32	6.54
27	31	Slovenia	6.22	6.06
28	27 (tie)	Greece	6.19	6.47
29	27 (tie)	Czech Republic	6.09	6.47
30	30	Hungary	6.07	6.22
31	29	Chile	5.97	6.35
32 (tie)	36	Poland	5.53	5.41
32 (tie)	32	South Africa	5.53	5.79
34	39 (tie)	Slovakia	5.51	5.33
35	33	Malaysia	5.43	5.61
36	39 (tie)	Mexico	5.21	5.33
37	34	Latvia	5.11	5.60
38	35	Brazil	5.07	5.56
39	37	Argentina	5.05	5.38
40	38	Lithuania	5.04	5.35
41	n/a	Jamaica**	4.82	n/a
42	42	Bulgaria	4.68	4.71
43	45	Turkey	4.58	4.51
44	43	Thailand	4.56	4.69
45	44	Venezuela	4.53	4.53
46	48	Saudi Arabia	4.38	4.38
47	50	Romania	4.19	4.23
48	41	Colombia	4.18	4.76
49	46	India	4.17	4.45
50	47	Peru	4.07	4.44
51	49	Philippines	4.03	4.35
52	55	Russia	3.98	3.74
53	51	Egypt	3.90	4.08
54	52 (tie)	China	3.85	3.96
55	56	Ecuador	3.83	3.70
56	52 (tie)	Sri Lanka	3.80	3.96

contd...

...contd...

2005 e-Readiness Rank (of 65)	*2004 Rank*	*Country*	*2005 e-Readiness Score (of 10)**	*2004 Score*
57	54	Ukraine	3.51	3.79
58	58	Nigeria	3.46	3.44
59	57	Iran	3.08	3.68
60	59	Indonesia	3.07	3.39
61	60	Vietnam	3.06	3.35
62	63	Kazakhstan	2.97	2.60
63	61	Algeria	2.94	2.63
64	62	Pakistan	2.93	2.61
65	64	Azerbaijan	2.72	2.43

Note: * Substantial differences between our 2005 and 2004 scores mainly reflect changes in methodology.

** Jamaica is new to the annual rankings and was not ranked in 2004.

Source: Economist Intelligence Unit (2005).

2 Inter-State Migration and Trickle-Down Effect

Introduction

India has seen many high growth spells between 1980-2010. During the relatively lower growth period between 1960-1980, most states grew slowly around the average all-India figure, but after 1980 some states grew much more rapidly than others. States like Karnataka, Andhra Pradesh, Tamil Nadu, Maharashtra and Gujarat grew at rates much higher than the national average, while the more populous states such as Bihar and Uttar Pradesh till recently fell well below the national average[1] (Purfield, 2006). The difference in the rates of growth meant that opportunities for employment arose in the higher growth states and inter-state migration therefore increased significantly (by nearly 55 per cent) from the lower growth states to the higher growth states.[2] There was nearly a doubling of inter-state migration into Maharashtra, Delhi and West Bengal between 1991 and 2001.[3] Potentially, inter-state migration could be an important agent of trickling down the benefits of growth from high to low growth states.

Inter-state migration has always been prevalent in the Indian economy. The difference that high growth rates have brought is that the number of destination states have increased. While earlier inter-state migration was focussed on metros such as Calcutta, Delhi and Mumbai, high growth rates have increased the attraction of destinations such as Jaipur, Bangalore, Pune and other such cities.[4] The growth of secondary

---

1. See Introduction for data on growth rates of different states of India.
2. Ibid.
3. Data highlights Tables D1. D2, D3 from the National Census of India 2001. *http://www.censusindia.net*
4. "More Migrations, New Destinations". *http://www.indiatogether.org/2009/aug/psa-behram.htm*

cities which accompanied economic growth in India has meant that inter-state migration has become more widespread, offering greater opportunities for trickle down.

India has 10 of the 30 fastest-growing urban areas in the world and, based on current trends, it is estimated that a massive 700 million people (roughly equivalent to the entire current population of Europe) will move to cities by 2050 (Goldman Sachs, 2007). This will have significant implications for demand for urban infrastructure, real estate and services. At the same time urbanisation offers opportunities for bettering incomes and lifestyles.

While migration could potentially be an important process for trickling down growth, it has also contributed positively to growth in GDP. During the high growth period of this century starting 2003, the movement of surplus labour from low-productivity agriculture to high-productivity industry and services contributed about 1 percentage point to annual GDP growth (Goldman Sachs, 2007). India is well-positioned to reap the benefits of an 'urbanisation bonus,' over the long term due to the continued movement of labour from rural agriculture to urban industry and services.

In contrast to this narrative, some studies based on the NSS Survey tend to underemphasise the importance of migration and may even draw the conclusion that population mobility is decreasing. Kundu calculates that RU migration has declined by 1.5 percentage points, even allowing for a decline in the fertility rate, increases in urban boundaries and the emergence of new towns (Kundu, 2003). These results are in sharp contrast to the micro survey studies that show both an increase in remittances and in inter-state migration. In fact the micro studies emphasise the poverty alleviating aspects of inter-state migration, and show that migration may be an important livelihood option for the poor (Deshingkar, 2004; Srivastava, 2003). The disjunct between micro and macro studies is in part explained by the inability of conventional surveys, such as the NSS, on occupation and residence to capture information related to temporary movement and part-time occupations.

The crucial question is not about the volume of trends of migration itself, but what kind of opportunities are available for what groups of people, and whether the type of migratory work allows the migrants and their families to improve their assets and 'human capital'. Effects of out-migration depends to some extent on an ability to maintain labour inputs and to invest remittances productively. The issue of assets has been little explored in literature. This chapter particularly focusses on asset building by migrants along with other issues of remittance uses. The focus on asset building can be explained by the fact that asset building reduces poverty especially in the informal sector (see Chapter 3). As shown in chapter 3 informal employment is dominant in the Indian economy, so it can be assumed that a large proportion of migrants go to the informal sector. Hence, asset building subsequent to migration would have an important bearing on reducing poverty and would be a good measure of trickle down through migration.

Explanations on trickle down based on surveys may be regarded as anecdotal and therefore difficult to replicate in all states and all situations. This chapter thus explores some relationships between variables that directly and indirectly contribute to trickle down at the macro level. Using growth data from the CSO and the Census data on migration as well as other secondary sources of informal asset building such as that developed by Marjit and Maiti (2005), this chapter examines the effects of out-migration on asset building and remittances into states of origin. It also examines the effects of out-migration on the convergence of inequality in incomes between states. Further through case studies based on interviews with migrants across the major destination states, the chapter analyses the major variables which determine asset growth in the states of origin as well as consumption in the destination states. It looks at the role of variables such as education and gender in determining the effects of out-migration. The chapter starts with a brief review of the literature on migration in Section I. Section II examines whether migration behaviour in India is consistent with economic theories of migration. Section III analyses the effects of migration in India drawing upon secondary literature. Using an econometric model, Section IV examines whether incomes, or poverty between states has converged as a result of inter-state migration in the Indian context. Using a survey of about 200 migrants, Section V arrives at some stylised facts about migrants and then using econometric techniques evaluates the factors that could accelerate trickle down through migration.

Essentially the section examines the factors that lead to asset formation in migrant families. Finally, the chapter concludes with policies that could strengthen trickle down through migration in the current growth dynamics of the Indian economy (Section VI).

I

Theories of Migration

Early theories of migration were presaged on the assumption that surplus labour in agriculture in the rural areas would migrate to urban areas in search of higher wages and higher productivity. In fact, most developed countries followed this pattern in their early stages of development. Some authors, like Lewis (1954) and Fei and Ranis (1965), assumed that a reduction of the labour force in agriculture, because of the widespread disguised unemployment, would not reduce agricultural production. This was one of the first theories which recognised though not explicitly the role of migration in trickling down the benefits of growth. However, Lewis (1954) did recognise that rural urban migration could cause a worsening of conditions for labour in the initial stages.

Ravenstein (1889) propounded that the principal reason for migration was overpopulation and undeveloped resources in rural areas, thus, providing opportunities for higher wages in other areas such as urban areas. The Harris-Todaro (1970) model assumed that people will make rational economic decisions to migrate from rural to urban areas based on expected higher income differentials. However, this theory assumed competitive and unsegmented homogeneous labour markets and no information asymmetries. This is certainly not the case in developing economies such as India.

Migration according to these early theories was explained in terms of push factors—conditions in the rural areas on account of drought, or fragmentation of land through population increase. This induced either individuals or families or the skilled and able family members to leave their homes. In addition there are pull factors—the perceived better economic circumstances in cities or other states that attract people to move there. General examples of push factors include drought, the loss of a job, political persecution, or even caste subjugation. Examples of pull factors include job opportunities, friends and family or a city lifestyle seen on the television. In many ways, however, these factors work together. For example, a farmer in rural Bihar whose land is increasingly unproductive due to its uneconomic size, would not be 'pushed' off his land and decide to move to Delhi unless he was also aware of the presence of opportunities to improve his economic situation there. In the context of urban growth, people often emphasise pull factors in that the city is seen as a magnet or a place where people believe there are better opportunities, higher incomes, and better lifestyles.

Several other theories have advanced reasons which determine an individual or a family's decision to migrate. These factors typically include the availability and remuneration of local jobs at destination, the existence of local amenities, the cost and availability of public goods, or even institutional factors such as better governance at destination areas (Lall *et al.*, 2006). The absence of a rural credit market may also act as a push factor when migration of a family member is used to generate remittances in order to overcome credit constraints and finance rural productive investments (Kats and Stark, 1987). Of course, migration decision also depends on its monetary and non-monetary costs. Distance to potential destinations has been shown to deter migration (Schwarts, 1973; Greenwood *et al.*, 1981). A few studies suggest that migration is facilitated by the concentration of the migrant pool (of same origin) in the area of destination (Mora and Taylor, 2005).

Recent job-search models show that migration can improve job matches or be used as a way to circumvent rural constraints, such as credit market and insurance imperfections. Some empirical evidence shows that internal migration contributes to the development of rural areas through remittances by enabling the financing of productive investment and by reducing poverty even though its effects on inequality are mixed. Most studies show that, remittances are spent on both consumption and investment, enabling both short-term increases in the standard of living and long-term development in rural areas. In urban areas, internal migration does not necessarily cause massive unemployment as suggested by Todarian models, and studies on the labour market assimilation of migrants indicate that migrants can catch up with natives under certain circumstances. These elements support the view that migration can be beneficial or at least can be turned into a beneficial phenomenon (Lall *et al.*, 2006).

Remittances of migrants are used for a variety of purposes (Rapoport and Docquier, 2005). Remitting might serve to take care of the migrants' assets and relatives back home (Cox *et al.*, 1998), to invest in one's parents to secure potential bequests (de la Brière *et al.*, 2002), to insure one's family against volatile incomes (Gubert, 2002), or to repay a loan (Ilahi and Jafarey, 1999). Remitting can also be justified by sheer altruism or social norms (Asam and Gubert, 2002). Interestingly, remittances sent to rural areas might benefit different populations depending on the context, which implies that remittances do not systematically benefit the poor or the rich. The diversity of contexts also explains that remittances serve a variety of uses. They can be used for consumption (Banerjee, 1984), for housing investments when anticipating the event of return migration (Osili and Paulson, 2004), as well as capital expenditure (Lucas and Stark, 1985).

In developing countries, remittances to rural areas contribute to rural development—both directly if used in education and productive investments, and indirectly via higher consumption levels. But, on the other hand, internal migration from rural to urban areas can exert a lot of pressure on cities who may not have the capacity to absorb large population flows and to provide migrants with an adequate level of public goods. This can lead to slum formation and in extreme cases to internal crime and unrest. Urbanisation may also lead to an unbalanced distribution of the population and contribute to increasing disparities between rural and urban areas.

The negative effects of migration and that it may be an undesirable outcome is the premise of some modern theories on migration. It is argued that the public and private modern sectors are not keeping pace with job creation for an increasing labour force in urban areas, poor migrants and commuters in the city tend to find work in the urban informal or unorganised sector. These activities generally involve petty business, services or non-farm labour including street vending, shoe shining, bicycle-riskshaw driving, loading and unloading, cleaning etc. Conventional development theory conceptualises a dual labour market in urban areas where the informal sector is disadvantaged, poorly paid and unprotected and where workers go if they are unable to find work in the superior, formal sector. The 'over-urbanisation' theory for instance, predicts that migrants supply far more labour than the organised sector can absorb (Hoselits, 1957). Labour absorption by the unorganised sector then leads to low productivity and limited prospects for exiting poverty. Thus, migrants may move from one poor situation to another. The experience of several decades in India has shown that most migrants never 'graduate' to the formal sector, by contrast with the oft-cited conceptualisation of Harris and Todaro (1970). There is usually marked occupational segmentation in the informal sector where workers in particular occupations tend to come from the same areas of origin or ethnic communities (Breman, 1985).

Structuralists such as Breman (2003) maintain that migrants will always remain underpaid and never be able to move out of a survival situation because most of the profits from their work are creamed off by the exploitative activities of middlemen and contractors. The Marxists accuse economists who view migration as voluntary as politically naïve because they refuse to recognise oppression and debt-bondage (Olsen and Ramana Murthy, 2000).

Myrdal (1957a) further advanced reasons why trickle down need not happen through migration. He considered a type of multiplier-accelerator mechanism whereby supply and demand are no longer considered as independent, but interact to produce cumulative movements away from the original equilibrium, i.e., the cumulative expansion of the prosperous region at the expense of backward region. 'There is no tendency towards automatic self-stabilisation...(and) the system is constantly on the move away from such a situation' (Myrdal, 1957b). For example the initial labour migration from rural to urban areas reduces human capital and depresses demand for goods, services and factors of production in rural areas. The same movements will stimulate business and the demand for products in urban areas, further increasing the demand for labour as well as attracting capital to urban areas. These 'backwash effects' perpetuate or even worsen development differentials between regions. These backwash effects may be countered by the beneficial spread or trickle-down effects—the favourable effects on the backward regions of growth in the expanding regions. These positive effects would be mediated not only through remittances of the migrants, but also through technology and knowledge spillover effects and the increased demand for goods from rural areas from the increased real income of the migrants in the urban areas. Myrdal (1957b), however, considered these effects to be weak and outweighed by the stronger backwash effects.

The gravitation towards a low level equilibrium was further strengthened by the importance of the informal sector in developing countries. Portes and Schauffler (1993) emphasised the importance of the informal economy, not as a transitional stage in development, but as a means of deliberately organising production and marketing while meeting the challenges of global competition.

In several developing countries including India, concentration on the modern sector led to an increasing regional disparity, rural-urban migration, urban unemployment, a decrease in agricultural production and hindrance in industrial development because of a lack of purchasing power in the rural areas. The anticipated trickle-down effects hardly ever happened at least till the 1990s. In *praxis*, development plans following this line of thinking led to failures like the early Indian development planning. Therefore, other authors like Jorgenson (1961) and Lele and Mellor (1981), emphasised the important role of agriculture at the beginning of development, i.e., preceding or parallel to industrial development in order to provide enough internal resources for the development process. In fact the green revolution and the subsequent development in the 1980s in India was a testimony to this strategy.

The 'backwash effects' logic could be said to apply to inter-state inequality in India. However, this does not explain why some states such as Rajasthan which were at the bottom of the spectrum have worked their way out of its low-level equilibrium. Even backward states such as Bihar and Orissa have improved their economic positions. It also does not explain why rural-urban poverty differentials have been narrowing, while inter-state poverty differentials at least for some states may be widening in India.

The important issue is what causes low-level equilibrium traps to break and develop virtuous circles of growth. In the context of migration, the question that arises is when do incremental increases in migrant incomes and remittances reach a critical and irreversible stage. Is this similar to Rostow's takeoff when trickle-down effects of growth become self-generating?[5]

5. *http://www.mtholyoke.edu/acad/intrel/ipe/rostow.htm*

The important variable that has been left out of Myrdal's backwash effects is land. In a land scarce country such as India which accounts for 2.4 per cent of global land and over 15 per cent of global population, the opportunity cost of leaving land to low productivity uses in agriculture can be very high. High growth rates have introduced income earning opportunities through alternative land uses. The role of this missing variable is analysed in Section II. The section however begins with an analysis of traditional push and pull factors in the context of India.

II

How do these Theories Apply to India

How High is Inter-State Migration in India

Studies on migration in India have not distinguished inter-state migration from other forms of migration such as rural-urban or intra-state. This is because most studies on migration in India do not focus on the trickle-down effects of growth. High rates of growth are a relatively recent phenomenon in India and studies which examine growth with equity have not analysed the effects of inter-state migration on equity. There is also a paucity of data on inter-state migration. The most reliable data is unfortunately dated and relates to the last Census in 2001. However since the break in growth rates, i.e., its upward trend was already visible at the time of the last Census, trends of migration are unlikely to have changed much.

Of the 1.02 billion people in India in 2001, roughly 307 million or 30 per cent were reported to be migrants. This is higher than the 27 per cent of the population which was listed as migrant in the 1991 Census. A back of the envelope calculation of the elasticity of inter-state migration to GDP shows that it was about 0.9 (calculated from the Census and CSO).[6] This implies that for every per cent increase in GDP, it is likely that inter-state migration will increase by about 0.9 per cent. Extrapolating on this basis, it appears that inter-state migration would have increased by about 48 per cent between 2001 and 2007. This could be explained by the fact that higher growth rates in the some states have generated income-earning

6. Census (2001) and *Economic Survey 2002*. Published by the Planning Commission, Government of India.

opportunities leading to higher migration. It is to be noted that inter-state migration has grown by over 50 per cent between 1991-2001, showing much higher growth rates than inter-district or intra-district migration.[7]

The highest proportion (36%) of inter-state migrants are in the age group of 35-59 years or the most productive period of their lifetime. This is followed by migrants in the age group of 25-34 which accounts for roughly 25 per cent of total inter-state migration. The next age group is 15-24 which accounts for 15 per cent of the inter-state migrants. Thus, a majority of inter-state migration is economic migration in the most productive age groups.[8]

Rural to urban migration accounts for nearly 40 per cent of inter-sate migration. Another 27 per cent is urban to urban migration. The rest is rural-rural and urban-rural migration. The most popular destinations of inter-state migration were Maharashtra, Delhi, Gujarat, Haryana and Karnataka in the decade between 1991-2001.[9] West Bengal and Rajasthan are also significant destinations of inter-state migration. While one reason for migration before 1991 was natural calamities, i.e., distress migration, after 1991, work and employment along with business became very important accounting for roughly 40 per cent of the total migration.[10] The major destination states are precisely those which have shown the highest increase in the state domestic product (SDP) with an average rate of growth exceeding 9 per cent during 1991-2001. States from which the maximum number of migrants came were Bihar and Uttar Pradesh, which are precisely the states which have grown the slowest during the decade 1991-2001, again emphasising the importance of pull factors.[11]

This trend has been substantiated by other studies, which show that rural migrants from Bihar to rural Punjab in the early 1990s, have now changed their migration destination to urban centres in Delhi, Maharashtra, Karnataka and even Rajasthan (Karan, 2003). Similarly, rural to rural migration from tribal Orissa in the 1980s has now shifted to urban centres

7. Census (2001).
8. Ibid.
9. Ibid.
10. Ibid.
11. Ibid.

in Delhi, Kolkata and Mumbai (Jha, 2005). Remittances have also had a poverty reducing role in the decade between 1991-2001. Migrants had a better diet, spend more on education and health than non-migrants. The effects of migration on inequality is mixed and contextual (Karan, 2003).

Anti-migration policies include restricted access to public services by below poverty line (BPL) cardholders to food, education and health care in the destination cities. Rural employment programmes are also expected to reduce migration especially to urban areas. Regular slum clearances are also expected to discourage migration. The recent slogan of 'Maharashtra for Maharashtrians' is the most regressive anti-migration political move.[12]

An Analysis of the Economic Conditions of the States of Origin: The Push Factors[13]

Bihar was one of the slow growing states of India till 2005 and had a per capita income of about half the national average. A total of 30.6 per cent lived below the poverty line against India's average of 22.15 per cent in 2005.

The rate of inter-state out-migration from the state increased by over 132 per cent over the period 1991-2001. Roughly 80 per cent of the total migrants from Bihar were inter-state, and of the total labour force inter-state migrants accounted for roughly 8 to 10 per cent.[14] As most inter-state migrants captured by the Census from Bihar were of a long-term nature, their remittances would also have an important role to play in the economy of Bihar. The most significant effect of remittances from migrants may be reflected in the literacy rates in Bihar. The male literacy rate went up to 60.32 per cent in 2001 from 51.47 per cent in 1991, while the female literacy rate went up to 33.57 per cent in 2001 from 21.99 per cent in 1991.[15]

---

12. "Raj Thackeray says his Struggle for a Maharashtra for Maharashtrians will Continue", Saturday, February 9, 2008. *http://www.thaindian.com/newsportal/india-news*

13. The information in this section has been obtained from *India Fact Sheet 2009*.

14. Census (2001).

15. *http://gov.bih.nic.in/Profile/CensusStats-03.htm*

The economy was mainly based on agricultural and trading activities. The vast swath of extremely fertile land made it ideal for agriculture. Despite a number of rivers and good fertile soil, investment in irrigation and other agriculture facilities has been grossly inadequate. Previously, there were a few half-hearted attempts to industrialise the state: an oil refinery in Barauni, a motor scooter plant at Fatuha and a power plant at Muzaffarpur. However, no sustained effort had been made in this direction, and there was little success in its industrialisation. All these factors led to substantial out-migration from Bihar to other states during the 1990s.[16]

Uttar Pradesh (UP) has witnessed significant outflow of migrants to other states. In 2001 Census, 3.8 million migrated out of the state. The ratio of the two sexes among the out-migrants from the state is skewed in favour of males. The rate of inter-state out-migration increased by about 73 per cent between 1991 and 2001. Of the total working population, inter-state migrants account for roughly 10 per cent.

Uttar Pradesh is also a predominantly agricultural economy, with agriculture accounting for roughly 73 per cent of the total employment and 46 per cent of the state SDP. In the last decade, industrialisation and services have also become important in the state economy. Nearly 40 per cent of the total population of UP lives below the poverty line, which accounts for the high proportion of inter-state migration to high growth states from UP.[17]

Orissa has abundant natural resources and a large coastline. It contains a fifth of India's coal, a quarter of its iron ore, a third of its bauxite reserves and most of the chromite. Rourkela Steel Plant was the first integrated steel plant in the public sector in India. It received unprecedented investments in steel, aluminium, power, refineries and ports. India's topmost IT consulting firms, including Satyam Computer Services, Tata Consultancy Services (TCS), MindTree Consulting, Hexaware Technologies, PricewaterhouseCoopers and Infosys have large branches in Orissa. IBM, Syntel, Bosch and Wipro are setting up development centres in Orissa. So far, two of the S&P CNX 500 conglomerates have corporate offices in Orissa *viz.*, National Aluminium

16. Ibid.

17. *www.planningcommission.gov.in*

(2005 gross income Rs 51,162 million) and Tata Sponge Iron (2005 gross income Rs 2,044 million).

The Central government has agreed to accord special economic zone (SEZ) status to eight sites in Orissa among which are Infocity at Bhubaneswar and Paradip. Orissa has a population of 32 million.

These developments have slowed out-migration from Orissa to otherstates. Orissa no longer ranks among the top states which have high rates of out-migration.[18]

West Bengal had the third largest economy (2003–04) in India, with a net state domestic product (NSDP) of US $21.5 billion. During 2001–02, the state's average SDP was more than 7.8 per cent—outperforming the national GDP growth. The state has promoted foreign direct investment, which has mostly come in the software and electronics fields; Kolkata is becoming a major hub for the information technology (IT) industry. However, the rapid industrialisation process has given rise to debate over land acquisition for industry in this agrarian state. NASSCOM–Gartner ranks West Bengal power infrastructure the best in the country. West Bengal's SDP grew in 2004 with 12.7 per cent and in 2005 with 11.0 per cent. The rate of out-migration from West Bengal slowed down between 1991 and 2001.[19]

The other big source of out-migration is the northeast of India, especially Mizoram, Tripura and Nagaland. The great majority of Mizoram's population comprises several ethnic tribes who are either culturally or linguistically linked. A significant proportion of the population account for all kinds of migration as life in Mizoram is difficult.

Tripura's GSDP for 2004 was estimated at $2.1 billion in current prices. Agriculture and allied activities was the mainstay of the people of Tripura and provides employment to about 64 per cent of the population. There is a preponderance of food crop cultivation over cash crop cultivation in Tripura. At present about 62 per cent of the net sown area is under food crop cultivation. Paddy is the principal crop, followed by oilseed, pulses,

18. Census (2001).

19. Census (2001).

potato and sugarcane. Tea and rubber are the important cash crops of the state.

Tripura ranks 22nd in the human resource development index and 24th in the poverty index in India according to 1991 sources. The literacy rate of Tripura is 73.66 per cent, higher than the national rate of 65.20 per cent. Out-migration from Tripura especially in the services sector tends to be high.[20]

Agriculture is the most important economic activity in Nagaland, with more than 90 per cent of the population employed; crops include rice, corn, millets, pulses, tobacco, oilseeds, sugarcane, potatoes and fibres. However, Nagaland still depends on the import of food supplies from other states. The widespread practice of *jhum*—clearing for cultivation—has led to soil erosion and loss of fertility, particularly in the eastern districts. Nagas out-migrate to several states of India and work in various capacities including domestic help.[21]

An Analysis of the Major Destination States: The Pull Factors

Maharashtra witnessed largest in-migration of population between 1991-2001 from different states. The total number of in-migrants into the state was 3.2 million. Out of 3.2 million in-migrants from other states during the past decade, 2.6 million (or 79.6 per cent) moved into urban areas. Important states from where they migrated into Maharashtra were Uttar Pradesh (0.9 million), Karnataka (0.4 million), Madhya Pradesh (0.27 million), Gujarat (0.24 million), Bihar (0.22 million) and Andhra Pradesh (0.19 million). Among inter-state male migrants, work/employment has been cited as the primary reason for migration (e.g., Uttar Pradesh: 73.0 per cent; Bihar: 79.1 per cent).[22]

Delhi, is the next in series, which attracted very high number of migrants from other states in the last decade. Total number of in-migrants in Delhi between 1991-2001 years was 2.2 million. Major influx of

---

20. Census of India (2001).
21. *http://www.mapsofindia.com*
22. Census (2001): Tables D1, D2 and D3.

population into Delhi was from Uttar Pradesh (0.88 million), Bihar (0.42 million) and Haryana (0.17 million). Sex ratio of net migrants into Delhi was only 673 females per 1,000 males. Migrants from all these states cited 'work/employment' as the most important reason for migration during the last decade.[23]

Punjab is another state with interesting migration profile. Though the total number of migrants from outside the state and outside the country are 0.81 million and 0.02 million respectively, there is significant out-migration from the state (0.5 million). The number of male out-migrants is less than female out-migrants. As a result, the net migrant in to Punjab is only 0.33 million, the sex ratio stacked highly in favour of males (313 females per 1,000 males). States from where sizeable number of in-migrants came to Punjab are: Uttar Pradesh (0.24 million); Haryana (0.11 million) and Bihar (0.14 million). Male in-migrants from Uttar Pradesh and Bihar cited 'work/employment' as the main reason for migration (72.1 per cent and 82.2 per cent respectively).[24]

There are clearly multiple rationales for the use of migrant labour in destination areas. While shortages of local labour provides one important rationale, virtually all available evidence shows that recruitment of immigrants is as much motivated by strategies of labour control and wage cost reduction (Singh and Iyer, 1985; Oberai and Singh, 1980).

The Missing Element in Migration Analysis: Land in India

Apart from these push and pull factors, one issue which is very important for explaining migration in India relates to land use. Although India occupies only 2.4 per cent of the world's land area, it supports over 15 per cent of the world's population.[25] This immediately puts it in the category of land-scarce countries. The imminent shift in land from agriculture to urban use and industry constitutes an important source of potential productivity gain. Land is a critical input that is needed to keep the development process moving, allowing for the shift of people from the

23. Ibid.
24. Ibid.
25. *http://www.state.gov/r/pa/ei/bgn/3454.htm*

rural to the urban sector. Access to land is needed for factories, housing projects and to create tens of millions of jobs in construction in the short-run, as well as longer-run jobs. Witness the development of the National Capital Region around Delhi, the development of the Mumbai-Pune industrial corridor, the development of peri-urban areas around Bangalore, Jaipur, Hyderabad, Lucknow and now even some of the lesser towns such as Patna in Bihar (Shaw and Satish, 2005). While this move started during the 1980s, it accelerated in the high growth periods of 1990s and from 2000 onwards. Land prices around towns have increased, rural landowners have often sold their land upto a 100 km radius from the metro cities. The discounted value of land price premiums is obviously much higher than a stream of lifetime earnings from agriculture. However, wealth effects as most economists know is not similar to income effect. Do these people who sell their land then swell urban slums or do they participate in the higher productivity uses of land?

When land moves from low-productivity agriculture to urban use and higher productivity sectors, overall productivity improves. However, India would need investments in agriculture to boost productivity, especially in rural connectivity, storage, etc., to improve the yield of remaining agricultural land. The creation of the new SEZs holds the potential of transforming the productivity of agricultural land. For example a Maharastrian village decided to develop a SEZ from village land which has ceased to become productive.[26] At the same time the protests, deaths and killing at Nandigram in West Bengal when land had to be acquired for constructing a SEZ shows that the population was resistant to dispossession of land.[27] So again there is likely to be a divergence in land use patterns between rich and poor states.

Productivity gains for the economy tend to be a cumulative process. Higher productivity leads to more confidence and increased openness, which means more technology and investment, and sustained productivity growth. The building of highways will not only lower costs for companies but also enable rural-urban migration, development of cities and the process of

26. *SEZs and Land Acquisition: Factsheet for an Unconstitutional Economic Policy. http://www.sacw.net/Nation/sesland_eng.pdf*

27. Ibid.

moving land from agriculture to industry and services. These in turn attract more investment through agglomeration effects, and thus sustain growth. However, not all states of India are likely to improve their productivity simultaneously. Growth is likely to proceed in concentric circles around the high growth metros and high growth states. In these circumstances, inter-state migration becomes a viable option for spreading the benefits of growth.

In India, labour is nearly four times more productive in industry and six times more productive in services than in agriculture, where there is a surplus of labour (Goldman Sachs, 2007). Indeed, economic theory tells us that as labour moves from low-productivity sectors such as agriculture to high-productivity sectors such as industry or services, overall output must improve. Lewis (1954) had already established the notion of gains to labour productivity in both sectors due to the movement of surplus labour from agriculture to industry. The gain is relatively small as migration is still in its initial stages. Goldman Sachs (2007) estimates that the output gains due to labour migration from agriculture to services and industry has contributed upwards of 0.9 percentage point to overall growth. The gains are roughly equally split between agricultural labourers moving to industry and to services.

Given that the movement from agriculture to other sectors (which in India's case is roughly equivalent to the move from rural to urban areas) is still in its initial phase, it is expected that the gains will continue to increase for several decades. Indeed, agriculture still employs close to 60 per cent of the labour force with negative marginal productivity (Goldman Sachs, 2007).

According to Goldman Sachs (2007) projections, another 140 million rural dwellers will move to urban areas by 2020, while a massive 700 million people will urbanise by 2050. This is because India's urbanisation rate of 29 per cent is still very low compared to 81 per cent for South Korea, 67 per cent for Malaysia and 43 per cent for China. Rural-urban migration in India has the potential to accelerate to higher levels, as judging by the experiences of other countries, migration tends to hasten after a critical level of 25-30 per cent urbanisation is reached, and faster economic growth considerably increases the rate of migration.

The effects of land scarcity and falling agricultural productivity has also been reflected in the 2001 census. The rates of urbanisation in 2011 stood at nearly 32 per cent of which a large proportion was accounted for by the redesignation of rural land to urban land. This overall figure bears testimony to the fact that rural land is being sold for urban usages.

III

Effects of Migration: Reviewing Contrasting Views

One of the first studies to look at the effects of migration on equity was a study by Bhanumurthy and Mitra (2003). This study decomposed changes in poverty into a growth effect, an inequality effect and a migration effect for two periods: 1983-1993/94 and 1993/94-1999/2000. The decomposition analysis showed that rural-to-urban migration contributed to poverty reduction in rural areas by 2.6 per cent between 1983 and 1993-1994. Poverty in the urban sector increased during the same period, but by a smaller rate than the reduction of poverty in rural areas. Therefore, the net poverty incidence for the country as a whole decreased over the period studied. Similar findings were reported for the 1993/94-1999/2000 period. Rural poverty declined by 1.64 per cent as a result of rural to urban migration, while urban poverty increased by 1.43 per cent. The first period was a higher growth period than the second one.

Older studies on migration (Ramana Murthy, 1991; Rao, 1994; Reddy, 1990) emphasised the distress dimensions of migration, where it was regarded as a means of survival in a situation of drought, crop failure and poor terms of trade. Thus, push factors dominated migration.

Later research has shown that sending one or more persons to work in a distant location for part of the year has become a livelihood strategy for many rural households (Rao, 2001; Deshingkar, 2004). Village studies from India conducted from 1995-2000 show a marked increase in temporary migration. While some of these studies are based on surveys of villages (Singh and Karan, 2001; Karan, 2003; Dayal and Karan, 2003), others have used recall to arrive at this conclusion (Rao, 2001; Dayal and Karan, 2003; Rogaly *et al.*, 2001; Rafique and Rogaly, 2003).

A major attraction for the poor working in the farm sector is the part-payment in cooked food. Although this has been perceived as exploitative by some, the labourers themselves see it as an important way of coping and surviving during economically lean times when casual work in the cities may be scarce. In fact rural to rural migration has resulted in a high level of remittances to the state of origin, considerably alleviating poverty in the households which receive remittances. The same can be observed for households which send maids from the northeast, as consumption in destination states does not eat away a large part of the earnings of the migrants.[28]

In contrast to the trickle-down theory, studies have emphasised the abysmal living conditions of migrants in urban areas. Most migrants live in open spaces or makeshift shelters in spite of the Contract Labour Act (1970) which stipulates that the contractor or employer should provide suitable accommodation (Ministry of Labour, 1991; NCRL, 2011). Food costs more for migrant workers who are not able to obtain temporary ration cards. Labourers working in harsh circumstances and living in unhygienic conditions suffer from serious occupational health problems and are vulnerable to disease. As there are no crèche facilities, children often accompany their families to the workplace to be exposed to health hazards. They are also deprived of education: the schooling system at home does not take into account their migration pattern and their temporary status in the destination areas does not make them eligible for schooling there (Rogaly *et al.*, 2001).

The effects of migration on the conditions of living in the rural areas according to different studies may also not be positive. Male out-migration has been seen to influence the participation of women in the directly productive sphere of the economy as workers and decision-makers and increase the level of their interaction with the outside world. The impact of male migration can be especially adverse for girls, who often have to bear additional domestic responsibilities and take care of younger siblings. The absence of male supervision further reduces their chances of acquiring education (Srivastava and Sasikumar, 2003).

---

28. Author's own survey. See Section V for stylised facts from the survey.

Why does Migration Take Place at All? What is the Counterfactual?

Some studies do show that seasonal out-migration potentially has the effect of smoothing out employment over the annual cycle. While rural out-migration could in theory cause a tightening of the labour market in some circumstances, empirical evidence from out-migrant areas does not often attest to this (Connell *et al.*, 1976; Srivastava, 1998). However there is also evidence that greater mobility of rural labour households has led to a less isolated and more generalised agriculture labour market and an upward pressure on wages (Bird and Deshingkar, 2008).

Field evidence right from the 1970s has established that the informal sector presents a strong pull in the process of migration and can in fact reduce poverty (ILO, 1972). Harris (2004) cites the example of Bangalore where the urban slum and squatter population doubled from 1.12 million in 1991 to 2.2 million in 1998/99, a period in which poverty in the state of Karnataka, of which Bangalore is the capital, fell from 54 to 33 per cent.

Contrary to the expectations of earlier migration theories, a majority of workers never 'graduate' to formal sector employment but remain in the informal sector. 'In many economies, the character of the informal sector as dynamic and growing is sharply accentuated when juxtaposed against a stagnant and shrinking formal sector' (Phillipson, 2004). Indeed several observers suggest that migrants have been able to escape poverty, even by remaining in the unorganised sector. A study of migrant labour in Delhi slums showed that with experience, migrants were likely to move from low income, casual jobs to higher income, regular jobs (Gupta and Mitra, 2002). A study on West Bengal showed that migration was a way of accumulating a useful lump sum, rather than simply surviving (Rogaly and Coppard, 2003). Migration has allowed numerous lower caste people in Madhya Pradesh and Andhra Pradesh to break out of caste constraints (which are especially strong in rural areas of India), find new opportunities and escape poverty (Deshingkar and Start, 2003). Papola (1981) noted in the case of Ahmedabad city in India that although a majority of the migrants were in the informal sector employment, their urban earnings after migration were double their rural earnings. It has also been noted that urbanisation of the poor had the potential to bring many more of the poor to the locations most favourable to overcoming poverty (Harris, 2004).

The 'pull' of informal sector work in urban areas is partly explained by the persistence of low wages in rural areas. In India nearly 40 per cent of the working population is employed as agricultural labourers (Shanmugam and Vijaylakshmy, 2005). Agricultural labourers are one of the most dispossessed and socially and politically deprived groups. They are usually from the lower castes that were historically disadvantaged. Agricultural labour contracts are verbal almost everywhere and the terms for the labourer range from exploitative to remunerative. The strongest determinant of wages is agricultural productivity with high-productivity crops offering the highest wages. However in low-productivity situations, wages are low and often lower than the statutory minimum because of the monopoly or monopsony power exercised by landlords and other locally powerful people in controlling access to credit and employment and keeping wages down. The poor are usually trapped in a situation of permanent debt and are in 'interlocked' trading arrangements where they sell (labour) cheaply and buy (credit, food etc.) expensively from their patrons. Owing to the highly seasonal nature of rainfed farming, most labourers traditionally do not earn enough throughout the year to escape debt and do not have the capital, skill or connections to diversify into other occupations. Migration offers them an option to earn during the lean season, escape local caste domination and save money.

Are Remittances used for Alleviating Poverty or for Generating Income Earning Assets?

In some regions of the country, one-quarter to one-third of the households receive remittances. Field studies show that a majority of seasonal migrants either remit or bring home savings. In many cases, a substantial proportion of household cash income is attributed to migrant earnings (Haberfeld *et al.*, 1999; Rogaly *et al.*, 2001; Mosse *et al.*, 2002). Moreover, it does appear that the income and consumption level of migrant households is generally higher than that of similarly placed non-migrants (Sharma, 1997; Krishnaiah, 1997).

Remittances are mainly used for purposes like consumption, repayment of loans and meeting other social obligations. These constitute, in effect the 'first charge' on migrant incomes. The evidence on investment is, however, mixed. Investment by migrant households on housing, land and consumer durables is common and migrant income is also used to finance working capital requirements in agriculture (de Haan *et al.*, 2000).

The major category on which remittances are spent is the repayment of debts. In some cases, it was the primary reason for migration. These included borrowing for agricultural purposes, health, boring of wells, marriages and festivals. In the absence of formal institutional credit to cater to the varied needs of migrants, private moneylenders have been used, but are the last resort due to the steep price in terms of high interest rates (Krishnaiah, 1997; Rao, 1994; Ravinder, 1989; Reddy, 1990).

Remittances are also utilised for health: 42 per cent of the migrants spent their earnings on health both at the destination and at the origin (Krishnaiah, 1997). The households utilised the remittances and took further loans often falling into debt due to expenditure for health and as a result of accidents at the workplace. As a result of the unhygienic conditions in which migrant workers are forced to live at the destination, they fall victim to all sorts of chronic diseases like diarrhoea, tuberculosis, jaundice and malaria. Their health is also affected by the poor quality food, the long working hours and the nature of their work, which often includes doing demanding, heavy manual work. They are deprived of public health facilities at the destination due to their temporary status, and visiting private hospitals is expensive and therefore not affordable. They carry these diseases with them when they return to the village (Krishnaiah, 1997).

Several households invest remittances in agricultural activities, which include the purchase of land and agricultural inputs like seeds, fertilisers and digging wells. It can be seen clearly in the villages that in spite of the accumulation of resources through long periods away, migrants who invested their remittances in agriculture-related activities still failed to get returns due to continuous drought and other institutional factors. This clearly attests to the necessity in these cases of moving out of agriculture to non-agricultural activities (Samal, 2006).

Remittances also went toward meeting the social expenditures of the households such as marriages and festivals. Remittances were sometimes invested in house construction especially in the case of long-term migrants (Samal, 2006).

Around 37 per cent of migrant households in particular areas invested their remittances in buying land and boring wells. A large number of households also invested remittances in buying livestock and some members of the migrant households went into vegetable vending. In a few instances, migrants have invested their remittances in buying tractors for the village, which they rent out, or auto rickshaws for local transportation, one migrant household has set up a small *kirana* (grocery) shop in the village. Many migrants have supplemented the lump sum amount of remittances with additional loans from private companies to undertake income generating activities, like buying tractors (Samal, 2006).

On the significance of remittances, it was believed by many scholars for a long time that remittances form an insubstantial part of village income. It was estimated that remittances accounted for only 2-7 per cent of village incomes, and less for poor labourers (Lipton, 1988; Connell *et al.*, 1976). However, new evidence suggests that this is not necessarily the case. Deshingkar and Start's (2003) research in unirrigated and forested villages of Madhya Pradesh showed that migration earnings accounted for more than half of the annual household earnings. In the more prosperous state of Andhra Pradesh the overall contribution was much lower but in the village that was unirrigated and poor, migration remittances contributed to 51 per cent of household earnings (Deshingkar and Start, 2003). Moreover, migration income was both from farm and non-farm sources and the relative importance of each depended on the particular skill base and historical migration pattern (Lakshmansamy, 1990). Recent research from Bihar suggests that migrant incomes contribute nearly 12 per cent of the state's SDP (Gerry Rogers, 2012, Forthcoming paper for the Institute of Development Studies, Delhi).

Additional questions that arise with respect to migration is when and under what circumstances are migrants likely to send higher remittances to the states of origin. This has significant implications for trickle down as higher the remittances, quicker the trickle-down effects of growth. Studies have found that seasonal and contractual labourers make regular and substantially greater remittances than short-term migrants. The majority of members (75%) migrating from 1990 onwards had not been able to save much due to the high cost of living at the destination. The hierarchy of expenses for migrants are food, rent for living and other expenses, such as health. Other major determinants of remittances are the size of the household, number of dependents (elderly people and children) and purpose (clearing debts, productive investment, consumption, among others). Large families usually send more members to urban areas to increase earning potential while the rest of the family take care of the household agricultural activities. Factors controlling the amount and duration of remittances are determined by the availability of work and the financial necessities at home. The duration of migration also mattered as staying for long periods especially in places like Mumbai, Hyderabad and Bangalore enabled migrants to earn more (Deshingkar, 2004).

To sum up, the existing literature on migration in India shows that in many cases it may alleviate poverty, but the overall picture is ambiguous. To obtain a wholistic and macro picture on the poverty alleviating results of migration other variables such as convergence of incomes should be examined. In theory, inter-state migration should also contribute to the convergence of state level rates of growth around the national average. It should also lead to a convergence in poverty rates which may be more sensitive to inter-state migration than per capita incomes. This is because the latter is particularly influenced by income inequalities. Moreover, poverty convergence is more likely to be sensitive to inter-state migration because it is the poor who constitute the majority of the migrants. The next section examines this hypothesis with the help of Census and CSO data bases as well as case studies conducted by the author.

IV

Convergence between States and Whether Inter-State Migration has a Role to Play

Views on convergence of growth rates between states differ. Further even studies which find that there has been convergence do not necessarily examine the role of inter-state migration in bringing this about. Some find evidence of convergence after controlling for initial economic conditions (Cashin and Sahay, 1996; Aiyar, 2001). Others find evidence of divergence (Rao *et al.*, 1999; Bajpai and Sachs, 1996). Various studies have made opposing claims of the effects of globalisation on convergence though few have conducted statistical tests. Bhattacharya and Saktivel (2004) and Kumar (2004) assert that growth rates have diverged during the reform period, whereas Ahluwalia (2002) asserts that growth rates have converged.

One of the few studies which analyses the effects of inter-state migration on convergence is by Cashin and Sahay (1996). The study claims that over 1961–1991, the dispersion of real per capita incomes across the Indian states had widened, except for the subperiods 1962–1968, 1972–1975, 1977–78 and 1980–1984. The dispersion of real per capita NDP across the states narrowed between 1961 and 1971 owing to robust growth rates in initially poor states (Manipur, Kerala and Himachal Pradesh) and slow growth rates in initially rich states (Delhi, West Bengal and Maharashtra). However, in the 1971–1981 and 1981–1991 subperiods, the initially poor states (Manipur, Bihar and Orissa in 1971; Bihar, Assam and Orissa in 1981) and the initially rich states (Delhi, Punjab and Haryana in 1971; Delhi, Punjab and Maharashtra in 1981) had similar rates of economic growth.

An important mechanism by which differences in cross-regional per capita incomes can be equalised within national economies is by population movements from relatively poor to relatively rich states. The relationship between the annual average net immigration rate between 1961 and 1991 and real per capita income in 1961 was visibly positive, which is evidence in favour of the proposition that net immigration is positively affected by cross-state differentials in per capita incomes (Cashin and Sahay, 1996).

Migration from poor to rich states should accelerate the speed of convergence of per capita incomes across the 20 states of India. After taking into account exogeneous shocks and the effect of migration, the results of this study yield the same rate of convergence (of about 1.5 per cent per year) as when only exogeneous shocks were considered (Cashin and Sahay, 1996). This suggests that the process of migration has had little effect on the convergence of per capita incomes across the states of India.

The essential question that this chapter seeks to answer is whether the magnitude and effects of inter-state migration during the period of high growth following 1991 led to poverty convergence.

Three growth periods have been identified. The first is from 1980-1990. The second from 1990-1995 and the third from 1995-2000. State domestic product (SDP) data has been obtained from the Central Statistical Office (CSO). Migration data has been obtained from the Census and to that extent it only captures permanent migration. However, if circular migration or temporary migration were to be included, the correlations obtained would be much more robust as it is estimated that temporary migration accounts for the movement of about 10 million people on an annual basis (Banerjee, 2004).

Several relationships which examine the contribution of migration to convergence have been examined. First of all the initial gap in the SDP from the national average was taken as an explanatory variable in determining the convergence of per capita income. The assumption was: higher the initial state SDP, higher should be the convergence of per capita domestic product with the national average. Secondly, the level of asset formation in the state of origin of the migrants was considered. Again economic logic dictates that higher is the asset formation in the state of origin, higher should be convergence of per capita domestic product. Poverty level was taken as another explanatory variable. Again it is assumed that higher the poverty level in a state, lower will be its convergence from the all India average per capita income.

Data Sources: The data for state level per capita SDP and SDP was been obtained from the CSO. The data for migration has been obtained from the Census 2001, tables D1, D2, and D3. The data for poverty has been obtained from the National Sample Surveys (NSS) at the state level. The data for asset formation refers to informal sector asset formation and has been obtained from Marjit and Maiti's (2005) paper on the informal sector.

The convergence variable was standardised by dividing with the overall standard deviation. This was to reduce the importance of extreme values in the data set and to normalise the series.

Table 2.1

Abbreviation of Variables

GpDP	Gap in the state domestic product from the national average
Ias	Growth of asset in the state of origin
Pov	Share of population below poverty level
DiAI	Difference from All India per capita income
Rom	Percentage of out-migrated people over state population
Std_	Standardised variable
Ln	Log of variable
***	Significant at 1 per cent
**	Significant at 5 per cent
*	Significant at 10 per cent

Standard deviations are in parenthesis

Table 2.2

Summary of Variables

	Mean	*Median*	*Std.*
GpDP	0.11	0.10	0.05
Ias	58.44	46.26	46.32
Pov	32.18	34.75	11.1
DiAI	-.00	2398	8972
Rom	0.03	0.02	0.03

Note: Thus, std DiAI= $\frac{\text{PCDP of ith state-AIPCDP}}{\text{Standard deviation}}$

And

Std DiAI= F(Rom, pov, Ias, GpDP)

Table 2.3

Convergence of Per Capita Incomes across States

Dependent Variable: Std_ DiAIExplanatory Variables	
Ln_Rom	-0.60*** (0.21)
Pov	0.048*** (0.01)
R-sq	0.57
Adj-Rsq	0.53
Root MSE	0.68
No Obs	27

Of all the variables examined above, only inter-state migration and the initial poverty level was found to satisfy statistical significance tests in explaining convergence. The other variables were not found to be significant. The fact that the initial gap in SDP was not found to be significant is explained by the fact that some of the most populous but poor states nevertheless have high SDPs. These include Uttar Pradesh and West Bengal. Similarly asset formation in the state of origin was not found to play a major role in determining convergence because migrants may not be investing in assets in their home states, but on the other hand may be acquiring assets in their state of destination. This is also supported by the fact that the Census data by and large captures permanent migration. The survey conducted by the author and other surveys show that while permanent migrants send remittances, they build assets in the state of destination.

The results of the above regressions show that migration contributes to convergence both in terms of absolute values and in the standardised variable. The difference in the per capita product from the national average decreases with increasing out-migration rates. Moreover higher the initial levels of poverty, higher is the divergence. This result does indicate that while higher poverty rates are associated with higher difference between the state and the national average domestic product, inter-state migration acts as an intermediating variable leading to convergence in the SDP per capita to the national average.

It should be understood that the empirical findings listed above are only partial equilibrium results. At any point of time there may be many other factors that could lead to divergence between per capita SDPs, such as land distribution, better focus of infrastructure in some states etc. What is important is to understand that the absence of inter-state migration would make convergence difficult, i.e., the regression only establishes the counterfactual. The absence of migration could lead to further divergence.

Apart from per capita incomes, to establish the trickle-down effects of inter-state migration, it may be more useful to examine either poverty convergence or human development value (HDV) convergence. This is because per capita income may be skewed by the higher income groups and need not capture the effects of inter-state migration on the lowest income groups. Moreover, GSDP figures may not be reliable. For example, West Bengal emerges as the state that has the highest growth rate of GSDP at constant 1993/94 prices of 7.05 per cent per year between 1993/94 and

2004/05. Our knowledge of the Indian economy leads us to state that this is not credible. It is true that the CSO makes some corrections on the GSDP data but the original data on production and prices reported by statistical departments of states is not tampered with in any way. Not only are GSDP figures unreliable but they are also, strictly speaking, not comparable across states.

Thus both from the view of equity as well as trickling down the benefits to the poor, it may be better to look at poverty figures. The dependent variables thus becomes a standardised poverty convergence variable and a standardised human development index (HDI) variable. To get robust results, the series on migration derived from the Census has been extended to 2004-05. The method used to extend the series is described below.

Methodology in Computation

First year-on-year percentage change in poverty level (Pov), human development value (HDV) and per capita income between 1990 and 2000 is calculated at the all-India level using data from the *Human Development Report* of the UNDP, data on poverty from the NSS, and data on per capita income from the CSO. Next, overall elasticities are obtained by dividing percentage change of HDV and percentage change in poverty by percentage change of per capita income for each year. These are then averaged out to get a unique value for the entire period 1990-2000.

These elasticities are then multiplied with percentage change in SDP for each year and each state for the period 1993-2004/05. This gives us the percentage change in poverty and HDV, for each year for each of the 20 states during the period 1993 to 2004/05. Next using the absolute value of poverty and HDV of 1993 (as a starting point) each years Pov and HDV is calculated for the years 1993-2004/05. Next for each year, the difference between state-level Pov and HDV, and all-state average, for each year is calculated to give a measurement of convergence of these variables. These are used as dependent variables in this regression.

Using the elasticity estimates of the first equation, the series on out-migration is extended upto 2004/05. Using GSDP for each year for each state, the estimated values of rate of out-migration are calculated for the entire period.

Regression of Convergence of Poverty and HDV and Growth of Informal Sector Wage

The first relationship that was measured was the correlation between poverty and HDV. This was done to examine whether they were correlated and if so both the variables would need to be examined separately in determining the underlying chain of causation introduced by inter-state migration. What is interesting is that the relationship between poverty and HDV works at lower rather than higher levels of poverty. Thus, if the population below the poverty line is below 33 per cent, the correlation between HDV and poverty is very high, but becomes much lower when poverty is higher than 33 per cent. Thus for states like Bihar and UP, which have poverty levels well above 33 per cent, it is to be expected that HDV would only be weakly correlated with poverty. This further emphasises the importance of measuring the effects of inter-state migration on poverty and HDV separately.

Table 2.4

List of Abbreviations

Dpov	Difference of percentage population below poverty line, between the state and all-India level. (state poverty – all-India level poverty).
DHdv	Difference of human development value, between state and all-India level. (state human development value – all-India level value).
Ln_Rom	Log of percentage of out-migration.
Year	Year is a time variable.
Rom	Rate of out-migration.
Hdv	Human development value.
Pov	Per cent of population below poverty line.
CIfWg	Growth in informal sector wage.
***	Significance at 1 per cent.
**	Significance at 5 per cent.

Table 2.5

Correlation between HDV and Pov

In aggregate	-0.58
If per cent of population below poverty line is above 33 per cent	-0.13
If per cent of population below poverty line is below 33 per cent	-0.79

The regression technique used here is a fixed effects regression model. This is because fixed effects regression is the model that can control omitted variables that differ between cases but are constant over time. It helps in accounting for the changes in the variables over time to estimate the effects of the independent variables on the dependent variable. It is also the main technique used for analysis of panel data which is the case in this regression.

Fixed Effects Regression

This regression shows that poverty rates have been converging over the years and going down. It also shows that inter-state migration has a converging effect on poverty rates. The important result is that inter-state migration has a statistically significant effect on the convergence of poverty rates. Such convergence is also seen in the case of rural-urban poverty rates which may also be caused by inter-state migration.

Table 2.6

Explaining Poverty Convergence through Inter-State Migration

Explanatory Variables	
Year	-0.57***
	(0.02)
Ln_Rom	-0.13**
	(0.05)
F(2,284)	702.21***
R-sq within	0.83
No. of groups	26

Table 2.7

Fixed Effects on HDV through Migration

Explanatory Variables	
Year	0.003***
	(0.0004)
Ln_Rom	0.018***
	(0.001)
F(2,152)	1731***
R-sq within	0.95
No. of groups	14

The effect of inter-state migration on HDV is positive. Again HDV has been increasing over time. This is the same trend as was the case with poverty. Further as poverty reduces below 33 per cent, HDV increases more than proportionately. Inter-state migration contributes to an increase in the absolute value of HDI. No statistically significant relation was found between convergence of HDI and inter-state migration. This could be explained by the fact that at rates of poverty over 33 per cent which accounts for the poverty level in a number of poor states such as Bihar and UP, inter-state migration is the highest. Yet the correlation of the levels of HDV would be weaker in these states, thus the effect on convergence would be weak.

Table 2.8

Fixed Effects on Informal Sector Wages through Migration

Explanatory Variables	
Ln_Rom	0.05*** (0.01)
F(2,259)	20.02***
R-sq within	0.07
No. of groups	26

The contribution that inter-state migration makes to real informal wage growth is shown by the above regression. Each percentage increase in inter-state migration leads to an increase in real informal wages by 0.05 per cent. This however refers to the real informal wage in the state of origin, showing labour market effects which arise locally when out-migration takes place. Thus, Lewisian effects are observed in the case of India. As inter-state migration takes place mostly from states which have surplus agricultural labour to states where industry and services are dominant, labour market effects can be observed both at the state of origin and the state of destination.

Table 2.9

Summary of Variables

	Mean	*Median*	*Std*
Rom	8.3	1.07	60.5
HDI	0.53	0.052	0.09
Pov	27.3	27.3	10.06

Lopes (2004) used a similar strategy and added a dynamic component. His results implied convergence in inequality over time, and a negative effect of initial GDP per capita on changes in inequality. This is consistent with the results above. Other studies found that inequality converges faster than growth, meaning that a policy that affects both growth and inequality may have a stronger effect on inequality in the short run and a stronger effect on growth in the long run (Bourguignon, 2004).

More interesting than the convergence of growth results, however, are studies on the convergence of both rural and urban poverty. Poverty trends between rural and urban areas across India show that they are converging and falling especially during the periods of high growth. This points to the importance of inter-state and rural-urban migration in achieving these results. The HDI based on indicators such as per capita expenditure, headcount poverty ratio, literacy rate, formal education rate, infant mortality, life expectancy, access to safe water and housing show that over time there has been convergence rather than divergence. They show that inter-state disparities have not worsened during the periods of high growth but have remained at the same level. This is despite the fact that HDI for high growth states has grown at faster rates than those of low growth states and thus points to the importance of transfers through inter-state migration from high growth states to low growth states (Siggel, 2010).

While these state-level results are interesting in themselves, it would be important to examine the chain of causation which is possible only at the micro level. This would require an examination of several explanatory variables which are best captured through a survey. To this effect, a survey of migrants was conducted of over 193 migrants in destinations such as Delhi, Punjab, Uttarakhand, Andhra Pradesh and Karnataka. These migrants were interviewed at different employment sites such as construction, homeworkers, hawkers, taxi drivers etc. While obvious shortcomings of a survey technique attend this survey, an extensive questionnaire which included several aspects of migration was used for group discussions and interviews. The interviews used recall method to understand the trickle-down effects of migration.

V

Factors Determining Trickle-Down through Inter-State Migration: A Case Study-based Approach

Before analysing the regressions generated by the survey, it would be useful to list some of the characteristics of the migrants surveyed. The survey was conducted in several destination states of India and people were chosen in an ad hoc manner. The interviewers went to several sites where migrant workers predominate and the major issues covered by the interviewers related to their income, living conditions, asset building, health expenditures etc., before and after migration. A copy of the questionnaire is attached as Annexure A-2.1. The interviewees were requested to recall expenditures on different items, poverty, unemployment, and other conditions deriving from migration. The case study was done by giving special attention to completeness in observation, reconstruction and analysis of the cases under study. It was done in a way that incorporated the views of the 'actors' in the case under study.

A frequent criticism of case study methodology is that its dependence on a single case renders it incapable of providing a generalising conclusion. Some commentators have considered case methodology 'microscopic' because it 'lacked a sufficient number' of cases (Yin, 1993). Others have forcefully argued that the size of the sample does not transform a multiple case study scenario into a macroscopic study (Hamel *et al.*, 1993). The goal of the study should establish the parameters, and then should be applied to all research. In this way, even a single case could be considered acceptable, provided it met the established objective. Case study can be seen to satisfy the three tenets of the qualitative method: describing, understanding and explaining. It is a fact that case studies do not need to have a minimum number of cases, or to randomly 'select' cases. The generalisation of results is made to theory and not to populations. Multiple cases strengthen the results by replicating the pattern-matching, thus increasing confidence in the robustness of the theory.

The methodology that has been used is more in the nature of exploratory case studies, where fieldwork and data collection have been undertaken prior to definition of the research questions and hypotheses. However, the framework of the study was created before the fieldwork. Survey questions were altered after a pilot of 50 interviews was conducted. Selecting cases, in this instance, migrants is a difficult process. The selection of states and job sites was made on the basis of best available opportunities to maximise what could be learned, knowing that time was limited. Hence, the cases that were selected were easy and willing subjects. Basically the use of multivariate cases and techniques promoted an analysis of pattern matching with the overall picture which has been described above from the Census data and other secondary sources.

Some Stylised Facts that Emerged from the Surveys

All the people surveyed were economic migrants and were thus predominantly male. They ranged between the ages of 15 and 40. Only about 2 per cent of the people surveyed were above 40 and 1 per cent were above 50. Nearly 70 per cent of the migrants were from scheduled castes or other backward castes. However, even the higher castes were doing the same work as those of the scheduled castes or the backward castes. Most had migrated because of the pull factor, i.e., work opportunities, though a few, about 5 per cent did state that their land had become unproductive or family quarrels had induced them to migrate.

Nearly 80 per cent of the migrants stated that they had no intention of returning to the villages except for occasional visits, whereas the rest were seasonal or circular migrants. Nearly 60 per cent of the migrants had come from other service sectors, i.e., urban to urban whereas the rest were primarily occupied in agriculture before migration, rural to urban. Most have seen a large increase of nearly 50-200 per cent in incomes and some 30 per cent had built assets subsequent to migration. Most migrants were living with dependents ranging between 4 and 11, and several families had more than one or two working members. Those who migrated alone were more able to build assets in their native places. Most of the remittances were however used for food, education of children and for health purposes.

Table 2.10

State-wise Percentage of Migrants

Native States	*Per cent of Migrants*	*Destination States*	*Per cent of Migrants*
Bihar	30	Delhi	50
Uttar Pradesh	30	Uttarakhand	20
Uttarakhand	15	Andhra Pradesh	11
West Bengal	7.5	Punjab	10
Others	16.5	Others	9

Table 2.11

Characteristics of Migrants

	No. of Migrants	*Illiterate*	*Working Age Group (15-50)*	*Permanent Migration*	*Married*	*SC/ST and Other OBCs*	*Economic Migrants*
Total	193	111	182	150	153	129	174
Male	180	100	169	138	141	121	171
Female	13	11	13	12	12	8	3

Table 2.12

Percentage Distribution of the Basis of Payment Made for Persons Covered by the Survey

Basis of Payment Made	*At Origin (Per cent)*	*At Destination (Per cent)*
In kind	28	0
Daily basis	44	33
Weekly basis	6	3
Monthly basis	24	64

The effects of migration on the migrants are shown by several factors. First of all 28 per cent of the migrants were paid in kind at the state of origin, whereas at the state of destination they were paid in cash. Payment in kind was generally much lower than payment in cash. Again payment on a daily basis implied that regular employment was not available to migrants before migrating. The fact that 64 per cent were paid monthly wages after migrating showed that a large proportion of them got regular employment after migrating.

Additionally, a large proportion of the migrant population was brought above the minimum wage level through inter-state migration. Where 51 per cent of the population earned wages which were below the minimum level before migration, only 28 per cent earned wages which were below the minimum wage level after migration.

Table 2.13

Percentage Distribution of Persons brought above the Minimum Wage Level through Migration

	Below Income Level of Rs 65 per day of Rs 2,000 per Month	*At or Above Income Level of Rs 65 per day of Rs 2,000 per Month*
At origin before migration	51%	49%
At destination after migration	28%	72%

Most of the migrants sent remittances and their remittances were used intensively for meeting food needs of their families at their states of origin. About 23 per cent of the migrants reported that their remittances were also used for education. About 30 per cent of the migrants reported that their remittances were used for health expenditures. Most remittances, however, appear to be used for meeting consumption deficits showing the low initial incomes of migrants.

Table 2.14

Use of Remittances by Migrant Families

Use of the Remittance for	*Percentage of Migrants Reporting Use of Remittances*
Food	94
Health	30
Education	23
Improving house	13

Asset building was, however, an important objective of migration. From the people surveyed, about 63 per cent built assets in their places of origin and only 22 per cent built assets at their places of destination. Migrant remittances thus were important in determining asset building.

Table 2.15

Asset Building by Migrants

	Proportion without Assets before Migration	*Proportion with Assets after Migration*
Assets in place of origin	37%	63%
Assets in place of destination	78%	22%

Regression Results from Survey Analysis

As direct information was available on asset building either from the use of remittance incomes or at the state of destination, the factors that contribute to asset building of the migrant could be examined. If the gap between the per capita income between the state of origin and the state of destination (DSDP) was high, the migrant was more likely to send higher levels of remittances which was used for asset building. Thus, a positive correlation could be expected between DSDP and asset building. Similarly, younger people are likely to remit more and hence contribute to asset building. The higher the level of education, the higher is the likely level of remittances and the higher the asset building. Women and men may have different patterns of remittances and hence different contributions to asset building. Similarly, the higher the percentage increase in expenditure relative to the state of origin, the lower would be the remittances and hence the lower the asset building.

For examining these relationships a logit analysis was used. This is the appropriate method to use when the sample is skewed. In this multivariate analysis, the sample is extremely skewed as most were illiterate and most were men.

Not all variables showed a statistically significant relationship. The regression results showed that higher the gap between the per capita incomes of the destination state and the state of origin, higher was the migrant likely to remit incomes for building assets. Women were more likely to remit incomes for asset building and women from poorer states were even more likely to remit incomes for asset building.

The pattern of utilisation of remittances in the high growth period was different from the earlier studies which showed that payment of debt was the main motive for migration. In the sample surveyed, most migrants appear to

Table 2.16

List of Abbreviations

DSDP	Per cent gap in per capita NSDP between destination state and native state of the person.
Age	Age of the person.
Ed1	=1 if education of the person is equal to 0; and 0 otherwise.
Ed2	=1 if education of the person is equal to 2, i.e., at least Tenth pass; and 0 otherwise.
Gen	=1 if person is male; 0 otherwise.
Gensd	Gen dummy multiplied by DSDP.
Asbk	=1 if the person builds assets with remittances; 0 otherwise.
Exin	Per cent change in consumption expenditure in destination state relative to native state.

For Logit model, number of positive response=60, negative response=89.

move with a view to permanent settlement and for income earning purposes. There is also a relative breakdown of the link between rural areas, showing that the safety net offered by rural presence is not valued as much as was shown by the earlier literature. It also shows that migrants are more confident of their future in the place of destination than they were earlier, which could be a direct result of the opportunities brought about by growth in the place of destination.

Table 2.17

Logit Estimates of Asset Building with Remittances

Dependent variable: Asbk

Explanatory Variables	
DSDP	2.82*** (0.21)
Age	-0.009 (0.017)
Ed1	-0.08 (0.86)
Ed2	-0.63 (0.89)
Gen	23.6*** (1.08)
Gensd	-2.87*** (0.22)
Chi2(6)	14.98**
Pseudo R2	0.07
No. of observations	149

VI

Conclusions and Policy Recommendations

The push and pull factors for inter-state migration has changed considerably over the high growth period of the Indian economy. Inter-state migration subsequent to 1991 may have had a role to play in both asset building in the state of origin and in explaining the convergence of poverty between states. The character of migration has changed to more permanent forms of migration, as migrants move with their families showing a higher level of urbanisation than in the past. Migrants also appear to value their rural safety nets much less than in the past, showing confidence in the growth opportunities brought by migration. Urbanisation also appears to have reached a critical point of above at 30 per cent, beyond which rates of urbanisation are expected to grow much faster, judging by the experience of other countries. Information from 2011 Census of India shows that the natural migration has shown an increasing trend. Urbanisation in 2011 crossed the 31 per cent level, largely on account of reclassification of rural into urban areas and migration.

The important contribution of migration to poverty alleviation needs to be recognised. Migration permits the use of flexible labour policies which would help accelerate growth. But there is a need to build on the human skills of migrants so that their remuneration and opportunities increase over time. There is a need to support migrants by improving their access to renumerative work, schooling, health care, training, safe working conditions and adequate housing. The training schemes outlined in chapter 3 would equally apply to migrants. Moreover, it is important that anti-migration policies outlined above be stopped. Thus, the Federal or the Union government of India should put in place policies that do not discourage migration and at the same time discourage regional factionalism.

Given that India is a land-scarce country, economic development would involve several forms of urbanisation. As shown above, this would improve productivity and reduce poverty. It is important to note that in India, there is a continuum in terms of population density from remote villages to the large urban centres. The conventional dichotomy of rural *versus* urban areas still seems to dominate development thinking and poverty research. Furthermore, migration patterns are seldom reflected adequately in statistics on poverty and living conditions. Static measurements of per capita or household income, consumption or other indicators of well-being may conceal important cyclical patterns of movements of people and transfer of resources between households as well as within families.

Policies in India should be more concerned with influencing the direction of rural to urban migration flows—e.g. to particular areas—with the implicit understanding that migration will occur anyway and thus should be accommodated at as low a cost as possible. The idea is often to prevent massive inflows to large overcrowded cities while helping migrants of rural origin to find a job in smaller or medium-sized cities. This is usually advocated through the decentralisation of infrastructure and activities with a view to create new centres of growth that will be able to absorb the rural population influx (Skeldon, 2003). With the benefit of hindsight, industrial and urban decentralisation strategies have faced significant challenges in India but have become more successful in the recent past because of the software boom (Waddington, 2003). The software boom spread to secondary cities because of the presence of better infrastructure and the possibility to create infrastructure. The availability of skilled manpower was also important though not all important.

Thus if programmes for the creation of secondary towns and cities are to be generalised, should potential migrants be trained before or after migrating? What is the best way to facilitate information sharing in rural areas? How can potential migrants better choose where to migrate given their qualifications and the distribution of job opportunities in urban areas? Should recruitment agencies, analogous to those that are often already active in the context of international migration, help rural dwellers secure a job contract before migrating to the city? What types of specific savings and credit programmes could help workers finance migration costs? These questions need to be answered by policy planners in directing the growth of cities with different hierarchies. Urban structure and change are important for the socioeconomic development of India because they are related to the production and distribution of goods and services, the government's capacity to provide public facilities and amenities, and the degree of crowding and stress in the environment under which people live. In this light, policies to affect or respond to urban structural change are also important.

Broadly, policies to influence urban structural change aim to achieve a more balanced pattern of urbanisation with a more clearly articulated hierarchy of different size cities and towns, integrated spatial development and accelerated economic growth with equity. This has been noted by Rodinelli and Cheema (1983) who state that, 'experience with three decades of development in Asia suggests that a broad spectrum of human settlements—rural villages, market towns, small cities, intermediate regional centres, and large metropolitan areas—is needed to build strong internal economies...Cities of various sizes must be integrated with rural settlements through physical, social, economic and political linkages that forge them into a mutually sustaining network of production, exchange and consumption centres.' They further added that 'the objectives should be not so much to slow urbanisation as to develop more harmonious rural-urban linkage at the regional level, with the aim of an integrated economy where income and employment growth in rural areas and neighbouring towns are mutually supportive and the benefits are not "creamed" off by a few metropolitan areas.' The proliferation of smaller but economically important urban settlements throughout India is a testimony to these trends. The 2011 Census of India shows that reclassification of rural into urban areas is one of the major factor contributing to increased urbanisation. Further urban population in the last decade grew by 91 million in comparison to 90.6 million in rural areas. A village or other population unit is declared as town when its population crosses 5,000, when the percentage of male workers in agriculture falls below 25 per cent, and where population density is above 400 per square kilometre (Census 2001). Thus government efforts should focus on building infrastructure in small towns of India and road networks which would encourage this form of migration. Given that government efforts in delivering social justice has been abysmal (see Chapter 6), its efforts should be focussed on building infrastructure, which has been relatively more successful.

A burning question has been whether the government should in fact, intervene to affect urban structural change. Some theorists argue that as economic growth accelerates equity problems are ameliorated and spatial polarisation is reversed automatically through internal migration (Mera,

1975). But others point out that even if polarisation reversal 'is bound to happen eventually, it may not happen for a very long time and the continued polarisation in the meantime may conflict with national policy objectives' and that 'developing country concern with inter-regional equity, national spatial integration and other spatial objectives will have a strong incentive to "nudge" polarisation reversal along with policy measures. The problems are when to intervene and how to intervene' (Richardson, 1973).

It has been suggested that the prospects for decentralisation strategies are increased if policies are implemented close to the time when polarisation reversal begins rather than when polarisation forces are still strong. The efficiency cost of premature intervention may be very high. Primacy reversal has been considered as having begun when the 'backwash' effects of resource movements (including migration) into the core region begin to be outweighed by increasing spatial diffusion of technical knowledge, by a rising demand for complementary goods produced in lagging regions; and by the setting up of branch plants made viable by the expanding size of dispersed markets, lower input costs (especially of labour), inter-regional transportation improvements and mobile external economies (Richardson, 1993; 1981). India appears to have reached this stage and therefore unlimited expenditure on infrastructure is called for on the part of the government. This includes the kind of training infrastructure outlined in chapter 3.

It is not enough just to have a hierarchy of different-sized cities and towns. Different components of the spatial system playing different and crucial economic and social functions in the development process must be linked to each other through a network of physical (road and other transportation and communication networks), economic (production linkages, market interaction patterns, capital and commodity flows, service delivery), technological, social and administrative interactions. Such linkages are essential for generating and spreading economic growth, for helping to integrate regional spatial systems into a strong national space economy, for creating multiplier effects of further growth and change, and for building up the potential for mutually beneficial economic interaction (Lim, 1987). For example, improved transportation between villages and towns could help to reorganise and expand periodic and regular markets which, in turn, could change the flow of economic and social interactions and the movement of people and goods. Closer linkages among different-sized cities make it less expensive and more convenient to integrate technology and to distribute services more widely. In the words of Renaud (1979: 113), 'national economic planners must be made more aware that most of their decisions are not spatially neutral, and physical planners must acknowledge the limits placed on their plans by the state of the national economy, if national spatial policies are to improve the national environment.'

In the context of India, this would involve some federal planning to allocate the most appropriate land to agriculture. For example, Bihar has fertile agricultural land and no shortage of water. The Government should therefore invest in improving agricultural productivity in Bihar to an extent that it can feed a good part of India. The same applies to eastern Uttar Pradesh, Orissa and West Bengal. Arid parts of the country could be more urbanised though water scarcity for human consumption would need to be addressed. Building of infrastructure should be a priority both for the Central and the state governments. This would decrease urban overcrowding and help build a hierarchy of cities and townships.

References

Ahluwalia, Montek S. (2002). "Economic Reforms in India Since 1991: Has Gradualism Worked?", *Journal of Economic Perspectives* 16(3): 67-88, Summer.

Aiyar, S. (2001). "Growth Theory and Convergence across Indian States", in Tim Callen, Patricia Reynolds and Christopher Towe (eds.), *India at the Crossroads: Sustaining Growth and Reducing Poverty*. Washington: International Monetary Fund. pp.143-69.

Asam, J.P. and F. Gubert (2002). "Those in Kayes: The Impact of Remittances on their Recipients in Africa", *Mimeo*, University of Toulouse.

Bajpai, N. and J. Sachs (1996). "Trends in Inter-State Inequalities of Income in India", *Development Discussion Paper* No. 528, Harvard Institute for International Development.

Banerjee, Abhijit V. (2004). "Educational Policy and the Economics of the Family", *Journal of Development Economics* 74(1): 3-32.

Banerjee, Biswajit (1984). "The Probability, Sise and Uses of Remittances from Urban to Rural Areas in India", *Journal of Development Economics* 16: 293–311.

Bhanumurthy, N.R and Arup Mitra (2003). *Declining Poverty in India: A Decomposition Analysis*. No. 70/2003, *http://www.iegindia.org/dispap.htm*

Bhattacharya, B.B. and S. Sakthivel (2004). "Regional Growth and Disparity in India: Comparison of Pre- and Post-Reform Decades", *Economic and Political Weekly:* 1071-77, March 6.

Bird, Kate and Priya Deshingkar (2008). "Circular Migration in India", *Policy Brief No. 4*. Prepared for the *World Development Report 2009, http://www.odi.org.uk/resources/download/2506.pdf*

Bourguignon, F. (2004). "The Poverty-Growth-Inequality Triangle", *Mimeo*, The World Bank.

Breman, J. (1985). *Of Peasants, Migrants and Paupers, Rural Labour Circulation and Capitalistic Production in West India.* Delhi, Bombay Calcutta, Madras: Oxford University Press.

———. (2003). *The Labouring Poor in India, Patterns of Exploitation, Subordination, and Exclusion.* Oxford University Press.

Cashin, P. and R. Sahay (1996). "Internal Migration, Centre-State Grants, and Economic Growth in the States of India", *IMF Staff Papers* 43(1): 123-71.

Census of India (2011). "Provisional Population Totals: India Census 2011", *www.censusindia.gov.in*. Ministry of Home Affairs, Government of India.

Connell, J., B. Dasgupta, R. Laishley and M. Lipton (1976). *Migration from Rural Areas: The Evidence from Village Studies.* Delhi: Oxford University Press.

Cox, D., S. Eser and E. Jimenes (1998): "Motives for Private Transfers over the Life Cycle: An Analytical Framework and Evidence for Peru", *Journal of Development Economics* 55: 57-80.

Dayal, H. and A.K. Karan (2003). *Labour Migration from Jharkhand.* New Delhi: Institute For Human Development.

de Haan, Arjan, Karen Brock, Grace Carswell, Ngolo Coulibaly, Haileyesus Seba and Kasi Ali Toufique (2000). *Migration and Livelihoods: Case Studies in Bangladesh, Ethiopia and Mali.* Institute of Development Studies, University of Sussex, Brighton.

de la Brière, B., E. Sadoulet, A. de Janvry and S. Lambert (2002). "The Roles of Destination, Gender, and Household Composition in Explaining Remittances: An Analysis for the Dominican Sierra", *Journal of Development Economics* 68(2): 309-28.

Deshingkar, P. (2004). "Understanding the Implications of Migration for Pro-poor Agricultural Growth", Paper prepared for the *DAC POVNET Agriculture Task Group Meeting*, Helsinki, 17–18 June.

Deshingkar, P. and D. Start (2003). "Seasonal Migration for Livelihoods in India: Coping, Accumulation and Exclusion", *ODI Working Paper* 220. *http://www.odi.org.uk/publications/working_papers/wp220.pdf*

DFID (2007). *Moving Out of Poverty-Making Migration Work for Poor People.* London, UK: DFID.

Fei, J.C.H. and G. Ranis (1965) *Development of the Labor Surplus Economy.* Homewood, IL: Richard D. Irwin Inc.

Goldman Sachs (2007). "India's Rising Growth Potential", *Global Economics Paper* Number 152GS. January. Global Economic Website Economic Research from the GS Institutional Portal at *https://portal.gs.com*

Greenwood, M.J., J.R. Ladman and B. Siegel (1981). "Long Term Trends in Migratory Behaviour in a Developing Country: The Case of Mexico", *Demography* 18: 369-89.

Gubert, F. (2002). "Do Migrants Insure those who Stay Behind? Evidence from the Kayes Area", *Oxford Development Studies* 30(3): 267-87.

Gupta, I. and A. Mitra (2002). "Rural Migrants and Labour Segmentation, Micro-level Evidence from Delhi Slums", *Economic and Political Weekly*: 163–68, January 12.

Haberfeld, Y., R.K. Menaria, B.B. Sahoo and R.N. Vyas (1999) "Seaosnal Migration of Rural Labour in India", *Population Research and Policy Review* 18(4): 73–89.

Hamel, J., S. Dufour and D. Fortin (1993). *Case Study Methods*. Newbury Park, CA: Sage Publications.

Harris, J.R. and M.P. Todaro (1970). "Migration, Unemployment and Development: A Two-Sector Analysis", *American Economic Review* 60: 126-42.

Harris, N. (2004). *The Impact of the Reform of International Trade on Urban and Rural Change*. Draft Development Planning Unit, University College London. April.

Hoselits, Bert F. (1957). "Generative and Parasitic Cities," *Economic Development and Cultural Change* 3: 278–94.

Ilahi, N. and S. Jafarey (1999). "Guestworker Migration, Remittances and the Extended Family: Evidence from Pakistan", *Journal of Development Economics* 58: 485-512.

ILO (1972). *Incomes, Employment and Equality in Kenya*. Geneva: ILO. *http://www.ilo.org*.

Jha, V. (2005). "Migration of Orissa's Tribal Women: A New Story of Exploitation", *Economic and Political Weekly, Commentary*. April 9.

Jorgenson, Dale (1961). "The Development of a Dual Economy", *Economic Journal* 71: 309-34.

Karan, A. (2003). "Changing Patterns of Migration from Rural Bihar", in G. Iyer (ed.), *Migrant Labour and Human Rights in India*. New Delhi: Kanishka Publishers. pp.102-39.

Kats, Eliakim and Oded Stark (1987). "Migration, Information and the Costs and Benefits of signaling", *Regional Science and Urban Economics* 17(3): 323-31, August. *http://www.sciencedirect.com*

Krishnaiah, M. (1997). "Rural Migrant Labour Systems in Semi-arid Areas: A Study of Tow Villages in Andhra Pradesh", *The Indian Journal of Labour Economics* 40(1).

Kumar, Nagesh (2000). "Economic Reforms and their Macro-Economic Impact", *Economic and Political Weekly*: 803-12, March 4.

Kumar, Sanjay (2004). "Impact of Economic Reforms on the Indian Electorate", *Economic and Political Weekly:* 1621–30 (April 17), (New Delhi).

Kundu, A. (2003). "Urbanisation and Urban Governance: Search for a Perspective beyond Neo-Liberalism", *Economic and Political Weekly* 38(29), India.

Lakshmansamy, T. (1990). "Family Survival Strategy and Migration: An Analysis of Returns to Migration", *The Indian Journal of Social Work* 51(3): 473-85.

Lall, S.V., H. Selod and S. Shalisi (2006). "Rural Urban Migration in Developing Countries- A Survey of Theoretical Predictions and Empirical Findings", *World Bank Policy Research Working Paper* 3915. May. Published by the World Bank.

Lele, Uma and John Mellor (1981). "Technological Change, Distributive Bias and Labor Transfer in a Two-Sector Economy", *Oxford Economic Papers* 33(3): 426-41.

Lewis, W.A. (1954). "Economic Development with Unlimited Supplies of Labour", *Manchester School* 22:139–91.

Lim, Lin Lean (1987). "Socio-economic Implications of Urban Structural Change", *The Sian Conference on Population and Development in Medium Sized Cities. http://www.auick.org/database/conf/conf1987/05/001.htm*

Lipton, M. (1988). "Rural Development and the Retention of the Rural Population in the Countryside of Developing Countries", in J. Havet (ed)., *Staying On: Retention and Migration in Peasant Societies.* University of Ottawa Press.

Lopes, H. (2004). "Pro-poor-Pro-growth: Is there a Trade Off?", *The World Bank Policy Research Working Paper No.* 3378.

Lucas, Robert E.B. and Oded Stark (1985). "Motivations to Remit: Evidence from Botswana", *Journal of Political Economy* 93: 901–18.

Marjit, Sugata and Dibyendu S. Maiti (2005). "Globalization, Reform and the Informal Sector", *Working Papers* RP2005/12. World Institute for Development Economic Research (UNU-WIDER).

Massey, Douglas S., Jorge Durand and Nolan J. Malone (2002). *Beyond Smoke and Mirrors: Mexican Immigration in an Era of Economic Integration.* New York: Russell Sage Foundation. p.133.

Ministry of Labour (1991). *Report of the National Commission on Rural Labour (NCRL).* Government of India.

Mera, K. (1975). *Income Distribution and Regional Development.* Tokyo: University of Tokyo Press.

Mora, J. and J. Taylor (2005). "Determination of Migration, Destination and Sector Choice: Disentangling Individual, Household and Community Effects", Osden and Schiffs (eds.), *Inernational Migration, Remittances and the Brain Drain.* The World Bank and Palgrave Macmillan. pp.21-51.

Mosse, D., S. Gupta, M. Mehta, V. Shah, J. Rees and the KRIBP Project Team (2002). "*Brokered Livelihoods: Debt, Labour Migration and Development in Tribal Western India", Journal of Development Studies* 38(5): 59–87, June.

Myrdal, G. (1957a). *Rich Lands and Poor.* New York: Harper and Row.

———— . (1957b). *Economic Theory and Underdeveloped Regions.* Harper and Row.

NCRL (2001). *Report of the National Commission on Migrant Labour. http://www.docstoc.com/docs/44225278/Bibliography-On-Migration*

Oberai, A.S. and H.K.M. Singh (1980). "Migration, Remittances and Rural Development: Findings of a Case Study in the Indian Punjab", *International Labour Review* 119(2): 229-41.

Olsen, W.K. and R.V. Ramana Murthy (2000). "Contract Labour and Bondage in Andhra Pradesh (India)", *Journal of Social and Political Thought* 1(2), June. *http://www.yorku.ca/jspot/2/wkolsenrvramana.htm*

Osili, Una Okonkwo and Anna Paulson (2004). "Prospects for Immigrant-Native Wealth Assimilation: Evidence from Financial Market Participation", *Federal Reserve Bank of Chicago Working Paper* WP 04-18.

Papola, T.S. (1981). *Urban Informal Sector in a Developing Economy.* Vikas Publishing House.

Phillipson, R. (2004). *Rural-Urban Change & The Role Of Regional Policy Lessons From European Experience.* A Report to the Department for International Development's Urban and Rural Change Team. February.

Portes, Alejandro and Richard Schauffler (1993). "The Informal Economy in Latin America: Definition, Measurement and Policies", *Population and Development Review* 19(1).

Purfield, Catriona (2006). "Mind the Gap: Is Economic Growth in India Leaving Some States Behind?", *IMF Working Paper* No. 06/103. International Monetary Fund (IMF), April. *http://papers.ssrn.com*

Rafique, A. and B. Rogaly (2003). "Internal Seasonal Migration, Livelihoods and Vulnerability in India: A Case Study", Paper presented at Regional Conference on *Migration Development and Propoor Policy Choices.* June 22-24. Dhaka: Refugee and Migratory Movements Research Unit.

Ramana Murthy, R.V. (1991). *Seasonal Labour Migration in Semi-Arid Areas: A Case Study of Palamuuru Labour.* M.Phil. Thesis. Hyderabad: Department of Economics, University of Hyderabad.

Rao, G.B. (2001). *Household Coping/Survival Strategies in Drought-prone Regions: A Case Study of Anantapur District, Andhra Pradesh, India.* SPWD-Hyderabad Centre.

Rao, Usha (1994). *Palamoor Labour: A Study of Migrant Labour in Mahabubnagar District.* Hyderabad: C.D. Deshmukh Impart Centre, Council for Social Development.

Rao, M.G., R.T. Shand and K.P. Kalirajan (1999). "Convergence of Incomes across Indian States: A Divergent View", *Economic and Political Weekly* 34(13): 769-78.

Rapoport, Hillel and Frédéric Docquier (2005). "The Economics of Migrants' Remittances", *Discussion Paper Series.* Forschungsinstitut sur Sukunft der Arbeit, Institute for the Study of Labor. March. *http://ftp.isa.org*

Ravinder, A. (1989). "Labour Migration: A Dimension of Poverty". Unpublished Master of Philosophy dissertation. Hyderabad: Department of Economics, Osmania University.

Ravenstein, E. (1889). "The Laws of Migration: Second Paper", *Journal of the Royal Statistical Society* 52: 241-305. *http://www.geog.ucsb.edu/~tobler/publications/pdf_docs/movement/migration/Ravenstein.pdf*

Reddy, D. Narasimha (1990). *Rural Migrant Labour in Andhra Pradesh.* Report submitted to the National Commission on Rural Labour, Government of India.

Renaud, B. (1979). "National Urbanisation Policies in Developing Countries", *World Bank Staff Working Paper* No. 347, Washington D.C.: World Bank.

Richardson, H. (1973). *The Economics of Urban Size.* Farnborough, Hants: Saxon House.

————. (1981). "Defining Urban Population Distribution Goals in Development Planning", in United Nations, *Population Distribution Policies in Development Planning.* New York: United Nations.

Richardson, N. (1993). "Efficiency and Welfare in LDC Mega-cities", in J.D. Kasarda and A.M. Parnell (eds.), *Third World Cities: Problems, Policies, and Prospects.* Beverly Hills: Sage. pp.32-57.

Rodinelli, D. and D.S. Cheema (1983). "Implementing Decentralisation Policies", in D.S. Cheema and D. Rodinelli (eds.), *Decentralisation and Development.* London: Sage.

Rogaly, B., J. Biswas, D. Coppard, A. Rafique, K. Rana and A. Sengupta (2001). "Seasonal Migration, Social Change and Migrants Rights, Lessons from West Bengal", *Economic and Political Weekly:* 4547–59, December 8.

Rogaly, B. and D. Coppard (2003). "They used to Go to Eat, Now They Go to Earn: The Changing Meanings of Seasonal Migration from Puruliya District in West Bengal", *Journal of Agrarian Change* 3(3): 395, July.

Samal, Chandan K. (2006). "Remittances and Sustainable Livelihoods in Semi-arid Areas", *Asia-Pacific Development Journal* 13(2), December.

Schwarts, A. (1973). "Interpreting the Effect of Distance on Migration", *Journal of Political Economy* 81: 1153-69.

Shanmugam, T.R. and K. Vijaylakshmy (2005). *Determinants of Agricultural Labour Participation in Organisation in India. http://www.agriculturaits.csu.cs, Agricultura Tropica et Subtropica* 38(2).

Sharma, Alakh N. (1997). *People on the Move: Nature and Implications of Migration in a Backward Economy.* Delhi: Vikas.

Shaw, Annapurna and M.K. Satish (2005). "Metropolitan Restructuring in Post Liberalised India: Separating the Global and the Local", Presented at the *103rd Annual Meeting of the Association of American Geographers,* Denver, CO. April 5–9. *http://www.sciencedirect.com*

Siggel, Eckhard (2010). *Poverty Alleviation and Economic Reforms in India.* Montreal, Canada: Department of Economics, Concordia University.

Singh, M. and A.K. Karan (2001). *Rural Labour Migration From Bihar.* New Delhi: Institute for Human Development.

Singh, M. and G.K. Iyer (1985). "Migrant Labour in Rural Punjab", in U. Patnaik and M. Dingwaney (eds.), *Chains of Servitude: Bondage and Slavery in India. sar.sagepub.com/content/29/1/19.refs*

Skeldon, R. (2003). "Migration and Poverty", Paper presented at the conference on *African Migration and Urbanisation in Comparative Perspective.* Johannesburg, South Africa, June 4-7.

Srivastava, R.S. (1998). "Migration and the Labour Market in India", *Indian Journal of Labour Economics* 41(4).

Srivastava, Ravi (2003). "An Overview of Migration in India, its Impacts and Key Issues," in *Migration Development Pro-Poor Policy Choices in Asia.*

Srivastava, Ravi and S.K. Sasikumar (2003). *An Overview of Migration in India, Its Impacts and Key Issues.* Report prepared for Department for International Development (DFID), U.K.

Stark, Oded and J. Edward Taylor (1991). "Relative Deprivation and Migration: Theory, Evidence, and Policy Implications", *Policy Research Working Paper Series* 656. The World Bank.

Waddington, C. (2003). "Livelihood Outcomes of Migration for Poor People", *Globalisation and Poverty Working Paper* No. T1. Brighton: Research Centre on Migration, University of Sussex.

Yin, R. (1993). *Applications of Case Study Research.* Beverly Hills, CA: Sage Publishing.

Annexure A-2.1

Rural-Urban-Rural Migration

Questionnaire

Name: M/ F Gender: ☐ ☐

Native state:

☐ Bihar ☐ Orissa ☐ West Bengal ☐ Northeast

Destination state:

☐ Delhi ☐ Mumbai ☐ Punjab ☐ Maharashtra ☐ Karnataka ☐ Andhra Pradesh

Age of the migrant: ____________________

Martial status:

☐ Single ☐ Civil Marriage ☐ Customary Marriage ☐ Divorced

Education:

☐ Illiterate ☐ Matriculation ☐ Higher Secondary ☐ Graduate ☐ Post Graduate

Religious affiliation:

☐ Hindu ☐ Muslim ☐ Sikh ☐ Christian ☐ Buddhist ☐ Jain

Caste:

☐ Scheduled Caste ☐ Scheduled Tribe ☐ Other Backward Classes ☐ Others

Reason for migration:

☐ Education ☐ Work ☐ Marry ☐ Natural disaster ☐ Illness

☐ Death of an earner ☐ Quarrel ☐ Unproductive land ☐ Other (specify)

Type of migration:

☐ Seasonal (Harvest) ☐ Occasional (for construction activities, building roads etc.) ☐ Permanent

Sectoral shift in economic activity (from before migration to after migration):

☐ Agri to agri ☐ Agri to manuf ☐ Agri to services

☐ Manuf to agri ☐ Manuf to manuf ☐ Manuf to services

☐ Services to agri ☐ Services to manuf ☐ Services to services

Sector of economic activity of the migrant (before migration):

☐ Agriculture ☐ Allied activities (animal rearing, poultry, husbandry etc.)

☐ Industry ☐ Services

Specify the occupation of the migrant (before migration): ____________________

Present sector of economic activity of the migrant:

☐ Agriculture ☐ Allied activities (animal rearing, poultry, husbandry etc.)

☐ Industry ☐ Services

Specify the occupation of the migrant (after migration): ______________________

Employment status before migration:

☐ Self-employed ☐ Industrial outworker ☐ Farmer

☐ Civil servant ☐ Tertiary/services (specify)____________________

Employment status after migration:

☐ Self-employed ☐ Industrial outworker ☐ Farmer

☐ Civil servant ☐ Tertiary/services (specify)

The form of source of income of the migrant at the native place (before migration):

☐ Cash ☐ Kind

If the migrant's source of income (before migration) was in cash whether it was paid on:

☐ Daily basis ☐ Weekly basis ☐ Monthly basis

Specify the amount Rs. ____________

Migrant's source of income (after migration) in cash is paid on:

☐ Daily basis ☐ Weekly basis ☐ Monthly basis

Specify the amount Rs. ____________

Asset holding (at native place):

☐ No ☐ Yes

If yes, specify: ______________________

Do the migrant still avail benefits from the native holdings of assets?

☐ No ☐ Yes

If yes, specify (whether in cash or kind): __________________________

Asset Holding (at the destination state)

☐ No ☐ Yes

If yes, specify: ________________________

Dwelling place before migration:

☐ *Kuchcha* (*jhopadh*) ☐ *Pucca* (hut) ☐ Rented (*pucca*) ☐ Spatial *pucca* self-owned

Dwelling place at the destination state (after migration)

☐ *Jhuggis* (Slum) ☐ Rented ☐ Shared with others ☐ Own apartment ☐ Footpath

Members residing with the migrant (at the destination state):

☐ Alone ☐ Two members

☐ More than two (specify the number) __________

Availability of infrastructure (at the destination state):

☐ Electricity ☐ Water supply ☐ Transportation facility

Does the migrant support the household by sending or bringing back goods or money?

☐ No ☐ Yes

If yes, specify the form of support (Cash/kind): ____________________

Daily working hours before migration (in hours):

□ < 8 □ 8=<10 □ 10=<12 □ 12=<14 □ >14

Daily working hours after migration (in hours):

□ < 8 □ 8=<10 □ 10=<12 □ 12=<14 □ >14

Monthly living expenditure of the migrant (in Rs.) after migration:

□ < 50 □ 51-100 □ 101-1000 □ 1001-5000 □ 5000

Where are the remittances mainly used?

□ Food □ Clothes □ Education □ Health

□ Repaying debt □ Improving house □ Inputs/tools □ Others (specify)

Does the migrant's labour productivity increased?

□ No □ Yes

Who is then main beneficiary of the remittances?

□ Alone □ Spouse/partner □ Parents □ Others (specify)

Does the migrant get financial support from other members of the household after migration?

□ No □ Yes

If yes, mention the relationship with the migrant: ____________________

Monthly expenditure on consumption (in Rs.) or (calorie intake)* before migration:

For rural mass:

□ 0-224 (1383)	□ 225-254 (1609)	□ 255-299 (1733)
□ 300-339 (1868)	□ 340-379 (1957)	□ 380-419 (2054)
□ 420-469 (2173)	□ 470-524 (2289)	□ 525-614 (2403)
□ 615-774 (2581)	□ 775-949 (2735)	□ 950-more (3778)

For urban mass:

□ 0-229 (1398)	□ 300- 349 (1654)	□ 350-424 (1729)
□ 425-499 (1912)	□ 500-574 (1968)	□ 575-664 (2091)
□ 665-774 (2187)	□ 775-914 (2297)	□ 915-1119 (2467)
□ 1120-1499 (2536)	□ 1500-1924 (2736)	□ 1925-more (2938)

Monthly expenditure on consumption (in Rs.) or (calorie intake)* after migration:

***For rural mass*:**

□ 0-224 (1383)	□ 225-254 (1609)	□ 255-299 (1733)
□ 300-339 (1868)	□ 340-379 (1957)	□ 380-419 (2054)
□ 420-469 (2173)	□ 470-524 (2289)	□ 525-614 (2403)
□ 615-774 (2581)	□ 775-949 (2735)	□ 950-more (3778)

For urban mass:

▯ 0-229 (1398)	▯ 300-349 (1654)	▯ 350-424 (1729)
▯ 425-499 (1912)	▯ 500-574 (1968)	▯ 575-664 (2091)
▯ 665-774 (2187)	▯ 775-914 (2297)	▯ 915-1119 (2467)
▯ 1120-1499 (2536)	▯ 1500-1924 (2736)	▯ 1925-more (2938)

Note: * Figures in brackets are the calorie intake & other is the expenditure bracket for the migrant that incurred on his consumption.

Source: *Nutritional Intake in India*, NSS 55th Round, Report No.471.

Annexure A-2.2

Data Sets for Regression Analysis of Section IV and V

States	*index*	*time*	*riw*	*pov*	*gpov*	*ias*	*gsdp*
AP	1	1	-14.9383	28.91	-0.044093	-7.79	0.201333
AS	2	1	-12.5909	40.77	-0.047769	-6.83	0.127810
BH	3	1	-12.4796	62.22	0.001814	-16.84	0.132324
GJ	4	1	-8.01461	32.79	-0.034117	-3.72	0.165801
HY	5	1	-15.417	21.37	-0.046136	-2.32	0.175078
HP	6	1	-11.5206	16.4	-0.082434	16.63	0.170661
KA	7	1	-12.8237	38.24	-0.036012	-6.77	0.168655
KE	8	1	-14.8953	40.42	-0.037661	-18.85	0.150239
MP	9	1	-12.6123	49.78	-0.032372	-6.14	0.188344
MH	10	1	-6.4	49.78	-0.018193	0.8	0.188863
OR	11	1	-13.1553	65.28	-0.011393	-11.32	0.082931
PN	12	1	-15.1443	16.18	-0.026725	-12.21	0.163422
RJ	13	1	-15.4959	34.46	-0.013183	-8.27	0.223871
TN	14	1	-10.1074	51.66	-0.009521	-4.03	0.180432
TR	15	1	-14.3066	40.03	-0.049372	-3.16	0.132810
UP	16	1	-13.2014	47.07	-0.006727	-7.97	0.159215
WB	17	1	-11.2556	54.85	-0.015614	-4.83	0.123057
AN	18	1	-10.1074	52.13	-0.009894	-4.03	0.080536
CH	19	1	-15.1443	23.79	-0.021534	-12.21	0.163422
DN	20	1	-8.01461	15.67	-0.096460	-3.72	0.177562
DH	21	1	-13.2014	26.22	-0.035158	-7.97	0.137878
LA	22	1	-8.01461	42.36	-0.032929	-3.72	0.177562
PO	23	1	-8.01461	50.05	-0.010015	-3.72	0.098693
GO	24	1	-14.8953	18.9	-0.082057	-18.85	0.177562
JK	25	1	-15.1443	24.24	-0.062997	-12.21	0.065594
MA	26	1	-14.3066	37.02	-0.051811	-3.16	0.142556
ME	27	1	-14.3066	38.81	-0.049465	-3.16	0.188832
MI	28	1	-14.3066	36	-0.056331	-3.16	0.136637
NA	29	1	-14.3066	39.25	-0.049934	-3.16	0.187442
SI	30	1	-11.2556	39.71	-0.048249	-4.83	0.150807
AP	1	2	38.37914	25.86	-0.026374	-0.96	0.216029
AS	2	2	9.400387	36.21	-0.027961	-4.34	0.115929
BH	3	2	9.259229	52.13	-0.040541	-8.67	0.080175
GJ	4	2	5.856186	31.54	-0.009530	4.87	0.232823
HY	5	2	23.39205	16.64	-0.055334	2.7	0.161999
HP	6	2	-0.34082	15.45	-0.014481	-12.2	0.162883

contd...

...contd...

States	*index*	*time*	*riw*	*pov*	*gpov*	*ias*	*gsdp*
KA	7	2	21.54953	37.53	-0.004641	-2.62	0.210974
KE	8	2	12.55645	31.79	-0.053377	-2.29	0.248884
MP	9	2	22.41174	43.07	-0.033698	-2.45	0.121175
MH	10	2	9.7482	40.41	-0.047057	8.49	0.230346
OR	11	2	22.78583	55.58	-0.037147	12.01	0.229943
PN	12	2	12.20414	13.2	-0.046044	-3.63	0.179038
RJ	13	2	32.53101	35.15	0.005005	0.42	0.148023
TN	14	2	6.406688	43.39	-0.040021	3.84	0.229200
TR	15	2	14.89337	35.23	-0.029977	-0.001	0.101273
UP	16	2	18.00436	41.46	-0.029796	-0.19	0.135077
WB	17	2	11.41085	44.72	-0.046171	-2.77	0.157570
AN	18	2	14.62978	43.88	-0.039564	-2.26	0.182444
CH	19	2	19.21098	14.67	-0.095838	32.89	0.442705
DN	20	2	9.828439	67.11	0.820676	-5.65	0.247721
DH	21	2	13.26679	12.41	-0.131674	-3.47	0.193493
LA	22	2	-0.21334	34.95	-0.043732	-5.65	0.247721
PO	23	2	20.77112	41.46	-0.042907	-15.85	0.118688
GO	24	2	20.50309	24.52	0.074338	-8.18	0.247721
JK	25	2	20.71262	23.82	-0.004331	-8.18	0.136634
MA	26	2	24.9116	31.35	-0.038290	3.04	0.151482
ME	27	2	18.91503	33.92	-0.031499	15.74	0.127063
MI	28	2	19.93168	27.52	-0.058888	3.04	0.235049
NA	29	2	15.62657	34.43	-0.030700	-10.65	0.175258
SI	30	2	28.81384	36.06	-0.022979	36.85	0.141645
AP	1	3	0.351421	22.19	-0.023653	23.34	0.093771
AS	2	3	0.502013	40.86	0.021402	36.85	0.074589
BH	3	3	-0.91022	54.96	0.009047	13.12	0.104596
GJ	4	3	3.761828	24.21	-0.038733	33.1	0.071363
HY	5	3	-4.11872	25.05	0.084234	75.32	0.102168
HP	6	3	3.509483	28.44	0.140129	25.51	0.115610
KA	7	3	7.021524	33.16	-0.019406	50.75	0.119730
KE	8	3	2.686628	25.43	-0.033343	41.77	0.118458
MP	9	3	1.455013	42.52	-0.002128	34.05	0.083114
MH	10	3	5.247609	36.86	-0.014641	13.38	0.085707
OR	11	3	-2.38878	48.56	-0.021050	26.2	0.069233
PN	12	3	-1.06954	11.77	-0.018055	52.59	0.097347
RJ	13	3	-1.34439	27.41	-0.036699	18.82	0.094998
TN	14	3	14.13201	35.03	-0.032111	40.31	0.121940

contd...

...contd...

States	*index*	*time*	*riw*	*pov*	*gpov*	*ias*	*gsdp*
TR	15	3	-5.45877	39.01	0.017882	35.92	0.119805
UP	16	3	-1.58454	40.85	-0.002452	53.23	0.096088
WB	17	3	-7.25447	35.66	-0.033765	95.83	0.143383
AN	18	3	3.202789	34.47	-0.035741	27.56	0.051537
CH	19	3	5.496664	11.35	-0.037718	141.1	0.152757
DN	20	3	-4.01589	50.84	-0.040406	60.08	0.2
DH	21	3	20.39249	14.69	0.030620	141.1	0.119136
LA	22	3	9.929694	25.04	-0.047257	185.73	0.2
PO	23	3	-3.96475	37.4	-0.016320	102	0.304352
GO	24	3	0.947838	14.92	-0.065252	102	0.2
JK	25	3	2.838103	25.17	0.009445	65.98	0.117049
MA	26	3	-4.18481	36.86	0.029292	-9.61	0.130763
ME	27	3	-5.28746	37.92	0.019654	65.98	0.088880
MI	28	3	-6.92451	25.66	-0.011264	115	0.021111
NA	29	3	-1.96228	37.92	0.016894	-9.61	0.011232
SI	30	3	-0.01264	41.43	0.024819	95.83	0.099966
AP		4	5.54216				
AS		4	19.94701				
BH		4	37.41843				
GJ		4	9.471879				
HY		4	33.07289				
HP		4	24.55454				
KA		4	13.43834				
KE		4	21.20452				
MP		4	13.11878				
MH		4	11.28708				
OR		4	33.1919				
PN		4	44.061				
RJ		4	33.03571				
TN		4	11.49062				
TR		4	45.36927				
UP		4	26.79013				
WB		4	15.29931				
AN		4	2.910365				
CH		4	12.4677				
DN		4	37.7676				
DH		4	12.10498				
LA		4	7.832409				

contd...

...contd...

States	*index*	*time*	*riw*	*pov*	*gpov*	*ias*	*gsdp*
PO		4	-18.5548				
GO		4	23.74566				
JK		4	33.64066				
MA		4	26.83254				
ME		4	33.57459				
MI		4	24.69716				
NA		4	25.16228				
SI		4	42.15758				
States	*index*	*time*			*1st Period Poverty Rate*		
AP	1	1	39.31	28.91		-0.044093	
AS	2	1	57.15	40.77		-0.047769	
BH	3	1	61.55	62.22		0.001814	
GJ	4	1	41.23	32.79		-0.034117	
HY	5	1	29.55	21.37		-0.046136	
HP	6	1	32.45	16.4		-0.082434	
KA	7	1	48.78	38.24		-0.036012	
KE	8	1	52.22	40.42		-0.037661	
MP	9	1	61.78	49.78		-0.032372	
MH	10	1	55.88	49.78		-0.018193	
OR	11	1	70.07	65.28		-0.011393	
PN	12	1	19.27	16.18		-0.026725	
RJ	13	1	37.42	34.46		-0.013183	
TN	14	1	54.79	51.66		-0.009521	
TR	15	1	56.88	40.03		-0.049372	
UP	16	1	49.05	47.07		-0.006727	
WB	17	1	60.52	54.85		-0.015614	
AN	18	1	55.42	52.13		-0.009894	
CH	19	1	27.32	23.79		-0.021534	
DN	20	1	37.2	15.67		-0.096460	
DH	21	1	33.23	26.22		-0.035158	
LA	22	1	52.79	42.36		-0.032929	
PO	23	1	53.25	50.05		-0.010015	
GO	24	1	37.23	18.9		-0.082057	
JK	25	1	38.97	24.24		-0.062997	
MA	26	1	53.72	37.02		-0.051811	
ME	27	1	55.19	38.81		-0.049465	
MI	28	1	54.38	36		-0.056331	
NA	29	1	56.04	39.25		-0.049934	
SI	30	1	55.89	39.71		-0.048249	

	1980	*1985*	*1990*	*1st Period Growth Rate*	*1995*	*2nd Period Growth Rate*	*2000*	*3rd Period Growth Rate*
Andhra Pradesh	1467	2400	4816	0.201333	10018	0.216029	14715	0.093771
Assam	1329	2704	4432	0.127810	7001	0.115929	9612	0.074589
Bihar	1022	1785	2966	0.132324	4155	0.080175	6328	0.104596
Delhi	4145	6732	11373	0.137878	22376	0.193493	35705	0.119136
Goa	3200	4742	8952	0.177562	20040	0.247721	NA	0.2
Gujarat	2089	3468	6343	0.165801	13727	0.232823	18625	0.071363
Haryana	2437	4117	7721	0.175078	13975	0.161999	21114	0.102168
Himachal Pradesh	1820	2829	5243	0.170661	9513	0.162883	15012	0.115610
Jammu & Kashmir	2152	3482	4624	0.065594	7783	0.136634	12338	0.117049
Karnataka	1644	2699	4975	0.168655	10223	0.210974	16343	0.119730
Kerala	1835	2918	5110	0.150239	11469	0.248884	18262	0.118458
Madhya Pradesh	1609	2471	4798	0.188344	7705	0.121175	10907	0.083114
Maharashtra	2492	3915	7612	0.188863	16379	0.230346	23398	0.085707
Manipur	1396	2284	3912	0.142556	6875	0.151482	11370	0.130763
Meghalaya	1538	2543	4944	0.188832	8085	0.127063	11678	0.088880
Mizoram	1399	2885	4856	0.136637	10563	0.235049	11678	0.021111
Nagaland	1607	3042	5893	0.187442	11057	0.175258	11678	0.011232
Orissa	1352	2238	3166	0.082931	6806	0.229943	9162	0.069233
Punjab	2629	4500	8177	0.163422	15497	0.179038	23040	0.097347
Rajasthan	1424	2304	4883	0.223871	8497	0.148023	12533	0.094998
Sikkim	1545	2972	5213	0.150807	8905	0.141645	13356	0.099966
Tamil Nadu	1666	2913	5541	0.180432	11891	0.229200	19141	0.121940
Tripura	1645	2548	4240	0.132810	6387	0.101273	10213	0.119805
Uttar Pradesh	1402	2192	3937	0.159215	6596	0.135077	9765	0.096088
West Bengal	1925	3140	5072	0.123057	9068	0.157570	15569	0.143383
Andaman & Nicobar	4548	6936	9729	0.080536	18604	0.182444	23398	0.051537
Chandigarh	NA	4500	8177	0.163422	26277	0.442705	46347	0.152757
Pondicherry	3201	5127	7657	0.098693	12201	0.118688	30768	0.304352

Part II

3 Trickling Down Growth through the Informal Sector

Can Asset Formation Trickle Up Growth

India has experienced unprecedented high growth rates over the last 20 years approaching double digit rates. Economic theory suggests that such high growth rates should inevitably trickle down to the poor and poverty would eventually be ameliorated. However, poverty has been slow to decline and one of the reasons advanced for this slow progress on poverty is the overwhelming size of the informal sector.[1] Poverty is a key characteristic of the informal sector, and there appears to be a clear association between the incidence of poverty and participation in the informal sector. Measured on the basis of consumption expenditure, evidence from India shows that 43 per cent of informal sector participants were poor compared to only 6 per cent in the formal sector (Pradhan *et al.*, 1999). The Indian government has recognised the critical role of the informal sector in alleviating poverty and constituted the National Commission on Enterprises in the Unorganised Sector (NCEUS) to study the conditions of the informal sector. The NCEUS has generated a large volume of data which has helped develop a better understanding of the heterogeneity of the informal sector (NCEUS, 2009).

Economic logic suggests that India's high growth rates would trickle down to the informal sector. However, the rates of poverty alleviation are disappointing to say the least.[2] To understand the diagnostics of slow poverty alleviation, it would be important to carefully analyse the effects of the high growth rates on the informal sector. Preliminary evidence suggests that the size of the informal sector has remained stable over the last 30 years while

1. Ninety-three per cent in terms of employment and over 60 per cent in terms of output. National Commission for Enterprises in the Unorganised Sector (NCEUS) 2009.
2. See Introduction to the book.

its share of output has declined (Bairagya, 2010). While this may suggest an impoverishment of the informal sector and of the majority of the population of the country, it does not take account of the high growth rates and the fact that a declining share of a much larger GDP may still make the average person in the informal sector much better off than before. While the average incomes by this simple mathematic may have risen in the informal sector, of equal importance is the distributional effects of economic growth in the informal sector. For poverty alleviation it is important that the poor do not get poorer in the informal sector. Moreover, within the informal sector it is important that there is upward mobility, i.e., the proportion of the poor should be reduced incrementally with economic growth.

Given this background, this chapter analyses both the growth and distributional consequences of high GDP growth rates on the informal sector. Section I begins with a review of literature on the informal sector in developing countries. This section thus contextualises the Indian informal sector not as an aberrant but as a part of development in a globalising world. Section II then goes on to examine the literature on growth and the informal sector in India. This section uses data from secondary studies to examine the effects of increase in informal sector wages and asset building on poverty. Using cross-sectional analysis across the different states of India, and growth as a control variable, it tries to set out which variable i.e., increase in informal sector wages or asset building is crucial for poverty alleviation. It also clarifies whether the variable changes during a high growth phase in comparison to a low growth phase. Section III analyses the structural changes in the composition of the informal sector during the period of high economic growth. The purpose of this section is to analyse whether there is upward mobility within the sector and to establish that the poor are not getting poorer with higher economic growth. It also provides examples of grassroots capitalism as an example of the heterogeneity of the informal sector. Section IV identifies the catalysing variables which accelerate asset formation or improve wages in the informal sector during the high growth phase. The data for this econometric exercise has been generated through surveys conducted by the author. At the outset it must be stated that this chapter does not deny the poverty of the informal sector in India, but rather seeks to examine the dynamism that the informal sector has generated in a rapidly growing India. Having identified the catalysing variables, Section V analyses government policy and actions which have addressed these catalysing variables. It examines the shortcomings of some of these policies and makes suggestions for their improvement. The chapter concludes with specific recommendation on how government could promote the dynamism of the informal sector as an agent of trickle down. This dynamism if properly channelled would also trickle up growth.

I

Informal Sector in the Developing World

Theories on Informalism

Theories on the informal economy tend to be polarised. Some suggest that it is a direct consequence of over-regulation by the state, or of draconian labour laws which have outlived their utility. In contrast, the 'marginalisation' thesis sees the informal sector as a form of outmoded feudalism confined to cities in developing societies, or as a central feature of economic development under contemporary capitalism and globalisation (Castells and Portes, 1989; Sassen, 1991; 1998). The narrative of informal economy as a site of exploitation has generated widespread discourse of dualism, where its coexistence with a formal sector is considered intrinsic to modern globalisation. Prescriptions on the informal economy as a consequence promote stronger regulations and tougher enforcement designed to minimise illegal activities (Portes and Schauffler, 1993).

The informal sector as a concept was first introduced by Hart (1971), according to Bekkers and Stoffers (1995). However, Kabra (1995) claimed that the concept really built upon the earlier framework of the 'unorganised sector', which encompassed production units of small size, including handicrafts, which had a domestic or 'unorganised character' and may also be part of the 'non-monetary' sector of the economy.[3] As claimed by Bromley (1978), it may equally well be seen as a spin-off of the dual economy literature, originating with Lewis (1954) and Hirschman (1958), which conceptualised economic development as the emergence and growth of manufacturing sector (the 'modern' sector) through the absorption of

3. Report, 1951, by the Village Industries Commission, Government of India, *On Small Scale Industries*, *http://www.indialabourarchives.org/sources/nmml2.htm*

labour being freed from agriculture (the 'traditional' sector), due to the more efficient means of production in the former. Whereas the dual economy (the 'modern-traditional' dichotomy) literature mainly addressed the sectoral differences in terms of the 'technology' applied, a somewhat later related literature focussed more on the 'organisation' of the sectors (Sethuraman, 1976). The concept of the informal sector (IS) is a fuzzy one. Indeed Kabra (1995) states that some 30 terms including the survival sector, non-structured sector and transitional activities have been and/or are currently used to describe the IS.

Irrespective of the definition or the constitution of the informal sector, the literature on informal economies pays special attention to the linkages between formal and informal economies. There are three well-known schools of thought regarding the links between the informal and the formal economies: the proponents of these schools are referred to as, respectively, the dualists, the structuralists and the legalists. The stylised views of each of these schools can be summarised as follows. The dualists view the informal economy as a separate marginal sector—not directly linked to the formal sector—that provides income or a safety net for the poor (ILO, 1972). They argue that the informal economy exists or persists because economic growth or industrial development has failed, as yet, to absorb those who work in the informal economy. The structuralists view the informal economy as being subordinated to the formal economy (Castells and Portes, 1989). They argue that privileged capitalists in the formal economy seek to erode employment relations and subordinate those who work in the informal economy in order to reduce their labour costs and increase their competitiveness. The legalists view informal work arrangements—or, more specifically, unregistered businesses—as a rational response to over-regulation by government bureaucracies (de Soto, 1989). They argue that those who run informal businesses do so to reduce their own costs and increase profits.

Each of these has a different perspective on how the informal and formal economies interact. The dualists argue that informal units and activities have few (if any) linkages to the formal economy but, rather, operate as a distinct separate sector of the economy; and that informal workers comprise the less-advantaged sector of a dualistic labour market (Lewis, 1954; Sethuraman, 1976; Tokman, 1978). Unlike the dualists, structuralists see the informal and formal economies as intrinsically linked. To increase competitiveness, firms in the formal economy are seen to reduce their input costs, including labour costs, by promoting informal production and employment relationships with subordinated economic units and workers. According to structuralists, both informal enterprises and informal wage workers are subordinated to the interests of providing cheap goods and services (Moser, 1978; Portes *et al.*, 1989). The legalists focus on the relationship between informal entrepreneurs/enterprises and the formal regulatory environment, not formal firms. But they acknowledge that capitalist interests—what Hernando de Soto (1989) calls 'mercantilist' interests—collude with government to set the bureaucratic 'rules of the game'.

Facts on Informalism in the Developing World

The informal economy consists of a range of informal enterprises and informal jobs. Yet there are meaningful ways to classify its various segments, as follows:

1. *Self-employment in informal enterprises:* Workers in small unregistered or unincorporated enterprises, including:
   - employers;
   - own account operators: both heads of family enterprises and single person;
   - operators, and
   - unpaid family workers.
2. *Wage employment in informal jobs:* Workers without worker benefits or social protection who work for formal or informal firms, for households or with no fixed employer, including:
   - employees of informal enterprises,
   - other informal wage workers such as:
     - casual or day labourers,
     - domestic workers,
     - unregistered or undeclared workers and
     - some temporary or part-time workers.
   - industrial outworkers (also called home workers).

Informal employment broadly defined comprises one-half to three-quarters of non-agricultural employment in developing countries:

specifically, 48 per cent in North Africa; 51 per cent in Latin America; 65 per cent in Asia and 72 per cent in sub-Saharan Africa.[4] The share of informal employment in non-agricultural employment is 78 per cent in sub-Saharan Africa, excluding South Africa. South Asia's share is considerably higher than 65 per cent judging by the share of Indian informal employment.[5]

Some countries include informal employment in agriculture in their estimates. This significantly increases the proportion of informal employment: from 83 per cent of 'non-agricultural' employment to 93 per cent of 'total' employment in India; from 55 to 62 per cent in Mexico and from 28 to 34 per cent in South Africa.[6] Informal employment is generally a larger source of employment for women than for men in the developing world. Other than in North Africa, where 43 per cent of women workers are in informal employment, 60 per cent or more of women non-agricultural workers in the developing world are informally employed. In sub-Saharan Africa, 84 per cent of women non-agricultural workers are informally employed compared to 63 per cent of men; and in Latin America, the figures are 58 per cent of women in comparison to 48 per cent of men. In Asia, the proportion is 65 per cent for both women and men.[7]

As noted earlier, the informal economy comprises both self-employment in informal enterprises (i.e., small and/or unregistered) and wage-employment in informal jobs (i.e., without secure contracts, worker benefits or social protection). In developing countries, 'self-employment' comprises a greater share of informal employment outside of agriculture (and even more inside of agriculture) than wage employment: specifically, self-employment represents 70 per cent of informal employment in sub-Saharan Africa, 62 per cent in North Africa, 60 per cent in Latin America and 59 per cent in Asia.[8] If South Africa is excluded, since black-owned businesses prohibited during the Apartheid era have only recently been

4. Women in the Informal Globalising Economy (WIEGO), *http://www.wiego.org/main/ilocstats.html*
5. Ibid.
6. Ibid.
7. Ibid.
8. Ibid.

recognised and reported, the share of self-employment in informal employment increases to 81 per cent in sub-Saharan Africa.[9]

Informal 'wage' employment is also significant in developing countries, comprising 30 to 40 per cent of total informal employment (outside of agriculture).[10] As noted earlier, informal wage employment comprises employees of informal enterprises as well as various types of informal wage workers who work for formal enterprises, households or no fixed employer (Chen *et al.*, 2004).

Estimates concerning the income of informal producers have generally revealed that informal producers earn less than formal workers (Kelley, 1994). The explanations put forward for these differences include formal sector unionisation and labour legislation (Mazumdar, 1975), labour heterogeneity and efficiency wage arguments (Bardhan, 1988). There are significant gaps in earnings within the informal economy: on average, employers have the highest earnings; followed by their employees and other more 'regular' informal wage workers; own account operators; 'casual' informal wage workers and industrial outworkers.

Sethuraman (1997) reports that the majority of the working poor are in informal sector in Latin America (e.g., 66.2 per cent in Bolivia, 66.4 per cent in Brazil, 87.1 per cent in Panama and 57.4 per cent in Venezuela). However, the association between poverty and participation in the informal sector does not hold uniformly across all types of workers. The self-employed, particularly microenterprise owners, are found to have average earnings several times the minimum wage, leading to the possible inference of a lower likelihood of poverty among them (Ñopo and Valenzuela, 2007). Consequently, in many cases, it might be incorrect to claim that poverty is a defining characteristic of the informal sector as a whole though on an average poverty is higher in the informal sector.

How do these stylised facts on the informal economy apply to India? Does the informal sector behave differently when the economy is growing rapidly and opportunities are being created in the formal sector? In a rapidly globalising world, as was pointed out by de Soto (1989), would

9. Ibid.

10. Ibid.

formal sector growth attract more informal sector growth and perhaps an upward push of wages? Also given the heterogeneity of the informal sector, it is possible that there is upward mobility in jobs within the categories of the informal sector itself. This would undoubtedly have a positive effect on poverty. Notwithstanding the standard literature on the informal economy, it is possible that in high growth economies the informal sector may play a dynamic role in trickling up growth. To begin with, in India poverty ratio has decreased with increased growth. Would this imply that the informal sector has become an effective trickle down and trickle up agent? The subsequent sections analyse the manner in which this may be happening and what can be done to accelerate this trickle down.

Situating the Informal Sector in India in the Global Economy

There is no uniform definition of the informal sector in India. Productive institutional units characterised by a low level of organisation with no access to formal credit, little or no division between labour and capital, labour relations based on casual employment and/or social relationship, as opposed to formal contracts, labour-intensive technology, and low-skill labour are categorised as informal units. These units to a large extent belong to the household sector and cannot be associated with other organisations (Sinha, 2002). The National Commission for Enterprises in the Unorganised Sector estimates suggest that the informal sector vary between 89 and 93 per cent of total employment (NCEUS, 2009).

In the primary sector about 98-99 per cent of the workers were informally employed in 2005. In the secondary sector, the percentage of informal employment has increased from 85.56 per cent in 1999-2000 to 89.39 per cent in 2004-05. In the tertiary sector also the informal employment has increased from 75.83 per cent in 1999-2000 to 79.70 per cent in 2004-05 (NCEUS, 2009).

In terms of GDP, the share of the formal sector in 2004-05 was only 4 per cent in agriculture whereas 96 per cent was contributed by the informal sector (NCEUS, 2009). Thus, informal activities are mainly studied for the non-agricultural sectors only. In the manufacturing sector, 60 per cent share in NDP is in the formal sector while 40 per cent share is contributed by the informal sector. In services, 53 per cent of the output comes from the formal sector while 47 per cent of the share is contributed by the informal sector.[11] Thus in terms of output, the share of the informal sector is estimated to be between 50 and 60 per cent.[12]

However, the quality of employment is of vital importance in determining the poverty status of the informal sector (Table 3.2). While these figures apply to the entire labour force, given that 93 per cent of the total employment is in the informal sector, they also indicate the quality of employment in the informal sector. It shows that the proportion of unemployed, the severely unemployed and the underemployed have risen significantly in the decade from 1993-94 and 2004-05. In fact it has been much higher than the rate of growth of the labour force and the rate of growth of workers, showing that a significant proportion of the increments in the labour force are either unemployed or severely unemployed.

Table 3.1

Formal and Informal Employment in India

(in million)

	1983	*1988*	*1993-94*	*1999-2000*	*2004-05*
Estimated population	718	790	895	1004	1093
Labour force	309	334	392	406	—
Employed	303	324	374	397	457
Unemployed	6	9	7	10	—
Formally employed	24	26	27	35	39
Informally employed	279	299	347	362	423

Source: Various rounds of Employment-Unemployment Survey of NSSO, Expert committee of population projection, DGE&T and the National Commission for Enterprises in the Unorganised Sector (2008).[13]

11. "Delhi Group on Informal Sector and System of National Accounts", Paper compiled by Ramesh Kolli, Deputy Director General, Central Statistical Organisation, Ministry of Statistics and Programme Implementation, India. From the documents available with the Delhi Group Secretariat, *http://www.unescap.org/stat/apex/2/APEX2_S.5_India-SNA-informal.pdf*

12. Ibid.

13. Adapted from Bairagya (2010).

Table 3.2

Estimates of Labour Force, Employment and Unemployment

(in million)

	1993-94	*2004-05*	*Growth Rate (%)*
Labour force	341.15	429.88	2.02
Workers	326.97	401.13	1.88
Unemployed	18.18	28.74	4.25
Severely unemployed	18.08	28.65	4.27
Strictly part-time workers	10.75	13.06	1.78
Underemployed	5.54	9.57	5.10
Current weekly status worker	342.92	423.36	1.93

Note: Severely unemployed refers to those reporting unemployment for 3.5 days or more of the week; Strictly part-time workers refers to persons who worked for 0.5 to 3 days in the week and are not available for work even for 0.5 days during rest of the week; underemployed refers to persons who worked for 0.5 to 3 days in the week and are unemployed for at least 0.5 days in the week.

Source: NSSO 50th and 61st Round Survey on Employment-Unemployment. Computed by NCEUS.

The first question that needs to be asked in the context of the Indian informal sector is why is it so large? Despite economic reforms, starting a formal business in India requires 11 procedures and 71 days (down from 89 in 2009). In addition:

- dealing with licences requires 20 procedures and 270 days;
- export procedures take 36 days;
- import procedures take 43 days;
- there are 59 taxes, compliance with which takes about 264 hours, and
- overall, some 40 procedures and 425 days are required for a contract.

The 'rigidity of employment' index, which relates to difficulties in hiring and firing workers, ranks India 62nd on an index of 100—by far the highest in the region. And while starting a business is obviously difficult, closing a business is likely to be even more so. According to this report, bankruptcy procedures take 10 years in India (World Bank Group, 2010; WEF, 2009).

The second question that arises is whether the formation of the informal sector is a part of economic development and whether it would change with high rates of growth. At the core of the debate on the Indian informal economy is the oft-repeated question of whether and how to 'formalise' the informal economy.[14] However, it is not clear what is meant by 'formalisation'. For the self-employed, policymakers often suggest that formalisation could mean that informal enterprises should obtain a licence, register their accounts and pay taxes. But to the self-employed, and often the poor, these represent the costs of entry into the formal economy. They would like to receive the benefits of operating formally in return for paying these costs, including: efficient and effective electricity supply, security of operation, better freight and transportation for their products, effective marketing. The state is in no position to provide these facilities all of which have to be provided by the enterprises themselves, and thus often the cost of entry far exceeds the benefits of doing so.

For informal and casual workers, however, formalisation means obtaining a formal wage job—or converting their current job into a formal job—with secure contract, worker benefits and social protection. For them, it is a coveted situation with lower accountability and greater benefits. For the employers on the other hand, formalisation represents a situation of rising costs, often falling productivity and lower competitiveness. In a globalised open economy, competitiveness has become very important and thus the costs of formalising informal labour may be prohibitively high (Dreyer, 2009).

Taking into account the different meanings of formalisation, the feasibility of formalising Indian informal economy is unclear. First, government would not be able to handle the volume of licence applications and tax forms if all informal businesses are formalised. Second, employers would not in several cases be able to afford to offer incentives and benefits that formal sector receive. Third, while unemployment rates have been static or declining in India, at this present time supply of unskilled labour outweighs demand thus making high wage employment in the formal sector unattractive for employers.[15] Finally, available evidence suggests that employers are more inclined to convert formal jobs into informal jobs—rather than the other way around in a bid to remain competitive in the global economy. The policy challenge is to decrease the costs of working informally

14. Statements of the Left Party, National Commission for Enterprises in the Unorganised Sector, Government of India, 2007, *http://www.wsws.org/articles/2007/sep2007/indi-s15.shtml*

15. *http://www.ilo.org/employment/Areasofwork*

and to increase the benefits of working formally. This can only take place in an incremental fashion given the magnitude of informality in the Indian economy.

The recent re-convergence of interest in the informal economy stems from the recognition that the informal economy is growing; is a permanent, not a short-term phenomenon and is a feature of high growth and global integration of the Indian economy (NCEUS, 2007). For these reasons, the informal economy has to be viewed as the base of the total Indian economy.

Economic relations—of production, distribution and employment—tend to fall at some point on a continuum between pure 'formal' relations (i.e., regulated and protected with benefits) and pure 'informal' relations (i.e., unregulated and unprotected with little or no benefits), with many categories in between. Depending on their circumstances, workers and entrepreneurs are known to move with varying ease and speed from informal to formal, or to operate simultaneously at different points in the formal and informal sectors. Consider, for example, the self-employed garment maker who supplements her earnings by stitching clothes under a subcontract or shifts to working on a subcontract for a firm when her customers decide they prefer ready-made garments rather than tailor-made ones. Or consider the public sector employee who has an informal job on the side.

Moreover, the formal and the informal sectors are often dynamically linked. For instance, many informal enterprises have production or distribution relations with formal enterprises, supplying inputs, finished goods or services either through direct transactions or subcontracting arrangements. Also, many formal enterprises hire wage workers under informal employment relations. For example, many part-time workers, temporary workers and homeworkers work for formal enterprises through contracting or subcontracting arrangements.

The Indian informal economy is consistent with their other counterparts in the developing world. However, India has experienced high growth rates over the last 20 years and this should have changed the structure, wages and the scale of the informal economy. The next section examines the effects of growth on the informal sector of the economy.

II

Growth, Poverty and the Informal Sector: Reviewing Contrasting Points of Views on the Informal Economy in India

According to some economists such as Arup Mitra (2007), the labour absorption capacity of the informal sector is much more than its formal counterpart. The share of the informal sector is equally high in the states which are highly industrialised in comparison to the states which are industrially backward. Subcontracting and other indirect processes seem to be generating employment in the informal sector in the industrialised states, whereas artisanal employment has been the major source of employment in backward states. Both direct and indirect effects of industrial growth have been beneficial for living standards in the informal sector. On the whole, no strong evidence is found to suggest any deterioration in the informal sector living conditions during the process of growth. It is however, not clear whether the trickle-down effects are substantive (Mitra, 2007).

Given the dimension of informal labour markets in India, and the fact that the vast majority of poor, if not all, are actually unskilled workers whether in agriculture or in urban informal sectors, changes in the unskilled real informal wage and real agricultural wages should reflect the trickle-down effects of high growth. This hypothesis is further strengthened by a study by Deaton and Drèze (2002) which reveals a negative correlation between real agricultural wages and rural poverty: -0.87 in 1993-94 and -0.91 in 1999-2000. Another study by Marjit *et al.* (2003) also observes a negative correlation between the real informal wage and rural poverty at the state level in 1999-2000 estimated at -0.58 for the 30-day recall period and -0.57 for 7-day recall period based on the Deaton and Drèze (2002) adjusted poverty estimates. (Poverty estimates in India are based on the money value of the amount of calories consumed either for the 30 days or for the 7 days preceding the survey. Benchmarks for minimum calorific consumption for rural and urban areas have been established.)

The study by Marjit *et al.* (2003) further shows that the average annual growth rate of real informal wage (RIW) across 14 states declined between 1984-1989. This was the period of low GDP growth rates of only a little over 3 per cent annually. However, during 1989-90 to 1994-95, there have been complete reversals. Annual GDP growth rates increased quite significantly to a little over 5 per cent per annum, accompanied by an increase in RIW over the period for all these states. This increase may be attributed to the growing economy which raised the demand for informal unskilled labour.

Another study by Acharya (2006) shows that the annual growth in real wage for unskilled agricultural workers and informal sector wages increased steadily during 1993-94 to 2004-05. Thus, both real informal and agricultural wages for unskilled workers increased on an average during the high growth periods resulting, of course, from increased demand for unskilled workers employed in informal sectors and agriculture. However, whether such improvements in wages are due to the composition effect or pure growth effects is an open question. Whatever the cause, the fact that real wages in the poorest sectors, i.e., informal and agriculture increased during the high growth periods makes a persuasive case for trickle-down effects of growth through the informal sector.

Another study by Dasgupta and Singh (2006), using the data on registered and unregistered manufacturing sector from the Ministry of Industry, shows that both registered and unregistered manufacturing are highly positively related to state-GDP growth. The Beta coefficients for unregistered manufacturing are, if anything, greater than those for registered manufacturing. However, this result may not be reliable as the equations for registered manufacturing do not pass the various diagnostic tests. The equations for unregistered manufacturing do pass the diagnostic tests. In economic terms, it is interesting that there should be a highly positive correlation between unregistered manufacturing growth and state-GDP growth for both 1993-94 and 1999-2000. To the extent that unregistered manufacturing is representative of the informal sector manufacturing economy, the evidence from this study suggests that the informal sector is not just a residual sector but in fact it may be capable of dynamic growth (Dasgupta and Singh, 2006).

Another paper by Bhattacharya (1996), of the Heriot-Watt University (Scotland), highlights the role of the informal sector in the Indian economy. The paper notes that it was the informal sector (I-sector) which accounted for most of the increase in non-agricultural employment. Evidence further suggests that the I-sector was not a passive absorber of labour but a dynamic sector responding successfully to changing demand in the economy and contributing significantly to income and output. This argument implies that the I-sector trickled up growth. The paper also offers a hypothesis that, simultaneously with these changes in economic structure, there is likely to have occurred a change in the composition of rural-urban migrants with the share of those who go to the I-sector and have only I-sector jobs as their targets (usually members of the poorer households in the rural areas) increasing and that of those who go to the formal sector (usually well-educated members of the relatively well-to-do landowning families in the rural areas) declining; further, migration by the members of the poorer rural households is likely to have increased not because their rural income declined but because the informal sector income increased.

Another study by Bosworth *et al.* (2007) shows that output growth surged to 7 per cent per year during 1993-1999. During this period, formal employment decreased whereas informal employment increased. There was a particularly large jump in labour productivity—concentrated in services but evident in all sectors. It was associated with rises in both TFP and capital deepening. Output moderated somewhat during the period (1999-2004) with growth slowing in all sectors, in part due to the severe drought. Contributions from TFP and capital deepening slowed in both services and industry. Notably, investment failed to keep up with the more rapid employment growth, particularly in the informal sector. However, informal sector wages rose and at rates higher than the formal sector.

Effects of Informal Sector Wages and Assets on Poverty

While the theoretical and empirical justification for a strong inverse correlation between poverty and informal sector wages is evident from the preceding literature survey, the effects of economic growth on the informal sector is more nuanced. This section will empirically establish whether informal sector wages or informal sector asset formation had a significant correlation with poverty. It is expected that the correlation variable (i.e., informal sector wages or asset formation with poverty) may change during periods of high growth rates. Two time periods with different levels of GDP growth have been used in this analysis. The data has been used from a paper written by Marjit and Maiti (2005) for World Institute for Development Economics Research (WIDER) on both informal sector asset formation and informal sector wages. The periods used are immediately before economic reform, i.e., 1989/90 to 1994/95 and from 1994/95 to 1999/2000. The latter was a higher growth period than the former. Using growth rates across states as a control variable, the effects of informal sector asset formation and informal sector wages have been plotted on the levels of poverty across states in Figures 3.1 and 3.2.[16] (see Annexure A-3.1 for the datasets used in the regression analysis.) As Figure 3.1 shows, the effect of informal sector asset formation on poverty is higher in the high growth period rather than in the lower growth period. In the lower growth period the effects on poverty are higher with higher wages. Thus, using growth as a control variable illustrates differential effects on inter-state poverty between informal sector wages and informal sector asset formation.

Figure 3.1

1994/95 to 1999/2000 Poverty Reduction, Growth in Informal Sector Wages and Informal Sector Asset Formation

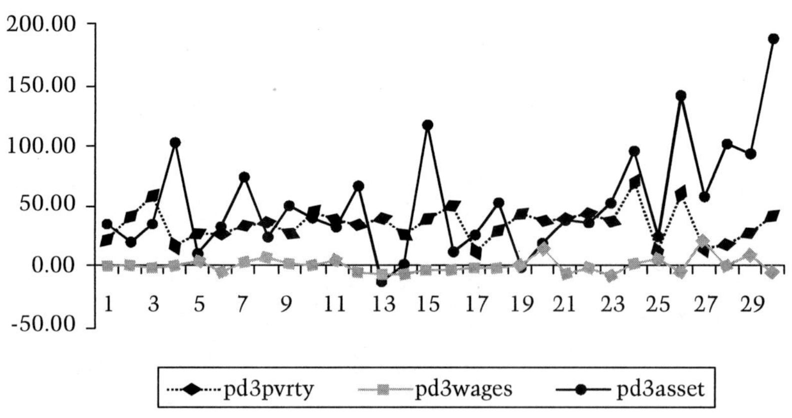

The x-axis indicates the state for which the variables poverty reduction rates, growth in informal sector wages, and growth in informal sector asset formation are plotted. As can be seen from Figure 3.1, the higher the asset formation for state, number 4 for example, the lower is the

16. *Economic Survey, 2005. http://exim.indiamart.com/economic-survey-2005-2006/*

level of poverty. This is despite the fact that level of informal sector wages were more or less stable across states for this entire period. This implied that the growth rates in wages during this high growth phase was close to 0 in most states. Despite this low growth in wage rates, the rate of growth of asset formation in most states was well above 0. The levels of poverty reduction closely followed the curve for asset formation across states.

As can be seen from Figure 3.2, the higher the wages the lower the poverty, with wages having a more decisive effect on poverty rather than asset formation. For the period of lower growth rates, the curve on poverty reduction more closely follows the curve of growth rates of wages in the informal sector. It is also to be noted that during the period of lower economic growth, the rate of asset formation is lower. This was despite the fact that except for a few states, wage increases were well above 0 in most states in the lower growth phase.

Figure 3.2

1989/90 to 1994/95 Poverty Reduction, Growth in Informal Sector Wages and Informal Sector Asset Formation

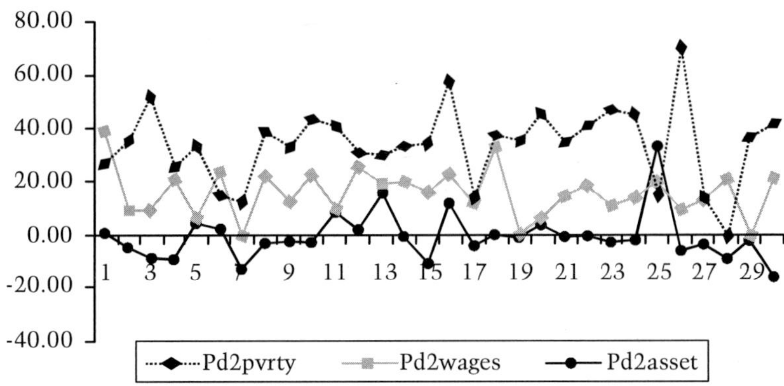

These correlations are further confirmed by the regression analysis for the first period. A detailed explanation of the data sources are provided in Annexure Tables. It is interesting to observe in the regression below that the rate of growth of assets has the most statistically significant effect on poverty. The rate of growth of informal sector wages had a statistically significant fixed effect. The rate of growth of the state domestic product (SDP) does not have a statistically significant effect on poverty. The elasticities with respect to asset formation and wages on poverty is much higher than with respect to SDP growth. Thus, every 0.3 per cent increase in informal sector assets and every 0.2 per cent increase in informal sector wages, decreases poverty by 1 per cent whereas every 1.1 per cent rate of growth of SDP reduces poverty by 1 per cent.

These results have significant policy implications. Government policy should thus focus on supporting asset formation in the informal sector. It is also important for the government to identify the variables that lead to higher asset formation in the informal sector. Similarly, it is important to identify the variables that could lead to higher wages. This is because governance deficits (see Chapter 6) in transferring incomes to the poor or building assets such as houses for the poor have led to poor outcomes. Thus, policy design has to take account of variables which lead to higher wages or higher levels of asset formation, as some of the identified variables may be easier to address through policy than others.

Table 3.3

Dependent Variable: Log (PPv) (For the Period 1984/85 to 2000/01) at 95 Per cent Level of Significance

Variables	*OLS*	*Fixed Effect*	*Random Effect*	*FGLS*
Δ As/As	-0.003*** (0.001)	-0.002*** (0.0006)	-0.002*** (0.0006)	-0.002*** (0.0003)
Δ W/W	-0.002 (0.003)	-0.003** (0.001)	-0.003* (0.001)	-0.004*** (0.0006)
Δ Y/Y	-1.06 (0.67)	0.244 (0.456)	-0.001 (0.444)	0.093 (0.223)
R-sq	0.11	-	-	-
F (3,86)	3.77***	-	-	-
R-sq-within	-	0.19	-	-
F(3,57)	-	4.58***	-	-
Wald chi2(3)	-	-	14.93***	59.59***
Hausman test: chi2 (3)	-	5.72	-	
Auto correlation coeff.	-	-		0.722
No. of observations	90	90	90	90

Note: Δ As/As: Growth rate of real informal sector real fixed asset; Δ W/W: Growth rate of real informal wage; Δ Y/Y: Growth rate of per capita domestic product; PPv: Percentage of population below poverty line; ***: Significance at 1 per cent; **: Significance at 5 per cent and *: Significance at 10 per cent.

III

Economic Growth and Structural Changes in the Indian Informal Sector[17]

The rates of growth of the Indian economy between 1993-94 and 1999-2000 averaged about 4.5 per cent per capita, whereas the growth rate per capita between 1999-2000 to 2004-05 averaged about 7 per cent per capita. The distribution of employment is indicative of the trickle-down effects of the high rates of growth. Throughout this period of high growth, there was a steady movement out of agriculture into non-agricultural activities in rural areas. During the first period with lower rates of growth, there was a decrease of over 5 per cent in households which were self-employed in the agricultural sector with a simultaneous increase of nearly 1 per cent in the non-agricultural sector (NCEUS, 2007). Using the framework of stylised facts derived by Martha Chen, the decrease in self-employed in agriculture, and the increase in agricultural labour would be indicative of a decrease in the rate of increase of rural incomes. By contrast, the number of self-employed in the urban areas increased marginally by 1 per cent, whereas the numbers of regularly employed fell by nearly 2 per cent. The incidence of casual labour increased by about 1 per cent (NCEUS, 2007). Whether the gainers compensate the losers in a net sense will depend on the wage rate increase in the informal sector which according to the NSS has been steady (NCEUS, 2007). Thus in the first period there should be an overall decrease in poverty, with urban poverty reducing at higher rates than rural poverty. In the second period by contrast, the reverse should be expected, i.e., rural poverty should decrease faster than urban poverty and in fact this is vindicated by NSS (NCEUS, 2007). From 2000-2005, the rate of growth in the agriculture sector was higher which along with higher proportion of self-employed households is indicative of better poverty impacts in the rural areas. In fact, the share of households in self-employment grew by 5.6 per cent just at par with the growth in their share in population. The decrease in agricultural labour both in terms of households and in terms of population is indicative of opportunities available elsewhere. The category of other labour, presumably

17. All the data used in this section unless otherwise specified has been obtained from the NCEUS report.

non-farm labour increased keeping pace with the population composition of this subsector.

The decline in share of 'others' in the labour force is outstripped by population composition of this category in the second period indicating again the relative importance of self-employment in rural areas. By contrast, the increase in share of self-employed households in urban areas was lower by almost one whole percentage point in comparison to their share in the population. This is indicative of slower opportunity growth in this subsector. The decrease in regular wage or salaried employment has been lower during the higher growth period, with the decline being somewhat lower than the decline in the share of population in urban areas. This would imply that the creation of jobs during the period of high growth in the formal sector just outstripped the increase in population though still declining marginally. The decline in the share of households and in population in the other categories are at par, again indicating the increase in opportunities elsewhere.

By all measures, it is the self-employed category which comprise over half the households in the rural sector and nearly 40 per cent of the households in the urban sector. Thus, it is this sector which is relatively less poor which should be studied more carefully for examining their potential for trickle down. According to a recent survey by the GoI, over 74 per cent of the self-employed category could be classified as poor and vulnerable, with an average expenditure of half a US$ per day per capita, whereas the rest would belong to middle and higher income groups. The latter comprises people with sufficient capital or skills such as professional lawyers, accountants etc. In the rural areas, only 1.1 per cent of the self-employed are landless, whereas nearly 55 per cent are small (1-2 ha of land) or medium and large landowners (over 2 ha of land). The rest have less than 1 ha of land. So by and large the self-employed do have some assets, though there is considerable variance in their level of assets. By contrast in the urban areas nearly 14 per cent of the self-employed are landless and nearly 90 per cent have less than 1 ha of land. Only over 10 per cent of the self-employed are either small or medium and large landowners. The change in the trend of the self-employed in rural households is therefore indicative of lower fragmentation of holdings and perhaps an exodus to urban areas. Both would be better for poverty alleviation in rural areas. The smaller landholdings in urban areas is indicative of the fact that skills such as education, rather than assets such as land may be better for the self-employed in urban areas in alleviating poverty.

Table 3.4

Distribution of Households by Type of Employment

(All-India)

Household Type	*Households*			*Population*		
	1993-94	*1999-2000*	*2004-05*	*1993-94*	*1999-2000*	*2004-05*
			Rural			
Self-employed in:						
Agriculture	378	327	359	424	371	398
Non-agriculture	127	134	158	131	139	167
Self-employed	505	461	517	554	509	565
Agricultural labour	303	322	258	275	301	241
Other labour	80	80	109	75	76	106
Rural labour	383	402	367	350	376	346
Others	112	137	116	95	114	88
All	1000	1000	1000	1000	1000	1000
			Urban			
Self-employed	337	344	375	388	393	433
Regular wage/salaried	434	417	413	428	402	396
Casual labour	132	140	118	129	141	118
Others	97	97	94	55	63	52
All	1000	1000	1000	1000	1000	1000

Source: NCEUS.

The education profile of the self-employed in the rural areas is also marginally better than that of the other categories. For example, the self-employed had a mean of 3.4 years of schooling in comparison to the other categories which had a maximum (agricultural workers) of 2.8 years of schooling. Both self-employed men and women had better schooling. In the urban areas too, self-employed men and women tend to be better educated than that of other unorganised sectors, with more than 60 per cent of them with an education of over 8 years of schooling. Self-employed in urban areas can be divided by categories of those who have physical assets, or those who have human capital to those which have none. The lowest category of self-employed consists of rickshaw pullers, street vendors, *beedi* rollers and the like with little access to any of these assets.

A poverty analysis of the different categories of informal workers also shows some interesting trends. The poverty levels of self-employed while higher than regular workers in the rural areas was only marginally so. The poverty levels of casual workers was much higher by about 8 percentage points in comparison to the self-employed. Thus, a higher growth in the proportion of self-employed in comparison to others may be indicative of trickle-down effects during high growth periods in agriculture. In addition, in the urban areas the poverty incidence of self-employed is less than half that of casual labour. Again the decrease in casual labour, accompanied by an increase in self-employment would be evidence of trickle down in higher growth periods. The fact that there is convergence between the poverty rates of regular and self-employment in the urban areas may be an indication of outsourcing industrial activities to the informal sector. This does not mean that the formal sector is being informalised (absolute numbers are more or less the same at slightly over 33 million workers between 2000-2005), but rather incremental gains in the formal sector are being made perhaps through outsourcing production to the informal sector (increase in formal sector employment of informal workers from 20 to 29 million during this period) (NCEUS, 2007). This may also be an important source of trickle down through the informal sector. In fact, this trend towards strengthening the formal-informal sector linkage is clearly a response to maintaining competitiveness in the face of uncertainty brought about by globalisation. Whatever the reason, it has undoubtedly helped reduce poverty.

The occupational profile of informal sector workers in the self-employed category, both in the agricultural and non-agricultural sectors also shows their high sensitivity to growth. The occupational profile of the self-employed in the non-agricultural sector are primarily in production for women and trade and sales for men. The occupational profile of men and women are not very different in the self-employed category in rural areas, though women account for a higher proportion of producers in rural areas. In the casual work category, however, the occupational profile is reversed, with most men in production and women in services and production-related categories. The NCEUS has also pointed out that the scheduled castes and tribes (SC/ST) are most vulnerable with a poverty incidence of over 40 per cent which is much higher than that of the casual informal labour. A higher proportion of labour from the SC/STs were likely to be casual in both rural and urban areas, which also explains the higher incidence of poverty for this social group. However, given the decline in the proportion of casual labour households in both rural and urban areas in the period of high growth (2000-2005), it is likely that some of this population is also getting into either regular employment or self-employment.

Analysing the Self-Employed in the Informal Sector

The self-employed which is the largest category of the informal sector has been further classified into three subcategories: (a) own account enterprises (OAE) accounting for 46 per cent of the total informal sector workers and two-thirds of the category of self-employed, (b) unpaid family labour, and (c) employers, i.e., those that hire at least 1 worker and up to 10 workers. In addition, homeworkers are also included in the self-employed categories. The category of self-employed is not necessarily and uniformly poor.

The objective function of the OAE, in which can be subsumed unpaid family labour, is to maximise the value added irrespective of how many family members are needed to work in this enterprise. About 37 per cent of these have assets of only Rs 5,000 (US $100) with a much higher concentration in rural areas, where 43 per cent have assets of only Rs 5,000 (US $100) in urban areas. Only 8 per cent of the rural OAE and 17 per cent of the urban OAE have assets more than Rs 10,000 (US $200). The rest have assets between Rs 20,000 (US $400) and Rs 70,000 (US $1,400). Most use their fixed assets and only a small proportion hire assets. OAEs are concentrated in food processing, tobacco, textiles and wearing apparel, and in producing non-metallic products.

The gross value addition per worker in OAEs in rural areas is Rs 1,167 (US $20) per month in comparison to the poverty line which is Rs 327 (US $8) per capita per month in rural households. In the urban areas the gross value addition per worker is Rs 2,175 (US $40) in comparison to the poverty line which is Rs 454 (US $9) per capita per month. This implies that if there are two full-time workers in OAEs households, in both rural and urban areas, a significant proportion of the population in India would clear the poverty line. However, the notional number of workers per household in OAEs was about 1.89. Further about 57 per cent of the rural OAEs and 30 per cent of the urban OAEs have incomes below the notional minimum for sustainable livelihoods (NCEUS, 2007).

Nearly 64 per cent of these enterprises believe they are stagnating, and 10 per cent felt that they were contracting. However, 18 per cent felt that they were expanding. Surprisingly, a high 30 per cent of the enterprises felt that they did not face any serious problems. Credit, infrastructure and lack of marketing facilities, as well as competition from large firms were the problems identified by this sector. Considering that less than 10 per cent of the rural and less than 25 per cent of the urban OAEs are not registered with any type of agency, lack of access to credit is not surprising.

The second category of self-employed with hired workers employ around 26 per cent of the workers in the informal enterprises. The value of assets with this group is an average of Rs 300,000 (US $8,500) and nearly 43 per cent of such enterprises have assets exceeding Rs 100,000 (US $2,500). The gross value added per worker in these enterprises is around Rs 26,303 (US $525) per annum in rural areas and around Rs 43,061 (US $800) per annum in urban areas. Obviously this is much above sustainable wage rates. About 50 per cent of the enterprises believe that they were stagnating and nearly 30 per cent believed they were expanding. Registration levels were also higher at nearly 43 per cent in rural areas and nearly 57 per cent in urban areas. Problems of credit were identified as crucial in this subsector too.

The information on the status of enterprises in the informal sector collected in the survey of NSSO in 1999-2000 showed the owner's impression about the growth of his enterprise over the last three years. Over 20 per cent of the entrepreneurs felt that their business activities have expanded over the three years preceding the date of survey. However, about 10 per cent entrepreneurs felt that their business has shrunk over the last three years. About 63 per cent of the entrepreneurs felt that their enterprises were stagnant while 7 per cent enterprises were started during the last three years only. Again this shows that in net terms informal enterprises have been doing better towards the end of the last century.

About 12 per cent of the self-employed workers are homeworkers. The percentage is much higher for women. In the manufacturing sector, 32 per cent are homeworkers and among the women 50 per cent of those employed are homeworkers. There are two kind of contracts for homeworkers, one which provides raw materials and the other which does not. In India, the predominant form of contracts, nearly 70 per cent, is of the first kind. This implies that the homeworker is dependent on the middleman or contractor for raw materials and the status of a homeworker is closer to a wage worker. The largest number of homeworkers are concentrated in tobacco and the wearing apparel industry.

Generally homeworkers receive lower wages, though living at home their expenses are lower. On an average the homeworkers received about 50 per cent of the minimum wage. Delayed payments, insufficient and low quality of raw materials, health problems because of poor home conditions were reported for this sector. The advantage of homeworkers who are on the lower end of the value chain is that employers have no outlay for infrastructure which would otherwise have been the case. Homeworkers can also adjust their timing to suit their domestic activities.

While the self-employed are relatively better off than casual or in some cases even regular workers, their conditions of living generally tend to be poor. They all share some common problems such as access to credit, poor living conditions, poor buildup of human capital. Absence of education and health acts as a debilitating factor for securing a reasonable living. Therefore, policies have to focus both on promoting the sustainability of such enterprises and to the provision of the labour involved in such enterprises with a living wage.

Success Stories of the Informal Economy

The preceding sections have reflected the dynamism of the informal economy and also identified variables which could accelerate this dynamism. While high growth rates have inevitably trickled down to the informal economy, it is also true that the informal economy is poor on an average. The average picture as seen above has to be nuanced with the vast differences that exist within the informal economy. This section gives some examples of how the informal economy has sought to make innovations to reach the poorest of the poor or what can be called 'grassroots capitalism'. The section concludes with some recommendations on how these examples can be multiplied and their core strengthened.

Grassroots Capitalism

Anecdotal examples of 'grassroots capitalism' thriving in India is also presented in a paper by Mitra (2006). Operating from small workshops, the informal sector can assemble a whole vehicle from scratch right under the roadside tree. In many parts of north India, these homemade vehicles are called *jugaad*, slang for 'quick fix'. Delhi generally provides used car parts like gearboxes, radiators, wheels and steering wheels. The mechanics start with an 8–12 horsepower agricultural diesel engine of the sort typically used to drive a water pump or other farm equipment. Then the chassis is welded, the engine is mounted, and the gearbox is connected to power the rear wheels. With a rudimentary bench as seat, the vehicle is ready to chug along at around 20 kilometres an hour, carrying around 25 people. To save on fuel, electric lights and horns are often eliminated. The vehicle costs from US $1,000 to US $2,000 (Mitra, 2006). Compare this to the price of a basic small car (800 cubic centimetres), which seats only four and costs US $5,000 (Mitra, 2006).

The competitive informal sector assemblers provide first-time buyers of personal computers (PC) the possibility of acquiring a locally assembled PC. The biggest advantage that the informal sector assemblers have is their flexibility to assemble a PC tailored to the customer's needs and financial constraints. For almost every major component, they provide a range of options, balancing quality and price. And, of course, they also provide on-site repair options.

Given the huge electricity deficits in India, local parallel grids developed by the informal sector are being run in many parts of urban India. Shop owners have set up businesses along road without the sanction of the civic administration. They collaborate to set up kerosene or diesel generator sets to supply lighting during the evening shopping hours. Typically, an informal sector entrepreneur wires 50 to 100 shops or vendors in one neighbourhood or at an informal marketplace. The fee charged is usually based on the number of light bulbs that are connected for a certain number of hours each evening. While the cost of electricity is much higher than it would be if it were available from the grid, the vendors have the flexibility to decide whether the benefits of attracting customers during peak shopping hours outweighs the costs of obtaining electricity.

As can be expected, informal sector entrepreneurs have entered education in a big way too. India always had some of the world's best private schools, but what has not been appreciated is the scale of educational service provided by the informal sector. According to some estimates, about 50 per cent of the poorest children in urban India are attending private neighbourhood schools, some run by charitable organisations and the majority run by local entrepreneurs. Tuition services to bring poor children upto grade level particularly in subjects such as english and mathematics is also available from the informal sector.

The Indian experience on the informal *hawala* system of international money transfers is also noteworthy. In Urdu, a language spoken primarily by the Muslim population in India and Pakistan, *hawala* means 'in the air.' In Arabic, it generally translates as 'transfer.' In other words, *hawala* is an invisible transfer of money from one country to another. *Hawala* also leveraged the gap between official channels available and the needs of the poor who have no bank accounts or other forms of assets to provide as guarantees to the formal banking systems. It has also served in times of foreign exchange crises to meet the needs of both the rich and the poor.

The informal sector has improvised to provide its own credit and savings facilities. Popularly known in Delhi as Committees in the poor classes, at almost every commercial complex in Delhi, people at the lowest income levels have tried to band together in small groups, led by a reliable coordinator. The members are typically 10 to 100 people working in the vicinity, or people who have known each other for a long time. They agree on various savings schemes in which the members may put in, say, US $1 a week or US $5 a month. The coordinator acts as a mobile bank, carrying the cash in his pocket and ready to disburse a loan on the spot. Every member has the opportunity to withdraw his contribution or to take a loan. The interest rate is determined by the members of the group themselves and is typically 2 per cent–5 per cent per annum.

These are only a few examples of the all pervading spirit of enterprise, particularly among people at the bottom of the economic ladder, in India today. They exhibit an uncanny ability to identify an unmet need and then find a way to supply that demand. Relative lack of formal education and training, or of capital and technology, are not obstacles. Of course the growth of these entrepreneurs has been much higher during the periods of high growth on account of increased demand for these services. While data on the growth of these services and goods are not systematic, anecdotal evidence suggests that this form of entrepreneurship may have grown substantially during the last 15 odd years.

So why are these examples of informal sector entrepreneurship not increasing significantly despite India's high growth rates. Some formal sector competitors complain that those who are involved in the large informal sector in India have an edge because they avoid paying taxes and do not bear the full cost of economic regulations. On the other hand, the single biggest obstacle to the informal sector is its vulnerability to extortion from law enforcing agencies. Strictly enforcing some of the regulations would gravely affect some of the poorest sections of society who are engaged in the whole range of informal economic activities. Political upheaval would inevitably follow. Because India is a democracy, its government has to maintain a balancing act. The other cost that the informal sector has to bear because of its extra legal status is the inability to raise the capital necessary to expand businesses even if they are competitive and have successful products or services.

This inability to capitalise assets, and the consequent underutilisation of capital for economic development, has been well researched by Peruvian economist Hernando de Soto (2000) in his book *The Mystery of Capital*. A corollary to this problem is the formal sector's difficulty in taking advantage of successful informal sector players' managerial and technical expertise by integrating them into their operations. This brief survey by Barun Mitra provides a glimpse of the culture of entrepreneurship that prevails in India. If these grassroots capitalist entrepreneurs were freed from the shackles of bureaucratic economic regulations, they could well take India to the top of the development ladder. It would not be too far-fetched to suggest that there is hardly any country in the world today where informal sector economic activity is as diverse and as widespread as it is in India. This activity is an unrealised potential just waiting to be harnessed. To multiply these examples of grassroots entrepreneurs, the government has to promote certain catalysing variables that will allow informal sector players to maximise their profit through asset building and incomes. The next section has identified these variables.

IV

Factors that Determine Informal Sector Asset Building and Incomes

Given the crucial role of informal sector asset formation and incomes in alleviating poverty in India, a survey of about 500 informal sector respondents, most of them self-employed was conducted by the author. For the identification of the sectors from which respondents would be chosen, first of all the data on formal and informal sectors by enterprises was collected. In the manufacturing sector, the subsectors in which formal firms account for 80 per cent of the total output was first tabulated from the *Annual Survey of Industries* (See Annexure A-3.2a). This pertains to the latest year for which information was available at the time of writing, i.e., 2003/04. A similar exercise was conducted for the services sector (see Annexure A-3.2b). From this list, in each item the data on the output of the top 500 firms was collected. Where the top 500 firms accounted for less than 25 per cent of total output, it was assumed that the majority of the production would be in the informal sector. These worked out to about 10 subsectors, about 5 in manufacturing and 5 in services. From each of these subsectors, 50 respondents were chosen. The questionnaire used for the interview is attached in Annexure A-3.3. The data generated by the surveys is presented in Annexure A-3.4 and Annexure A-3.5.

The survey showed the trickle-down effects through the informal sector during the high growth period, i.e., 2000-2007 was much higher than the trickle-down during the lower growth period, i.e., 1994/95-2000. This is shown by the fact that the majority of the respondents irrespective of the subsector to which they belonged had higher incomes post-2000 than pre-2000. The increase in incomes was higher in the manufacturing sector than in the services sector. The level of asset formation also in the informal sector was much higher during the high growth period than in the low growth period. Interestingly, but logically, the number of dependents and the number of working people in the family were closely associated with higher levels of asset formation.

The equation used to estimate the correlation coefficients was as follows:

Formation of Assets = f(health expenditure, transport expenditure, income, meals consumed, education, dependents, infrastructure)

Table 3.5

Abbreviations Used for Explanatory Variables

Linear Least Square Regression Explanatory Variables	
LN_AST	Logarithm of asset
Ln_HEE	Logarithm of health expenditure
Ln_TRP	Logarithm of transport
LN_INC	Logarithm of income
Ln_DPE	Logarithm of dependent
DM1	=1 if meal=0, & otherwise =0
DM2	=1 if meal=3, & otherwise =0
DE1	=1 if education=0, & otherwise =0
DE2	=1 if education=1, & otherwise =0
DE3	=1 if education=2, & otherwise =0
DF1	=1 if infrastructure=1, & otherwise =0
DF2	=1 if infrastructure=2, & otherwise =0
dT	=1 if the time is before, & otherwise =0

The explanatory variables detailed above need to be explained. A range of dummies have been used. If a person eats at least one meal, DM1=1, otherwise it is 0. For DM2 to be 1, a person has to eat all his three meals, and for it to be 0, all other situations are covered, i.e., 0, 1 or 2 meals. For education, three dummies have been used. DE1=1, if a person is literate and DE1=0 otherwise. DE2 is 1 if the person has finished high school, but 0 otherwise. DE3 is 1 if the person has finished his university education and 0 otherwise. Access to infrastructure again refers to either one type of infrastructure or two types of infrastructure. DF1 is 1 if the person has a *kuccha* (made of mud) house but does not have a *pucca* house (made of bricks and mortar, cement etc.). DF2 is 1, if the person has a *pucca* house but no access to electricity. dT refers to whether the assets were acquired before or after the high growth period. Thus, if the assets were acquired after the year 2000, dT=1, otherwise 0. Further the play of the explanatory variables would differ according to the subsector of employment of the informal sector worker. The workers were thus classified in three categories: agriculture, manufacturing and services (see regression below). It is expected that the returns to education would be higher in the industrial sector, for example in comparison to agriculture.

The summarised regression tables which have passed all the diagnostic tests for robust correlation are given below. Table 3.6 shows the role of different explanatory variables in explaining asset formation in the informal sector both in the economy as a whole and in the separate sectors. The sample design took account of professions which dominate informal sector employment. Nevertheless the sample can at best be considered representative, not exhaustive.

The correlation for different variables in the high growth period is indicated by the variable XdT. The table indicates that both during the high growth and the low growth period, access to transport was critical in determining the level of asset formation in the informal sector. The correlation with health and number of dependents was relatively weaker. However, the correlation with transport expenditure held at the 1 per cent level of significance. This is logical as those from the informal sector who owned their own means of transport were more likely to build other assets. In the lower growth period, the levels of education, the number of meals consumed, and access to infrastructure such as electricity, water and sanitation were important for asset building. However the correlation was negative, showing that for all sectors being educated could have a negative effect on asset building. This result on the face of it appears counter-intuitive, but if we look at the informal sector activities in general, formal education has little role in generating assets or income. It is skill formation which is important in this sector and that may not be related to formal education. In fact formal education could be a disincentive to skill formation, as people educated formally may consider informal sector activities as 'beneath their touch'. Skill formation takes place on the job which implies experience may be gained by people who have not been to formal schools. There is a need therefore to meld skill formation with formal schooling. Some suggestions for an effective school system have been developed in the last section.

Table 3.6

Regression Result from Survey Analysis

	Dependent Variable: Ln_AST			
Explanatory Variables	*Aggregate Study*	*Agriculture*	*Manufacturing*	*Services*
Ln_HEE	0.027 (0.038)	-0.093 (0.124)	-0.079 (0.08)	0.093* (0.056)
Ln_TRP	0.177*** (0.058)	0.400* (0.232)	0.260*** (0.097)	0.129 (0.086)
DM1	4.701*** (0.716)	4.80 (3.61)	4.33*** (1.16)	5.16*** (1.02)
DM2	0.601** (0.299)	-1.08 (1.57)	0.92** (0.48)	0.775** (0.408)
DE1	-2.912*** (0.508)	-0.07 (1.91)	-4.06*** (1.16)	-2.89*** (0.634)
DE2	-1.248** (0.511)	-1.65 (1.68)	-2.19** (1.17)	-0.856 (0.649)
DE3	-0.956** (0.528)	-3.27 (1.95)	-1.27 (1.17)	-1.09 (0.673)
DF1	-1.760*** (0.511)	-	-1.91** (0.88)	-1.85 (0.632)
DF2	-1.159*** (0.328)	-3.25 (1.95)	-0.599 (0.517)	-1.53 (0.445)
DM1× dT	-	-	-	-
DM2× dT	0.918** (0.459)	0.955 (2.15)	1.08 (0.839)	0.646 (0.598)
DE1× dT	1.573 (0.535)	-0.252 (2.54)	1.77** (1.00)	1.69** (0.676)
DE2× dT	0.804 (0.519)	1.82 (1.96)	0.284 (0.953)	0.613 (0.692)
DE3× dT	0.927* (0.540)	5.10 (3.12)	0.225 (0.863)	1.26* (0.733)
DF1× dT	0.166 (0.730)	-	0.051 (1.28)	0.311 (0.898)
DF2× dT	0.595 (0.455)	4.78 (3.28)	0.824 (0.723)	0.568 (0.621)
Ln_DPE	0.222 (0.168)	1.43 (1.20)	0.240 (0.201)	0.146 (0.320)
R-sq	0.417	0.57	0.47	0.42
F(16,483)	21.63***	-	-	-
F(14,23)	-	2.21**	-	-
F(16,177)	-	-	9.91***	-
F(16,251)				11.76***
Root MSE	2.10	2.31	2.05	
No. of observations	500	38	194	268

Table 3.7

Linear Least Square Regression

	Dependent Variable: Ln_INC			
Explanatory Variables	*Aggregate Study*	*Agriculture*	*Manufacturing*	*Services*
Ln_HEE	0.041 (0.069)	-0.022 (0.179)	-0.036 (0.136)	0.087 (0.100)
Ln_TRP	0.547*** (0.104)	0.363 (0.334)	0.749*** (0.164)	0.452*** (0.154)
DM1	6.07*** (1.29)	6.79 (5.19)	8.39 (1.97)	4.88*** (1.82)
DM2	-2.63*** (0.539)	-3.79* (2.25)	-3.20*** (0.826)	-1.48** (0.72)
DE1	-361*** (0.914)	4.60* (2.75)	-7.25*** (1.98)	-3.33*** (1.13)
DE2	-2.15** (0.920)	-1.03 (2.41)	-4.66 (1.99)	-1.27 (1.15)
DE3	-0.373 (0.951)	-1.98 (3.16)	-2.58 (2.00)	-0.668 (1.20)
DF1	2.32** (0.920)	-	1.57 (1.49)	2.18** (1.12)
DF2	0.163 (0.591)	-5.74** (2.80)	-0.528 (0.878)	0.958 (0.794)
DM1× dT	-	-	-	-
DM2× dT	3.62*** (0.827)	7.48** (3.09)	3.74*** (1.42)	2.59** (1.06)
DE1× dT	4.88*** (0.963)	-1.88 (3.65)	4.97*** (1.69)	5.15*** (1.20)
DE2× dT	3.59*** (0.934)	3.54 (2.81)	3.80** (1.61)	2.90** (1.23)
DE3× dT	1.67** (0.973)	4.41 (4.49)	1.27 (1.46)	2.10* (1.30)
DF1× dT	-2.15* (1.31)	-	-0.66 (2.17)	-2.16 (1.60)
DF2× dT	0.076 (0.819)	5.80 (4.72)	0.559 (1.22)	-0.224 (1.10)
Ln_DPE	0.644** (0.302)	0.201 (1.72)	-0.042 (0.342)	1.94 (0.57)
R-sq	0.48	0.79	0.62	0.42
F(16,483)	28.18***	-	-	-
F(14,23)	-	6.43***	-	-
F(16,177)	-	-	18.59***	-
F(16,251)	-	-	-	11.35***
Root MSE	3.78	3.33	3.46	3.77
No. of observations	500	38	194	268

During the lower growth period, lack of access to infrastructure also had a negative effect on asset building. The negative correlation between literacy, infrastructure and asset building was statistically significant.

During the high growth period, most of these variables were not statistically significant in determining informal sector asset building. However, access to meals and primary education was significant at the 5 per cent level in determining informal sector asset building. This was especially so for the manufacturing and services sector showing the importance of basic level of schooling or literacy in these sectors. In the services subsector, university education was positively correlated with asset building though at a 10 per cent level of significance.

Informal sector incomes in the high growth period depended crucially on education, access to infrastructure and on the number of dependents. Education upto secondary level increased incomes. University education did not necessarily generate higher incomes. This could be because the income group covered by the sample were all in the low income range where university education may not be important. Predictably, the returns to university education was significant in the services subsector. For both manufacturing and services, the returns to secondary education was significant and high. This implies that incomes increased when informal sector workers were educated upto the secondary level. In the agriculture sector, the correlation between education and income was not significant. Individuals who were able to eat three square meals also tend to have higher incomes. This was particularly true in agriculture signifying that better meals were associated with higher incomes. The most important determinant, however, was access to infrastructure. Lack of infrastructure actually decreased incomes. This could be because the sample consisted of a large number of home-based workers who could work longer hours if they had access to infrastructure such as electricity.

In the lower growth period, predictably education had a dampening effect on income. This negative correlation points to the very important role played by the control variable, i.e., growth. Interpreted otherwise, these results imply that only with high growth would education lead to higher incomes in the informal sector. In periods of low growth, the higher the health expenditure, the lower the income particularly in agriculture and manufacturing. This implies that absenteeism on account of poor health would decrease incomes especially in periods of low growth when employment contracts are of a casual nature. Access to transport shown by the positive correlation with transport expenditure provides better access to incomes even in low growth periods. Another significant relationship in low growth periods is the negative and significant correlation between meals and income. This implies that in low growth periods payment may often be in kind and lower cash payments may be disbursed. Access to infrastructure in periods of lower growth was important in raising incomes only in services. Low growth effects dominated incomes in both agriculture and manufacturing, i.e., lack of access to infrastructure continued to lower incomes.

These findings are of crucial importance as the policy implications would depend on whether the informal sector is operating in a high growth period or a low growth period. For protecting the informal sector asset building and incomes, governments would have to design health insurance schemes. Similarly, governments should increase their outlay on infrastructure so that in a high growth period the informal sector can increase both its incomes and asset building. As growth is likely to follow a cyclical pattern, it is of crucial importance to focus on these two key variables. Transport has emerged as a variable of crucial importance in determining asset formation and incomes in the informal sector. On the whole, building of physical infrastructure should be the focus of government policy for alleviating poverty in the informal sector. This applies particularly to the provision of public transport facilities and electricity to the informal sector. An important variable whose effects on the informal sector was somewhat nuanced was education. While literacy and primary education was of great importance in forming assets and increasing incomes in the informal sector, its importance was lower in the agriculture sector. It is important, therefore, in agriculture to focus more on skill formation and much less on formal education. In the services sector, more emphasis needs to be placed on formal education. In the industrial sector, the target of the government should be to ensure at least secondary education for informal sector participants along with vocational education. The government of India has recognised the importance of vocational education and infrastructure building for the informal sector. A critical assessment of these initiatives is carried out in the next section.

V

Initiatives of the Government of India for Improving Skill Development and Infrastructure of the Informal Economy

Current Initiatives in Training for the Informal, Unorganised Sector

Currently 'learning on the job' is the main method for skill acquisition both in the formal and unorganised sectors of the economy (King, 2007). Thus, interventions in skills development for the informal sector can scarcely avoid direct confrontation with this mainstream modality. One of the difficulties about the analysis of training in the informal sector is that there is not a single system of informal apprenticeship operating which can be built upon, improved or formalised. The main training mechanism is 'learning on the job', which does not sufficiently differentiate between training in established traditions of craft apprenticeship and on the job training in manufacturing, construction, services and agriculture. Chandra (2006) has argued that it should be possible to 'draw upon traditional arrangements for skill building and strengthen them instead of dismissing them as inadequate'. However, regarding the suggestions for developing and 'incentivising' the system, all assume that the trainers and employers can be persuaded to invest much more substantially in training their apprentices to a higher level of skills, and to provide training allowances; whereas it could be argued that it is precisely the very low cost of the current on the job training system that is so attractive to employers. Chandra notes that current training approaches can be highly exploitative: 'In informal apprenticeship arrangements, the trainee may not be paid for years and treated as unpaid worker.' He further notes that there is a need for 'effective advocacy for training' and that there needs to be a 'comprehensive strategy.' But, in a final comment, Chandra (2007) admits that there is a long way to go: 'This aspect [a comprehensive strategy] cannot be overemphasised, given that despite lip service for a long time, training for the informal economy remains a distant dream.'

The World Bank (2006a) has also given systematic attention to the role of vocational training in India, including the key role of training for the very large informal economy. What is surprising, however, is that despite its very detailed analysis of India's employment challenge, there is little attempt to connect the causes of the employment challenge to the particular challenge of training effectively in the informal sector. It merely acknowledges that non-government providers have proved to be more effective than the government, and that, rather than the government intervening in provision for the informal sector, an enabling environment for these non-public providers should be created. There is little acknowledgement of the fact that labour regulations which have encouraged dualism and informality would also discourage the private sector from investing in training for the informal sector.

Historically, employers in India (both formal and informal) have paid scant attention to in-service training. The World Bank (2006b) suggests that in India no more than 7 per cent of employees get access to any kind of formal in-service training in a given year. The World Bank and the Informal Sector Task Force were both aware that, in respect of formal in-service training, India compares very poorly with other countries in South Asia (apart from Pakistan which is even lower), and the gap is very much larger when India is compared to Malaysia and China (World Bank, 2006b; NCEUS, 2005).

Policies of the Government of India to Improve Skill Formation

The Government's main provision for vocational training, through the industrial training institutes (ITIs), has almost no connection with the informal economy, or of training for self-employment. Only 8-12 per cent of ITI graduates were running small businesses (ILO, 2001; 2003a; 2003b). The formal skill training system, because of its educational entry requirements and long duration of courses, is basically not designed to offer skills to the less educated people (Planning Commission, 2006).

The Government of India recommended the 'Setting up of an Apex Institute for Skill Building in Informal Sector'. This Apex Institute for Skill Building would be especially set up for testing and certifying in the area of construction, brassware, glasswork, fishing, *khadi* etc., with a capacity and output of 250,000 (Planning Commission, 2006). There is no discussion of the rather strange bed-fellows that are suggested for training in this Apex Institute and so far no progress has been made on this front.

A more structured approach to skill development was in the initiative to direct the NCEUS to set up a Task Force on Skill Formation in the Informal sector in 2005 (NCEUS, 2005). The Terms of Reference of the Task Force included an identification of the characteristics and specificities of skill formation, the adequacy of the existing training infrastructure for use by the unorganised sector, the demand and supply of skills, best practice in NGO and government programmes for this sector, and even the design of 'a National Skill Development Initiative for the Unorganised Sector' (NCEUS, 2005). The Task Force did not, in fact, expect to become involved in a major independent initiative in infrastructure development, such as building skill centres. Rather, it saw its own niche as making use of the existing buildings of the Industrial Training Institutes, the private training centres, especially the NGOs, and even the primary schools, in order to mount their own short-term evening courses. These are likely to be intensive short courses of 1 to 3 months, certified in an appropriate manner. The model has not yet been finalised, but there is discussion about a Rs 10,000 (US $200) package: Rs 3,000 (US $60) being allocated to the trainers (e.g. the NGO or the instructors in the Training Institute); Rs 1,000 (US $20) to the youth for their out of pocket expenses; and Rs 6,000 (US $120) as an incentive to the possible employer or, in the case of self-employment, help with startup funding (NCEUS, 2005). This model was going to be tried out with linked NGOs in some 10 small towns, but so far nothing has been put in place.

Suggestion for Improving Skill Formation in the Informal Sector

While on the job training may be the natural way to go and build on the existing systems of informal training, it needs to be supplemented with some formal schooling. This is to enable the informal sector participants to move to other occupations should they desire to do so. The apprenticeship system of the informal sector was normally based on family labour and it is possible that there may be several members of the family, leading to underemployment or that there may be talents (other than those of the family business) which some members of the family develop. The Swiss

Schooling system is a good model which melds formal schooling with on the job training. Nearly two-thirds of those entering upper-secondary education, after nine years of schooling at age 13 or 14, enter the vocational education and training system in Switzerland. At this level, vocational education and training is mainly provided through the 'dual system'. Students spend some of their time in a vocational school; some of their time doing an apprenticeship at a host company; and for most programmes, students attend industry courses at an industry training centre to develop complementary practical skills relating to the occupation at hand. Common patterns are for students to spend one-two days per week at the vocational school and three-four days doing the apprenticeship at the host company; also they alternate between some weeks attending classes at the vocational school and some weeks attending industry courses at an industry training centre. A different pattern is to begin the programme with most of the time devoted to in-school education and gradually diminishing the amount of in-school education in favour of more in-company training.

Switzerland draws a distinction between vocational education and training (VET) programmes at upper-secondary level, and professional education and training (PET) programmes, which take place at tertiary B level. In 2007, more than half of the population aged 25-64 had a VET or PET qualification as their highest level of education. In addition, universities of applied sciences (*Fachhochschulen*) offer vocational education at tertiary A level. Pathways enable people to shift from one part of the education system to another.[18] The informal sector could be a part of the vocational training system where a substantial part of the training could take place within the informal enterprise itself. This could be combined with the NCEUS Task Force recommendation of short vocational courses with appropriate certification.

Infrastructure Development Initiatives for the Unorganised Sector

The Task Force for Micro, Small and Medium Enterprises (MSMEs) recommended a national programme for renewal of industrial infrastructure

18. *http://www.oecd.org/dataoecd/12/5/42578681.pdf.* Learning for Jobs OECD Review of Switzerland, 2009.

to upgrade infrastructure for existing industrial estates, such as roads, drainage, sewage, power distribution (within industrial areas), water supply distribution, etc.[19] This programme was to build on two Central government programmes addressing similar objectives—namely Industrial Infrastructure Upgradation Scheme (IIUS), Department of Industrial Policy and Promotion and Integrated Infrastructural Development (IID) Scheme, Ministry of MSME. Given the different scales at which IIUS and IID schemes operate, a practical distinction could be drawn between industrial estates (based on area), which may qualify for assistance under IIUS/IID.

The two programmes would require additional funding support to assume the character of a National Mission. The funding under these schemes should be linked to certain reforms/measures to be taken by the state governments/local bodies. These reforms/measures may include:

- As a long-term measure, the industrial estates should be entrusted with the municipal functions including levy of taxes, responsibility to maintain the infrastructure within the industrial estates, etc.
- The state governments would undertake to provide dedicated power supply to the industrial estates. Alternatively, funding for common captive power generation in industrial estates would be encouraged through subsidies given to the Special Purpose Vehicle (SPV) managing such facility.
- The state governments would formulate a policy for incentivising private sector for setting up of new industrial estates.

Local bodies would earmark funds for industrial estates within their budgets. For this purpose, a tripartite agreement could be executed between the state government, local body and the SPV, which would be a body constituted by the occupants of the industrial estates.

A number of new industrial parks/areas were developed under various programmes of different ministries, where there is no specific provision for locating micro and small enterprises (MSEs). It may be made mandatory to earmark at least 40-45 per cent of available land for MSEs in such areas, given the existing and envisaged role of MSEs in the production chain.

19. *http://msme.gov.in/PM_MSME_Task_Force_Jan2010.pdf*

Flatted factory complexes may be set up, particularly in and around large cities for MSEs. On similar lines, dormitories for industrial workers in industrial estates may be set up on public private partnership (PPP) mode. Setting up of common facility services in the industrial estates/clusters should be encouraged by providing adequate assistance under various on-going schemes of the ministry of MSE. There is a need to encourage setting up/earmarking of at least one industrial estate in each block for MSEs.

All these schemes were presaged on the relocation of the unorganised sector enterprises to industrial estates. The informal sector is typically dispersed and based on homeworkers. A large proportion of home-based workers are women who for cultural reasons among others are reluctant to work outside their homes. This is the main reason why most of these initiatives have not seen the light of the day. It is important to improve infrastructure of the entire economy with the help of the informal sector. The informal sector has generated in many cases its own infrastructure and it is necessary to build on these initiatives of self-generation. These informal initiatives could then be linked with formal initiatives. For example, while the generation of power could be the responsibility of the government, its distribution could be left to the informal sector in rural and urban slums. It is also important to ensure that infrastructure is fairly decentralised and interest capture is prevented. In any case, building infrastructure should be a priority of the government to ensure that its high economic growth rates are maintained. Some states such as Rajasthan have seen a moderate degree of success in building roads while the hilly states have become self-sufficient in the generation of electricity. These models should be spread to other states too.

VI

Conclusions and Policy Recommendations

The presence or absence of economic growth has a crucial effect on the informal economy. In a rapidly growing India, informal enterprises are likely to find greater opportunities for profitable investment than in a stagnant one. As shown above, growth has trickled down to the informal sector as shown by the increase in the share of self-employed in the overall informal economy. The self-employed have better incomes and better conditions of living than casual workers and almost as much as regular workers in many cases. However, the fact that the trickle down of growth has been insufficient is shown by an average employment of 1.88 per family in the informal sector in self-employment. As shown above, an average employment of 2 would be required to alleviate poverty. This would require either higher growth rates or a more enabling environment for the informal sector to generate jobs. It is the neglect of these factors—the relationship between micro and macro levels—which seems to explain why the current interventions have failed to produce any visible impact on the informal sector. The challenge is therefore how to create an 'appropriate' macroeconomic environment so that the informal sector will have greater opportunities for participation in the market, both formal and informal.

Sustaining high growth rates is a precondition for the improvement of incomes and asset building in the informal sector. Both have a decisive effect on poverty, though in the informal sector asset building has a more statistically significant effect on poverty in periods of high growth. Hence in India's present growth environment, government policy should focus on factors that are of importance in building assets in the informal sector.

The defining characteristic of the informal sector is that its participants generate incomes for themselves by interacting with various markets directly. Viewed in this perspective one can ask whether they can be assisted in any way so that they can help themselves i.e., interact with markets more effectively, without necessarily depending on external intermediaries. As shown by the above analysis, informal sector asset building and incomes are particularly sensitive to easy access to transport facilities and to infrastructure. Government policy should thus focus on infrastructure building.

In providing better infrastructure, government could draw upon the entrepreneurial capacities of the informal sector. This would necessitate a reorientation and restructuring of supply sources of infrastructure (i.e., credit, training, technical know-how, information, electricity etc.). While most of them are in the formal sector, linking them to their informal counterpart would be a step in the right direction but poses a formidable challenge. For instance it may involve privatisation of certain sources of supply, increasing the number of outlets from which the informal sector may obtain its requirements and the creation of a competitive atmosphere. Improving access to infrastructure in cities likewise would entail a review of existing legislations regarding land use, ownership, tenure and rental, etc.; and regulations regarding supply of power, water, communication facilities, most of them under the control of urban authorities. It would be interesting to examine possibilities of using the informal sector for provisioning such public services as shown above in the section on grassroots capitalism.

Education was also identified as an important factor in informal sector income generation and asset building. Formal education was found to be inadequate for the informal sector and may even have a negative effect on their income generation and asset building capacities. There is a need to build through appropriate interventions a market to provide training and information (as many NGOs have been doing already) to the informal sector. This has to be combined with formal education to provide maximum flexibility to informal sector participants. One good example of such melding is the Swiss School system as shown above.

Another important issue is that while formalisation of the informal sector may not be a possibility, the existing formal institutions (and firms) such as commercial banks, technology and training institutions have failed to respond to the needs of the informal sector. This has led, as shown above in the section on grassroots capitalism, to the creation of parallel structures and mechanisms, be it for the delivery of credit, training, technology, information or other kinds of services. While this approach has proved useful in reaching specific target groups and making resources accessible to them, especially the poor, it may have also increased the risk of creating parallel economies and markets within the same society.

An alternative way to avoid parallel structures would be to establish linkages between the informal and the formal institutions e.g., informal credit organisations linked to formal financial institutions, informal training systems linked to formal training institutions and so on. The purpose of such linkages could be to help upgrade the informal systems in a gradual manner. For instance, skills in the informal sector could be upgraded by strengthening the informal apprenticeship systems. In the case of credit the formal banks can channel funds to the informal sector through informal credit mechanisms that already exist e.g., rotating credit and savings associations at the community level, chit funds or the equivalent known under various names in India such as 'Committee' as shown above. The scattered experiences show that it is possible to integrate the formal and informal support systems though it may not be easy. This remains a major challenge in drawing effective strategies for this sector that requires further exploration.

Creation of such an environment would seem easier when the Indian economy is growing rapidly; increased economic opportunities may generate less resistance from interest groups to bring about a change in the environment. It would, therefore, seem desirable that strategies to promote incomes in the informal sector be accompanied by complementary policies and measures to generate economic growth.

The organisation of informal sector enterprises could also serve as a mechanism to overcome infrastructural constraints and market imperfections. The very fact that the informal sector, which accounts for over 90 per cent of India's employment and over 50 per cent of GDP, is deprived of even basic infrastructure, should be a matter of policy concern. Though India is faced with real constraints in terms of finance and space, the failure to recognise the role of infrastructure in raising productivity and incomes of those in this sector and to improve it can only be attributed to the absence of organised pressure from below. The informal sector organisations could also help overcome certain market imperfections. One can cite a number of examples where informal producers have been able to improve their incomes through collective action e.g., buying key raw materials directly from the source without having to depend on intermediaries and thus benefit from price discounts. In some cases they have successfully persuaded the government to obtain access to certain production facilities that are in the public sector. These organisations have also served in some cases as the channel for delivery of credit, inputs or services, including electricity. In these cases the costs of delivery are internalised i.e., borne by the beneficiaries. This is most evident when the organisations take the form of cooperatives.

To sum up, policy interventions by both the Government of India and donors have been limited to addressing the micro aspect of informal enterprises. It was assumed that once the missing resources or inputs are made available, those in this sector would automatically be able to avail the opportunities that become available in the development process and participate in it. But the evidence discussed above do not lend support to this view. The regressions show that these interventions would only lead to higher incomes and higher asset formation in the informal sector if and when the rates of growth of the economy are high. So the first and foremost requirement to ensure that growth trickles down is to maintain a high rate of growth in the Indian economy. Along with high growth rates it is necessary to find mechanisms to link formal and informal mechanisms for skill generation and infrastructure provision. This implies that there should be some symmetry between the two sectors in terms of skill generation, access to information on markets, technical know-how and credit.

References

Acharya, Rajat (2006). "Trade Liberalisation, Poverty and Inequality in India", *INRM Policy Brief* No.10. *http://www.adb.org/Documents*

Bairagya, Indrajit (2010). "Liberalization, Informal Sector and Formal-Informal Sectors' Relationship: A Study of India", Paper Prepared for the *31st General Conference of The International Association for Research in Income and Wealth*. St. Gallen, Switzerland. August 22-28.

Bardhan, P. (1988). "Alternative Approaches to Development Economics", in H. Chenery and T.N. Srinivasan (eds.), *The Handbook of Development Economics*. Amsterdam: North Holland. pp.39-72.

Bekkers, Hans and Wim Stoffers (1995). "Measuring Informal Sector Employment in Pakistan: Testing a New Methodology", *International Labour Review* 134.

Bhattacharya, Prabir C. (1996). "The Role of the Informal Sector in Structural Transformation: Some Indian Evidence", *Journal of International Studies* 8. *http://ideas.repec.org/a/wly/jintdv*

Blunch, Niels-Hugo, Sudharshan Canagarajah and Dhushyanth Raju (2001). *The Informal Sector Revisited: A Synthesis Across Space and Time*. Social Protection Unit, Human Development Network, The World Bank.

Bosworth, Barry, Susan M. Collins and Arvind Virmani (2007). "Sources of Growth in the Indian Economy", *NBER Working Paper* No. 12901. February. NBER Program(s): IFM. *http://www.nber.org/papers/w12901.pdf*

Bromley, Ray (1978). "Organization, Regulation and Exploitation in the So-Called `Urban Informal Sector': The Street Traders of Cali, Colombia", *World Development* 6(9/10).

Carr, Marilyn (ed.) (2004). *Chains of Fortune: Linking Women Producers and Workers with Global Markets*. London: Commonwealth Secretariat.

Castells, Manuel and Alejandro Portes (1989). "World Underneath: The Origins, Dynamics, and Effects of the Informal Economy", in Alejandro Portes, Manuel Castells and Lauren A. Benton (eds.), *The Informal Economy: Studies in Advanced and Less Developed Countries*. Baltimore: The John Hopkin University Press.

Chandra, A. (2006) "Vocational Education and Training in India: A Perspective for Change", Draft of October 30. New Delhi.

————. (2007). "Training for the Informal Economy in India", in A. Chandra and M. Khanijo (eds.), *Training for Informal Economy*. New Delhi: Excel Books.

Charmes, J. (1990). "A Critical Review of Concepts, Definitions, and Studies in the Informal Sector", in D. Turnham, B. Salomé and A. Schwarz (eds.), *The Informal Sector Revisited*. Paris: OECD.

————. (2000). "The Contribution of Informal Sector to GDP in Developing Countries: Assesssment, Estimates, Methods, Orientations for the Future", *4th Meeting of the Delhi Group on Informal Sector Statistics*. Geneva. August 28-30.

Chen, Martha Alter, Joann Vanek and Marilyn Carr (2004). *Mainstreaming Informal Employment and Gender in Poverty Reduction: A Handbook for Policy-makers and Other Stakeholders*. Commonwealth Secretariat, IDRC, WIEGO. Published by the Commonwealth Secretariat.

Dasgupta, Sukti and Ajit Singh (2006). "Manufacturing, Services and Premature Deindustrialization in Developing Countries: A Kaldorian Analysis", *Working Papers* RP2006/49. World Institute for Development Economic Research (UNU-WIDER).

de Soto, Hernando (1989). *The Other Path: The Invisible Revolution in the Third World*. New York: Harper & Row.

————. (2000). *The Mystery of Capital: Why Capitalism Triumphs in the West and Fails Everywhere Else*. Basic Books.

Deaton, Angus and Jean Drèze (2002). "Poverty and Inequality in India: A Reexamination", *Working Papers*, Princeton Univeristy, Woodrow Wilson School of Public International Affairs, Research Program on Development Studies. *http://ideas.repec.org/s/pri/rpdevs.html*

Dreyer, Iana (2009). "India Unbound: Growing Might—Preparing for the Next Stage of Growth: Deepening India's Integration in the World Economy", in *The India Economy Review* VI, March 31. The IIPM Thinktank. *http://www.iipmthinktank.com/publications/archive/ier/ier-march-2009.pdf*

Field, G. (1990). "Labor Market Modelling and the Urban Informal Sector: Theory and evidence", in David Turnham, Bernard Salome and Antoine Schwarz (eds.), *The Informal Sector Revisited*. Paris: OECD. pp.49-69.

Hart, K. (1971). "Small Scale Entrepreneurs in Ghana and Development Planning", *Journal of Development Planning*, July.

Hirschman, Albert O. (1958). *The Strategy of Economic Development*. *http://homepage.newschool.edu/het/profiles/hirschm.htm*

International Labour Office (ILO) (1972). *Employment, Incomes and Equality: A Strategy for Increasing Productive Employment in Kenya*. Geneva.

————. (2001). *Training for Employment Promotion in Muktsar District, Punjab* (V. Gasskov and M. Burns). New Delhi: ILO.

————. (2003a). *Industrial Training Institutes of India: The Efficiency Study Report* (V. Gasskov *et al.*). New Delhi: ILO.

————. (2003b) *Industrial Training Institutes of India: The Efficiency Study Report*. New Delhi: ILO Office and Geneva: ILO.

Kabra, K.N. (1995). "The Informal Sector: A Reappraisal", *Journal of Contemporary Asia* 25(2): 197-232.

Kantor, P., U. Rani and J. Unni (2006). "Decent Work Deficits in Informal Economy: Case of Surat", *Economic and Political Weekly*, May.

Kelley, B. (1994). "The Informal Sector and the Macroeconomy: A Computable General Equilibrium Approach for Peru", *World Development* 22(9): 1393-411.

King, Kenneth (2007). "Training in the Informal Sector of India: An Asian Driver?", Paper delivered at the national conference on *Approaching Inclusive Growth through Skills Development*. New Delhi: MHRD/Ministry of Labour and Employment, GTZ and UNESCO. February 12-13.

Lewis, Arthur (1954) *Economic Development with Unlimited Supplies of Labor.* Manchester School. *http://homepage.newschool.edu/het/profiles/lewis.htm*

Lubell, H. (1991). *The Informal Sector in the 1980s and 1990s.* Paris: OECD.

————. (1993). "The Informal Sector in Southeast Asia", in *Work Without Protections: Case Studies of the Informal Sector in Developing Countries.* US Department of Labor.

Marjit, Sugata and Dibyendu S. Maiti (2005). "Globalization, Reform and the Informal Sector", *Working Papers* RP2005/12. World Institute for Development Economic Research (UNU-WIDER).

Marjit, Sugata, Saibal Kar and Punyabrata Sarkar (2003). "Trade Reform, Internal Capital Mobility and Informal Wage: Theory and Evidence", April. *http://website1.wider.unu.edu*

Mazumdar, D. (1975). "The Urban Informal Sector", *Working Paper* 211. Washington, DC: World Bank.

Mitra, Arup (2007). "Industry and Informal Sector in the Context of Globalisation", Paper presented on the seminar on *India and Globalisation. http://www.ris.org.in/India_Globalisation_Industry and Informal sector Arup Mitra.pdf*

Mitra, Barun (2006). "Grass Roots Capitalism Thrives in India", in *2006 Index of Economic Freedom.* Washington, DC: The Heritage Foundation. *http://www.strathmore.edu/essay/policy/intros/pre_97_mitra_capitalism_india.htm*

Moser, Caroline O.N. (1978). "Informal Sector or Petty Commodity Production: Dualism or Dependence in Urban Development?", *World Development* 6(9/10): 1041, 64.

NCEUS (2009). *The Challenge of Employment in Development in India: An Informal Economy Perspective.* NCEUS working draft for comments only. New Delhi.

————. (2007). *Conditions of Work and Promotion of Livelihoods in the Unorganised Sector.* New Delhi. *http://nceus.gov.in/Condition_of_workers_ sep_2007.pdf*

————. (2005). *Constitution of Task Force on Skill Formation in the Unorganised Sector.* Government of India. June 09.

Ñopo, Hugo and Patricio Valenzuela (2007). "Becoming an Entrepreneur", *Discussion Paper* No. 2716, Germany: Inter-American Development Bank, Institute for the Study of Labour (IZA). March.

Planning Commission (2006). *Report of the Working Group on Skills Development and Vocational Training for the Next Five Year Plan, 2007-2012.* New Delhi: Government of India. pp.27-28.

Portes, A. and J. Böröcz (1989). "Contemporary Immigration: Theoretical Perspectives on its Determinants and Modes of Incorporation", *International Migration Review* 28(4): 606-30.

Portes, A. and R. Schauffler (1993). "Competing Perspectives on the Latin American Informal Sector", *Population and Development Review* 19: 33-60.

Pradhan, Basant K., P.K. Roy and M.R. Saluja (1999). "Informal Sector in India: A Study of Household Saving Behaviour", *Contribution of the Informal Sector to the Economy*, Report no. 1. New Delhi: National Council of Applied Economic Research. August.

Quasem, M.A., A.H. Mondal and S. Mahmud (1998). "A Study of the Informal Sector in Bangladesh", *Bangladesh Institute of Development Studies Research Report* No. 158.

Sassen, Saskia (1991). *The Global City: New York, London, Tokyo.* Princeton, NJ: Princeton University Press.

————. (1998). *Globalization and Its Discontents: Essays on the New Mobility of People and Money.* New York: The New Press.

Sethuraman, S.V. (1976). "The Urban Informal Sector: Concept, Measurement and Policy", *International Labour Review* 114(1): 69-81.

————. (1997). *Urban Poverty and the Informal Sector: A Critical Assessment of Current Strategies.* Geneva: ILO.

————. (1998). "Gender, Informality, and Poverty: A Global Review", *Background Paper* for World Bank *World Development Report 2000.* Washington, D.C.

Sinha Anushree (2002). "Income Distribution and Employment", Presented at the *14th International Input-Output Conference* held in Montreal (October).

Tokman, V.E. (1978). "An Exploration into the Nature of Informal-Formal Sector Relationships", *World Development* 6: 1065-75.

UN (2000). *The World's Women 2000: Trends and Statistics.* New York: UN Statistical Division.

WEF (2009). *India Competitiveness Report. http://www.slideshare.net/itsgowri/wef-india-competitiveness-report-2009*

World Bank (2006a) *India's Employment Challenge: Creating Jobs, Helping Workers.* Report No. 35772–IN. Washington: Poverty Reduction and Economic Management, South Asia, World Bank.

————. (2006b) *Skills Development in India: The Vocational Education and Training System.* Washington: Human Development Unit, South Asia Region, World Bank.

World Bank Group (2010). *Doing Business, http://www.doingbusiness.org/economyrankings/*

Annexure A-3.1

Data Table for Regression 1 Analysis

States	*pd 1pvrty*	*pd2pvrty*	*pd 1wages*	*pd 2wages*	*pd1asset*	*pd2 asset*
Andhra Pradesh	26.59	23.47	38.37	0.35	0.96	36.85
Assam	35.28	41.81	9.40	0.50	-4.34	23.34
Bihar	51.57	57.43	9.25	-0.91	-8.67	36.85
Goa	26.44	17.02	20.50	0.94	-8.18	102.00
Gujarat	33.00	26.23	5.85	3.76	4.87	13.12
Haryana	14.96	28.31	23.39	-4.11	2.70	33.10
Himachal Pradesh	12.86	32.60	-0.34	3.50	-12.20	75.32
Karnataka	38.40	35.78	21.54	7.02	-2.62	25.51
Kerala	33.06	27.97	12.55	2.68	-2.29	50.75
Madhya Pradesh	43.18	43.53	22.41	1.45	-2.45	41.77
Maharashtra	41.12	39.22	9.74	5.24	8.49	34.05
Manipur	30.87	34.80	24.91	-4.18	3.04	65.98
Meghalaya	29.92	38.73	18.91	-5.28	15.74	-9.61
Mizoram	33.12	26.83	19.93	-6.92	0.00	0.00
Nagaland	33.74	38.97	15.62	-1.96	-10.65	115.00
Orissa	56.98	48.84	22.78	-2.38	12.10	13.38
Punjab	13.48	12.89	12.20	-1.06	-3.63	26.20
Rajasthan	36.69	29.83	32.53	-1.34	0.42	52.59
Sikkim	35.17	42.40	0.00	-0.01	0.00	0.00
Tamil Nadu	44.78	37.81	6.40	14.13	3.84	18.82
Tripura	34.60	39.92	14.89	-5.40	0.00	40.31
Uttar Pradesh	41.36	42.79	18.00	-1.58	-0.19	35.92
West Bengal	46.53	37.38	11.41	-7.25	-2.76	53.23
Andaman & Nicobar	45.44	69.82	14.62	3.20	-2.26	95.83
Chandigarh	15.22	12.47	19.21	5.49	32.89	27.56
Dadra & Nagar Haveli	69.82	57.58	9.82	-4.01	-5.56	141.10
Delhi	14.03	15.98	13.26	20.39	-3.47	60.08
Daman & Diu	0.00	18.08	20.50	0.94	-8.18	102.00
Lakshwadeep	36.60	26.93	-0.21	9.92	-2.26	95.83
Pondicherry	42.13	40.54	20.77	-3.96	-15.85	185.73

Source: Marjit and Maiti (2005) and *Economic Survey*, 2006.

Annexure A-3.2a

Sectors in Manufacturing where Formal Firms Account for 80 Per cent of Total Output

(All figures in lakh)

Code	Description	Value of Output		% Output
A.				
1. Food & Beverages				
151	Food	5,687,680		4.42
152	Dairy	2,151,018		1.67
153	Grain mill	4,267,499		3.31
154	Other food products	4,544,405		3.53
155	Beverages	1,381,935	18,032,537	1.07
2. Textiles				
171	Textiles	7,900,393		6.14
172	Other	937,890	8,838,283	0.73
3. Paper & Publishing				
210	Paper & paper products	2,053,396		1.60
221	Publishing	678,954	2,732,350	0.53
4. Petroleum				
232	Petroleum	17,277,783	17,277,783	13.42
5. Chemicals				
241	Basic chemicals	9,051,155		7.03
242	Other	8,311,694	17,362,849	6.46
6. Rubber & Tyres				
251	Rubber & tyres	1,632,558		1.27
252	Plastic	2,497,277	4,129,835	1.94
7. Non-Metallic Minerals				
269	Non-metallic mineral	3,578,610	3,578,610	2.78
8. Steel & Metal				
271	Basic iron & steel	11,927,154		9.26
272	Precious metals	3,061,365		2.38
273	Casting of metals	914,685		0.71
281	Metal products	1,003,906		0.78
289	Fabricated metal products	2,037,708	18,944,818	1.58
9. Machinery				
291	General machinery	2,591,738		2.01
292	Special machinery	2,360,971		1.83
311	Electric motors	1,387,493	6,340,202	1.08
10. Motor Vehicles & Accessories				
341	Motor vehicles	4,064,564		3.16
342	Bodies of motor vehicles	122,276		0.09
343	Accessories	2,837,548	7,024,388	2.20
	Total of above (A)	104,261,655		
	Total	128,738,002		

Add: Sectors where informal firms dominate

B.			
160	Tobacco	1,207,516	0.94
173	Fabrics	871,996	0.68
181	Apparels	1,706,769	1.33
182	Fur	13,899	0.01
191	Leather	559,597	0.43
192	Footwear	583,416	0.45
201	Wood	52,301	0.04
202	Wood plaiting materials	309,295	0.24
222	Printing	393,661	0.31
223	Reproduction	31,818	0.02
231	Coal tar	568,917	0.44
243	Manmade fibres	640,228	0.50
293	Domestic appliances	518,872	0.40
300	Office machines	682,484	0.53
313	Wires & cables	763,193	0.59
314	Batteries	275,511	0.21
315	Lightening equipment	216,524	0.17
319	Other electrical equipment	241,814	0.19
321	Valves and tubes	680,468	0.53
322	TV & radio	432,725	0.34
323	Receivers of television & radio	1,725,831	1.34
331	Medical instruments	703,989	0.55
332	Optical instruments	58,636	0.05
333	Watches & clocks	111,175	0.09
351	Ships	252,843	0.20
352	Railway locomotives	181,958	0.14
353	Aircrafts	45,727	0.04
359	Transport equipment	2,755,508	2.14
361	Furniture	312,412	0.24
369	N.E.C	2,144,245	1.67
371	Recyclining metal waste	26,778	0.02
372	Recyclining non-metal waste	9,017	0.01
261	Glass	452,028	0.35
Other	Miscellaneous	3,335,702	2.59
	Total of above (B)	22,866,853	

Add: Industry items not belonging to the manufacturing sector:

C.			
014	Agro-based services	963,431	0.75
142	Mining & quarrying	11,493	0.01
	Total of above (C)	974,924	
	Grand Total (A+B+C)	128,738,002	

Annexure A-3.2b

Sectors where Formal Firms Dominate in Delivery of Services

Statement of 10: Gross Domestic Product by Economic Activity (Only Services Sector Considered Here) (At Current Prices)

(in Rs crore)

Sectors		*FY 2005-06*	*Per cent Share**
4 Electricity, gas & water supply		65,979	2.20
5 Construction		222,110	6.80
6 Trade, hotels & restaurant		540,415	15.50
6.1 trade	493,755		14.20
6.2 hotels & restaurants	46,660		1.30
7 Transport, storage & communication		284,521	10.10
7.1 railways	32,995		1.20
7.2 transport by other means	182,206		5.40
7.3 storage	2,307		0.10
7.4 communication	67,013		4.00
8 Financing, insurance, real estate & business services		464,493	13.80
8.1 banking & insurance	180,205		6.10
8.2 real estate, ownership of dwellings & business services	284,288		7.6
9 Community, social & personal services	468,128		14.20
9.1 public administration & defence	208,343		5.90
9.2 other services	259,785		8.30
10 Gross domestic product at factor cost (1 to 9) (Total GDP amount of all sectors)	3,250,932		62.60

Note: *The percentages here are as a per cent of total GDP of all sectors.

Source: National Accounts Statistics, 2007. Prepared by CSO, Ministry of Statistics and Programme Implementation.

Annexure A-3.3

Questionaire for the Informal Sector Survey

1. Name: ____________________
2. Age: ____________________
3. Gender:

   ☐ Male ☐ Female
4. Marital Status:

   ☐ Married ☐ Unmarried
5. Total number of members in the family: ____________________
6. Number of males and females in the family:

   ☐ Males ☐ Females
7. Number of working members in the family: ____________________
8. Total monthly income (in Rs.) generated by the working members in the family:

☐ Less than 100	☐ 301-400	☐ 601-700	☐ 901-1000
☐ 101-200	☐ 401-500	☐ 701-800	☐ 1001-2000
☐ 201-300	☐ 501-600	☐ 801-900	☐ > 2000

9. Number of children: ____________________
10. Education status: ____________________

    ☐ Illiterate ☐ Senior secondary

    ☐ Literate but below primary ☐ Graduate

    ☐ Matriculation ☐ Diploma/certificate course
11. Education status of children: ____
12. Access to basic infrastructure facilities:

Electricity	Drinking water	Sanitation
☐ Yes	☐ Yes	☐ Yes
☐ No	☐ No	☐ No

13. Current economic activity:

    ☐ Agriculture and allied activities:

    ☐ Agriculture & animal husbandry activities

    ☐ Horticulture activities

    ☐ Floriculture ☐ Mining & quarrying

    ☐ Market gardening ☐ Others, specify:

    ☐ Manufacturing sector: Manufacturing of:

    ☐ Food & beverages ☐ Textiles & apparel ☐ Basic metals

- [ ] Wood products
- [ ] Chemical & products
- [ ] Transport equipment
- [ ] Rubber & plastic
- [ ] Electronics & apparatus
- [ ] Paper & products
- [ ] Construction
- [ ] Mason, head loaders
- [ ] Painters
- [ ] Plumbers
- [ ] Labourers
- [ ] Others,_______

- [ ] Services:
  - [ ] Cooks, bartenders
  - [ ] Maid & housekeeping worker
  - [ ] Securitymen
  - [ ] Launders
  - [ ] Cargo handling
  - [ ] Mechanic
  - [ ] Sanitation worker
  - [ ] Rickshaw pullers
  - [ ] Tailors

14. Current monthly wage level (in Rs.):
   - [ ] 50-150
   - [ ] 451-550
   - [ ] 851-950
   - [ ] 151-250
   - [ ] 551-650
   - [ ] 951-1050
   - [ ] 251-350
   - [ ] 651-750
   - [ ] 1051-1150
   - [ ] 351-450
   - [ ] 751-850
   - [ ] More than 1150
15. How many days a month do you work?
   - [ ] Monthly
   - [ ] Weekly
   - [ ] Daily
16. Current activity status:
   - [ ] Self-employed:
   - [ ] Worked in household enterprises as own account operators.
   - [ ] Worked in household enterprise as employer.
   - [ ] Worked in household as helper.
   - [ ] Regular/salaried wage employer.
   - [ ] Casual labourer.
     - [ ] Worked as casual labourer in public works.
     - [ ] Worked as casual labourer in other types of work.
     - [ ] Did not work but there was work in households/had regular wage employment.
17. Wages in cash or kind:
   - [ ] Only cash
   - [ ] Only kind
   - [ ] Cash and kind
18. Market for home-based workers:
   - [ ] Urban market
   - [ ] Semi-urban market
   - [ ] Rural market
   - [ ] Semi-rural market
19. Type of enterprise worker is engaged in:
   - [ ] Non-directory enterprise
   - [ ] Directory enterprise

☐ Perennial enterprise ☐ Seasonal enterprise

☐ Casual enterprise ☐ Household enterprise

20. Location of work/enterprise:

☐ Owner's home ☐ Formal enterprise

☐ Service outlet ☐ Market area

☐ Footpath/street corner ☐ No fixed location

21. Number of years worked in the informal sector since 1991:

☐ Less than 4 years ☐ 9-11 years

☐ 5-8 years ☐ 12-16 years

22. Work experience in the formal sector since 1991:

☐ Zero years ☐ 9-11 years

☐ Less than 4 years ☐ 12-15 years

☐ 5-8 years

23. Rate of job switch over since 1991:

Formal to informal

☐ Less than a month ☐ 3-6 months ☐ More than one year

☐ 1-3 months ☐ 6 months-1 year

Informal to informal

☐ Less than a month ☐ 3-6 months ☐ More than one year

☐ 1-3 months ☐ 6 months-1 year

24. Duration of the contract in the informal sector:

☐ Weekly ☐ 3 month basis ☐ Yearly

☐ Monthly ☐ 6 month basis

25. Does the worker engage himself/herself in subsidiary activity apart from the principal work activity in the informal sector?

☐ Yes ☐ No

If Yes, mention the occupation & duration of work: ______________________

26. Reason for labour mobility:

☐ To supplement income ☐ Not enough work & to supplement income

☐ Not enough work ☐ Lack of job security

☐ Work place too far ☐ Others, specify:

27. Presence of sub-contract type of work with the formal sector:

☐ No contract ☐ Yes

28. Frequency of sub-contract in a 6 month period since 1991:

☐ 1-4 ☐ 9-14 ☐ More than 20

☐ 5-9 ☐ 15-20

29. Duration of contracts:

☐ Less than a month ☐ 1-3 month basis

☐ 4-6 month basis ☐ More than 6 months

29. Consumption pattern of the informal workers:

☐ Number of meals taken during a day

☐ Quality of meals taken during a day (* enter the code)

* Code for assessing the quality of food intake:
Cod 1: inferior quality of food: rice, *bajra*, poor quality of wheat
Cod 2: medium quality of food: cereals, *ghee*, barley, millets, milk, vegetables.
Cod 3: medium to superior quality: meat, butter, *vanaspati*, fruits
Cod 4: superior quality: dry fruits, fruits, vegetables, pure *ghee*.

30. Amount of calorie intake on daily basis:

☐ Less than 50 ☐ 1001-1500 ☐ 2501-3000

☐ 51- 500 ☐ 1501-2000 ☐ 3001-3500

☐ 501-1000 ☐ 2001-2500 ☐ 3501-4000

31. Asset building after joining work in the informal sector:

☐ *Kuccha* house ☐ *Pucca* house ☐ TV

☐ Motor vehicles ☐ Furniture ☐ Fridge

☐ Others, specify:

32. Monthly living wage level:

Rs. 150-250 Rs. 251-350

Rs. 351-450 Rs. 451-550

More than Rs. 551, specify: ______________________________

33. Monthly health expenditure:

☐ Less than 100 ☐ Rs. 101-200 ☐ Rs. 201-300

☐ Rs. 301-400 ☐ Rs. 401-500 ☐ Rs. 501-600

☐ Rs. 601-700 ☐ Rs. 701-800 ☐ Rs. 800 & above

34. Monthly transport expenditure:

☐ Less than Rs.100 ☐ Rs. 101-200 ☐ Rs. 201-300

☐ Rs. 301-400 ☐ Rs. 401-500 ☐ Rs. 501-600

☐ Rs. 601-700 ☐ Rs. 701-800 ☐ Rs. 801 & above

35. Does the worker support the members of the family at the native place?

☐ No ☐ Yes

If yes, specify the form (cash or kind): ________________________

36. Lean periods:

☐ Goes back to native place ☐ Stays near the place of work

☐ Finds some work ☐ Finds work in some other profession

36. Former economic activity engaged in:

☐ Agriculture and allied activities:

☐ Agriculture & animal husbandry activities ☐ Mining & quarrying

☐ Horticulture activities ☐ Others, specify:__________

☐ Floriculture

☐ Market gardening

☐ Manufacturing sector: Manufacturing of:

☐ Food & beverages ☐ Textiles & apparel ☐ Basic metals

☐ Wood products ☐ Chemical & products ☐ Transport equipment

☐ Rubber & plastic ☐ Electronics & apparatus ☐ Paper & products

☐ Construction ☐ Mason, head loaders ☐ Painters

☐ Plumbers ☐ Labourers ☐ others,

☐ Services:

☐ Cooks, bartenders ☐ Maid & housekeeping worker ☐ Securitymen

☐ Launders ☐ Cargo handling ☐ Mechanic

☐ Sanitation worker ☐ Rickshaw pullers ☐ Tailors

37. Monthly wage level (in Rs.) in the previous profession:

☐ 50-150 ☐ 451-550 ☐ 851-950

☐ 151-250 ☐ 551-650 ☐ 951-1050

☐ 251-350 ☐ 651-750 ☐ 1051-1150

☐ 351-450 ☐ 751-850 ☐ More than 1150

38. Employer status in the previous profession:

☐ Usual status

☐ Current weekly status

☐ Current daily status

39. Activity status in the former profession:

☐ Self-employed:

☐ Worked in household enterprises as own account operators.

☐ Worked in household enterprise as employer.

☐ Worked in household as helper.

☐ Regular/salaried wage employer

☐ Casual labourer.

☐ Worked as casual labourer in public works.

☐ Worked as casual labourer in other types of work.

☐ Did not work but there was work in households/had regular wage employment.

40. Asset building before joining work in the informal sector:

☐ *Kuccha* house	☐ *Pucca* house	☐ TV
☐ Motor vehicles	☐ Furniture	☐ Fridge

☐ Others, specify: ____________________

41. Consumption pattern of the worker before entering in informal sector:

☐ Number of meals taken during a day.

☐ Quality of meals taken during a day (* enter the code).

> * Code for assessing the quality of food intake:
> Cod 1: inferior quality of food: rice, *bajra*, poor quality of wheat
> Cod 2: medium quality of food: cereals, *ghee*, barley, millets, milk, vegetables.
> Cod 3: medium to superior quality: meat, butter, *vanaspati*, fruits
> Cod 4: superior quality: dry fruits, fruits, vegetables, pure *ghee*.

42. Amount of calorie intake on daily basis before joining informal sector:

☐ Less than 50	☐ 1001-1500	☐ 2501-3000
☐ 51- 500	☐ 1501-2000	☐ 3001-3500
☐ 501-1000	☐ 2001-2500	☐ 3501-4000

43. Monthly health expenditure before getting employment in informal sector:

☐ Less than 100	☐ Rs. 101-200	☐ Rs. 201-300
☐ Rs. 301-400	☐ Rs. 401-500	☐ Rs. 501-600
☐ Rs. 601-700	☐ Rs. 701-800	☐ Rs. 800 & above

44. Monthly transport expenditure before joining informal sector:

☐ Less than Rs. 100	☐ Rs. 101-200	☐ Rs. 201-300
☐ Rs. 301-400	☐ Rs. 401-500	☐ Rs. 501-600
☐ Rs. 601-700	☐ Rs. 701-800	☐ Rs. 801 & above

Annexure A-3.4

Summarised Results from Answers Obtained from the Questionire Survey

	Employee Code	*1*	*2*	*3*	*4*	*5*	*6*	*7*	*8*	*9*	*10*
1	Dependents	4	7	3	14	6	7	5	3	6	9
2	Working members	1	3	2	4	1	2	2	1	2	4
3	Education status Code	Illiterate 0	BP 1	G 3	SS 2	LBP 1	LBP 1	Illiterate 0	LBP 1	LBP 1	LBP 1
4	Basic infrastructure Code	EW 2	EW 2	ES 2	DWES 3	DWE 2	WSP 3	EDW 2	PWS 3	PWS 3	PWS 3
5	Profession (current) (after) Category (current)	Labour RPE	Labour SI	OoRS Service outlet	Cook MH	Factory welder SI	Labour SI	Worker SI	Worker SI	Worker SI	Worker SI
6	Income monthly wage (in Rs) (after) Code (lower slab)	50-150 50	> 1150 1150	951-1050 951	951-1050 951	>1150 1150	> 1150 1150	> 1150 1150	> 1150 1150	> 1150 1150	> 1150 1150
7	Meals Consumption pattern (after) Code	 1	 3	 2	 3	 2	 3	 2	 3	 3	 2
8	Asset building (after) Code	KH 0	KH 0	MV 1	PH,F,TV 3	KH,TV, 2	KH 0	PH 1	PH,TV 2	PH,TV 2	KH,TV 1
9	Monthly health expenditure (after) Code (lower slab)	< 100 0	< 100 0	201-300 201	< 100 0	101-200 101	101-200 101	201-300 201	< 100 0	101-200 101	< 100 0
10	Monthly transport expenditure (after) Code (lower slab)	401-500 401	< 100 0	<100 0	101-200 101	< 100 0	< 100 0	201-300 201	801 & above 801	< 100 0	< 100 0
11	Income monthly wage (before) Code (lower slab)	50-150 50	 0	351-400 351	> 1150 1150	 0	 0	 0	 0	151-250 151	 0
12	Profession (before)	Self-emp	NWB	TB	F&B	None	None	None	None	BM	None
13	Asset building (before) Code	KH 0	None 0	None 0	None 0	None 0	None 0	None 0	KH,TV 1	None 0	None 0
14	Meals consumption pattern (before) Code	 1	 1	 2	 1	 2	 1	 1	 3	 1	 1
15	Monthly health expenditure (before) Code (lower slab)	< 100 0	< 100 0	< 100 0	< 100 0	< 100 0	< 100 0	< 100 0	< 100 0	< 100 0	< 100 0
16	Monthly transport expenditure (before) Code (lower slab)	101-200 101	< 100 0	< 100 0	< 100 0	< 100 0	< 100 0	< 100 0	< 100 0	< 100 0	< 100 0

contd...

...contd...

	Employee Code	*11*	*12*	*13*	*14*	*15*	*16*	*17*	*18*	*19*	*20*
1	Dependents	10	8	7	12	6	4	2	2	3	8
2	Working members	2	4	4	1	3	1	1	2	1	2
3	Education status	LBP	LBP	SS	SS	Illiterate	Illiterate	Matriculation	D/C C	D/C C	Matriculation
	Code	1	1	2	2	0	0	1	2	2	2
4	Basic infrastructure	E	EW	PWS	EWS	EWS	W	EW	EWS	EWS	EWS
	Code	2	2	2	3	2	3	2	3	3	3
5	Profession (current) (after)	CBT	CHK	Mechanic	Cook	Tailor	Cargo	CJ	WPCP	EED	Salesman
	Category (current)	HI	MH	Mechanic	MT	Tailoring	Cargo	Chemist	PHW	EA	F & B
6	Income monthly wage (in Rs) (after)	> 1150	451-550	1051-1150	451-550	651-750	251-350	751-850	> 1150	951-1050	251-350
	Code (lower slab)	1150	451	1051	451	651	251	751	1150	951	251
7	Meals Consumption pattern (after)										
	Code	2	2	3	2	1	1	3	3	2	3
8	Asset building (after)	PH (SOR)	KH,Fu	PH,TV, MV, fri	PH & Fu	PH & Fu	KH	PH,TV,Fu,Fri	PH,TV,Fu,Fr	PH,TV, Fu,Fri	PH,TV,Fu,Fri
	Code	0	2	4	2	2	0	4	4	4	4
9	Monthly health expenditure (after)	< 100	< 100	301-400	< 100	Rs101-200	Rs101-200	301-400	701-800	< 100	Rs.201-300
	Code (lower slab)	0	0	301	0	101	101	301	701	0	201
10	Monthly Transport expenditure (after)	Rs 701-800	101-200	< 100	501-600	< 100	< 100	< 100	Rs 201-300	Rs 401-500	Rs.201-300
	Code (lower slab)	701	101	0	501	0	0	0	201	401	201
11	Income monthly wage (before)	151-250	50-150	151-250	151-250	50-150	351-450	351-450	351-450	251-350	
	Code (lower slab)	151	50	151	151	50	351	351	351	251	
12	Profession (before)				Self-emp	Self-emp	Self-emp	Regular	Regular	Self-emp	Regular (Salesman)
13	Asset building (before)	none	none	none	PH	KH	KH	PH,Fu	PH,Fu,TV	PH,Fu	PH,Fu,Fri
	Code	0	0	0	1	0	0	2	3	2	3
14	Meals Consumption pattern (before)										
	Code		2	2	2	1	1	3	3	2	
15	Monthly health expenditure (before)	< 100	101-200		< 100	201-300	< 100	301-400	401-500	101-200	401-500
	Code (lower slab)	0	101	0	0	201	0	301	401	101	401
16	Monthly transport expenditure (before)	< 100	401-500		201-300	< 100	< 100	< 100	201-300	< 100	Rs.101-200
	Code (lower slab)	0	401	0	201	0	0	0	201	0	

Note: W- Water; E- Electricity; BP- Below primary; G- Graduate; SS- Senior secondry; LBP- Literacy below primary; EW- Electricity, water; ES- Electricity, sanitation; EWS- Electricity, water sanitation; DWES- Drinking water electricity sanitation; DWE- drinking water electricity; WSP- Water, sanitation, power; EDW- Electricity, drinking water; PWS- Power, water sanitation; RPE- Rubber and plastic equipments; SI- Steel industry; SO- Service outlet; OoRS- Owner of rental store; MH- Mussoorie hotel; KH- *kuccha* house; PH- *Pucca* house; MV- Motor vehicles; Fu- Furniture; Self-emp- Self-employed; NWB- Not worked before; TB- Telecom bussiness; F&B- Food & beverages; BM- Basic metals; CBT- Cook Bartender; CHK- Cook and housekeeper; HI- Hotel Industry; MT- Mussoorie tourism; CJ- Chemical job; WPCP- Wood products and chemical products; EED- Employer in electric department; PHW- Paint and hardware; EA- Electrical appliance; SOR- staying on rent; Fri- fridge.

Annexure A-3.5

Summarised Results from Answers Obtained from the Questionire Survey

Income	*Assets*	*Dependent*	*Infrastructure*	*Meals*	*Working Member*	*Education*	*Health Expenditure*	*Transport*	*Profession*
0	0	6	3	2	3	2	50	50	Not worked before
0	1	6	3	2	3	3	50	800	Not worked before
1150	0	5	3	2	1	2	450	50	Printing press (Indore)
900	0	2	3	2	1	2	50	550	Self-employed casually
0	1	5	3	2	2	2	250	250	Not worked before
1150	3	4	3	2	1	2	50	450	National Cables (Operator, Okhla Phase-II)
800	0	7	3	2	2	2	250	800	Others (printing) labour
400	0	7	3	2	3	2	250	150	Others (Hindustan Injection)
600	1	6	3	2	1	1	350	450	Agriculture (Aluminium washing)
1150	0	5	3	2	1	1	800	350	Printing & packaging (regular employee)
600	2	5	3	2	1	2	450	450	Household agriculture
0	0	7	3	2	2	2	50	50	Not worked before
0	2	4	3	2	1	2	150	150	Not worked before
0	0	5	3	2	1	2	50	150	Not worked before
1100	0	3	2	3	1	1	50	350	Basic metals (labour)
0	0	4	3	2	2	3	50	50	Not worked before
0	0	6	3	2	2	3	50	50	Not worked before
0	0	7	3	2	5	3	50	50	Not worked before
0	0	5	3	2	1	3	50	50	Not worked before
0	0	8	2	2	1	1	50	50	Not worked before
0	0	6	3	2	1	1	50	50	Not worked before
0	0	5	2	2	1	3	50	50	Not worked before
0	0	4	3	2	1	3	50	50	Not worked before
0	0	6	3	2	1	0	50	50	Not worked before
0	0	6	3	2	3	3	50	50	Not worked before
0	0	4	3	2	2	2	50	50	Not worked before
0	0	7	3	2	2	3	50	50	Not worked before
0	0	5	3	2	2	3	50	50	Not worked before
0	0	6	3	2	1	2	50	50	Not worked before
0	0	3	3	2	1	3	50	50	Not worked before
0	0	11	3	2	1	3	50	50	Not worked before
0	0	12	3	2	5	3	50	50	Not worked before
0	0	6	3	2	2	2	50	50	Not worked before
0	0	7	3	2	1	3	50	50	Not worked before
0	0	5	3	2	1	3	50	50	Not worked before
0	0	6	3	2	1	3	50	50	Not worked before
0	0	6	3	2	1	3	50	50	Not worked before
0	0	6	3	2	1	3	50	50	Not worked before
0	0	4	3	2	1	3	50	50	Not worked before
0	0	7	3	2	1	3	50	50	Not worked before
0	4	3	3	2	1	3	50	50	Not worked before

contd...

...contd...

Income	Assets	Dependent	Infrastructure	Meals	Working Member	Education	Health Expenditure	Transport	Profession
0	0	5	3	2	1	2	50	50	Not worked before
0	0	4	3	2	1	3	50	50	Not worked before
0	0	1	3	2	1	3	50	50	Not worked before
0	0	4	3	2	1	3	50	50	Not worked before
0	0	4	3	2	1	3	50	50	Not worked before
0	0	4	3	2	2	2	50	50	Not worked before
0	0	5	3	2	1	3	50	50	Not worked before
0	0	4	3	2	1	1	50	50	Not worked before
0	0	4	3	2	1	1	50	50	Not worked before
0	0	8	3	2	3	0	50	50	Not worked before
0	0	3	3	2	1	0	50	50	Not worked before
0	0	9	3	2	2	0	50	50	Not worked before
0	0	10	3	2	4	0	50	50	Not worked before
0	0	4	3	2	1	0	50	50	Not worked before
0	0	5	3	2	1	1	50	50	Not worked before
0	0	6	3	2	1	1	50	50	Not worked before
0	0	2	2	2	1	0	50	50	Not worked before
0	0	2	3	2	1	0	50	50	Not worked before
0	0	3	3	2	1	1	50	50	Not worked before
0	0	5	3	2	1	1	50	50	Not worked before
0	0	3	3	2	1	0	50	50	Not worked bfore
0	0	5	3	2	1	1	50	50	Not worked before
0	0	6	3	2	1	0	50	50	Not worked before
0	0	6	3	2	2	0	50	50	Not worked before
0	0	5	3	2	1	1	50	50	Not worked before
0	0	7	3	2	1	0	50	50	Not worked before
0	0	4	3	2	1	0	50	50	Not worked before
0	0	5	3	2	1	1	50	50	Not worked before
0	0	9	3	2	1	0	50	50	Not worked before
0	0	6	3	2	2	0	50	50	Not worked before
0	0	4	3	2	1	1	50	50	Not worked before
1150	1	2	3	3	1	0	350	50	Food & beverages (labour)
0	0	5	3	2	1	0	50	150	Not worked before
0	1	4	3	3	1	2	150	250	Not worked before

contd...

...contd...

Income	*Assets*	*Dependents*	*Infrastructure*	*Meals*	*Working Member*	*Education*	*Health Expenditure*	*Transport*	*Profession*
1100	0	6	3	2	3	2	150	150	Printing & packaging (labour)
1150	1	6	3	2	3	3	50	800	Printing & packaging (labour)
1150	0	5	3	2	1	2	450	550	Printing & packaging (labour)
1150	1	2	3	2	1	2	50	250	Printing (labour)
900	1	5	3	2	2	2	50	50	Printing (labour)
1150	0	4	3	2	1	2	800	550	Printing (labour)
500	0	7	3	2	2	2	150	800	Printing & packaging (labour)
500	0	7	3	2	3	2	450	250	Printing (labour)
900	1	6	3	2	1	1	350	450	Printing (regular)
1150	2	5	3	2	1	1	350	550	Printing & packaging (regular)
1150	3	5	3	2	1	2	450	550	Dhaba (self-employed)
1150	1	7	3	2	2	2	350	150	Tea stall (regular)
500	3	4	3	2	1	2	350	150	Printing (Regular)
1150	3	5	3	2	1	2	50	350	Packaging (Regular)
1150	0	3	2	3	1	1	150	50	Basic metals (Labour)
1150	5	4	3	3	2	3	50	800	Paper & products
1150	4	6	3	3	2	3	750	750	Paper & products (labour)
1150	3	7	3	3	5	3	550	650	Paper & products (labour)
1150	5	5	3	3	1	3	800	800	Paper & products (labour)
1150	1	8	2	3	1	1	350	150	Paper & products (labour)
1150	4	6	3	3	1	1	800	800	Paper & products (labour)
1150	3	5	2	3	1	3	250	450	Paper & products (labour)
1150	5	4	3	3	1	3	800	50	Paper & products (labour)
1150	4	6	3	3	1	0	50	50	Paper & products (labour)
1150	4	6	3	3	3	3	800	800	Paper & products (labour)
1150	4	4	3	3	2	2	750	450	Paper & products (labour)
1150	4	7	3	3	2	3	800	800	Paper & products (labour)
1150	4	5	3	3	2	3	750	750	Paper & products (labour)
1150	3	6	3	3	1	2	750	750	Paper & products (labour)
1150	0	3	3	2	1	3	50	50	Paper & products (labour)
1150	4	11	3	3	1	3	450	550	Paper & products (labour)
1150	4	12	3	3	5	3	750	800	Paper & products (labour)
1150	2	6	3	2	2	2	50	150	Paper & products (labour)
1150	0	7	3	2	1	3	450	450	Paper & products (labour)
1150	4	5	3	3	1	3	750	800	Paper & products (labour)
1150	4	6	3	2	1	3	800	800	Paper & products (labour)
1150	4	6	3	3	1	3	800	800	Paper & products (labour)
1150	4	6	3	3	1	3	50	50	Paper & products (labour)
1150	0	4	3	2	1	3	750	750	Food & beverages (household)
1150	4	7	3	3	1	3	750	750	Food & beverages (household)

contd...

...contd...

Income	*Assets*	*Depen-dents*	*Infrast-ructure*	*Meals*	*Working Member*	*Education*	*Health Expenditure*	*Transport*	*Profession*
1150	4	3	3	2	1	3	750	800	Food & beverages (household)
1150	4	5	3	3	1	2	450	450	Food & beverages (household)
1150	4	4	3	3	1	3	350	350	Food & beverages (household)
1150	3	1	3	3	1	3	350	350	Food & beverages (household)
1150	4	4	3	3	1	3	350	350	Food & beverages (household)
1150	4	4	3	3	1	3	350	350	Food & beverages (labour)
1150	4	4	3	3	2	2	350	450	Food & beverages (labour)
1150	3	5	3	2	1	3	750	750	Food & beverages (labour)
1150	1	4	3	3	1	1	150	50	Food & beverages (labour)
1150	1	4	3	3	1	1	50	50	Food & beverages (labour)
1150	0	8	3	3	3	0	50	50	Food & beverages (labour)
1150	1	3	3	3	1	0	150	250	Food & beverages (household)
1150	1	9	3	3	2	0	250	50	Food & beverages (household)
1150	3	10	3	3	4	0	50	150	Food & beverages (household)
1150	1	4	3	3	1	0	250	250	Food & beverages (household)
1150	0	5	3	3	1	1	150	250	Food & beverages (household)
1150	0	6	3	3	1	1	50	50	Food & beverages (household)
1150	3	2	2	3	1	0	50	50	Food & beverages (labour)
1150	1	2	3	3	1	0	50	50	Food & beverages (labour)
1150	0	3	3	3	1	1	150	50	Food & beverages (labour)
1150	1	5	3	3	1	1	250	50	Food & beverages (labour)
1150	1	3	3	3	1	0	50	50	Food & beverages (labour)
1150	0	5	3	3	1	1	50	50	Food & beverages (labour)
1150	2	6	3	3	1	0	150	50	Food & beverages (labour)
1150	0	6	3	3	2	0	50	50	Food & beverages (labour)
1150	1	5	3	3	1	1	50	250	Food & beverages (labour)
1150	1	7	3	3	1	0	50	50	Food & beverages (labour)
1150	1	4	3	3	1	0	250	50	Food & beverages (labour)
1150	0	5	3	3	1	1	50	50	Food & beverages (labour)
1150	1	9	3	3	1	0	50	50	Food & beverages (household)
1150	0	6	3	3	2	0	50	50	Food & beverages (household)
1150	1	4	3	3	1	1	50	50	Food & beverages (household)
1150	1	2	3	3	1	0	550	50	Food & beverages (labour)
1150	2	5	3	2	1	0	50	350	Printing (regular) (employee)
1150	4	4	3	3	1	2	250	350	Textiles & apparel (supervisor)

contd...

...contd...

Income	*Assets*	*Dependents*	*Infrastructure*	*Meals*	*Working Member*	*Education*	*Health Expenditure*	*Transport*	*Profession*
0	0	8	3	2	2	0	50	50	Not worked before
1000	0	5	2	2	1	0	250	750	Others (printing) labour
0	0	4	3	2	1	2	250	450	Not worked before
1150	0	4	3	2	1	2	250	450	Others (HBT), services (operator)
1000	0	4	3	2	1	0	250	150	Others (hindustan injection)
0	0	4	3	2	2	3	150	150	Not worked before
600	2	8	2	2	5	0	350	350	Household (agriculture)
1150	1	3	3	3	2	3	550	800	Household (agriculture)
0	0	5	3	2	1	3	50	50	Not worked before
0	0	4	3	2	2	3	50	50	Not worked before
0	0	5	3	2	2	3	50	50	Not worked before
0	0	5	3	2	1	3	50	50	Not worked before
0	0	10	0	2	1	3	50	50	Not worked before
0	0	10	3	2	1	3	50	50	Not worked before
0	0	5	3	2	1	2	50	50	Not worked before
0	0	10	3	2	5	0	50	50	Not worked before
0	0	6	3	2	1	3	50	50	Not worked before
0	0	6	3	2	1	3	50	50	Not worked before
0	0	5	3	2	1	3	50	50	Not worked before
0	0	7	3	2	1	3	50	50	Not worked before
0	0	5	3	2	2	3	50	50	Not worked before
0	0	5	3	2	2	2	50	50	Not worked before
0	0	6	3	2	3	3	50	50	Not worked before

contd...

...*contd*...

Income	*Assets*	*Depen-dents*	*Infrast-ructure*	*Meals*	*Working Member*	*Education*	*Health Expenditure*	*Transport*	*Profession*
1150	0	8	3	2	2	0	550	50	Labourer (farms)
1150	0	5	2	2	1	0	250	750	Self-employed (farms)
1150	0	4	3	2	1	2	150	350	Labourer (farms)
1150	0	4	3	2	1	2	450	550	Labourer (farms
1150	0	4	3	2	1	0	150	450	Labourer (farms
1150	3	4	3	3	2	3	750	750	Regular labour (farms)
1100	2	8	2	2	5	0	800	450	Labourer (farms)
1150	1	3	3	3	2	3	800	550	Household (agriculture activities)
1150	5	5	3	3	1	3	50	800	Household (agriculture activities)
1150	0	4	3	2	2	3	350	750	Casual labourer (farms)
1150	0	5	3	2	2	3	750	450	Casual labourer (farms)
1150	4	5	3	2	1	3	550	800	Casual labourer (farms)
1150	0	10	0	2	1	3	50	50	Casual labourer (farms)
1150	4	10	3	2	1	3	450	550	Casual labourer (farms)
1150	4	5	3	2	1	2	800	800	Self-employed (agriculture)
1150	0	10	3	2	5	0	750	800	Self-employed (agriculture)
1150	4	6	3	3	1	3	550	450	Horiculture activities (labour)
1150	4	6	3	3	1	3	350	350	Horiculture activities (labour)
1150	4	5	3	3	1	3	750	450	Horiculture activities (labour)
1150	0	7	3	2	1	3	550	350	Household (agriculture activities)
1150	0	5	3	2	2	3	800	800	Casual labourer (farms)
1150	0	5	3	2	2	2	150	450	Casual labourer (farms)
1150	0	6	3	2	3	3	800	750	Casual labourer (farms)

contd...

...contd...

Income	*Assets*	*Dependents*	*Infrastructure*	*Meals*	*Working Member*	*Education*	*Health Expenditure*	*Transport*	*Profession*
1150	0	4	2	2	2	0	250	50	Services (rikshaw pullers)
1150	0	5	2	2	2	2	50	50	Services (rikshaw pullers)
1150	0	6	3	2	1	1	50	50	Services (cooks, bartenders)
0	0	5	3	2	1	1	50	50	Not worked before
0	0	7	3	2	2	2	50	50	Not worked before
0	0	5	3	2	2	3	50	50	Not worked before
0	0	3	3	2	2	2	50	50	Not worked before
0	0	5	3	2	1	3	50	50	Not worked before
0	0	4	3	2	2	3	50	50	Not worked before
0	0	4	3	2	2	3	50	50	Not worked before
0	0	7	3	2	1	3	50	50	Not worked before
0	0	4	3	2	1	3	50	50	Not worked before
0	0	3	3	2	2	2	50	50	Not worked before
1150	0	7	3	3	1	1	150	150	Services (cooks, bartenders)
700	0	4	2	2	1	2	250	150	Labourers (farms)
700	0	3	0	2	2	0	150	50	Household (agriculture)
0	0	3	3	2	3	3	50	50	Not worked before
0	0	5	3	2	2	3	50	50	Not worked before
0	0	8	3	2	1	2	50	50	Not worked before
0	0	5	3	2	1	3	50	50	Not worked before
0	0	5	3	2	1	1	50	50	Not worked before
0	0	5	3	2	2	2	50	50	Not worked before
0	0	5	3	2	1	3	50	50	Not worked before
0	0	6	3	2	2	3	50	50	Not worked before
0	0	4	3	2	2	3	50	50	Not worked before
0	0	3	3	2	1	2	50	50	Not worked before
0	0	3	3	2	2	3	50	50	Not worked before
0	0	4	3	2	1	2	50	50	Not worked before
0	0	2	3	2	2	2	150	150	Not worked before
1150	0	3	3	3	1	0	150	150	Mechanic (household)
0	0	6	3	2	2	2	50	50	Not worked before
1150	0	7	2	2	1	0	150	50	Rikshaw pullers (self-employed)
1150	0	7	2	2	3	2	150	50	Rikshaw pullers (self-employed)
500	0	1	2	2	1	0	250	50	Rikshaw pullers (self-employed)
0	0	5	3	2	2	0	50	50	Not worked before
1150	0	5	3	2	1	0	150	50	Cargo handling (self-employed)
0	0	5	3	2	2	2	50	50	Not worked before
1150	4	5	3	3	1	1	150	150	Tailors (regular/salaried wage employer)
1150	2	4	3	3	2	1	150	150	Tailors (regular/salaried wage employer)

contd...

...contd...

Income	*Assets*	*Depen-dents*	*Infrast-ructure*	*Meals*	*Working Member*	*Education*	*Health Expenditure*	*Transport*	*Profession*
1150	1	3	2	3	1	0	150	150	Textiles & apparel (tailors)
1150	2	4	3	3	1	2	150	50	Textiles & apparel (tailors)
0	2	3	3	3	1	1	150	50	Not worked before
0	0	6	3	2	3	1	50	50	Not worked before
1150	1	5	3	3	1	1	250	50	Textiles & apparel (tailors)
0	1	4	3	3	1	2	150	250	Not worked before
0	1	13	3	3	5	2	150	50	Not worked before
0	1	4	3	3	1	1	150	150	Not worked before
1150	0	8	3	3	3	1	150	50	Textiles & apparel (tailors)
1150	2	4	3	3	1	0	150	150	Textiles & apparel (tailors)
0	3	4	3	3	2	2	250	450	Not worked before
0	2	5	3	3	2	2	150	150	Not worked before
600	1	6	2	2	6	0	50	50	Maid & housekeeping (worker)
100	1	3	2	2	1	1	50	50	Food & beverages (labour)
600	1	5	2	2	4	0	50	50	Maid & housekeeping (worker)
600	1	5	2	2	2	2	50	50	Maid & housekeeping (worker)
1100	1	5	3	2	2	1	250	250	Household
600	0	3	2	2	1	0	50	50	Sanitation worker
1150	2	5	3	2	3	1	350	350	Sanitation worker
1150	3	2	3	2	1	2	450	350	Bartenders
0	2	5	3	3	3	1	50	50	Not worked before
0	0	3	3	2	1	1	50	50	Not worked before
0	0	6	3	3	2	1	50	50	Not worked before
0	0	3	3	3	2	1	50	50	Not worked before
0	0	5	3	3	4	1	50	50	Not worked before
0	0	3	3	3	2	1	50	50	Not worked before
0	0	2	3	3	2	1	50	50	Not worked before

contd...

...contd...

Income	*Assets*	*Dependents*	*Infrastructure*	*Meals*	*Working Member*	*Education*	*Health Expenditure*	*Transport*	*Profession*
1150	0	4	2	2	2	0	250	50	Services (rikshaw pullers)
1150	0	5	2	2	2	2	250	50	Services (rikshaw pullers)
1150	2	6	3	3	1	1	450	250	Services (cooks, bartenders)
1150	1	5	3	3	1	1	450	250	Services (hotel-housekeeping)
1150	2	7	3	3	2	2	250	150	Services (housekeeping)
1150	2	5	3	3	2	3	250	550	Services (tour guide)
1150	1	3	3	3	2	2	250	150	Services (driver)
1150	2	5	3	3	1	3	550	250	Services (hotel-room service)
1150	0	4	3	3	2	3	150	150	Services (tour & travel)
1150	2	4	3	3	2	3	250	550	Services (tour operator)
1150	4	7	3	3	1	3	750	550	Services (hotel clerk cum cashier, room service)
1150	1	4	3	3	1	3	450	550	Services (hotel clerk/ cashier, restaurant)
1150	0	3	3	3	2	2	450	250	Services (hotel industry-front office)
1150	1	7	3	3	1	1	450	450	Services (cooks, bartenders)
1150	1	4	2	2	1	2	250	50	Rikshaw pullers (self-employed)
1150	0	3	0	2	2	0	250	50	Rikshaw pullers (self-employed)
1150	2	3	3	3	3	3	450	250	Taxi driver (self-employed)
1150	1	5	3	3	2	3	250	450	Tour guide (self-employed)
1150	2	8	3	3	1	2	250	150	Hotel-housekeeping
1150	2	5	3	3	1	3	450	350	Hotel-housekeeping
1150	3	5	3	3	1	1	550	250	Hotel-taxi driver
1150	2	5	3	3	2	2	450	250	Travel & tour labour
1150	4	5	3	3	1	3	550	750	Travel & tour labour
1150	0	6	3	3	2	3	250	350	Hotel-store clerk
1150	0	4	3	3	2	3	250	450	Hotel-front office
1150	4	3	3	3	1	2	450	50	Hotel-office clerk/peon
1150	1	3	3	3	2	3	450	350	Hotel-front office
1150	3	4	3	3	1	2	750	250	Hotel-room service
1150	0	2	3	2	2	2	250	50	Hotel-room service
1150	1	3	3	2	1	0	150	150	Mechanic (services)
1150	4	6	3	2	2	2	150	150	Securitymen (services)
1150	0	7	2	3	1	0	150	50	Rikshaw pullers (self-employed)
1150	0	7	2	2	3	2	150	50	Rikshaw pullers (self-employed)
1150	0	1	2	2	1	0	250	50	Rikshaw pullers (self-employed)
1150	0	5	3	2	2	0	50	50	Cargo handling (self-employed)
1150	0	5	3	2	1	0	150	50	Cargo handling (self-employed)

contd...

...contd...

Income	*Assets*	*Dependents*	*Infrastructure*	*Meals*	*Working Member*	*Education*	*Health Expenditure*	*Transport*	*Profession*
1150	0	5	3	3	2	2	250	50	Cargo handling (self-employed)
1150	4	5	3	3	1	1	250	150	Tailors (regular/salaried wage employer)
1150	2	4	3	3	2	1	150	50	Tailors (regular/salaried wage employer)
1150	1	3	2	3	1	0	150	50	Textiles & apparel (tailors)
1150	4	4	3	3	1	2	250	150	Textiles & apparel (tailors)
1150	3	3	3	3	1	1	250	150	Textiles & apparel (tailors)
1150	3	6	3	3	3	1	150	50	Textiles & apparel (tailors)
1150	2	5	3	3	1	1	250	150	Textiles & apparel (tailors)
1150	4	4	3	3	1	2	250	350	Textiles & apparel (supervisor)
1150	1	13	3	3	5	2	150	50	Textiles & apparel (tailors)
1150	4	4	3	3	1	1	150	150	Textiles & apparel (tailors)
1150	0	8	3	3	3	1	250	50	Textiles & apparel (tailors)
1150	3	4	3	3	1	0	250	250	Textiles & apparel (tailors)
1150	4	4	3	3	2	2	250	350	Cooks, bartenders
1150	4	5	3	3	2	2	250	350	Cooks, bartenders
1150	3	6	2	2	6	0	250	150	Maid & housekeeping worker
400	1	3	2	2	1	1	50	50	Maid & housekeeping worker
500	1	5	2	2	4	0	150	250	Maid & housekeeping worker
900	3	5	2	2	2	2	250	150	Maid & housekeeping worker
1150	2	5	3	2	2	1	250	50	Rikshaw pullers (self-employed)
1100	1	3	2	2	1	0	150	50	Rikshaw pullers (self-employed)
1150	2	5	3	2	3	1	250	350	Tailors (household)
1150	4	2	3	2	1	2	250	550	Tailors (household)
1150	2	5	3	3	3	1	50	50	Cook, bartender
1150	0	3	3	3	1	1	50	50	Cook, bartender
1150	1	6	3	3	2	1	50	50	Cook, bartender
1150	2	3	3	3	2	1	50	50	Cook, bartender
1150	2	5	3	3	4	1	50	50	Cook, bartender
1150	0	3	3	3	2	1	50	50	Cook, bartender
1150	0	2	3	3	2	1	50	50	Cook, bartender

4 Trickling Up Growth through Gender Parity

Introduction

The last three chapters have shown that economic growth trickled down *albeit* slowly to the informal sector and the poor. The same trickle down effects should be observed on gender disparities. Theoretically, rising income and falling poverty levels would in general reduce gender disparities in education, health and nutrition. Higher productivity and new job opportunities brought about by rising income levels often reduce gender inequalities in employment. Higher income levels when accompanied by government investment in the provision of basic water, energy and transportation infrastructure help reduce gender disparities in workloads.

However, as shown below, gender disparities have not reduced substantially during the period of high growth in India. Because economic growth may not have been high enough or sustained enough to reduce poverty, active measures are needed to redress persistent gender disparities in the short to medium term. Empirical work in recent years has brought out very clearly how the relative respect and regard for women's well-being is strongly influenced by such variables as women's ability to earn an independent income, to find employment outside the home, to have ownership rights and to have literacy and be educated participants in decisions within and outside the family. Indeed, even the survival of disadvantaged women compared to men in developing countries seems to go up sharply—and may even get eliminated—as progress is made in these agency aspects. Progress in one area (that of being able to work outside the household) seems to help to foster progress in others (in enhancing freedom from hunger, illness and relative deprivation).

This chapter investigates a complex situation where increasing economic growth has been accompanied by deteriorating gender development index for India. The different indicators of gender inequality show divergent trends. These trends need to be investigated as policy responses would necessarily need to take account of the factors that have led to these divergent trends. What is even more interesting is the reverse causation, i.e., restoring gender parity has trickled up growth in the Indian economy. While the effects of gender parity on economic growth may not be pronounced, this chapter shows that its effect on poverty reduction is much clearer. Section II documents a literature review of economic growth and gender relationships and shows that causation either way may not be strong. However before doing so, the chapter tries to outline an operational concept of gender parity in Section I. Section III outlines India's growth experience and gender equality. Section IV examines the correlations between gender equality and growth. Section V focusses on gender parity in education and health with growth. Before concluding in Section VII, Section VI discusses gender and poverty.

I

Operational Concepts of Gender Parity

The term gender equality has been defined in multiple ways in the development literature and has been the subject of great debate in the UN. It often means women having the same opportunities in life as men, for instance equality of access to education and employment, which does not necessarily lead to equality of outcomes. Three primary domains of equality between men and women emerge:

1. capabilities,
2. access to resources and opportunities, and
3. agency or the ability to influence outcomes.

The capabilities domain refers to basic human abilities as measured through education, health and nutrition. It is the most fundamental of all the three domains and is necessary for achieving equality in the other two domains. Access to resources and opportunities, the second domain, refers primarily to equality in the opportunity to use or apply basic capabilities through access to economic assets (such as land and property) and resources (such as income and employment). The third domain, agency, is the defining element of the concept of empowerment and refers to the ability to make choices and decisions that can alter outcomes. Gender equality in this domain can only result from an equalising in the balance of power between women and men in the household and societal institutions.

These three domains of equality are inter-related. Progress in any one domain to the exclusion of the others is insufficient to meet the goal of gender equality. While they are inter-related, the three domains are not necessarily dependent on each other. So, for instance, illiterate women may organise, thereby building their agency to influence outcomes for themselves and their households. Not surprisingly, women then use that agency to demand capability (better health or education) and opportunity (access to decent work). Similarly, women with capabilities (as measured by education) may have no economic opportunity, as is evidenced in many Middle Eastern countries.

Explicit measures of gender inequalities are: sex ratio, literacy rates, health and nutrition indicators, wage differentials, ownership of land and property. The implicit measures of gender inequalities are those embedded in relations of power and in hierarchies and are more difficult to measure. Located in the household, in custom, religion and culture, these intra-household inequalities result in unequal distribution of power, control over resources and decision-making, dependence rather than self-reliance, control rather than autonomy and unfair, unequal distribution of work, drudgery and even food. Current development debate has resulted into generation of meaningful indicators of women and development. In 2010, India ranked 134 out of 182 nations in terms of human development, but in gender development index (GDI) India's rank was 139 out of 155 countries.[1] Comparative data of 155 countries regarding gender-related development index reveals that gender equality does not depend entirely on the income level of society. The human development approach which focusses on demographic, health, education, employment and human rights issues of women provides realistic insights to address women's

1. *Human Development Report*, published by the United Nations Development Programme. Accessed from *www.undp.org*

concerns. Thus, gender sensitive human development ensures an inclusive growth. In other words, addressing gender disparities through positive measures would trickle up growth and more importantly reduce poverty.

II

Trickling Up Growth through Gender Parity

The effect on growth of increased gender equality of opportunity has been examined extensively. Growth regressions have serious limitations, and those that use gender-disaggregated data are no exception. The most important limitation is that of endogeneity: gender equality affects growth, but growth presumably also affects gender equality. Finding valid instrumental variables to correct for this endogeneity is challenging to say the least. One empirical paper employing growth regressions explicitly addresses this simultaneity by instrumenting. In a cross-country panel regression of over 100 countries for the 1975-1990 period, Dollar and Gatti (1999) find that increases in per capita income are associated with increases in gender equality along three dimensions: secondary school attainment, wage gaps and women in parliament. The effect of income on gender equality becomes stronger as countries move from low-middle income to high income.

Economic growth appears to be positively correlated with gender equality. This latter finding is sensitive to changes in the length of the period over which per capita GDP growth rates are averaged and to one alternative measure of gender equality (the GDI-HDI ratio). When gender equality is measured by the gender empowerment measure (the GEM), however, the relationship is not statistically significant. (World Bank, 2001). What is quite interesting is that the effects of gender parity on growth is much more evident than the reverse. This implies that restoring gender parity actually trickles up economic growth. There are several aspects of gender parity, but some of the important ones which have helped trickle up growth are discussed below.

Gender Parity in Education and Growth

Equality of opportunity in education has received particular attention, for two simple reasons. First, education and, more broadly human capital, is easily incorporated into two frequently-used econometric models of economic growth: the augmented Solow model and endogeneous growth models. Second, educational inequalities are both easily measurable and these measures are widely available.

The first generation of panel regression studies examining the relationship between gender disaggregated measures of educational attainment and growth in per capita GDP find little difference between the effect of male and female education. Two well-known studies (Barro, 1991; Barro and Lee, 1994) even find that base-period female educational attainment is negatively related to subsequent rates of growth.

More recent studies have addressed the econometric and specification problems in this first generation of studies, and typically find a larger impact of female education on growth than of male education on growth (Abu-Ghaida and Klasen, 2004). Dollar and Gatti (1999), for example, find that negative returns to female education disappear once regional dummy variables are included in the specification; they hypothesise that the earlier result was driven by the low growth and high education for women that characterised Latin America for the period of the study. Klasen (2002) estimates the effect of the gender gap in years of total schooling in the adult population on per capita income growth, using cross-country and panel regressions for the 1960-1992 period for 109 industrial and developing countries. He estimates both a structural model (which includes a direct impact of education on growth, an indirect effect via increased investment, an indirect effect via lower population growth, an indirect effect via the interaction of population growth and investment, an indirect effect via labour force growth and an indirect effect via the interaction of labour force growth and investment) and a reduced form model. His findings are striking: the direct and indirect effects of gender inequality in educational attainment account for 0.95 percentage points of the 2.5 percentage point gap in growth rates between South Asia and East Asia, 0.56 percentage points of the 3.3 percentage point gap between sub-Saharan Africa and East Asia, and 0.85 percentage points of the 1.9 percentage point gap between the Middle East/North Africa and East Asia.

What is the intuition behind these results? Klasen (2002) argues that assuming that boys and girls have a similar distribution of innate abilities, gender inequality in education implies that less able boys will have access to education. If human capital is some combination of innate ability and education, this means that the overall level of human capital in society will be lower than it would be in the absence of gender inequality in education, and overall economic growth rates would suffer. A simulation assuming a 70-30 per cent male-female split of those children receiving education—as opposed to a 50-50 per cent split—leads to a decline of 12 per cent in average human capital, assuming innate ability is normally distributed and assuming that 50 per cent of all children go to school. Using the estimated relationship between human capital and GDP growth from a well-known panel study yields a 0.3 percentage point decline in annual growth (Klasen, 2002) through gender inequality.

Abu-Ghaida and Klasen (2004) project the costs of missing the United Nation's Millennium Development Goals (MDGs) in gender equity on growth for 25 countries. They find that more unequal countries would average 0.4 per cent per year higher growth during 2005-2015, if they achieved the MDG gender equity goals in 2005.

Gender Parity in Employment and Growth

Inequalities in opportunities are not limited to education. Numerous studies document large gaps in wages or hourly earnings between men and women, even after accounting for education and other forms of human capital. The allocation of talent and entrepreneurial skills to productive activities is a powerful source of growth; conversely, if this talent is dedicated to rent-seeking behaviour, long-run growth will suffer (Murphy *et al.*, 2001). An analogous argument can be applied to occupational segregation by gender: to the extent that the concentration of women in low productivity occupations is non-voluntary, the misallocation of talent may have large growth costs via efficiency losses.

Surprisingly, few studies have looked at the impact of occupational segregation on growth rates. Tzannatos (1999) using data from the 1980s from 11 Latin American and Caribbean countries, calculates the impact of the elimination of occupational differentials within industries on women's wages, men's wages and output. While men's wages fall by between 6 and 13 per cent, women's wages rise by significantly more: from 24 to 96 per cent. Output increases range from 2 to 9 per cent of GDP (Tzannatos, 1999). Tzannatos (1999: 559) interprets these impacts as what 'can happen in the long run when: a) women and men are equally endowed with human capital; b) there is no employer discrimination; c) family constraints are no more binding upon women than men; and d) the gender specific effects of social norms and other institutional factors have withered away.'

Gender wage gaps *per se* have an ambiguous relationship with growth rates. On the one hand, one analysis based on panel data found that gender wage inequality in export-oriented middle income countries boosts economic growth presumably via its effect on firm profits and investment (Seguino, 2000a). On the other hand, greater wage inequality may be associated with lower aggregate saving in these countries, which is likely to hamper long-run growth rates (Seguino and Floro, 2003). Both these results should be viewed as tentative and preliminary, given that the robustness of these results has not been tested with other model specifications and a larger sample of countries.

Women's Agency and Socioeconomic Variables

Apart from the studies linking gender inequality to economic growth, there are a large number of studies that link gender inequality in education to fertility and child mortality (e.g., Murthi *et al.*, 1995; Summers, 1994; King and Hill, 1995). For example, Summers (1994) shows that females with more than seven years of education have, on average, fewer (two) children in Africa than women with no education. King and Hill (1995) find a similar effect of female schooling on fertility. Over and above this direct effect, lower gender inequality in enrollments has an additional negative effect on the fertility rate. Countries with a female-male enrollment ratio of less than 0.42 have, on average, 0.5 more children than countries where the enrollment ratio is larger than 0.42 (in addition to the direct impact of female enrollment on fertility). Similar linkages have been found between gender inequality in education and child mortality (Murthi *et al.*, 1995; Summers, 1994). Thus, reduced gender bias in education furthers two very important development goals, namely reduced fertility and child mortality, quite apart from its impact on economic growth (Sen, 1999).

The findings in the studies cited above are corroborated by international as well as national studies, and they demonstrate the powerful role of women's agency and women's educational empowerment in reducing desired family size, fertility, population growth, child morbidity, child mortality and gender bias in child mortality, while at the same time showing that men's education mattered comparatively less to these important social outcomes.

Sometimes referred to as the 'good mother hypothesis', the argument is that income under women's control is more likely to be spent on child's well-being than income under men's control. Female influence over household consumption is of course directly linked to women's bargaining power, proxied by various measures such as education, assets at marriage, spheres of decision-making, divorce law and relative status within the household and society (Quisumbing, 2003). A number of studies show positive correlations between women's bargaining power and children's education and health (Murthi *et al.*, 1995; Quisumbing, 2003; Quisumbing and Maluccio, 2003; Schultz, 2001; World Bank, 2001). That women invest a greater proportion of their resources in the household is perhaps not surprising, as women's spheres of influence do not often extend beyond the household (World Bank, 2005).

Another link between gender equality and growth may be via differential marginal propensities to save, although the empirical evidence on this score is relatively weak. Seguino and Floro (2003) and Stotsky (1997) note that women may have greater incentives to save than men, reflecting: i) women's role as 'principal home builders' (Stotsky's term); ii) the fact that men may have greater recourse to social insurance, thus reducing the need to save in order to smooth consumption expenditures; and iii) women's stronger bequest motives and intergenerational altruism. Seguino and Floro (2003), in a cross-country panel study of semi-industrialised countries, find that an increase in women's wage share relative to men is associated with increase in the domestic savings rate.

The positive externalities of gender norms also come up in studies of corruption and growth. Behavioural studies show that women tend to be more trustworthy and public-spirited than men; higher proportions of women in government or the labour force are negatively correlated with corruption (Dollar *et al.*, 2001; Swamy *et al.*, 2001). Gender distribution of income also matters for aggregate savings. Using panel data for a set of semi-industrialised countries between 1975 and 1995, Seguino and Floro (2003) test whether macroeconomic measures of female bargaining power—women's share of the wage bill and the gap between male and female educational attainment—have an effect on aggregate savings. The hypothesis is that women differ from men in their propensities to save because of their differing institutional positions: in the labour market, in the household, in the community and in their access to state-provided social insurance. They find that an increase in women's share of the wage bill is positively correlated with aggregate savings, though the gender education gap variable does not perform as consistently.

Lower fertility is also correlated with higher female labour force participation and gender wage equity (Galor and Weil, 1996; World Bank, 2001). The familiar logic is that as the opportunity costs of women's time increases, parents opt for more child quality over quantity. With women doing most of the childcare, it is essential that the opportunity costs of women's time increase relative to men's, as increases in male incomes will simply raise the demand for children.

In sum, the evidence linking greater gender parity to growth is mixed. There are several cross-country growth regression studies that suggest that greater equality in access to education may pay growth dividends, but growth regressions suffer from several important weaknesses. Studies on the effects of wage gaps on growth are more convincing. Studies need to be cognisant of cultural aspects of gender inequalities. While the effects of gender parity on growth is mixed, there is some literature on the indirect effects of gender equality on growth that are transmitted via the impact of gender equality on poverty alleviation.

In the context of the Indian experience, what is of more relevance is the effect of gender parity on poverty alleviation. Given the increasing inequality associated with economic growth (see Introduction), it is of utmost importance to examine the agencies that reduce poverty. This chapter through statistical work and the underlying economic intuition delves into the relationship between poverty and gender parity. However before doing so, it is worthwhile getting a state of play, i.e., what has been the result of India's growth experience on gender parity.

III

India's Growth Experience and Gender Equality

Overall labour participation levels in the Indian labour force have been relatively stable since the 1970s to about 1990, for both men and women, implying that employment rates were growing at the same level as the work- force. The growth effects on female labour force have been felt much more strongly from 2001-2007. Gender indicators have generally been assumed to be not sensitive to economic growth, except in the organised labour sector as shown below. In fact, as the scatter in Figure 4.1 and Table 4.1 suggests, female labour force participation rates increased significantly but in the later periods of high growth.

Figure 4.1

Economic Growth and Female Labour Force Participation

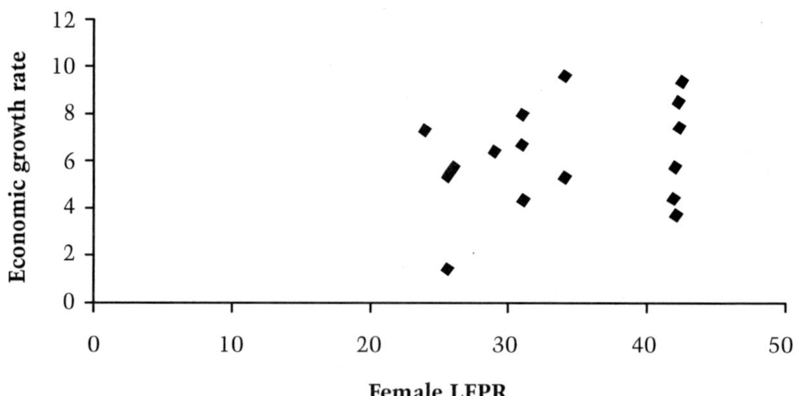

Again as in the organised sector (see below), it can be observed from Figure 4.1, that at rates of economic growth over 5 per cent, female labour force participation responded positively to economic growth.

The employment situation in India, as revealed by the study of available data, suggests the presence of discrimination against women at all levels. This disparity is a source of some concern, for high labour participation rates for women have been shown to raise nutrition levels for their children, lower mortality rates and raise sex ratios by combating traditional male biases (Agnihotri and Neetha, 1997). Many have argued that the labour participation of women is one of the most important indicators of women's empowerment, access to resources and decision-making ability, and thus must be made a central focus of policy. The score for female LFPR remained static at 42 per cent and went down during periods of high growth, i.e., in 2007/08.

However, as shown by Figure 4.1 and Table 4.1, the overall female participation rate increased at higher rates of growth. This shows the importance of focussing policies on maintaining high rates of economic growth so that the organic changes accompanying growth can improve the labour force participation rates for women.

Table 4.1

Economic Growth and Gender Indicators

Year	*Growth (Real GDP at Factor Cost) (Financial Year Figures)*	*Life Expectancy at Birth (Years)*	*Maternal Mortality Rate per 100,000 Live*	*Literacy Rate 15 Years & Above (%age)*	*Women in Labour Force (Rate % of Total)*	*Women in Parliament (% of Seats Occupied by Women)*
1990	5.3	59	340	29	34	7.9
1991	1.4	59.1	340	29	25.6	9
1992	5.4	59.3	550	34	25.6	8
1993	5.7	59.3	550	40	26	7
1994	6.4	59.9	550	40	29	7
1995	7.3	60.4	460		24	
1996	8	60.7	570	36	31	8
1997	4.3	61.4	570	36.1	31	7.3
1998	6.7	61.8	570	37.7	31	7.3
1999	6.4	62.9	570	39.4	29	8.3
2000	4.4	63.3	410	43.5	41.8	8.9
2001	5.8	63.3	410	44.5	42	8.8
2002	3.8	63.8	540	45.4	42.1	8.9
2003	8.5	64	540	46.4	42.2	9.3
2004	7.5	64.4	540	46.4	42.4	9.3
2005	9.4	65	540	47.8	42.5	9.3
2006	9.6	65.3	540	47.8	34.0	9.2
2007-08	8.4	65.3	540	47.8	34.0	9.0

Sources: *Human Development Report*, various issues, *Economic Survey of India*, various issues, Ministry of Labour, *Annual Reports*.

But data on LFPR masks inherent inequalities. John and Lalita (1995) have effectively shown that LFPRs are additionally affected by caste and communal differences that interact with gender to influence employment status. Dalit males and females are more likely to be concentrated in casual employment. Dalit women are less likely than other groups to be involved exclusively in domestic work, and thus actually have a higher LFPR than other groups of women, though their employment may be concentrated in low-paying casual labour. The gap between the LFPRs of Muslim women and men was also found to be much higher than average, as was the case with upper caste Hindu families. Such variation across groups indicates that the relationship between LFPRs and income must not be assumed, for no easy categorisation of this relationship exists. Intervention measures to aid any of these groups must take into account the particular characteristics of their employment—such as heavy involvement of the Dalit community in casual labour—to most effectively meet their needs. A greater detail of group-differentiated data is, thus, critically needed.

Table 4.2

Labour Force Participation Rates

Year	*Rural*		*Urban*	
	Male	*Female*	*Male*	*Female*
1977-78	63.7	30.5	60.1	17.1
1983	62.6	29.1	60.3	14.8
1987-88	61.4	29.2	59.6	14.6
1989-90	54.6	25.4	52.4	12.9
1990-91	54.9	24.3	53.2	13
July-Dec. 1991	54.8	24.7	53.5	12.7
1992	55	25.3	52.6	13.4
Jan-June 1993	61.7	27.9	59	13.3
1993-94	63	27.2	60.1	14.5
1994-95	55.3	23.8	53.4	11.7
July 1995-June 1996a	55	23.6	54.4	11.1
Jan-Dec 1997a	55	22.4	53.7	11.7
Jan-June 1998a	54.3	21.2	53.4	10.8
1999-2000	53.3	23.5	53.9	12.6
July 2000-June 2001*	54.08	22.25	58.8	12.05
July 2001-June 2002*	53.8	24.6	57.1	11.5
July-Dec. 2002*	54.7	21.6	55.16	12.6

Source: Indiastat.com

Socioeconomic factors are also important in determining women's participation rate. Studies have found that a complex situation in which a U-curve of women's employment by education levels is caused by a mixture of economic and cultural factors (Olsen and Mehta, 2005). Thus, labour force participation is higher among illiterates than among the literate women. However, as women reach higher levels of education, their participation in the labour force increases. The U-curve was explored in some detail using both descriptive and regression statistics. Rural/urban, religious and state differences in patterns of labour force participation were considered. The typical scenario at the bottom of the U-curve was among middle-class educated women. It was noted that the standard norms for housewives are adapted for poor women, who often have a double or triple burden of work, and for rich women who can employ others to assist them whilst still being the manager of a household. The U-curve may explain the criticality of higher growth rates which offer better employment opportunities to women and hence increases the labour force participation of women. In fact, part of the rationale of the U-curve may also be explained by the wage differentials which typically tends to be lower for the illiterate and at higher levels of qualification.

The most prominent feature that emerges from the study of LFPR of females is the changing role of women in the micro and small enterprises (MSEs) in the post-reform period. There is now more active participation of female workers even in the non-traditional sectors, and a more even distribution of them both over different industrial activity groups and across regions. However, the absolute numbers of female workers is increasing in the urban areas but decreasing in the rural areas. The share of hired workers within female workers has also increased marginally. A major development has been the drastic increase in the share of part-time workers within female workers at the cost of full-time female workers. There is thus a prominent trend towards change in the status of female workers from fulltime to part-time which is a reflection of outright casualisation. This has serious policy implication in the sense that it brings out the vulnerability of women in the labour market. Industrial activity level study reveals that the share of women is increasing in the so called non-traditional sectors like machinery & equipment etc., and decreasing in the traditional sectors like tobacco & beverages, textiles, etc., thereby making the distribution more even (*indiastat.com*).

Regional study shows that the southern states top the list regarding share of women in total employment, while the shares are low in the northern and western states. Here also, the regional disparity is decreasing over time. It is also observed that factors like incidence of poverty, female literacy levels, female work participation rate and per capita state national product of the states are important factors affecting the magnitude and share of women employment in the MSEs (*indiastat.com*).

Economic Growth and Female Employment in the Organised Sector

Perhaps the most dramatic effect of economic growth on female employment can be observed in the organised sector. While the organised sector only accounts for 4 per cent of female labour force *versus* 10 per cent for men, this sector also has the highest employment growth rates for women: 3.6 per cent; for men: 2.5 per cent. High growth rates have, therefore, translated to more employment for women. Within this, 62 per cent are employed within the public sector, making them more vulnerable to the effects of disinvestment in state-owned enterprises. What is also important to observe is that most of the increase in female employment has taken place at growth rates well above 5 per cent. For the organised sector, there is a direct correlation between the increase in the economic growth rate and female employment: the higher the growth rate the greater the share of female employment.

Figure 4.2

Economic Growth and Female Labour Participation in the Organised Sector

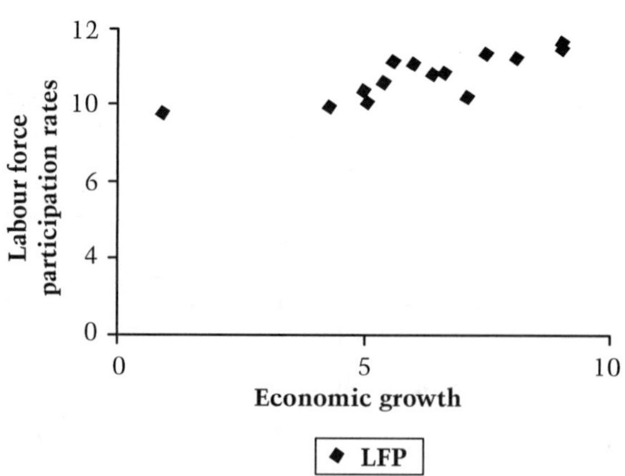

Source: Indiastat.com

India's overall index score on women's advancement (reflecting largely organised sector employment) decreased marginally to 37.8 in 2009 from 39.4 in 2008. This was despite a slight increase in the number of women per 100 men considering themselves to be in the managerial positions (rising from 9 women per 100 men in 2008 to 12 women per 100 men in 2009). The drop was driven by the decrease in the proportion of women to men perceiving themselves to be earning above median income. The number of women per men dropped from 32 women per 100 men in 2008 to 22 women per 100 men in 2009.[2]

Besley *et al.* (2004) provide an Indian case study that considers the cross-regional effects of gender gaps in access to managerial positions and general employment on per capita income between 1961 and 1991. They find that a 10 per cent increase in the female to male ratio of managers raises non-agricultural output by 2 per cent; a 10 per cent increase in the female share of the labour force raises overall output by 8 per cent.

Economic Growth and Female Employment in Agriculture

The largest sector in the Indian economy in terms of employment is agriculture. Dalit and tribal women account for half of female agricultural labourers and almost all of them are landless. Studies show a shift from farm to non-farm employment in the agricultural sector among men, but not among women. This is to the disadvantage of women who: (a) lost out on higher wages in the non-farm sector, and (b) bear the brunt of the stagnation in the agricultural farm sector (Papola, 1999). It also points to their relatively lower mobility within the rural labour market. Figure 4.3 shows that female rural employment was generally found to be unresponsive to growth rates, even declining with higher growth rates. Growth rates (in employment and overall) in the agricultural sector have been found to be stagnating averaging at around 2 per cent for the entire period from 1991-2007. This is the period covered by the scatter in Figure 4.3.

2. *http://www.adb.org/documents/events/2009/poverty-social-development/growing-disparity-in-india-Kundu-paper.pdf*

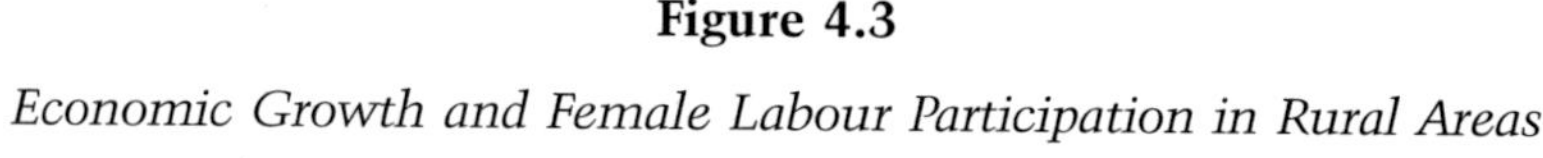

Figure 4.3

Economic Growth and Female Labour Participation in Rural Areas

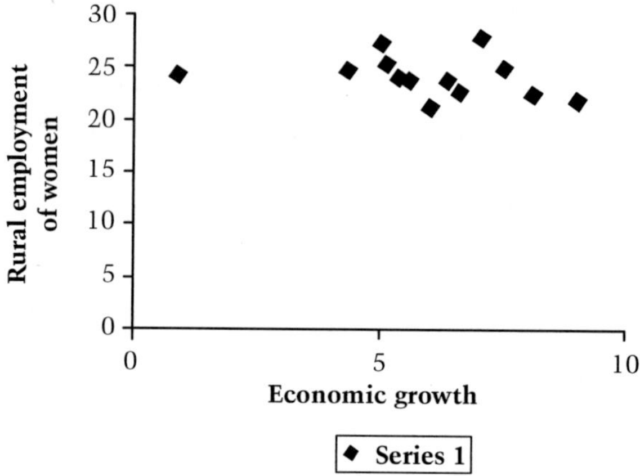

Paradoxically, the wage gap between men and women in agriculture is the lowest in the poorest states. For example, Bihar, West Bengal and Orissa show the smallest gap between the wages of men and women in rural areas. This is suggestive of out-migration of men from these states to other states in search of work. In fact, Chapter 2 on migration has shown that this is indeed the case. In addition, between 2001-2005, the gap in these poor states also widened slightly, indicating a growth in opportunitites in the non-farm sector for men. This is also vindicated by other studies (Sen and Mukherjee, 2007).

Economic growth is not just an exogeneous rise in income, but usually results from a change in productivity that can significantly alter the returns to investments in human capital. Income effects can be small, but growth-induced changes in returns to investments can have large effects. The Indian 'green revolution', for example, substantially increased the productivity of agricultural production in many areas of India and raised the returns to schooling for men and women, particularly in those areas where the new crop varieties were most productive (Foster and Rosenzweig, 1996; Behrman *et al.*, 1999).

A study using panel data from India during the period of the initial years of the green revolution, re-assessed: (i) whether gender differences in survival rates reflect gender differentials in the value of human capital, and (ii) to what extent policies promoting economic growth can affect the female survival deficit in the absence of fundamental changes in cultural practices that differentiate the roles of men and women. Adopting a general equilibrium framework in which sons contribute to parental household incomes and daughters do not, it was found that growth in agricultural productivity can improve the survival chances of girls. While these effects may be weak, the local demand for literate wives increases significantly in areas in which agricultural growth is expected to rise. Thus, agricultural growth is also likely to have a positive effect on literacy.

Economic Growth and GDI in India

Figure 4.4 shows the scatter of the gender development index (GDI) with the economic growth rate of India. The GDI is a composite index developed by the UNDP to reflect different measures of gender inequality. The GDI provides a composite measure of three dimensions of gender development: living a long and healthy life (measured by the difference in life expectancy of women and men), being educated (measured by the difference between men and women with regard to adult literacy and enrollment at the primary, secondary and tertiary level) and having a decent standard of living (measured by the difference between men and women's purchasing power parity, PPP, income). The closer the index is to 1 the lower is the gender disparity. Figure 4.4 clearly shows an improvement in the GDI index at higher rates of economic growth.

Figure 4.4

Growth and Gender Development Index

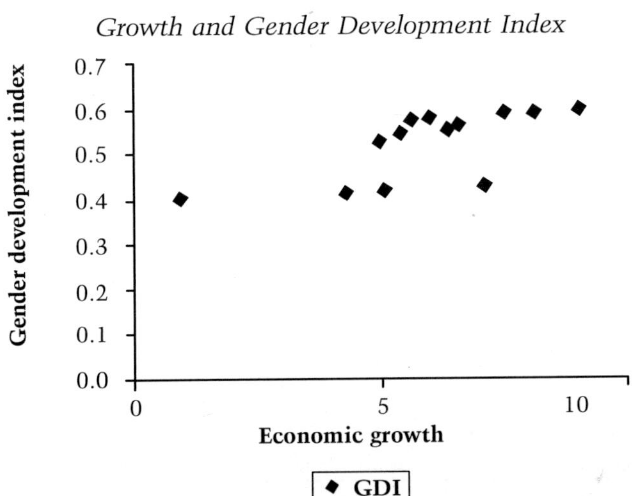

From Figure 4.4 it is clear that higher growth rates would generally translate to greater gender equality. Greater gender equality should in turn lead to poverty alleviation. While examining all these factors is beyond the scope of this chapter, empirical work on India for the high growth period is scarce. This chapter tries to examine some of the correlations between gender equity and growth, narrowing on factors which matter most from a policy point of view.

IV

Examining Correlations between Gender Equality and Growth

To examine the complex correlations between economic growth and gender equality in India, a number of multiple regressions were carried out. These showed interesting correlations between different variables and helped narrow the policy variables. Most of the data on gender indicators was available only till 2005, but as India's growth story is of more recent origin, i.e., post-2005, the data was extrapolated to 2008. As is shown in Table 4.3 and from the multiple regressions below, social indicators for

Table 4.3

Definition of Variables

Var	*Name*
PSDP	Per capita state domestic product at 1993 constant prices
FeIN	Number of females in unorganised sector
IHe	Index of health of women
IEd	Index of education of women
IEr	Index of access of economic resources to women
Ca	Capital asset
Abs(WD)	Absolute value of wage difference between women and men
Pov	Percentage of people below poverty line
S1	Composite index-1 (with: IHe, IEd)
F1	Composite index-1 (with: IHe, IEd and IEr)
***	Significant at 1 per cent level
**	Significant at 5 per cent level
*	Significant at 10 per cent level
NB	Parenthesis contain the estimated standard error of estimates

women has been sticky upwards and are less sensitive to growth. Labour force participation rates, education and literacy rates have however responded positively to economic growth. A particularly worrisome indicator is the maternal mortality rate which has shown little response to economic growth (See Table 4.1), showing the dominance of social and cultural factors which does not accord pregnant women due care even if they are economically independent. However, with constant interventions by the govt. this figure came down in 2009.

Table 4.4

Sources of Data

Var	*Name*
PSDP	Proceedings of the National Seminar on Gender Statistics, 2004, CSO
FeIN	National Commission for Enterprises in Unorganised Sector, November 2008
IHe	2004, CSO
IEd	2004, CSO
IEr	2004, CSO
Abs(WD)	2004, CSO
PSDP	CSO
Pov	Planning Commission and *Economic Survey* 2007/08

The first relationship which was examined was whether wage inequality between men and women affects the growth of per capita domestic product. Using panel data across the 27 Indian states for the high growth periods, it was found that as the gap in wage rates increase so does the per capita state domestic product (SDP). In fact the reverse causation was found to be even stronger, i.e., as the SDP increases the wage differential increases. While the elasticity in the first case was weak, the elasticity in the second case was stronger. Two equations were examined:

PSDP= f(Ca, Abs(WD),...)

and

Abs(wd)=f(Ca, PSDP, ...)

Table 4.5

Regression Results

	Dependent Var: Log (PSDP)
Explanatory Variables	
Log(Ca)	0.008 (0.048)
Log{Abs(WD)}	0.027** (0.011)
F (2,15)	3.17*
R-square	0.29
No. of observations	18

In the first scenario a relatively weaker correlation was observed than in the second scenario. The R-square was also relatively weak pointing to a number of missed variables. In the second case, the R-square grew stronger and the correlation coefficient more significant, pointing to the fact that higher growth rates may actually exacerbate the wage differential between men and women.

Table 4.6

***Reverse Regression*

	Dependent Var: Log{Abs(WD)}
Explanatory Variables	
Log(Ca)	0.038 (0.041)
Log (PSDP)	0.650*** (0.200)
F (2,15)	6.73***
R-square	0.47
No. of observations	18

This ties up with earlier empirical findings (cited above) on the ambiguous role of wage inequality on economic growth. The intuition behind the second stronger result lies in the fact that states which experienced high rates of growth particularly in the second half of the last decade were those which had high rates of growth in services and export sectors. Hence, higher rates of growth increased the disparity in wages between men and women.

A simple explanation for this phenomenon can be found by looking at the data on wage differentials in agricultural activities in India across states. The overall wage differentials in a state would normally be influenced more than proportionately by the wage differential in agriculture, as agriculture still accounts for a large share of employment across India. Paradoxically the poorer the state, the lower the wage difference between men and women in agriculture, perhaps because of the substantial out-migration that takes place from poorer states such as Bihar to richer states such as Maharashtra and Karnataka. In fact instead of taking the absolute wage differential, if the wage differential is indexed, a weak inverse relationship with per capita SDP is observed.

Table 4.7

Wage Differentials in Agricultural Occupations between States

States	*February 2005*	
	Men	*Women*
Andhra Pradesh	46	37.92
Assam	60.4	52
Bihar	52.69	50.39
Gujarat	53.64	52
Haryana	87.57	73.83
Himachal Pradesh	@	-
Jammu & Kashmir	@	-
Karnataka	52.84	41.13
Kerala	@	101.65
Madhya Pradesh	45.71	@
Maharashtra	63.05	40.43
Manipur	60	55
Meghalaya	@	@
Orissa	49.17	46.33
Punjab	87.83	@
Rajasthan	@	@
Tamil Nadu	67.35	42.46
Tripura	70	-
Uttar Pradesh	56.78	51.5
West Bengal	53.72	50.17
India	60.46	50.97

Note: @ - No information provided.

Source: *Indiastat.com*

Wage differentials have been extensively documented in all sectors of the Indian economy. Within the workforce, two kinds of wage differentials have been found to exist. In the informal sector—where most women are employed—there is evidence of women directly being paid lower wages than men, especially in the agricultural labour sector and the urban informal labour sectors where little effective legislation exists as a disincentive for this practice. In the organised sector, where equal renumeration laws are more directly enforceable, pure wage discrimination (differential pay for the same job) has not been found to exist. However, differential levels of education and differential returns to that education implies that women are usually less skilled than men and thus can attain only lower level jobs even within the organised sector, leading to a high wage differential.

FeIN=F(PCSDP, ...)

In fact the correlation between economic growth across sectors and informal sector employment of women has been found to be negative. This is contrary to the findings of the informal sector in general, where informal employment rises with growth in income. The simple explanation for this can be found in the increase in male non-agricultural employment over the high growth period and no commensurate increase in female non-agricultural employment. Part of the explanation may also lie in the U-curve, i.e., as the family becomes richer women devote their time to housework. The elasticity with respect to growth in SDP and informal employment amongst women is significantly negative.

Table 4.8

Regression Results

	Dependent Variable: Log(FeIN)
Explanatory Variables	
Log (PSDP)	-2.23***
	(0.729)
F (1,30)	9.37***
R-square	0.23
No. of observations	32

Table 4.9

Regression Results

Explanatory Variables	
Log(Ca)	0.059 (0.03)
Log(IHe)	0.46 (0.467)
Log(IEd)	1.59** (0.64)
R-square	0.69
F (3,13)	10.10***
No. of observations	17

Education has been found to greatly influence wage differentials. Studies found that the female-male wage ratio in urban India was 0.59 for female illiterates and 0.82 for literates (Deshpande and Depshpande, 1992). Another study by Kingdom *et al.*, however, found that even after controlling for gender, only 22 per cent of the gap in wages could be explained by the lack of female education—78 per cent of the wage gap, thus, is due to differential returns to education. Barriers to education and employment of women must be studied, given that differential rates of return on education brings the level of direct economic return of female education into question. It must also be kept in mind that different caste, religious and income groups will have widely varying incentives to either educate, or conversely not educate, their daughters as opposed to their sons.

V

Examining Gender Parity in Education and Health with Growth

A large body of microeconomic evidence shows that increases in women's education generally lead to increases in their labour force participation as well as in their earnings. Educated women's greater participation in labour market, work and their higher earnings are thought to be good for their own status (economic models say 'bargaining power') within the household and are good for their children because it appears that a greater proportion of women's income than men's is spent on child goods.

On the down side, it may be thought that educated women's greater labour force participation takes them away from their children for longer periods of time (than is the case with uneducated or less educated women) and this may disadvantage educated women's children through neglect. At present this is a relatively unresearched issue. However, limited evidence suggests that children whose mothers work have just as good or better educational outcomes than children whose mothers do not work (Olsen and Mehta, 2005).

How does economic growth affect education and health of women? Given the critical role of education and health in female LFPR, it is expected that India's growth experience should have had a positive effect on both these variables. Table 4.8 presents the regression results of per capita SDP with the index of health of women and the index of education of women. The index of education attainment compiled by the CSO includes the female literacy rate and the percentage of girls between 6 and 17 attending school. The index of nutrition and health includes a measure of the percentage of women with anaemia, the percentage of women with body mass index below 18.5 and the female infant mortality rate (CSO, 2004). The result indicates that the higher is the education for woman, the higher will be the per capita income. This correlation is significant at the 5 per cent level. However, the impact of the health index on incomes is less significant. On the other hand, the correlation between education and health is very large, showing that educated women are more likely to be healthy than otherwise. From Table 4.10, it can be seen that this correlation is 0.76, i.e., over three-quarters of the women who are educated are also likely to be healthy. This shows that there is a high degree of multicollinearity between the health index and the education index for women in India. Multicollinearity could also explain in part the lack of traction between the health index of women and incomes.

Table 4.10

Correlation Results

Variable	*Log(IHe)*	*Log(IEd)*
Log(IHe)	1.00	
Log(IEd)	0.76	1.00

In order to address the problem of multicollinearity, a composite index that can represent the impact of health and education was constructed. The eigenvalues that represent the composite component of health and education are presented in Table 4.11. The eigenvalues reflect the spread of the composite index. The first component was selected and this composite index is called S1 which is the predicted composite index with log of health and log of education. Table 4.12 presents the regression of log of per capita SDP on S1. The result indicates that the estimated parameter of the composite index is positively significant. It reflects a situation where it could be said that the improvement of education of female or/and their health should improve the per capita income. In other words, there is a positive significant impact of both health and education on per capita SDP.

Table 4.11

Composite Component with Log(IHe), Log(IEd)

Principle Component (Eigenvalues)

Variable	*Eigenvalues*
1st component	1.76
2nd component	0.23

Principle Component (Eigenvectors)

Variable	*Eigenvalues*
Log(IHe)	0.707
Log(IEd)	0.707

Table 4.12

Regression Results

Explanatory Variables	
Log(Ca)	0.053 (0.032)
S1	0.293*** (0.054)
R-square	0.68
F (2,14)	15.17***
No. of observations	17

Thus as the health and education index of women improves, the per capita SDP goes up. The logical reasoning behind this correlation has to do with the pattern of India's growth rate. India has seen a service-led growth which has shown increasing returns to education. Thus, states with higher levels of literacy and particularly higher tertiary education for women would also be states which are growing relatively rapidly. On the other hand, the low growth states have a higher participation of women in agriculture.

National income is growing, as is the urban organised sector. Female literacy and health care indicators show vast improvements in the late 1990s and the rising involvement of NGOs is raising the number of successful community-based programmes in social service sectors. The next decade, however, will be critical in terms of creating policy that is tailored to the needs of specific communities in order to be most effective in terms of delivering on the universal education objective. To attain such policies with regards to gender and development, it is critical to understand the gendered impact of economic policies and social policies. The correlations above show the importance of education of women in generating the right growth impulses in the Indian economy.

VI

Gender and Poverty

While the effects of improved female health and education on economic growth has been shown to be positive, of greater importance are the poverty-related outcomes. Though the measurement of poverty as a paucity of sufficient income has traditionally dominated academic thinking, discourses on the gendered experience of poverty seek to widen this perspective. Though hard to empirically define and analyse, there exist specific processes and indicators—intra-household processes and incidences of female headship in households, in particular—that indicate that men and women experience poverty differently, and use different methods to cope with that experience. Overall trends in poverty depend on the method of analysis being used.

But as was shown above in the case of economic growth and gender inequality indicators, not all indicators of gender inequality would impact significantly on poverty reduction. Three variables which could be important for gender development aspects could include health, education and female labour force participation rates as shown above. The first two variables were selected because it was found earlier that the income of the state was particularly sensitive to these variables. Access to economic resources is another variable which has been introduced over here, as wage inequality was not found to be very sensitive to economic growth or per capita incomes. Access to economic resources reflects female labour force participation rates over the age of 15 (CSO, 2004).

Table 4.13 presents the correlation between log of these three variables, index of education, health and LFPR. It can be seen that the correlation between LFPR with the other two variables is quite weak. In addition, as before, the correlation between education and health is large. The correlation raises the possibility that a woman who is healthy and educated may nevertheless not participate as an economic agent in the labour force. This is consistent with the U-curve hypothesis observed for educated women in India. A composite index that can be related with gender, however, should include all these three aspects. This is particularly true as with higher rates of growth, female LFPRs were seen to rise (see Table 4.1).

Table 4.14a presents the eigenvalues of three composite indices. The first composite index is selected. The first-index eigenvalue is 1.83. Table 4.14b presents the eigenvectors. The coefficient on education and health is large relative to access to resources. Table 4.15 presents the regression result of log of poverty on the composite index for gender. The coefficient is negative and significant. It reflects that as the gender indicators improve the proportion of people, who are below poverty line, would decrease.

Table 4.13

Correlation Results

Variable			
Log(IEr)	1.00		
Log(IEd)	-0.09	1.00	
Log(IHe)	-0.23	0.76	1.00

Table 4.14

Composite Component with Log(IHe), Log(IEd) & Log(IEr)

a. Principle Component (Eigenvalues)

	Eigenvalues
1st component	1.83
2nd component	0.94
3rd component	0.21

b. Principle Component (Eigenvectors)

Variable	*1st Component*
Log(IHe)	0.69
Log(IEd)	0.66
Log(IEr)	-0.26

Table 4.15

Regression Results

Explanatory Variables	
Log(Ca)	-0.030 (0.037)
F1	-0.280*** (0.078)
R-square	0.42
F (2,18)	6.6***
No. of observations	21

Thus improving health, education and LFPR of women has a significant effect on poverty reduction. While this is an overall picture, it is important to see the vulnerable groups among poor women, as policy must address such groups specifically. It was noted earlier that women and men face poverty in different ways. An increasing burden of poverty is thought to affect women more than men. Women suffer from biases in intra-household nutrition and resource allocation and thus have to bear the brunt of the reduced availability of resources. In addition, women are often not in positions to influence how earned income is spent. It has already been argued that several factors—stagnation in the agricultural sector and the shift to non-farm employment, rising rural poverty, marginalisation of female workers in manufacturing sector etc.—are leading to an increasing burden of poverty that is pushing many women and children into informal sectors of the economy and possibly increasing levels of female child labour.

The Feminine Face of Extreme Poverty in India

Female-Headed Households

Women's experience of poverty can be further exacerbated in the case of female-headed households (FHHs). Studies estimate that between 30-35 per cent of households are exclusively female-headed. The relationship between the number of FHHs and female poverty is hard to ascertain—one cannot say which has a causal effect on the other. Indeed a correlation cannot be assumed, and when and where there is a correlation, it depends on such factors as why the household is female-headed. What one can argue, however, is that in the case of economic hardship, women in FHHs have few options of support without an economically supportive family. The lack of fair property and inheritance laws, microcredit facilities, alimony payments for divorcees, or pension payments for widows makes the situation of these women even more precarious (Swarup *et al.,* 1994). More data on FHHs, their prevalence amongst different income, religious, and caste groups and explanations of their regional disparity is needed in order to understand the relationship between FHHs and poverty.

A recent study, however does show that FHHs were likely to be less poor than male-headed households (MHHs) especially in the rural areas. In urban India, FHHs were more likely to be poorer than MHHs. This differential increased with higher growth rates (Gangopadhyay and Wadhwa, 2003). However, another study for rural Orissa found that at different levels of poverty more FHHs rather than MHHs were likely to be poor. On the basis of primary data collected, the paper suggests that poverty and female headship were strongly linked in rural Orissa. For example, 12 per cent of people living in MHHs are poor as compared with 33 per cent of people living in FHHs. Thus, female headship can be a better targetting indicator for poverty alleviation in rural Orissa. The results further suggest that the use of resources are significantly different between the two types of households. Labour force participation data indicate that female heads are more likely to work in the market place than women who are spouses of male heads of household. The differences are large: on average 74 per cent *versus* 54 per cent. The comparison of household expenditures indicates that, FHHs spend relatively less on higher quality food items such as meat, vegetables, milk and other dairy products. However, there is some evidence that they spend less on personal consumption such as alcoholic beverages. Overall, the differences are pronounced between these households. Finally, the findings show that children in FHHs are disadvantaged both in terms of access to social services and actual welfare outcomes (Ganesh-Kumar *et al.*, 2004).

Widows in Modern India

Eight per cent of Indian women are widowed, compared to only 2 per cent of Indian men. This numerical disparity is attributed to a higher incidence of remarriage amongst the men. The plight of an estimated 33 million widows in India is one of the most neglected aspects of gender and development studies of India. Mortality rates have been estimated to be 86 per cent higher among elderly widows than married women of the same age. Chen and Drèze (1992) and Drèze and Sen (1995) highlight the plight of widows by identifying the following major concerns:

(a) Violation of the legal rights of widows, especially in terms of property and inheritance rights.

(b) Widows are expected to stay in the husband's village and face social isolation. They have limited freedom to remarry.

(c) Given the fact that most widows are elderly and that the labour market is already highly segmented, few employment opportunities exist for widows.

(d) Barred from employment, most widows additionally get little economic support from their families/communities. There is little evidence to show that joint families care for widows—most stay with unmarried children or as dependents on adult sons.

In rural India, the plight of widows highlights existing inequities in the ownership of land and the lack of any gender focus to the government's land reform initiatives. Though it is estimated that 20 per cent of rural households in India are *de facto* female-headed, few women own the title to their land, and even fewer actually exercise control over it. Given that women, lacking the option to seek non-farm employment (especially as widows), are even more dependent on agriculture than men, transferring ownership of actual assets to women needs to be made a priority for any future policy undertakings.

Gendered experiences of poverty also assert the fact that simply transferring income to the people living in poverty will not change biases in inter- and intra-household resource allocation. Intervention programmes must thus focus on the empowerment of women themselves and enable them to gain decision-making power.

From the above discussions, it is clear that socioeconomic biases are still prevalent in the Indian economy and society. Although efforts are being taken by the Government to cope with this issue, still it has been found that to a large extent women have limited means to seek empowerment, for seeking ways to with their deprivation. While gender inequalities have shown some sensitivity to higher growth rates, the economic status of women could improve significantly if education and specially vocational training were to be the focus of gender empowerment programmes. As the regressions above show, this is the single most important variable which can lead to positive income and poverty impacts.

Several gender-related issues have to be solved by education, thereby leading to better employment opportunities. Programmes linked with empowerment and employment of women are increasingly focussing on the quality of education which would pave the way for the upliftment of women, economically and socially, in the long run.

VII

Conclusions and Options

This chapter has attempted to distill the state of knowledge about the links between gender equality, on the one hand, and poverty reduction and economic growth on the other in India. The relationships are far from simple, and our knowledge is far from complete. At the macro level, there has been significant work done exploring the links between gender equality and economic growth. The simple scatter plots presented in this chapter hint at a positive relationship, as do (somewhat) more sophisticated panel regressions. Yet there is abundant reason to be skeptical of these results:

one should never take simple correlations very seriously, and panel regressions are plagued by a number of shortcomings especially the difficulty of establishing causality.

With regard to the macro-level links between gender equality and poverty reduction, the macro correlations are stronger than those for gender equality and growth and more robust to different measures of gender equality. Here, not surprisingly given the easier applicability of the concept of poverty at the micro (household) level, there is more micro research buttressing this link. Ample evidence suggests that greater gender equality in resources such as education, health and access to employment (economic resources) can reduce the likelihood of a household being poor.

While female labour force participation has increased with growth, this increase has been concentrated at higher education levels. This suggests that as economic opportunities increase, educated women are more likely to enter the work force. The policy variable that has emerged as crucially important from the above analysis is education. Education is seen to affect both health and access to economic resources.

For policy purposes two factors stand out in the case of India. One that high growth rates will lead to better gender indicators and reduce gender inequality. Hence, it is first of all crucially important to maintain high rates of economic growth. To accelerate the trickle-down effects of growth on poverty, education and particularly vocational education of women should be targetted by government policy.

References

Abu-Ghaida, Dina and Stephan Klasen (2004). "The Costs of Missing the Millennium Development Goal on Gender Equity", *World Development* 32: 1075-107.

Agnihotri, Indu and N. Neetha (2007). "Data on Indian Women", in *National Conference on All India Democratic Women's Association* (8th: Kolkata), Organised by All India Democratic Women's Association, November 1-4, CD-759.5a. pp.22-31.

Anker, R. (1998). *Gender and Jobs: Sex Segregation of Occupations in the World.* Geneva: ILO.

Barro, R. and J. Lee (1995). "International Measures of Educational Achievement", *American Economic Review* 86: 218-23.

Barro, R. and X. Sala-i-Martin (1995). *Economic Growth*. New York: McGraw-Hill.

Barro, Robert J. (1991). "Economic Growth in a Cross Section Countries", *Quarterly Journal of Economics* 106: 407-43.

Barro, Robert J. and J.W. Lee (1994). "Sources of Economic Growth", *Carnegie-Rochester Conference Series on Public Policy* 40: 1-46.

Behrman, Jere R., Andrew D. Foster, Mark R. Rosenzweig and Prem Vashishtha (1999). "Female Schooling, Home Teaching, and Economic Growth", *Journal of Political Economy*, August.

Bergmann, Barbara (1974). "Occupational Segregation, Wages and Profits When Employers Discriminate by Race or Sex", *Eastern Economic Journal* 1(2): 103-10.

Berik, Gunseli, Yana van der Meulen Rodgers and Joseph E. Zveglich Jr. (2004). "Does Trade Promote Gender Wage Equity?", in William Milberg (ed.), *Labor and the Globalization of Production: Causes and Consequences of Industrial Upgrading.* London: Palgrave Macmillan.

Berik, Günseli, Yana van der Meulen Rodgers and Joseph E. Zveglich Jr. (2004). "International Trade and Gender Wage Discrimination: Evidence from East Asia", Review of Development Economics 8(2), May.

Besley, T., R. Burgess and B. Esteve Volart (2004). *Operationalising Pro-Poor Growth: India Case Study.* Mimeographed, DFID.

Birdsall, Nancy, David Ross and Richard Sabot (1995). "Inequality and Growth Reconsidered: Lessons from East Asia", *The World Bank Economic Review* 9(3): 477-508.

Braunstein, Elissa (2007). "The Efficiency of Gender Equity in Economic Growth: Neoclassical and Feminist Approaches", *GEM-IWG Working Paper* 07-4. March. The International Working Group on Gender, Macroeconomics, and International Economics Working Paper Series GEM-IWG. *www.genderandmacro.org*

Central Statistical Organisation (2004). *Annual Report.* Delhi.

Chen, M., and J.P. Drèze. (1992). "Widows and Well-Being in Rural North India", *Working Paper #40*. Development Research Program, London School of Economics.

Deshpande, S. and L.K. Deshpande (1992). "New Economic Policy and Female Employment", *Economic and Political Weekly* 27 (14).

Dollar, D., R. Fisman and R. Gatti (2001). "Are Women Really the "Fairer" Sex? Corruption and Women in Government", *Journal of Economic Behavior & Organization* 46: 423-29.

Dollar, David and Roberta Gatti (1999). "Gender Inequality, Income and Growth: Are Good Times Good for Women?", *Policy Research Report on Gender and Development Working Paper Series* No. 1. Washington, D.C.: World Bank.

Drèze, J. and A. Sen (1995). *India Economic Development and Social Opportunity.* New Delhi: Oxford University Press.

Foster, Andrew D. and Mark R. Rosenzweig (1996). "Technical Change and Human Capital Returns and Investments: Evidence from the Green Revolution", *American Economic Review,* September.

Galor, Oded and David N. Weil (1996). "The Gender Gap, Fertility, and Growth", *American Economic Review* 86(3): 374-87.

Ganesh-Kumar, A., Srijit Mishra and Manoj Panda (2004). "Employment Guarantee for Rural India", *Economic and Political Weekly*: 5359-61. 18 December.

Gangopadhyay, S. and W. Wadhwa (2003). *Are Indian Female Headed Households More Vulnerable to Poverty.* India Development Foundation.

John, M. with K. Lalita (1995). *Background Report on Gender Issues in India.* Bridge: Brighton. Available at: *http://www.ids.ac.uk/bridge/*

Kessel, Kitty Van. (2004). *Women's Empowerment and Health. http://www.carped.org/index.php/Reports-and-Studies/womens-empowerment-a-health.html*

King, E. and A. Hill (1995). *Women's Education in Development Countries.* Baltimore: Johns Hopkins Press.

Klasen, Stephan (1999). "Does Gender Inequality Reduce Growth and Development: Evidence from Cross Country Regressions", *Policy Research Support on Gender and Development, Working Paper Series* No. 7. The World Bank Development Research Group/Poverty Reduction and Economic Management Network

————. (2002). "Low Schooling for Girls, Slower Growth for all? Cross-country Evidence on the Effect of Gender Inequality in Education on Economic Development", *World Bank Economic Review* 16: 345-73.

Lipton, Michael and Martin Ravallion (1995). "Poverty and Policy", in Jere Behrman and T.N. Srinivasan (eds.), *Handbook of Development Economics.* Volume 3. Amsterdam: North-Holland.

Murphy, Kevin M., Andrei Shleifer and Robert W. Vishny (2001). "The Allocation of Talent: Implications for Growth", *Quarterly Journal of Economics* 106: 503-30.

Murthi, Mamta, Anne-Catherine Guio and Jean Dreze (1995). "Mortality, Fertility, and Gender Bias in India: A District-Level Analysis", *Population and Development Review* 21(4): 745-82.

Olsen, W.K. and S. Mehta (2005). *The Right to Work and Differentiation in India.* Conference paper. Delhi: The Indian Society for Labour Economics.

Papola, T.S. (1999). "Scope for Economic Diversification", *News Letter.* Kathmandu, Nepal: ICIMOD.

Quisumbing, Agnes R. (2003). "What Have We Learned from Research on Intrahousehold Allocation?", in Agnes R. Quisumbing (ed.), *Household Decisions, Gender and Development: A Synthesis of Recent Research.* Washington, D.C.: International Food Policy Research Institute.

Quisumbing, Agnes R. and John A. Maluccio (2003). "Resources at Marriage and Intrahousehold Allocation: Evidence from Bangladesh, Ethiopia, Indonesia, and South Africa", *Oxford Bulletin of Economics and Statistics* 65(3): 283-327.

Schultz, T. Paul (2001). *Why Governments Should Investment More to Educate Girls*. Yale University. Manuscript.

Sen, A. (1999). *Development as Freedom*. New York: Knopf.

Sen, Survana and Ishita Mukherjee (2007). *The Changing Status of Women in India: The Challenges Ahead.* Accessed from SSRN, *http://papers.ssrn.com*

Seguino, Stephanie (1997a). "Gender Wage Inequality and Export-Led Growth in South Korea", *Journal of Development Studies* 34(2): 102-32.

————. (1997b). "Export-Led Growth and the Persistence of Gender Inequality in the Newly Industrialized Countries", in Janet Rives and Mahmood Yousefi (eds.), *Economic Dimensions of Gender Inequality: A Global Perspective.* Westport, CT: Praeger. pp.11-33.

————. (2000a). "Gender Inequality and Economic Growth: A Cross-country Analysis", *World Development* 28: 1211-30.

————. (2000b). "Accounting for Gender in Asian Economic Growth", *Feminist Economics* 6(3): 27-58.

————. (2000c). "The Effects of Structural Change and Economic Liberalization on Gender Wage Differentials in South Korea and Taiwan", *Cambridge Journal of Economics* 24(4): 437-59.

————. (2006). *Gender, Distribution, and Balance of Payments Constrained Growth in Developing Countries.* University of Vermont.

Seguino, Stephanie and Maria Sagrario Floro (2003). "Does Gender have any Effect on Aggregate Saving? An Empirical Analysis", *International Review of Applied Economics* 17(2): 147-66.

Standing, Guy (1989). "Global Feminization through Flexible Labor", *World Development* 17(7): 1077-96.

————. (1999). "Global Feminization through Flexible Labor: A Theme Revisited", *World Development* 27(3): 583-602.

Stotsky, Janet G. (1997). "Gender Bias in Tax Systems", *Tax Notes International*: 1913-23. June 9.

Summers, L. (1994). *Investing in All the People*. Washington DC: The World Bank.

Swamy, A., S. Knack, Y. Lee and O. Azfar (2001). "Gender and Corruption", *Journal of Development Economics* 64: 25-55.

Swarup, H.L., Niroj Sinha, Chitra Ghosh and Pam Rajput (1994). "Women's Political Engagement in India", in B. Nelson and N. Chowdhury (eds.), *Women and Politics Worldwide.* London: Yale University Press.

Tzannatos, Zafiris (1999). "Women and Labor Markets Changes in the Global Economy: Growth Helps, Inequalities Hurt and Public Policy Matters", *World Development* 27: 551-69.

World Bank (2001). *Engendering Development through Gender Equality in Rights, Resources and Voice.* Washington D. C.: World Bank.

————. (2005). *World Development Report 2006: Equity and Development.* Washington, D.C. and New York: World Bank and Oxford University Press.

Part III

5 Can Philanthropy Accelerate Trickle Down

Introduction

India has long established traditions of philanthropy. Prominent kings, merchants and agrarian families have been important philanthropists in Indian history. There are estimated to be hundreds of thousands of philanthropic non-profit and civil society organisations in India. Charities Aid Foundation (India) under the auspices of the Planning Commission of India has validated 1,350 voluntary organisations nationwide and believe that there may be up to 3 million more (Ambrose, 2005). Estimates of total philanthropic contributions range from roughly 0.6 per cent of GDP to 1 per cent of GDP (Sheth, 2010). However, systematic data on philanthropy has not been collected though there are point sources obtained from surveys conducted by various sources such as Sampradan and the Planning Commission. The terminology used by the surveys differ and hence these point sources are not strictly comparable. The Planning Commission uses the term voluntary sector which could be said to comprise not just philanthropists, but non-profit organisations (NPOs), non-governmental organisations (NGOs) and community-based organisations (CBOs). Others use terms such as the third sector referring to the sector which is neither government nor private.

The liberalisation of the Indian economy and its aggressive new focus on manufacturing, services and technology has resulted in changes in terms of philanthropic funding and priorities by India's wealthy individuals and corporations, many of whom rank high amongst the globally wealthy. There are over 115,000 high net worth individuals in India today. Since 2000, this elite group has grown an average of 11 per cent annually. Between 2006 and 2007, the number of wealthy individuals in India surged by 23 per cent—possibly the highest growth rate in the world (Sheth, 2010). The collective wealth of these 100 richest Indians, which includes 52 billionaires as against 27 a year ago, is 276 billion dollars which corresponds to almost one-fourth of the country's GDP (Sheth, 2010). India's youthful and cosmopolitan entrepreneurs and venture capitalists are investing and partnering in social change and community development, rather than merely donating funds for short-term charitable relief. As with some other emerging economies, India's new technologies and resources are being used to improve and transform the daily lives of its poor and underprivileged communities.

Government policy on philanthropy or the voluntary sector as it is called by the Planning Commission recognises that it has contributed significantly to finding innovative solutions to poverty, deprivation, discrimination and exclusion, through means such as awareness raising, social mobilisation, service delivery, training, research and advocacy. It is also felt that this sector acting as intermediaries may effectively link the common man to the government. Government policy recognises the important role that the voluntary sector has to play in various areas and affirms the growing need for collaboration with philanthropists, as well as by the private sector, at the local, provincial and national levels.

Yet, philanthropy has not systematically addressed the country's most fundamental development problems. Philanthropy has provided charitable relief to those in need, but addressed the underlying causes of poverty only to a limited extent. While many individuals, families and corporations give generously, many more need to become involved if philanthropy is to make a significant dent in India's poverty levels. The prevailing mindset—that government should be the sole provider of social services needs to be changed. Philanthropy needs to increase in scale and the third sector needs to be better organised.

This chapter is an overview of philanthropy in India, including its early traditions, more modern influences and the current landscape of social sector investment by the voluntary sector. Throughout, it seeks to examine whether and how philanthropy trickles down to the poor thereby supporting or accelerating a process of equitable social and economic development in India. The last section of the chapter offers some recommendations and considerations for how to strengthen the nexus between philanthropy and equitable development.

I

History of Philanthropic Traditions in India

Philanthropic activity in India has a very long tradition and history. *Rig Veda,* an ancient Indian text makes ample references to charity as a duty and responsibility of the citizen and the benefits that one earns through an act of charity (*Rig Veda*, 10 *Mandala*, *Suktha*: 6-47, 8-4-20, 13-2, 46-31, 10-17-1 to 7).[1] The concept of *daana* (giving) was essentially the root of the voluntary/ non-profit sector. Charity inspired by religious beliefs and values continued to remain popular and fairly widespread in pre-colonial India.

Historically, the concept of giving for charity was well established with individuals offering alms for ascetics and the *brahmins* (Hindu priests). This practice arose from the belief that charitable activities lead to 'Nirvana' or ensures that you are not born again. Religious obligations encompass a duty to help the needy) (Dadrawala, 2001). All the major religious scriptures advocate and encourage charitable giving. The cultural roots of philanthropy in India are ancient and deep, and have given life to long established traditions of philanthropic engagement, social service and voluntary work. Religion has always played a major role in philanthropic giving in India and continues to be a profound influence on giving. However various other factors—social, economic and political—have affected and accelerated the emergence of civil society in modern India and shaped the role and practice of philanthropy today.

The worthiness of social service was and is deeply engraved in India's social consciousness; individual and unorganised giving have existed in various forms from time immemorial. The concepts of *daana* (giving) and *dakshina* (alms) in Hinduism, *bhiksha* (alms) in Budhhism and *zakaat* (prescribed offerings) and *sadaqaat* (voluntary offerings) in Islam have been a part of Indian culture for many centuries (Dadrawala, 2001). With the advent of Buddhism, through the order of monks (*sanghas*) and later with Christianity, philanthropy became an organised institutional concern. The gospel of service was preached through the establishment of schools, hospitals, leper homes and homes for the aged and the needy.

1. Swami Dayanand Saraswati's *Introduction to the Vedas*, Part 5, *http:// www.vjsingh.info/int5.html*

Some form of philanthropy was ingrained in the joint family system of hindu societies. As in several other societies, the relationships between individuals and groups were established to ensure that the care of the underprivileged and vulnerable members of family was entrusted to the more able family members. Society was built into social institutions and structures which upheld the values of a joint family, i.e., families where several nuclear units coexisted. Social and often family institutions provided mechanisms to help meet the needs of the old, the sick and the handicapped, as well as other helpless sections of the community. For example, the joint family, caste members and community councils often took responsibility for individuals who needed support.

The contemporary non-government, non-profit and voluntary sector in India owes its origin to Gandhian principles, philosophy and practices. Inspired by Gandhi, committed and charismatic individuals such as Vinobha Bhave established village-oriented community organisations throughout the country (Dalal, 2006). These organisers guided, motivated and assisted the community in addressing their economic and social needs and most importantly, in giving a voice to the unheard. Many of these community groups emerged as organised, informal representatives of the people who could challenge and confront the establishment (Desai, 1999). Subsequently, many developed into powerful and effective organisations, capable of delivering social services in an efficient and cost-effective manner.

Institutionalised philanthropy also gained momentum after the industrialisation processes of the late 19th century. Gradually, corporate gains began to trickle towards welfare and development. Several business houses that emerged during rapid industrialisation laid the foundation for a philanthropic tradition that have been followed and strengthened by succeeding generations. Notable among the pioneering efforts were the industrial houses of Tata, Birla, Godrej, Mahindra, Shri Ram group and Bajaj. Several large landowners built schools and hospitals in their neighbourhoods. Noted social reformers such as Raja Ram Mohun Roy and the families of Rabindranath Tagore worked for social causes and donated a large share of their wealth too. The tradition of philanthropy became intricately woven with the tradition for social reform in the 19th century (Sharma, 2001).

Development of the voluntary sector during the colonial phase, which began during the late 18th century, is closely linked with the social reform and freedom movement. At the same time, the British colonial administration also supported some religious and private organisations engaged in providing social services (Asia Pacific Philanthropy Consortium, 2001). The activities in the voluntary sector during the late 19th century and early 20th century were coloured by nationalist sentiments. Institutionalised philanthropy also received an impetus with the industrial revolution in India, as corporate wealth began to be channelled towards welfare and development work. It is possible that at this point of time corporate welfare may have been an alternative to organised labour and trade union movements which characterised post- independence India. Volunteerism also found a new meaning in the wake of India's struggle for freedom, with Mahatma Gandhi giving India a vision of *swaraj* (self-rule), *ahimsa* (non-violence) and *seva* (service) (Ibid).

The first 20 years of independence (often referred to as India's era of nation building) thus saw the three sectors—the state, the market and the voluntary sector—join together to tackle the emerging tasks of nation building, focussing on extension work in such areas as agriculture, health, community development (Charities Aid Foundation (CAF), 2003). This, in fact, heralded the beginning of a much broader civil society participation in nation-building.

Today, there are a wide range of actors and activities on India's philanthropic landscape. Yet philanthropy—as traditionally practiced by private trusts, family foundations, corporate donors and intermediary agencies—has had only a limited impact on bridging the equity divide. While a variety of foundations and trusts have made strategic and systematic investments in the social space, the inputs and supplements provided by the private sector have been minimal. However, the world is changing rapidly, and so, too, is the situation in India.

Many trusts established by corporate leaders are increasingly strategic in addressing societal challenges. The information technology revolution has had a significant and positive impact on philanthropic investment trends. Diaspora philanthropy is significant, and has made particularly strategic investments in education and the digital divide. There is the beginning of a philanthropic infrastructure to support and nurture philanthropic engagement. Increasingly, philanthropic and social investment capital in India targets such areas as education, health care, population, gender issues, natural resource management, energy and enterprise development; many initiatives are focussed on rural India.

Organised philanthropy is part of the larger voluntary/non-profit sector that includes public charitable trusts, societies and NPOs defined as 'promoting commerce, art, science, religion, charity or any other useful object.' The nature and character of NPOs or voluntary organisations (VOs) have undergone a noticeable change in the last decade and a half. A large number of organised, development-oriented, charitable and voluntary institutions have emerged that are led by professionals, and employ full-time, paid staff, who are trained to meet the needs and demands of the sector more effectively. These voluntary organisations are not run for profit, whether personal or organisational. They may organise and implement profit-earning programmes but the earnings are not disbursed to the members.

In the past 15 years, i.e., since liberalisation India has seen a surge in volunteerism from both within and outside India. Several organisations in India accept international volunteers for short-term assignments. Employees of corporate houses are increasingly volunteering their time and skills towards strengthening programme and institutional capacities of organisations.

In a societal context, voluntary organisations constitute the 'third sector', the first sector being the government and the second sector being the market or private business. The 'third sector' is also known as the 'independent sector', which emphasises the important role VOs play as an independent force outside the realm of government and private business (though, in financial terms, this sector depends heavily on both the government and private business).

Development organisations today encompass a wide-ranging field of activities, including designing and implementing innovative programmes in various sectors of development. Their activities also include work in various areas of research, reporting, documentation and training to support grassroot initiatives, and also involve highly technical and technological outputs.

II

An Analysis of Philanthropic Point Sources of Information

NGOs in modern India have traditions that can be traced back to the ideologies of the religious and reformist institutions such as the Ramakrishna Mission, Mahatma Gandhi, Sarvodaya, Jesuit Missions and even Marxism (Copal Partners, 2006). Most non-profit charities in India are included within the NGO or the voluntary sector. However, the voluntary sector need not only consist of philanthropic activity, it would also include member-driven activities which is paid for by the membership of the society.

What is the key factor that distinguishes an ordinary organisation from a 'voluntary organisation' in India? Largely, it is the significant input that volunteers give to the management and operation of the organisation. It is this factor that gives voluntary organisations the other commonly used name 'non-profit' or 'not-for-profit' organisation. 'Non-profit' or 'not-for-profit' emphasises the fact that the organisation does not exist primarily to generate profits for its owners, managers or members.

There are certain common factors (Asia Pacific Philanthropy Consortium, 2001) that characterise VOs in India, which are typically:

- Formal: institutionalised, to some extent, registered, demonstrating a definite programme or aims and objects, as well as rules and regulations of governance.
- Private: institutionally separate from the government.
- Self-governing: not controlled by the government or any other outside entity.
- Not-for-profit: non-profit distributing.
- Voluntary: involving some meaningful degree of voluntary participation, either in the actual conduct of the organisation's activities or in the management of its affairs.
- Non-religious: not primarily involved in the promotion of religious worship or religious education.

- Non-political: not primarily involved in promoting candidates for elected office, etc.

Key Facts and Figures

The non-profit sector in India is quite widespread with huge scale in terms of employment, revenue and types of activities. While there is no official, ongoing effort to maintain statistics on India's non-profit sector, several independent NGOs have conducted surveys at different points of time to estimate the size of this sector. Estimates range from as little as US $2 billion to over tens of billions of US$s (Sheth, 2010).

While there is no definitive study on the size of the sector, there are several estimates and projections. It is estimated that there are between 2-3 million charities or NGOs in operation in India, but according to Arpan Sheth, partner at Bain & Co., only 500 of them operate on a scale large enough to be effective (income over US $100,000) (Sheth, 2010). The factors that have contributed to this astronomical increase in the number of NPOs in the last few decades include weakening government delivery systems, widespread poverty and deprivation and increasing inequity, rising awareness and social concern about underdevelopment and inequity, and the influx of increased funding—both indigeneous and foreign—for development purposes.

The Indian government may be the largest source of funding for charities in India, and estimate their contribution at about $3 billion (Rs 131 billion) (Copal Partners, 2006). This is mostly directed to foundations and other NGOs for delivery of social services. Funding from the Indian diaspora comprises just over $1.2 billion (Rs 55 billion), the second largest source, and contributions from Indian corporations and individuals amount to around $447 million (Rs 20 billion) (Copal Partners, 2006). Most individual giving is directed towards religious institutions (temples, *gurudwaras* etc.), which are not technically qualified as charity. Individual and corporate giving tends to be higher during times of national calamities.

The Society for Participatory Research in Asia (PRIA) (2000; 2001; 2002), a civil society organisation focussed on development issues, conducted studies between 2000 and 2002 to examine the state of the philanthropy sector in India.

Key findings from this report reveal the existence of a substantial charity sector. The number of charities in India are estimated to be about 1.2 million (some estimates suggest it to be as high as 4 million). About 20,000 of them are fairly active in developmental work. The PRIA study had estimated the size at Rs 200 bn (US $ 4 bn) in 2002, of which foreign contribution was Rs 50.5 billion (approx. US $1 billion). US contributions comprise about Rs 14.9 billion (approx. US $ 270 million) while donations from the UK and Germany have come in at around Rs 6.7 billion each (approx. US $1.2 million).

Fifty-three per cent of charities operate in rural areas. Nearly half of these charities may be unregistered. About 500 charities have annual income above Rs 4.5 million (about US $100,000); most of others have annual income less than Rs 450,000 (about US $10,000).

A large percentage of charities operating in India are involved in social development, though many are associated with religious organisations. Religious organisations in India are also the largest recipients of donations and have floated affiliated organisations to undertake developmental activities (29%). Other popular activities in the voluntary sector are community/social service (22%), education (23%), promotion of sports & culture (19%) and health (7%). The formal voluntary sector in contemporary India is fairly vibrant.

The percentage of registered NPOs is highest in Maharashtra (74%) and lowest in Tamil Nadu (47%). An overwhelming majority of these registered NPOs are registered under Societies Registration Acts. Most of the unregistered NPOs are in rural areas. But even in urban Delhi, nearly 30 per cent of NPOs are not legally incorporated. Informal and organised characteristics of the NPOs are the most challenging realities today. Indian NPOs are essentially small: nearly three-fourth of all NPOs have only volunteers or at most 1 paid staff. Only one in 12 NPOs (8.5%) employs more then 10 paid staff.

Nearly 20 million persons work on a paid or volunteer basis in NPOs. This is 3.4 per cent of total adult population. As an illustration it can be observed that:

- In Delhi, one out of every eight adult persons is working in a NPO.
- In West Bengal, 90 per cent of all the persons working in NPOs are volunteers.
- Overall, volunteers are nearly five and a half times more than paid staff in NPOs nationwide.
- Nationwide, NPOs have nearly 27 lakh (2.7 million) full-time equivalent paid employees.

All these point to the vibrant and large NPO sector in India. With growth in the decade 2000-2010, preliminary findings of the Planning Commission suggest that this sector grew steadily.

How does it Compare Internationally?

Salamon *et al.* (2003) report that average for 22 countries (developed and Latin American) taken together shows the following patterns:

- Fifty-one per cent NPOs in India are self-generated *versus* 49 per cent internationally.
- Seventeen per cent NPOs use private funds *versus* 11 per cent internationally.
- Thirty-two per cent NPOs use government funds *versus* 40 per cent internationally.

Do Foreign Funds Matter for Indian NPOs?

The percentage of foreign funds in total receipts of NPOs during 1999-2000 was as follows:

- Nationwide, only 7.4 per cent of total receipts of NPOs are foreign funds.
- Foreign funds constitute nearly one-eighth of total receipts for Tamil Nadu and Delhi.
- Foreign funds as share of total receipts of NPOs in West Bengal are insignificant.

Who Gives Funds?

- Nationwide, more than 75 million households give for charitable causes—nearly two-fifth (40.7%) of all households in India.
- Two-thirds (68%) of all givers live in rural areas.
- Nearly two million households give in Delhi—more than four-fifth (80.7%) of all households in Delhi.
- The pattern for Meghalaya and West Bengal shows that more than two-thirds of all households are givers (72.5% in Meghalaya and 66.6% in West Bengal).
- Nearly a quarter of all households in Maharashtra give for charitable causes.
- In Tamil Nadu, the giver households account for one-tenth of all households.

Economic Profile of All Givers Presents an Interesting Picture

- Nationwide, two-fifth of all givers are poor households (annual income below Rs 25,000 (US $450).
- Only a small percentage of givers are from households whose annual income is above income tax paying level (Rs 1 lakh (US $2,000) per annum).
- A majority of givers in Delhi and West Bengal are from poor households; nearly a third of all givers in Maharashtra are from poor households.

And how much do Indians give to NPOs?

Average amounts per giver vary significantly across states and income categories:

- Poor in Delhi and Tamil Nadu (at Rs 553 and Rs 2,333 (between US $10 and US $40) per annum per household) give more than the middle income group (at Rs 470 (US $8) and Rs 1,039 (US $20) respectively).
- In West Bengal, Maharashtra and Meghalaya, middle income giver gives substantially more per annum than the poor household

(Rs 445 *versus* Rs 200 (US $8 *versus* US $5) in West Bengal, Rs 849 *versus* Rs 245 (US $15 *versus* US $6) in Maharashtra and Rs 758 *versus* Rs 272 (US $12 *versus* US $7) in Meghalaya).

- The richer households give substantially more in all the states—Delhi: Rs 1,402 (US $14); Meghalaya: Rs 3,770 (US $32); Tamil Nadu: Rs 7,515 (US $150); West Bengal: Rs 1,077 (US $20); Maharashtra: Rs 1,122 (US $22).
- Overall Indians give Rs 4,214 crore (US $1 billion) per year; nearly 55 per cent of these resources go to individuals, balance to organisations.

Fundraising by Philanthropies, NGOs and NPOs

The only source of reliable data on foreign inflows (not diasporic flows) to NGOs in India are those maintained by the Home Ministry under the statutory Foreign Contribution (Regulation) Act (FCRA). It is impossible from this data to separate the fraction of FCRA funds originating from the diaspora, from that emanating from other sources—namely international NGOs and non-diaspora foreign citizens.

Table 5.1

Trends of Foreign Contributions to Charities in India

Year	*Foreign Contribution ($million)*
1991-92	344
1992-93	445
1993-94	838
1994-95	587
1995-96	1359
1996-97	726
1997-98	526
1998-99	650
1999-2000	734
2000-01	1008
2001-02	1082
2002-03	1121
2003-04	1134
2004-05	1390
2005-06	1751
2006-07	2731

Source: FCRA, *Annual Report 2008*. Government of India, Ministry of Home Affairs.

Only about half the organisations registered, report their FCRA contributions. This implies that the actual inflows are a lot higher than that suggested by the data above. More than 80 per cent of the FCRA donations are from Christian organisations (Nayyar, 2010). This does not imply that other organisations are not sending money. In fact remittances in 2010 totalled US $55 billion. Though data on FCRA contributions to charities is not available for 2010, assuming a normal increase, it is unlikely to exceed US $4 billion in 2010. This implies that remittances by overseas diaspora which also includes philanthropy among other purposes was more than 12 times as much as FCRA contributions (Nayyar, 2010).

The Government of India is a major source of funding for NGOs. Their contribution was estimated at about $3 billion (Rs 131 billion) in 2006. Funding from overseas for charities comprised just over $1.2 billion (Rs 55 billion), the second largest source, and contributions from Indian corporations and individuals was around $447 million (Rs 20 billion) in 2006 (Copal Partners, 2006). While more recent figures are not available it is unlikely that the composition of funding for charities would have changed substantially.

The nature of issues addressed by the voluntary organisations and their scale and spread have changed considerably over the years; today they cover a wide spectrum of activities, ranging from basic social issues of education, health and family welfare to emerging areas like environment protection, gender equality, wildlife protection and human rights. Their chief strength lies in the fact that they work at the grassroot level and are directly involved with people in these areas.

The relationship between the NGO sector in India and the government is one of collaboration more than competition. The government has set up Central and state welfare boards to promote and fund the sector and to provide technical support. From the very first five-year plan, budget allocations have been made for providing assistance to the voluntary sector as policymakers have felt that this sector can deal with socioeconomic problems that the state is unable to address effectively. The government also grants tax relief to individuals and organisations that donate to the voluntary sector.

The growth of the Indian voluntary sector—post-Independence—has been significant, yet it remains somewhat vulnerable. Although there is limited data, it appears that one of its greatest vulnerabilities is its dependence on funds from government and international aid agencies. The preferences of potential donors and the patterns of philanthropic giving suggests that fundraisers and others who seek to encourage and promote more philanthropy need to build greater understanding of motivations, practices and barriers into their approaches and strategies.

International Foundations and Charities

Many international foundations and charities provide funding for development activities in India. While some, e.g., the Ford Foundation, are exclusively grant-making, the majority—including ActionAid, CARE, Christian Children Fund, Oxfam (UK), Plan International, Save the Children Fund, World Vision, the Aga Khan Foundation, the International Development Research Centre (IDRC) from Canada and Charities Aid Foundation also operate their own programmes. According to a study by CAF-India (2002), in 1997-98 'the total foreign funding was Rs 2,760 crore (US$0.7b) and is estimated to have touched Rs 4,000 crore (US$1b) in 1999.'

The primary assumption underlying these agencies is that it is right to provide financial assistance from financially more wealthy societies to assist with disaster situations and poverty in India. In some situations the motivation has been 'charitable' (for example Oxfam supporting relief during the Bihar famines of the mid-1950s); in other situations it has been 'political' (for example much of USAID assistance could be categorised as 'political'). A third category is to sponsor research into social development as is done by the IDRC.

This international aid, mostly in the form of grants to voluntary organisations and the governments, has in general not taken into account 'indigeneous' philanthropy—the assumption being that if the grant would not be provided, the work would not be done. This would have been at least partly true. A consequence of this type of aid, presumably not foreseen, is that it will gradually promote an ethos that the work and service to be done in India needed a grant from either the Indian government or from a foreign source. This ethos could be counterproductive.

Regranting Organisations

A fairly recent and promising development is the emergence of Indian donor agencies that both raise and distribute (or 'regrant') funds locally to address a specific issue or vulnerable population. While data is limited, such focussed efforts appear to be successful both in stimulating philanthropy as well as in addressing some of India's most critical development and equity challenges. Examples of regranting organisations include:

- HelpAge, registered in 1978 (with the support of 'Help the Aged' in the UK), began work as an Indian agency with an Indian board to promote care of the aged in India.[2] From the beginning efforts were made to raise resources within India; this has continued and expanded, with Indian resources being supplemented by resources from the international network of HelpAge members.
- In 1979, Child Rights and You (CRY) was formed by a small group in Mumbai to raise resources to support work with children.[3] It has grown into a nationally respected agency. Ninety per cent of its resources are raised from public and corporate donations within India; 10 per cent comes from the international non-resident Indian community mostly living in the USA.[4]

It is worth noting that several other international, national and local groups have begun to successfully mobilise Indian philanthropy to support their own work. Notable among these groups are Lok Kalyan Samiti in New Delhi (an eye care programme), which raises all its resources within India through direct mail; the Hindu Mission Hospital in Chennai, which has built a very diversified system of local resource mobilisation to enable its hospital to expand and provide rural health care; and World Vision which established a local affiliate with an Indian board and is actively raising resources from fundraising programmes to seek individual, corporate and foundation donations (Viswanath and Dadrawala, 2004).

---

2. *http://www.helpageindia.org/faq.php*
3. *http://www.scribd.com/doc/36010999/Child-Relief-and-You-Cry-India-A-Case-Study*
4. Ibid.

III

Models of Philanthropy in India

Giving in India is more often than not individual giving. Philanthropy is guided by the religious rules, regulations and demands of caste, clan, family and/or community. Giving is primarily directed towards religious organisations like temples and churches. However, giving to the needy has also occupied a significant place.

The propensity to give is a function of many factors. The greater the wealth the more is the philanthropic activity. However, the ability to give must be distinguished from the 'willingness to give' and the presence of distribution channels that are able to translate a 'latent willingness' to realised flows. The willingness to give is a function of the relationship between the philanthropist and his roots. Distribution channels affect both the volume and purposes of philanthropy. High transaction costs, low recipient transparency and limited coordination mechanisms and low social capital all adversely affect the volume of flows.

The principal distribution channels of philanthropy are:

1. informal family and personal networks or individual philanthropy,
2. religious charities,
3. diasporic philanthropy,
4. corporate philanthropy, and
5. international aid.

While the ethos of 'giving' in India is clearly 'personal', in contrast with the institutionalised charitable giving practiced in the West, the last decade in particular has witnessed a trend towards more organised charitable giving.

Individual Philanthropy

Surveys conducted on the reasons for philanthropy suggests that the most important reason was a feeling of compassion (68%). The second most important reason was that the giver feels good (48%). Religious beliefs and practices (46%) are the third most important reason. Twenty-nine per cent respondents donated because they believed in the cause of the organisation. The survey showed that for the donors reduction of taxes was the least important reason (Dadrawala, 2001).

Another study on individual giving in five southern cities (Dongre, 2003) has also recorded a high incidence of giving, both in terms of size and frequency, among particular income groups. The study showed that a sample of 200 individuals donated an amount of Rs 0.5 million in one year. The study indicates that in urban high salaried class giving has become more rationalised and people are willing to give to big foundations that can channel the funds more effectively rather than to governmental and religious institutions.

Besides giving in cash and kind, Indians contribute their time, labour and other capacities to charitable causes in society. For instance, members of the Sikh community—irrespective of their social and economic status, volunteer at *gurudwaras* (Sikh temples) sweeping the floor, washing the dishes, polishing shoes, cooking food for devotees—the activities generally considered menial otherwise. In India, philanthropy evolved more in terms of time and work, called 'shram'. People did not have much money but were willing to give their time and labour to good causes and for the benefit of society. It is perceived that most of this time was contributed to religious organisations like temples and churches (Dadrawala, 2001).

Voluntary organisations or the NPO sector in India clearly lack skills, methodology, and any strategic plan for tapping this very important source of funds. Many experts believe that, due to lack of transparency and accountability, voluntary organisations suffer from serious crises of credibility and this often deters individuals from contributing to welfare or developmental projects. Perhaps for these reasons, as well as lack of good communication, it has been observed that some of the poorest states in India like Bihar, Uttar Pradesh, Madhya Pradesh and Rajasthan receive much less from various sources (individual, corporate, local and foreign foundations) than Tamil Nadu, Karnataka and Kerala. This of course exacerbates existing inequality between states as philanthropic non-state provision of basic services also concentrates on states that are relatively better off.

In addition to this broad philanthropic participation, there are several highly prominent individual philanthropists in India. These individuals are important not just for their own significant philanthropic investments, but for the attention they bring to philanthropy and the role they set for others. Because many of these individuals come from the corporate sector and/or have established foundations or trusts, there activities are profiled in other sections. Nevertheless, it is certainly important to recognise them as individuals, including: Ratan Tata, N.R. Narayana Murthy, Azeem Premji, K.V. Kamath, Rahul Bajaj, Anand Mahindra, K.M. Birla, Anji Reddy, Dhirubhai Ambani, Rajan Nanda, Jamshyd Godrej, Vikram Lal, Brijmohan Lal, M.V. Subbiah and Arun and Manju Bharat Ram (Viswanath and Dadrawala, 2004).

While charities are supposed to spend most of their revenues on programme expenditure, administrative costs and other overheads can be significant, particularly fundraising costs, which can often comprise 10 per cent of revenues.

Table 5.2

Indicative Economic Model for Charities

Gross income	100 per cent
Fundraising cost	8 per cent-12 per cent
Programme expenditure	60 per cent-85 per cent
Administrative expenses	5 per cent-15 per cent
Depreciation	1 per cent-2 per cent
Surplus	0 per cent-15 per cent

Source: PRIA (2002).

Challenges for any charitable organisation include inefficient access to capital, underscored by high fundraising costs—22 per cent to 43 per cent in the US and around 25 per cent in the UK. Indian NGOs spend an average of 10 per cent to 12 per cent of revenue on fundraising. This is in contrast to the bloated fundraising models that a number of US and UK charities have incurred. Nevertheless, even this low outlay is beyond the reach of most charities.

However, wealthy individuals in India give much less in charity than their counterparts in the US or UK. In fact, the wealthiest, or 'upper class,' have the lowest level of giving at 1.6 per cent of household income. The high class, which is ranked one level below the 'upper class' on the income and education scale, donates 2.1 per cent to charity. Even the middle class gives 1.9 per cent of household income to philanthropy (Sheth, 2010).

Further individual charities follow specific philosophies and there is little pooling of funds. Individual and corporate donations make up only 10 per cent of charitable giving in India. By contrast three-fourths or 75 per cent of the funds in the US comes from individuals or corporations. The balance of the philanthropy comes from foreign organisations and the government. In fact, nearly 65 per cent is donated by India's Central and state governments with a focus on disaster relief (Sheth, 2010). Diasporic philanthropy and religious philanthropies are also important.

Religious Philanthropy

Funds available with religious trusts are generally earmarked for general maintenance of the associated place or places of religious worship, rituals, and other activities connected with the place of worship, most of which are ameliorative, e.g., programmes for feeding the poor, religious discourses, devotional songs and dance programmes, etc. With few exceptions (e.g., a handful of larger organisations) there are no reliable data or statistics on the use of religious funds for development activities. In some ways, religious philanthropy offers stiff competition to the evolution and growth of secular organised philanthropy. Substantial numbers of Indians in India and elsewhere are aware of the development activities of religious groups like the Swami Narayan Mandir, Sri Sathya Sai Central Trust, the Ramakrishna Mission and the Chinmaya Mission, and support the activities of these trusts generously (Viswanath and Dadrawala, 2004).

Some temple trusts in the city of Mumbai are spending their funds for educational purposes. Examples that immediately come to mind are the Shree Mahalaxmi Temple Charitable Trust, Mumbadevi Temple Trust and the Shree Siddhivinayak Ganapati Trust. In South India, Tirupati Devasthanam has also devoted some of its funds to secular activities such as establishing colleges and hospitals.

There is some evidence that Indians residing outside India provide significant support to religious philanthropic groups. For example, the Sri Sathya Sai Central Trust and the Ramakrishna Mission are preferred giving options for a number of non-resident Indians in the United States. In addition, a number of households (the female) in California's Silicon Valley give to the Ramakrishna Mission and the Chinmaya Mission, both renowned for their work in education. Religious sentiments are not of primary concern to these households where the average income per household is over US $200,000. The brand identity of the two organisations *vis-à-vis* development work influences and inspires women particularly to extend generous support. Members of the Indian diaspora in this region are articulate and informed and justify their giving by quoting examples of the exemplary development work undertaken by several Trust, e.g., Sri Sathya Sai Central Trust's water project in India, which is also one of the largest in Asia.

Indian Diasporic Philanthropy

It is estimated that between 1975-2000, $97 billion was received from the diaspora (Kapur, 2003). However, disaggregated data on contributions by non-resident Indians (NRIs) is not available. Diasporic inflows can come through both formal and informal channels. There are reasons to believe that a greater fraction of diasporic inflows—especially from NRIs—comes through informal channels and is therefore largely undocumented. The potential size of diasporic philanthropy is an increasing function of the income/wealth of a diaspora and the propensity to give. In turn the total wealth of a diaspora is an increasing function of the size of the diaspora, its income and its vintage. Diasporic philanthropy focusses on those issue areas where affinities, self-interest and distribution channels are strongest. However, such an approach may exacerbate inequities and even channel resources to causes with negative welfare consequences. Thus to the extent that the diaspora (in the US) comes from those geographical regions that are relatively richer (metropolitian cities, richer states like Kerala, Gujarat and Punjab), they are more likely to channel resources to these areas exacerbating inequities.

Natural disasters: Diasporic philanthropy increases markedly when a shock occurs in the country of origin. Although most shocks are natural disasters, a similar response is likely in the case of (man-made) economic shocks. The Orissa cyclone of 1998, and the Maharashtra and Gujarat earthquakes of 2002 are examples where the Indian diaspora's response was particularly salient (Kapur, 2003). The Report of High Level Committee on Indian Diaspora, Government of India (2001) observed that, 'Indian Diaspora has contributed in national crisis like the Kargil War, the cyclone in Orissa and the earthquakes in Maharashtra and Gujarat. It has donated generously to charities in India for reconstruction, disaster relief, rural development, literacy, child-care and women's empowerment.' The Indian community in Kuwait contributed US $1 million and 11 containers containing relief material towards the PM's Relief fund in the wake of the

Gujarat earthquake. Contributions are made either on an individual basis or through religious groups, student organisations or other Indian associations abroad. Donations and services have been received from all sections of the Indian diaspora, irrespective of income differentials (Ibid.).

Education: Another area where the diaspora is likely to be more forthcoming is education. The examples of IIT Kharagpur, the oldest of IITs is instructive. It has an alumni network of about 6,800 alumni. The IIT Foundation, a non-profit organisation registered in the US, was the first of similar organisations started in the case of individual IITs by its overseas alumni, specially in the US. Recently, it has launched Vision 2020, a $200 million initiative by 2020. As of 2001, the assets of the IIT (Kharagpur) Foundation was 2.4 million dollars. Similar counterpart organisations have been created in India, reflecting the dialectic between the diaspora and India (Kapur, 2003). To enhance research facilities at the IIT, two of its alumni donated US $6 million as a 'give back' during its golden jubilee celebrations (Shourie, 2003).

Religious philanthropy: In recent years, diasporic financial contributions to sectarian and religious groups has attracted attention. Sometimes this kind of philanthropy can be used to fuel extremist sentiments, e.g. funding for RSS or so called religious conversions to christainity in the tribal belt (Sidel, 2003). Some also believe that such funding could cause some security concerns (Vishwanath, 2003).

India is motivated strongly by religious beliefs. Many secular organisations lack the commitment that often underpins the work of religious organisations irrespective of the religion. The success of faith-based charities is a response to the failure of state to provide basic needs, especially education and health, to marginalised groups over the past 60 years or so. The philanthropic community has not found a way to deal with the negative externalities associated with religious philanthropy. The critical weakness is the protection offered to religious charities and places of worship from public scrutiny. Unless this changes the potential for abuse will remain and indeed perhaps grow.

Corporate Philanthropy

According to a study of Indian companies with stated and unstated policies on philanthropic activity, as many as 83 per cent of the surveyed companies saw themselves as major players in everything from rural community development to running projects for the disabled, to upgrading infrastructure facilities for the underprivileged (Dadrawala, 2001). The following are some of the reasons indicated by the survey companies for adopting a philanthropic policy (ActionAid India):

- Seventy per cent believe they have an obligation towards the society upon whose resources they are drawing;
- Fifty per cent felt concern for a specific group;
- Forty per cent felt concern for the underprivileged, and
- Twenty-three per cent cited benefits to the organisation.

Table 5.3

Diasporic Philanthropy and Religion

(in per cent)

	Buddhist	*Christian*	*Hindu*	*Muslim*	*Sikh*	*Other*
Andhra Pradesh	0	92	3	3	0	2
Arunachal Pradesh	14	29	57	0	0	0
Assam	0	67	0	33	0	0
Bihar	11	63	11	11	0	4
Chandigarh	0	63	25	0	13	0
Chhattisgarh	2	92	4	1	0	0
Dadra & Nagar Haveli	0	100	0	0	0	0
Delhi	3	74	10	6	1	6
Gujarat	0	69	13	10	0	8
Haryana	0	86	6	3	6	0
Himachal Pradesh	66	28	0	3	3	0
Jammu & Kashmir	29	57	7	7	0	0
Jharkhand	1	88	7	2	0	2
Karnataka	3	88	5	3	0	1
Kerala	0	92	1	6	0	0
Madhya Pradesh	0	92	4	2	0	0
Maharashtra	2	85	4	6	0	4
Manipur	0	94	3	2	0	1
Meghalaya	0	96	3	0	0	1
Mizoram	0	100	0	0	0	0
Nagaland	0	100	0	0	0	0
Orissa	3	78	17	0	0	2
Pondicherry	5	90	0	5	0	0
Punjab	0	90	1	0	6	3
Rajasthan	0	76	13	11	0	0
Tamil Nadu	0	83	4	2	0	11
Tripura	0	80	20	0	0	0
Uttar Pradesh	3	73	12	11	0	1
Uttarakhand	13	60	23	0	0	4
West Bengal	1	66	24	6	0	3
Others	4	93	1	2	0	1
Total	2	84	6	5	0.18	3

Source: Kapur (2003).

According to the same survey, the following are some of the 'benefits' perceived by the companies for being philanthropic:

- satisfaction in fulfilling social obligations (45%);
- improved credibility with the general public and the government (28%);
- builds confidence and pride in staff (19%), and
- tax benefits (9%).

Some of the factors influencing corporate giving in India include:

- Is the project for the community in which the industry operates?
- Is there scope for the company in projecting a 'caring-sharing' image about itself?
- Is there any tax benefit?
- Is it a long-term investment for the company? (e.g. economic growth of the community leading to increased consumerism or a better educated or technically skilled community leading to a better work force for the company.)
- Is there a possible link between the company's philosophy and goal and the project? (e.g., a pharmaceutical company supports a community health programme or a housing development corporation supporting a project for low cost housing.)

The survey by ActionAid in 1999 explored the philanthropic practices of 600 companies (ActionAid India, 2001). The survey found that 69 per cent were involved in social development activities of some kind. Of these, 17 per cent were working or had worked in partnerships with NGOs/ developmental agencies. Another 14 per cent seemed positive about working with the NGOs, while 31 per cent did not see any role for NGOs in their company's social development activities. The report also noted that most companies (78%) provided monetary contributions, while some also made 'in-kind' contributions such as the use of company facilities.

Experts in India also suggest that voluntary organisations should look beyond large corporate houses to small traders, merchants, entrepreneurs and professionals. Presently, corporate philanthropy in India is perceived to have become sluggish with a recession afflicted market. Corporate giving in India during the year 2000 was estimated to be Rs 200 crore (US $0.5 billion immediately after the recession). Some examples of important corporate philanthropy are listed below.

Tata Sons are considered leaders not only in their industrial endeavours but in philanthropic activity as well. The Tata Trusts control 65.8 per cent of the shares of Tata Sons, the holding company of the group. The Sir Dorabji Tata Trust has promoted six pioneering institutions of national importance. Four of these were established in Mumbai: the Tata Institute of Social Sciences (TISS), in 1936; the Tata Memorial Centre for Cancer Research and Treatment (TMC), in 1941; the Tata Institute of Fundamental Research (TIFR), in 1945, and the National Centre for the Performing Arts (NCPA), in 1966.[5]

The Bajaj Group has also been a leader in corporate philanthropy in India working in the areas of the education of women, abolition of child marriage, education, promotion of forestry and the popularisation of *khadi* and village industries. In 1942, The Jamnalal Bajaj Seva Trust was set up with an initial corpus of Rs 500,000 (US $10,000); representing Jamnalal Bajaj's entire share in the family wealth. After Jamnalal's death, his wife also surrendered her wealth for development and relief efforts.[6]

The Social Initiatives Group (SIG) of ICICI is a permanent and full-time group concentrating on development-related initiatives. Through the SIG, ICICI seeks to define and effectively fulfill its responsibilities as a corporate citizen. A particularly innovative ICICI-supported programme is the new GIVE Online, promoted by Give Foundation, a not-for-profit organisation whose mission is to help non-profit organisations raise funds and promote greater accountability and transparency in the non-profit sector in India. This is a charity portal that allows people to donate online, with a high degree of personalisation and assurance.[7] The ICICI Foundation established in early 2008 with a commitment of 1 per cent of

5. "Giving Journeys: Philanthropy & Indian Corporations", July 15, 2010. Asian Philanthropy Forum.mht. Mumbai: Centre for Advancement of Philanthropy. Philanthropy newsletter in December 2009.

6. Ibid.

7. *www.icici.com*

ICICI Bank's profit is today looking at education, health, financial inclusion, civil society and the environment.

The Citibank India Community Support Programme was launched in June 1997 to focus on microcredit organisations working to empower underprivileged urban women through income generation. The programme is based on the 'Banking on Enterprise' programme and builds on Citibank's extensive experience in supporting NGOs that serve the underprivileged across the world. The programme is based on the philosophy of self-reliance and volunteerism. Citibank works with five local NGOs to implement the programme. Citibank India's Microcredit Community Support Programme has been acknowledged as a 'unique example of public-private partnership.'[8]

New Indian Corporate Philanthropy

In 1996, two of India's flagship companies Infosys Technologies and Dr Reddy's Laboratories set up the Infosys Foundation and Dr Reddy's Foundation respectively. While the latter known as the 'Hyderabad' model works in the areas of livelihoods, the former known as the 'Bangalore' model focusses on education, health care, rural development, arts and culture.[9]

In 2001, Azim Premji founder of Wipro established the Azim Premji Foundation, a not-for-profit organisation that today reaches out to over 2.5 million children in more than 20,000 schools across India. The foundation works in partnership with government and other non-profit organisations with a similar vision. In 2006, Bharti Foundation committed Rs 200 crore (US $40 million) to a corpus to open 500 primary and 50 senior secondary-cum-vocational training schools for underprivileged children across rural India under its Satya Bharti School Programme.[10]

The aspiration of old and new companies to be active in the philanthropy space is on the rise. Profits, government and big business will find ways of optimising use of resources to build a more equitable world. However, they together with individual philanthropy only account for 10

---

8. *www.gcweb.citibank.com*
9. Giving Journeys, n.5.
10. Ibid.

per cent of total philanthropic expenditure in India. The bulk, i.e., 75 per cent of the expenditure by NGOs on social development is done by the Government of India (Sheth, 2010). In fact the 10 per cent spent by the private sector on philanthropy is a miniscule part of their wealth. The combined fortune of India's 100 richest is $276 billion, almost one-fourth the country's GDP in 2009 (Kamali, 2009).

Primary Education

The Premji Foundation has adopted 200 government-run schools in Karnataka and worked with the state government on improving primary education in those schools. The Foundation is planning to expand its primary education programming to Andhra Pradesh and other states in which Wipro has strong professional and commercial links, in collaboration with state education authorities.[11] The Foundation, since its inception in 2001, has been working in the area of elementary education with a view to bringing about systemic change in India's 1.3 million government-run schools. The Foundation also focusses on working in rural areas, where a majority of these schools exist. The programmes of the Foundation had already touched over 25,000 schools and over 2.5 million children. The key focus of the University which has been set up by the Foundation is to prepare a large number of committed education and development professionals, who can significantly contribute to meeting the needs of the country.

Other IT successes such as Narayana Murthy of Infosys have provided support for computer science faculty at leading Indian engineering colleges and universities to understand IT trends. The corporation has also contributed to primary and secondary education. A 'Catch-them-Young' programme 'identifies bright high school students for short-duration courses in programming fundamentals.' A 'Computers@Classrooms' programme provides used PCs and Microsoft-donated software to schools. And the 'Rural Reach' programme 'aims to increase awareness of computers among children in the semi-rural areas. Local language interfaces have been created using specialised software to make the learning experience more meaningful.'

---

11. "How Premji's Philantrophic Trust is Educating Children", February 1, 2011. *http://www.azimpremjifoundation.org/foundation-in-the-news.html*

Giving by the Indian diaspora community also frequently focusses on primary education. In late 1999, for example, the Indian co-founder of US technology firm Exodus Communications, B.V. Jagadeesh, committed $1 million towards improvements in primary education in Bangalore, and other Indians in the diaspora have reportedly provided substantial resources for primary education in Bangalore and other parts of India (Sidel, 2001).

Strengthening Higher Education

Philanthropic gifts to higher education in India by entrepreneurs based within and outside India have garnered significant attention in recent years. Infosys Technologies has made significant gifts to the Indian Institute of Information Technology (IIIT-Bangalore) to establish an information technology library, and to engineering colleges and universities to upgrade the skills of computer science faculty (Sidel, 2001). Diaspora and domestic entrepreneurs have made substantial donations to the new Indian School of Business (ISB) in Hyderabad.

Infrastructure and Civic Development in Bangalore

The new wealthy in Bangalore have also committed funds and time for infrastructure and civic development in Bangalore, not only in primary education but in other areas of social services as well. Infosys and its key executives have taken a leading role in the Bangalore Agenda Task Force, which brings together public and private actors to improve the infrastructure of Bangalore for citizens and businesses, a private-public partnership that epitomises one of the goals of the Indian new economy philanthropy. Nandan Nilekani and Infosys personnel (including Narayana Murthy) have devoted substantial time to the work of the Task Force (Sidel, 2011).

Infosys has donated corporate funds for Bangalore's improvements, including a 1997 donation of funds for an ambulance and motorcycles for police traffic management. Nilekani and Sudha Murthy, Director of the Infosys Foundation (spouse of Narayana Murthy), have each committed extensive personal funds to improving sanitation and other civic amenities in Bangalore as part of the public-private partnership through the Bangalore Task Force. Other wealthy individuals and companies have also contributed, both to the work of the Bangalore Agenda Task Force and for specific civic amenities in Bangalore.

Rural Development

The Naandi Foundation in Hyderabad set up by IT billionaires in Hyderabad provide support for lift irrigation projects, farmer management of lift irrigation projects, construction of village sanitary facilities, promotion of self-reliance in tribal areas of Visakhapatnam district, and promotion of science and environmental education in rural schools and communities. All are being implemented by well-known, Andhra-based NGOs (Sidel, 2011).

Philanthropic projects include an Andhra-based agricultural training centre, the KCK Raju Krishi Vigyana Kendra, a 'young farmers development programme' that seeks to train young resource people in improving agricultural productivity, several adopted villages, most near Nagarjuna plants, and a green belt near its primary fertiliser and chemical production facilities.

Beyond these, other organisations concerned with the development of philanthropy in Hyderabad and Andhra Pradesh include the Cooperative Development Foundation, which has convened regional and national discussions on the Societies Registration Acts that govern the formation and operation of many Indian non-profits organisations, and which seeks to support and promote the work of cooperatives.

Child Development

The Foundation for Human and Social Development of the Dr Reddy's group—currently the most active corporate philanthropy and social responsibility programme in Andhra Pradesh, and one of the most active in India—supports a used clothes bank for poor families, initiated in Hyderabad and planned for expansion to other major Indian cities, entrepreneurship training for rural women and street children (including a Livelihood Advancement Business School (LABS), a joint venture with the city of Hyderabad and UNICEF), symposia and other activities on the social issue of children at risk, a Child and Police Programme (CAP) intended to reduce child labour, livelihood promotion and microcredit, vocational training, and other activities.

The new Indian philanthropy seeks, at least in rhetorical terms, to be as socially innovative as its underlying corporate foundations have been innovative in the economic and technological arenas. But at least in its early years, this new philanthropy was finding it more difficult to locate and pursue approaches to social innovation than it did in its core businesses. And the pro-state, anti-intermediary and anti-institutional focus of the new Indian philanthropists is under pressure as philanthropic donations increase and ways need to be found to evaluate and track grant-making.

IV

Intermediary Philanthropy Organisations

To take care of some of these problems, intermediary organisations such as community foundations are under discussion in Ahmedabad, Bangalore, Delhi and elsewhere. Several other intermediary organisations to assist philanthropy especially corporate philanthropy has already been established. Some examples include:

The Centre for Advancement of Philanthropy (CAP) was established in October 1986 to provide professional assistance to philanthropic organisations in the area of charity laws, effective administration, financial management, taxation, investments and resource mobilisation. The Centre also undertakes research and critical appraisal of public policies affecting philanthropy and serves as a clearing-house for information in the field.

The Sampradaan Indian Centre for Philanthropy (SICP), a national non-profit organisation, founded in 1996, dedicated to promoting and strengthening philanthropy in India. The organisation works to foster co-operation between the state, the corporate sector and civil society organisations. It promotes networking among donors and NGOs. Its strategic programme areas include networking and advocacy, research and documentation, communications, and the promotion of educational material and campaigns to promote giving.

The National Foundation for India (NFI), established as a non-profit, philanthropic, fundraising and grant-making foundation, supports voluntary action for national development. The mission is one of stimulating and supporting the creative potential of people and community organisations to build a prosperous, progressive and united India. The Foundation aims to mobilise public opinion as well as resources for supporting development action, and lays great stress on networking between non-governmental social action groups, the media, the corporate sector and academic and research agencies, and on forging partnerships between organisations sharing similar concerns.

Charities Aid Foundation (CAF) India, which seeks to help create a sustainable voluntary sector through the development of resources that reflect a trusted relationship and shared vision between donors and NGOs. CAF India has pioneered corporate community initiatives with several companies and established payroll giving programmes through its offices in Delhi and Bangalore.

Partners in Change, a not-for-profit organisation that was initiated by ActionAid in 1995 with support from the Department for International Development of the British government. Partners in Change seeks to increase corporate involvement in addressing and remedying the challenges faced by poor and marginalised communities.

Several other groups, including the United Way of Mumbai, the Business and Community Foundation, New Delhi, and the Confederation of Indian Industry (CII)-Social Development and Community Affairs Council are prominent intermediaries working to promote and raise corporate-NGO interface.

V

Legal Provisions for Philanthropy

Charities can be formed in multiple ways and may be subject to various acts of legislation. Different legal provisions exist at the national and state level. Some states in India have enacted their own law to govern certain forms of charities. NPOs are not permitted to be involved in any 'political activity'. Bombay Public Trusts Act even puts 'political education' outside the scope of 'charitable purpose'. However, Section 20 of the Societies Registration Act allows registration of a society whose object may be 'diffusion of political education' (Agarwal and Dadrawala, 2002). India, being a secular state, does not allow distinction of caste, colour and creed in formation of a charity. However, it is possible to create a valid trust for the benefit of a particular section of the community. Although, this kind of trust would not enjoy income tax exemption.

As far as law is concerned, the various Trusts Acts, the Societies Registration Act and the Income Tax Act do not mention voluntary organisations specifically, but only refer to 110 organisations of 'Charitable Purpose'. A number of voluntary organisations, though forced to register under some of these rather archaic Acts, do not quite identify themselves as 'charitable' or their work as being for 'charitable purpose.' This is particularly the case with regard to modern development-oriented voluntary organisations.

Religious trusts established for the benefit of a particular religious community are also not exempt from income tax. Some of the important Acts governing the charity sector in India are discussed below:

- Public Trusts Acts: Some states (Maharashtra, Gujarat, Madhya Pradesh etc.) have formed their own Public Trusts Acts, which primarily control the Public Trusts created in these states. Some of these states have also created a Charity Commissioner, which operates at state level. The states which do not have their own legislation mostly rely on the Indian Trusts Act, 1882, which is a national act and primarily deals with private trusts.
- The Registration of Societies Act, 1860: It is a Central Act but modified versions operate at state level; 'Registrar of Societies' at state level deals with the registered organisation.
- The Companies Act, 1956: It is a Central Act and Section 25 deals with non-profit companies. 'Registrar of Companies' at state level deals with registered organisations under the Act.
- The Income Tax Act, 1961: A Central Act applicable uniformly to all states. It governs tax exempt status of charities as well as exemption available to donations to charities.
- The Foreign Contribution (Regulation) Act, 1975: Regulates receipt and spending of foreign funds. The Ministry of Home Affairs handles registration under this Act.

The government is increasingly looking at voluntary organisations to implement social development projects. But the rules and regulations governing the voluntary sector are not simplified enough to help them function effectively. In fact, there are many instances where, the government machinery goes to scuttle the good work done by voluntary organisations. In the words of Amartya Sen, the relationship between the two is one of 'cooperative conflict' (Kothari, 2002).

The tax exemption given to corporate organisations for charitable donations was curtailed by the Finance Act of 1983, which resulted in a decline in the corporate donations. As an alternate policy, the government established the National Fund for Rural Development to channel corporate funding for development activities. Although, the provisions of tax exemptions to the corporate bodies, which contributed money to this fund, existed, the fund did not pick up due to a lack of patronage by the corporate. Corporate houses preferred setting up their own trusts and voluntary organisations to donate to and undertake development activities.

Through co-option, the state offered increased funding, allowed more activity areas in which the voluntary organisations could be involved and reduced bureaucratic hurdles. Through this, the voluntary organisations would be dependent on the funding from the state, which would reduce the scope to criticise the state's policies and action. These policies did have their impact and increasing number of voluntary organisations moved away from 'activism' and adopted 'development orientation' with liberal funding both from government as well as international funding agencies, which in many cases routed their resources through the Government of India.

Charity is a matter of state control, so different states in India have different legislations (i.e., trusts or endowment Acts) to govern and regulate public charitable voluntary organisations, for example:

- Bombay Public Trusts Act in the state of Maharashtra regulates all public charitable trusts. The Act also operates in the state of Gujarat.
- Rajasthan has a Trusts Act of 1959, and Madhya Pradesh has its own (1951) Act.

- In certain southern states (e.g. Andhra Pradesh) there are Endowment Acts, whereas a number of southern, northern and northeastern states in India do not have Public Trusts Act at all.
- The capital of India, New Delhi, does not have Trusts Act to specifically cover the trusts formed for the public causes. In such states, NPOs are registered under the Societies Registration Act (passed by the concerned states) or Section 25 of the Companies Act, 1956 or under the Indian Trusts Act.

There is no single law catering to all NPOs in India. The multiplicity of legislations and the web of restrictive provisions in these laws is also an indication of state's desire to regulate the activities of NPOs.

VI

Is Trickle Down Accelerated through Philanthropy?

Using an econometric model to find out whether higher rates of growth is leading to higher philanthropy, it was found that the per capita incomes in 2003/04 across states were affected positively by an aggregation of the previous period's income and philanthropy. In other words, the higher the level of philanthropy the higher is the trickle down. Interestingly, the initial levels of per capita income has a much higher coefficient than philanthropy, but per capita philanthropy tends to be higher in the poorer states than in the richer states. This shows that even though a per cent point increase in per capita philanthropy increases the per capita SDP only by 0.27 of 1 per cent, poorer states with higher per capita philanthropy are likely to benefit more. If such states also start growing at higher rates than the impact of philanthropy would be better through better initial conditions.

The trickle down is also affected by the past per capita SDP which enters the equation with a negative sign. This implies that the positive trickle-down effects of philanthropy is further heightened in low-income states as the higher the previous period's income the lower is the income effect in future periods in this equation. Thus, the trickle-down effects of philanthropy are likely to be positive and higher in low-income states.

Table 5.4

Regression Results

		1999/2000	2000/01	2001/02	2002/03	2003/04	2004/05	2001/02	
States	*vol*	*psdp1*	*psdp2*	*psdp3*	*psdp4*	*psdp5*	*psdp6*	*pop*	*volp*
Andhra Pradesh	50045326	15049	16708	17932	19087	21372	23153	75727541	0.6608603
Bihar	85935956	4794	5161	5004	5606	5362	5772	82878796	1.036887
Gujarat	93227663	18831	17938	19713	22624	26672	28355	50596992	1.842553
Himachal Pradesh	10231630	18160	19925	21570	22902	25059	27485	6077248	1.683596
Karnataka	12714617	16345	17816	18091	19576	21238	23945	52733958	0.2411087
Kerala	38160365	18117	20107	20287	22776	24492	27048	52733958	0.7236393
Madhya Pradesh	20375056	11764	10777	12209	11500	13722	14069	60385118	0.3374185
Maharashtra	103959528	22978	21891	24044	26858	28848	32170	96752247	1.074492
Manipur	5987100	11070	11066	12683	12878	13732	14901	2388634	2.506495
Orrisa	17916268	9507	9245	9879	10164	12645	13601	36706920	0.4880897
Rajasthan	54914343	12765	12514	13621	12641	15738	16212	56473122	0.9723979
Tamil Nadu	17314134	18337	20346	20326	21740	23358	25965	62110839	0.2787619
Uttar Pradesh	40416724	8970	9162	9320	9963	10637	11477	166052859	0.2433967
West Bengal	44511966	14817	16146	17499	18494	20548	22497	80221171	0.5548656
Madurai	4656199								
Mizoram	13669175	14909	18491	19704	22207			891058	15.34039

Note: vol – Volume of philanthropy.

PSDP – Per capita state development product.

Source: Data obtained from *Indiastats.com*

Impact of Philanthropy on Health and Education Sectors in India

The responsibility of providing education in India mainly rests with the government. But the vastness of the universe to be covered has left huge space for non-profit sector to extend its support. All private, non-government educational institutions in India are run by NPOs, their role is more pronounced in primary, secondary, adult education and literacy programmes.

Nearly 20 per cent of the children between 8-14 years attend a private school, or a NPO. The percentage of children attending philanthropic schools are much higher, closer to 50 per cent in the northeast, Punjab, Haryana and Kerala. In other states it is closer to 15 per cent, and is the lowest in West Bengal at 3 per cent (ASER Report, 2007). The quality of education obtained in philanthropic schools is generally considered better than government schools.

The private sector plays a major role and accounts for about 80 per cent of all primary health care and 40 per cent of tertiary medical care. However, because of lack of a nationwide system of registering either practitioners or institutions providing health care in the private and voluntary sectors, it is difficult to accurately assess impact and extent of services.

Although many look to the government to improve infrastructure and implement health care, many more turn to provide free clinics and emergency medical treatment. There are believed to be over 7,000 non-profit initiatives providing health care services—from implementing Government programmes to providing basic health care or else specific care for diseases like leprosy and cancer. This excludes a host of rural-based voluntary organisations for whom conducting health awareness programmes is a common activity. The corporate sector has opened a number of charitable hospitals like the Escorts Heart Institute and Research Centre in New Delhi, Lupin Human Welfare and Research programme which runs an effective TB programme and Tata Memorial Hospital, a premier cancer hospital in Mumbai. Many religious institutions and *mutts* too have started hospitals, mostly incorporated as NPOs. Majority of these institutions have a dual policy of collecting high fees from those who could afford to do so and providing concessions or free medicines to the economically weaker groups.

Table 5.5

Results of Principle Component Analysis

PSDP01/02, PSDP02/03, Pvol; [PSDP: Percapita SDP; Pvol: percapita voluntary exp]				
Component	*Eigenvalue*	*Variables*	*Eigenvectors*	*Scoring Coefficient*
1	2.07	PSDP02/03	0.68	0.68
2	0.91	PSDP01/02	0.67	0.67
3	0.008	PVol	0.27	0.27

Component Z2= (0.68 * PSDP02/03) + (0.67 * PSDP01/02) +(0.27 * PVol)

PSDP99/00, PSDP00/01				
Component	*Eigenvalue*	*Variables*	*Eigenvectors*	*Scoring Coefficient*
1	1.96	PSDP00/01	0.70	0.70
2	0.03	PSDP99/00	0.70	0.70

Component Z1= (0.70 * PSDP00/01) + (0.70 * PSDP99/00)

Regression Log(PSDP03/04) on Log(Z2) Log(Z1)

Variables	
Log(Z2)	0.23** (0.73)
Log(Z1)	-0.08 (0.069)
R-square	0.91
Root MSE	0.04

VII

Conclusions and a Way Forward

As illustrated above, the charitable impulse is well established in India. A plethora of individuals, families and corporations are engaged in providing assistance and relief to those in need. And, as noted, there are indeed many excellent examples of philanthropists who seek to go beyond charity and use philanthropy to address the underlying causes that make charity necessary. But such efforts are limited. The concept and practice of strategic philanthropy aimed at true, equitable, social change—often referred to as 'social investing' is still new to India. During the course of this research, many leaders from both the corporate and non-profit sector were interviewed; most had not heard the term and had some difficulty interpreting its meaning.

The potential to promote more—and more strategic—social investment in India is tremendous. Perhaps more than most other countries, India is ready and fertile for the infusion of private funds into development initiatives. The Government of India, more than ever before, is ready for partnership and has, in fact, opened up key social sectors to third-sector investment. The challenge before the voluntary sector is to evolve mechanisms and strategies for domestic philanthropy and social investment. Communication and fundraising are two sides of a coin. How effectively the sector positions itself to attract private investment is the challenge for this century. There are fairly diverse philanthropic organisations that address social ills and are competent to champion philanthropic giving. These organisations will, however, need to look keenly at addressing issues of mistrust, accountability, transparency and governance—critical in hampering partnership and investments for development.

More specifically, the following obstacles and barriers need to be addressed in order to promote social investing.

Knowledge and Information Gap

The single largest deterrent to promoting social investing is the existing knowledge gap in philanthropy. Data on the sources, amounts, recipients and impact of philanthropy simply does not exist. By way of example, there is no study on the numbers, activities and contribution of the many family foundations and trusts in India. Without such information, the 'big philanthropists' will continue to get the spotlight, perhaps overlooking the extensive contributions of others. And without such knowledge, it is difficult to effectively make a case for the potential roles of private investing in the social space.

Philanthropic Infrastructure

With the exception of the Ford Foundation in India, Charities Aid Foundation, the Sir Ratan Tata Trust and Sir Dorabji Tata Trust, few organisations or funding agencies have invested in the promotion of philanthropy in India. Organisations promoted/funded by these agencies have a long way to go before they can become sustainable. Establishing a new institution or developing the capacity of an existing organisation to support philanthropy in ways similar to the Philanthropic Initiative in Boston or similar 'one stop institutions' is critical to the promotion of social investing.

In addition, there are too few (only a handful) of philanthropy professionals in India. While 'Moving Away From Aid' is the new mantra of the Indian Government, there are few ideas and resources to strengthen local resource mobilisation, skills and knowledge. A second tier of resource persons in philanthropy is virtually absent. For effective and sustainable social investment, an investment in building human resources/ philanthropy professionals is critical.

Legal and Regulatory Changes

Two major issues facing NPOs in India are archaic laws and excessive government control. Consistent efforts are needed to advocate for a more enabling and encouraging legal environment.

Current laws—e.g., the Societies Registration Act (1860) and the Public Trusts Act—date to 1860 and do not adequately cover organisations working in areas of developmental support and activities. Even the federal Income Tax Act grants tax exemptions only to organisations having a 'charitable purpose'. Developmental organisations today undertake wide-ranging activities, including research, documentation and training as well as the operation of development programmes. The Societies Registration Act, which was initially conceptualised in 1860 as a membership forum for professional and fraternal associations working in areas of literature, science, etc., is hardly a suitable choice for registering development-implementing agencies. As a result, organisations addressing the wide and varied issues facing modern society experience considerable frustration. There is a need for a separate legislation under which voluntary organisations working in the field of development can register themselves.

In India today, excessive government oversight and bureaucratic requirements also limits the effectiveness and efficiency of voluntary organisations. NPOs must register with and report to a number of government authorities. At the state level, the organisation has to register either with the Office of the Charity Commissioner, the Registrar of Societies, or the Registrar of Companies. At the federal level, they must register with the income tax authorities and if they receive foreign contributions, then they must also register with the Home Ministry. Separate returns must be filed annually with all three authorities.

While a friendlier Foreign Exchange Management Act (FEMA) has replaced the Foreign Exchange (Regulation) Act (FERA) applicable to commercial organisations, the Foreign Contribution (Regulation) Act or FC(R)A continues to be a 'thorn in the flesh' for most NPOs. There are endless delays in granting registration under the FC(R)A and organisations that are less than three years old are even refused registration. Even 'prior permission' to receive foreign funds is often denied without ascribing any reason.

In addition, while it is beyond the scope of this paper to review tax law in detail, it is worth noting that the tax deductions for philanthropic contributions are probably not sufficient to promote greater levels of philanthropy. For example, the tax rebate of 50 per cent is no longer attractive for corporate donors, especially since corporate taxes have been reduced.

India's economic and political liberalisation has opened doors for private participation in spheres hitherto the province of the state. Such participation has brought a sea change in areas such as education and health. However, to tap these sources effectively government support will be crucial.

It must also be recognised that so far philanthropy has been directed to better governed states which have a good climate for investment. This may have exacerbated inter-state inequalities. It is necessary to direct policies that would target the states which are relatively worse off such as Bihar and Orissa, Madhya Pradesh and possibly West Bengal. This would require organisations which can deliver philanthropic outcomes in a positive and transparent manner. Moreover, the use of philanthropic cover for terrorist and anti-social activities also needs to be curbed. It must also be noted that while corporate philanthropy, especially the new corporate philanthropy is delivering better public services, it may also lead to rent- seeking behaviour for commercial purposes by the corporate entities. Corporate philanthropy has extended the reach of new IT firms much beyond that of mere business. Besides while partnership with the government is desirable, it may reduce the capacity of the third sector to raise issues about faulty government practices and policies. On the other hand the third-sector risks becoming just another wing of the government.

Strategic Diasporic Philanthropy

A critical weakness in diasporic philanthropy (even the newer and better endowed organisations) is a lack of a strategic view on how best to leverage the philanthropy. The example of Bangalore where the new high-tech philanthropy has been involved in augmenting municipal services is a good example in this regard. It is one thing to give money for the health and education of slum children and quite another to give money to change the book-keeping practices of Bangalore Development Authority from single entry to double entry book-keeping and reforming property tax systems; and in this process sharply turning around the financial fortunes of Bangalore city. This strategic philanthropy has considerably increased the local government's overall resources, thus augmenting resources for public services consumed by the poor. It must be re-emphasised that the greater part of public services for the poor still comes directly or indirectly from the state. Consequently strategic investments by NGOs which reshape state policies, priorities and the quality and quantity of public expenditure can have more far-reaching effects than what an NGO might do directly with the same money.

However, one should be careful that attempts to strategically leverage diasporic philanthropy result in a broad increase in societal welfare and not an amplification of existing inequities. The strategic intervention should focus particularly on those areas which extend the horizons (or equivalently the discount rate). The intervention of Rockefeller and Ford Foundation in the 1950s and 1960s in agricultural research and scientific institution is a case in point. The returns were extremely high to Indian society as a whole. However, in recent years groups like the Ford Foundation have been more reluctant to support long-term institution building efforts specially in areas like scientific research (however, the Gates Foundation may be filling this gap). Funding for institution strengthening is also hard to come by. It is much easier to persuade to give funds to a specific village or for the education of a specific child. It is much harder to do so to strengthen an organisation so that it can hire better professionals who, in turn, can increase the long-term effectiveness of the organisation.

References

ActionAid India (2001). *Changes* (Special Issue by Partners in Change). October-December.

Agarwal, Sanjay and Noshir Dadrawala (2002). *Philanthropy and Law in India. http://uttardayee.freewebspace.com/Handbooks/PALISA/3. per cent20India.pdf*

AIESEC & Business and Community Foundation (1999). *Corporate Social Responsibility: Initiatives and Future Challenges.* Background note to national seminar. February. Delhi: AIESEC & Business and Community Foundation.

Ambrose, Natalie (2005). *An Overview of Global Philanthropy.* Council of Foundations. *http://www.cof.org/files/Documents/Family_Foundations/Family-and-Global-Philanthropy/Overview-of-Global-Philanthropy-COF.pdf*

ASER (2007). *Annual Status of Education Report.* Produced by Pratham. *http://www.pratham.org.uk*

Asia Pacific Philanthropy Consortium (2001). "Strengthening Philanthropy in the Asia Pacific: An Agenda for Action", *Background Paper: India.* September. *http://unpan1.un.org/intradoc/groups/public/documents/apcity/unpan005483.pdf*

Business & Community Foundation (2000). *Managing and Sustaining Partnerships for Sustainable Development.*

CAP (Center for the Advancement of Philanthropy) (1993). *Philanthropy: Newsletter of the Center for Advancement of Philanthropy.* No. 30.

———. (1994). *Philanthropy: Newsletter of the Center for Advancement of Philanthropy* 34, 35 & 39.

———. (1995). *Philanthropy: Newsletter of the Center for Advancement of Philanthropy* 43.

———. (1998). *Philanthropy: Newsletter of the Center for Advancement of Philanthropy.* 56.

———. (1999). *Philanthropy: Newsletter of the Center for Advancement of Philanthropy* 66, 67.

———. (2001). *Philanthropy: Newsletter of the Center for Advancement of Philanthropy* 74, 75, 76, 77, 78 & 79.

———. (2001a). *Laws Governing Voluntary Organisations in India.*

———. (2002). *Philanthropy: Newsletter of the Center for Advancement of Philanthropy* 80.

Charities Aid Foundation (CAF-India) (2000). *Dimensions of Voluntary Sector in India: CAF's Validated Database 2000.* New Delhi: CAF-India.

———. (2002). *CAF-India Annual Report. 2000-01.* March. New Delhi: CAF-India.

———. (2003). *Working with the Non-Profit Sector in India.* New Delhi: CAF-India.

Chaturvedi, T.N. (2008). *Voluntary Organizations and Development: Their Role and Functions.* Catalyst Resources in book edited by Noorjahan Bawa on non-governmental Organisation in Development: Theory and Practice, Kanishka Publications, India.

Cherian, Mathew (2002). *Dimensions of Voluntary Sector in India.* New Delhi: Charities Aid Foundation-India.

CII (Confederation of Indian Industry) (2001). *Corporate Social Responsibility in South Asia: Mapping the Ground.* September. New Delhi: Confederation of Indian Industry Conference.

———. (2001a) *Business as a Social Partner: A Compendium of Case Studies.* Volume III. December. New Delhi: Confederation of Indian Industry.

Copal Partners (2006). *India's Charity Sector: An Overview and Analytical Approach. http://www.oneworldtrust.org/csoproject/images/documents/INDA5.pdf*

Culshaw, Murray (1998) (Compiled). *Profile 300: Selected Voluntary Organizations in India.* Mumbai: Center for Advancement of Philanthropy.

———. (2002a). *Growth of Fundraising in India: A Presentation.* Agra: The Resource Alliance Conference. March.

———. (2002b). *International Support for Philanthropy in India: An Overview.* Catalyst Resources. March.

Dadrawala, Noshir (1996). *Management of Philanthropic Organizations.* Bombay: Center for Advancement of Philanthropy.

———. (2001). "Strengthening Philanthropy in the Asia Pacific: An Agenda for Action", *Background Paper: India.* Asia Pacific Philanthropy Consortium. Bali, Indonesia. September. *http://www.asiapacificphilanthropy. org/files/backgrounder_ india.pdf*

Dalal, Ajit K. (2006). "Psychosocial Interventions for Community Development", in G. Misra (ed.), *Psychology in India.* Volume 3. New Delhi: Pearson. *http://ipi.org.in/texts/ajit/dalal-psychosocial-interventions-for-community-development.pdf*

Das, Gurcharan (2002a). *The Elephant Paradigm: India Wrestles with Change.* New Delhi: Penguin India.

———. (2002b). *India Unabound.* New Delhi: Penguin India.

Dasgupta, Sugata (1967). "The Professional Social Work Approach", in Sugata Dasgupta (ed.). *Towards a Philosophy of Social Work in India.* New Delhi.

Desai, Chitra (1999). *Gandhi's Concept of Social Welfare. http://www.gandhi-manibhavan.org/activities/essay_socialwelfare.htm*

Dongre, Yashavantha (2003). "Individual Giving as Rational Choice: A Study of High Salaried Urban Population in India", Masayaki Deguchi (ed.), *The Role of Volunteering and the Non-Profit Sector in Building Communities.* Tokyo: Teansart. pp.135-146.

Donor Agency Network (1997). *Report of the National Consultation of Donor Agencies.* July. Bangalore: Donor Agency Network.

Drèze, Jean and Amartya Sen (1996). *India: Economic Development and Social Opportunity.* New Delhi: Oxford University Press.

———. (2002). *India: Development and Participation.* New Delhi: Oxford University Press.

Gangadharan, Nalini (2002). *Building an Enabling Environment for Local Resource Mobilisation: A Presentation.* Agra: The Resource Alliance Conference, March.

Geithner, Peter F., Lincoln C. Chen M.D. and Paula D. Johnson (eds.) (2004). *Diaspora Philanthropy and Equitable Development in China and India.* Harvard University Press. *http://www.globalenvision.org/library/5/819*

Gore, M.S. (1989). "Historical Background of Social Work in India", in Sumitra Gupta (ed.), *Social Welfare in India..*

Government of India (2002). *National Human Development Report 2001.* Planning Commission. New Delhi: Oxford University Press.

Grand Metropolitan PLC. (1994). *Grand Metropolitan: Community Involvement.* Grand Metropolitan PLC.

High Level Committee on Indian Diaspora (2001). *The Report of the High Level Committee on Indian Diaspora.* New Delhi: Indian Council of World Affairs.

India Health Report 2003. New Delhi: Oxford University Press

Johnson, Paula (2001). *Global Social Investing: A Preliminary Overview.* The Philanthropy Initiative.

Kamali, N. (2009). "India's 100 Richest", *http://www.forbes.com/2009/11/18/india-100-richest-india-billionaires-09-wealth-intro.html,* 18 November 2009.

Kapur, Devesh (2003). "Indian Diasporic Philanthropy: Some Observations", Paper commissioned by the Global Equity Initiative for the *Diaspora Philanthropy to China and India* workshop. May.

Kothari, U. (2002). "Feminist and Postcolonial Challenges to Development", in U. Kothari and M. Minogue (eds.), *Development Theory and Practice: Critical Perspectives.* Palgrave. pp.35–51.

Mahindra, Anand (2002). *Business Today, Collector's Edition.* Volume II.

Lala, R.M. (1981). *The Creation of Wealth.* Bombay: India Book House.

———. (1998). *The Heartbeat of a Trust.* New Delhi: Tata McGraw-Hill.

Norton, Michael (1996). *The Non-Profit Sector in India.* Kent: Charities Aid Foundation-International

Nayyar, Sanjeev (2010). *Do Foreign Contributions To India Impact National Security: FCRA Report 2007-08.* April 13. Email: esamskriti@suryaconsulting.net. *http:// www. esamskriti.com/essay-chapters/Do-foreign-contributions-to-India-impact-national-Security-FCRA-Report-2007~2008-1.aspx*

Norton, Michael and Murray Culshaw (2000). *Getting Started in Fundraising*. New Delhi: Sage Publications.

Oza, D.K. (1991). *Voluntary Action and Gandhian Approach.* New Delhi: National Book Trust.

Partners in Change (PIC)(2000). *The Business of Social Responsibility: The Why, What and How of Corporate Social Responsibility in India.* Harsh Shrivastava & Shankar Venkateswaran. Bangalore: Books for Change.

PRIA (2000). *Defining the Sector in India: Voluntary, Civil or Non-profit.* New Delhi: Society for Participatory Research in Asia.

———. (2001). *Historical Background of the Non-Profit Sector in India.* New Delhi: Society for Participatory Research in Asia.

———. (2002). *Invisible, Yet Widespread: The Non-Profit Sector in India.* New Delhi: Society for Participatory Research in Asia.

PWC and PIC (PricewaterhouseCoopers & Partners in Change) (1999). *Social Responsiveness Award: Documents for the Jury.* PricewaterhouseCoopers & Partners in Change.

SAFRG (South Asian Fund Raising Group) (1997). *Philanthropy in a Changing World: A Report.* 9th South Asian Fund Raising Workshop. September. Hyderabad.

———. (2000). *Resource Mobilization for Voluntary Organizations in India.* June. South Asian Fund Raising Group.

Salamon, Lester M. and Helmut K. Anheier (1997). *Defining the Non-Profit Sector: A Crossnational Analysis.* Manchester: Manchester University Press.

Salamon, Lester M., S. Wojciech Sokolowski and Regina List (2003). *Global Civil Society: An Overview.* Johns Hopkins Center for Civil Society Studies. p.22. *www.jhu.edu/~ccss.*

Sarwal, Tarun (2000). *Mapping Exercise for the National Local Resource Mobilization Network.* April.

Sen, Amartya (1999). *Resources, Values and Development.* New Delhi: Oxford University Press.

———. (2000). *Development as Freedom*. New Delhi: Oxford University Press.

Sharma, Sanjay (2001). *Famine, Philanthropy and the Colonial State: North India in the Early Nineteenth Century*. New Delhi: Oxford University Press.

Sheth, Arpan (2010). *An Overview of Philanthropy in India*. March 19. Bain and Company.

Shourie, Dharam (2003). "IIT gets $6 mn from its Alumni", *Press Trust of India*. Sunday, January 19. *http://www.expressindia.com/fullstory.php?newsid=18492*

Shiveswarkar, Shymala (2002). Paper presented at the preparatory conference for the *World Summit on Sustainable Development*. 29 May. Bali.

———. (2004). *Mapping for Diaspora Investment in the Social Development Sector in India*. New Delhi: CAF India.

SICP (Sampradaan-Indian Center for Philanthropy) (1997a). "Charity for Social Change and Development: Essays on Indian Philanthropy", *Occasional Paper* No. 1. April. New Delhi: Sampradaan-Indian Center for Philanthropy.

———. (1997b). "Women and Philanthropy in India: Essays on Indian Philanthropy", *Occasional Paper* No. 2. April. New Delhi: Sampradaan-Indian Center for Philanthropy.

———. (1998). Sir Ratan Tata Trust. (*India Foundations Series*). New Delhi: Sampradaan - Indian Center for Philanthropy.

———. (1999). K.K Birla Foundation. (India Foundations Series). New Delhi: Sampradaan - Indian Center for Philanthropy.

———. (2000a). *Bombay Community Public Trust. (India Foundations Series)*. New Delhi: Sampradaan-Indian Center for Philanthropy.

———. (2000b). *Our Community Our Responsibility: An Introduction to Community Foundations*. November. New Delhi: Sampradaan-Indian Center for Philanthropy.

———. (2000c). *Population Foundation of India (India Foundations Series)*. New Delhi: Sampradaan-Indian Center for Philanthropy.

———. (2000d). *Rashtriya Gramin Vikas Nidhi (India Foundations Series)*. New Delhi: Sampradaan-Indian Center for Philanthropy.

———. (2000e). "Religious Philanthropy and Organized Social Development Efforts in India", *Occasional Paper* No. 3. July. New Delhi: Sampradaan-Indian Center for Philanthropy.

———. (2001a). *Bhoruka Charitable Trust (India Foundations Series)*. New Delhi: Sampradaan-Indian Centre for Philanthropy.

———. (2001b). *Directory of Donor Organization*. 2nd edition. New Delhi: Sampradaan-Indian Center for Philanthropy.

———. (2001c). *Investing in Ourselves: Giving and Fund Raising in India*. New Delhi: Sampradaan-Indian Center for Philanthropy.

———. (2001d). *National Foundation for India (India Foundations Series)*. New Delhi: Sampradaan-Indian Center for Philanthropy.

———. (2002). *Sampradaan: Indian Center for Philanthropy Newsletter* 24. January-February.

Sidel, Mark (2001). *New Economy Philanthropy in the High Technology Communities of Bangalore and Hyderabad, India: Partnership with the State and the Ambiguous Search for Social Innovation*. University of Iowa College of Law and Obermann Center for Advanced Studies. *http://www.rockarch.org/publications/conferences/sidel.pdf*

———. (2003). *Diaspora Philanthropy to India: A Perspective from the United States*. Global Equity Initiative, Harvard University.

SmithKline Beecham (1998) *SmithKline Beecham and the World Health Organization to Collaborate in Seeking to Eliminate One of the World's Greatest Scourges: Lymphatic Filariasis (Elephantiasis).* 26 January. Press Release, London.

South Asian Fund Raising Group (2000). *A Guide to Resource Mobilisation for Voluntary Organisations in India.*

Social & Rural Research Institute (SRRI) (2000). *Report on Survey on Corporate Involvement in Social Development in India.* Indian Market Research Bureau. New Delhi: Partners in Change.

SRTT (Sir Ratan Tata Trust) (2001). *Sir Ratan Tata Trust: Annual Report 2000-01.* Mumbai: Sir Ratan Tata Trust.

Srivastava, H. and V. Shankar (2000). *The Business of Social Responsibility: Partners-in-Change.*

Sundar, Pushpa (2000). *Beyond Business: From Merchant Charity to Corporate Citizenship.* New Delhi: Tata McGraw-Hill.

Thapar, Romila (ed.) (2000). *India: Another Millennium?.* New Delhi: Viking.

Vaidyanathan, A. (2003). *India's Economic Reforms and Development.* New Delhi: Academic Foundation.

Viswanath, Priya (1999). *Scoping Study on Socially Responsible Business.* Department for International Development (DFID), UK.

———. (2002a). *From Managing Investments and Assets in Financial Markets to Social Fund Management: Providing Leadership to the New United Way of Mumbai.* Mumbai : Centre for Advancement of Philanthropy.

———. (2002b). "Sir Ratan Tata Trust: A Presentation", *Asia Confers2 CAFO: Giving with a Difference in Asia.* Hong Kong.

———. (2003). *Diaspora Indians: On the Philanthropic Fast-Track.* Mumbai: Centre for Advancement of Philanthropy.

Viswanath, Priya and Noshir Dadrawala (2004). *Philanthropy and Equity: The Case of India.* Global Equity Initiative, Harvard University. June. *http://www.wingsweb.org/download/Phil_India_Case.pdf*

Voluntary Action Network of India (2000). *Social Action, An Indian Panorama.*

World Bank (2000). *India: Reducing Poverty, Accelerating Development.* A World Bank Country Study. New Delhi: Oxford University Press.

Useful Websites

www.cozUcare.org

www.cozUcare.org/cap

www.indev.nic.in

www.indev.nic.in/icp

www.propoor.org

www.indianngos.com

http://planningcommission.nic.in/

www.accountaid.net

www.ngoresearch.org

www.bcfindia.org

www.cafonline.org/cafindia
www.mssf.org
www.nfidel.tripod.com
http://actionaidindia.org
www.cfar.umd.edu/~venue/NFI
www.pria.org/cgi-bin

6 Governance Issues and Public Policy in Trickle Down

Despite the global economic crisis, there are grounds for optimism with regard to growth momentum and stability over the medium-term in India. The regular increase in gross domestic savings and total factor productivity (TFP) over the last 20 years[1] indicate increasing level of potential output. There are discernible elements of self-sustaining and accelerating competitive strengths, as evident from increasing global presence of Indian corporates and interest of global companies (UNCTAD, 2009) in India. The savings and investments balance as well as the external sector reflect the strength and the resilience in the Indian economy. However, the persistent fiscal and trade deficits over the past two years have weakened the capacity of the Indian economy to bear risks. The microstructural reforms undertaken in the real economy are bearing fruits in some states resulting in double-digit annual growth in their domestic product. Other states are trying to follow the example of these growth pioneers.

There are certain 'not easily quantifiable strengths' which the Indian economy possesses. A vast pool of science and technology graduates and the millions of people who are familiar with the english language are sources of strength. The familiarity with multiple languages in India prepares its people to adapt better to multicultural situations, making it easier for them to fit into international systems smoothly. The political climate is characterised by, what may be termed as, political system stability. India will remain one of the youngest countries in the world in the next few decades. This 'demographic dividend' is seen as an inevitable advantage provided pre-

1. Reserve Bank of India, *Annual Report-2009-10. http://rbi.org.in/scripts/AnnualReportPublications.aspx*

requisites such as skill upgradation and sound governance to realise it are put in place. In terms of business environment, the impressive growth coupled with market orientation of the economy has been a bottom-up exercise with a very broad-based and growing entrepreneurial class, including in the informal sector. However persistent inflation, especially the rise in prices of food and other essentials, over the past two years has diminished the capacity of the Indian economy to trickle down growth.

For some, Indian economic progress signifies the beginnings of a major economic powerhouse in the world. But this optimism over the medium-term has to be tempered by inadequate basic nutrition, clean water, safer sanitation, minimal housing, personal security and individual dignity for millions in India. The prospects for growth and stability in India are great, but greater are the challenges in fulfilling the very basic objectives of public policy (Reddy, 2003).

If we take a bird's eye view of the Indian economy, the unemployment rate based on periodical surveys shows an increase both in the rural and urban areas over the last 15 years, with sharper increase in the rural areas, reflecting a slowdown in agriculture. However, this does not take into account the growth in employment and wages in the informal sector as was shown in Chapter 1. The result of this increase in informal employment has been a decrease in poverty. While there has been a significant reduction in the poverty ratio, the number of poor is still high. In addition, poverty lines have been moved up to over US $2 a day. This would show no improvement in poverty rates as there is no retrospective correction for poverty rates of the past years.[2] Even if we ignore the controversy surrounding the estimates on the poverty ratio, the high rate of inequality calculated at close to a Gini of nearly 0.5 recently is a worrying phenomena (Himanshu, 2010). Naturally, the overarching priority for public policy is creating employment and reducing poverty and does not address directly the question of inequality. As Michael Walton of the Kennedy School of Government argues, the real obstacles to growth in India will be structural inequalities that result from the inefficiency of institutions, particularly market and public institutions. Structural inequalities revolve around identity-based differences (such as

2. *Economic Times*, 12th October 2009. Published by the Times of India Group, New Delhi, India.

caste, religion), spatial inequalities (across states and even within states) and across skills (Walton, Forthcoming). Public policy for reducing poverty in India range from public distribution of food grains, rural employment guarantee schemes, education and health schemes. However, the success of these schemes has been mixed at best and certainly not in keeping with the vast expenditure on these schemes.

There is a growing recognition in India that governance reforms are critical to strengthen state capacity and enable it to perform its core functions of public service delivery. The development of physical infrastructure is also one of the core functions of the government. The task of improving institutions of economic governance comprise, among others, many actions essential for efficient functioning of markets. The business community has, therefore, a vital stake in improving and empowering public institutions. This chapter explores governance issues associated with public policy aimed at poverty reduction. These policies are variously described as provision of social services, provision of social amenities or the common minimum programme of the Government of India. The question it seeks to answer is whether governance deficit should change the design of policy itself?

What is Good Governance?

Good governance can mean different things to different countries and can have different implications for policy and administrative reforms (Jabeen, 2007). While the ideological and theoretical basis of diverse views on governance is the same, they differ in their approach. Some focus on the normative (Kaufmann and Paublo, 1999; HDC, 1999; World Bank, 1999) others on the descriptive aspects of governance (Hyden and Court, 2002; UNDP, 1997). To some process is more important while to others outcome. Some focus on rules while others are inclined to concentrate on implementation of rules. The notion of good governance, as it is being used in India draws basically on two distinct but overlapping views on governance originating from the World Bank and the United Nations Development Programme (UNDP).

The World Bank (1992) defines governance as 'the manner in which power is exercised in the management of a country's economic and social resources.' It has identified three distinct aspects of governance: (1) the form of the political regime; (2) the process by which authority is exercised in the management of a country's economic and social resources for development; and (3) the capacity of governments to design, formulate, and implement policies and discharge functions. Although the Bank identified political, administrative and economic aspects of governance, it did not include the political aspects in its policies until recently. The World Bank has its own methodology of assessing the quality of governance popularly known as *Worldwide Governance Indicators* (WGI). The six indicators used in the latest governance assessment are: (1) voice and accountability, (2) political stability, (3) government effectiveness, (4) regulatory quality, (5) rule of law, and (6) control of corruption. These six dimensions cover the political, economic and institutional aspects of governance. These indicators are normative and have a high association with democracy and economic development (Kaufmann and Kraay, 2007).

UNDP (1997) defines governance 'as the exercise of economic, political, and administrative authority to manage a country's affairs at all levels.' It comprises mechanisms, processes and institutions through which citizens and groups articulate their interest, exercise their legal rights, meet their obligations and mediate their differences. This definition clearly identifies three governance arenas: political, economic and administrative. In its *Human Development Reports*, UNDP's Human Development Centre (HDC) defined good governance from the standpoint of human development. According to this definition, good humane governance is one which promotes human development. Humane governance is measured by the Human Governance Index (HGI), a composite measure of political, economic and civic governance.

The second extension of UNDP's view of governance has appeared in the form of a working definition for the World Governance Assessment Project (WGA). Drawing on the system perspective on politics (Easton, 1965), Hyden and Court identified six dimensions of governance with six corresponding institutional arenas. While the governance dimensions are socialising, aggregating, executive, managerial, regulatory and adjudicatory, the institutional arenas are civil society, political society, government, bureaucracy, economic society and judicial system. Good governance focusses on the formal and informal rules in each governance arena. Under WGA, quality of governance is assessed on the basis of six universally accepted values—accountability, transparency, participation, decency, fairness and efficiency—in each of the six governance arenas. The authors claim that this assessment approach provides a descriptive rather than normative tool for assessing the quality of governance in a country within its own institutional context.

Grindle (2004) has presented a strong case for good enough governance as a goal of good governance. She argued that a generic notion of good governance has generated an ambitious reform agenda without addressing basic questions such as what needs to be done, when it needs to be done, and how it needs to be done. Good enough governance is defined 'as a condition of minimally acceptable level of government performance and civil society engagement that does not significantly hinder economic and political development and that permits poverty reduction initiatives to go forward' (Grindle, 2004: 526). She argues that this definition may serve developing countries better, even though it is imprecise.

Surveys on Good Governance in India

Because operating conditions in India are significantly different from developed countries it is often argued that governance concepts need to be adapted. Indigenisation does not mean rejection of the concept of good governance, it means developing a strategy and viable action plan for good governance suitable to the institutional context of India. Indian cultural context may best be characterised by one where merit is often sacrificed to nepotism popularly known as *bhaichara*.

In India, paying bribes for obtaining legal or illegal, formal or informal licences and certificates is a common phenomenon. The findings of a survey on governance in India quoted comments of an Indian elite that, 'right from birth to death nothing happens without bribery and corruption. People can neither live nor die with dignity' (Court, 2001). The Bofors scandal in India involved two former prime ministers in corruption (Human Development Centre, 1999).

Several surveys have been conducted on governance in India. Some of the better known international surveys are summarised below:

1) The governance assessment conducted by the Dr Mahbub ul Haq Human Development Centre using the HGI calculated governance assessment for 58 countries on which data was available. According

to the data reported in its annual report in 1999, out of 58 countries, India was ranked at 42.[3]

2) In 2002, under the World Government Assessment (WGA) Project, 16 countries were surveyed to assess their quality of governance. On a 7 point scale, India scored 3.27 (Hyden *et al.*, 2003).

3) The findings of a survey to assess dissatisfaction with the Indian bureaucracy and justice system showed that a weak system of accountability coupled with political interference had deteriorated meritocracy; and equality of law existed merely in theory while in practice only for those with money and they buy justice (Court, 2001).[4]

4) The *Worldwide Governance Indicators* (WGI) launched by the World Bank in September 2006 also revealed a poor quality of governance in India. According to the *World Governance Report 2009,* the governance percentile of India on six governance indicators is in the middling level hovering around the 50th percentile mark for 2008.[5]

Table 6.1

WGI for India

	Governance Indicator	*Governance Percentile*
1.	Voice and accountability	59
2.	Political stability/no violence	17
3.	Government effectiveness	54
4.	Regulatory quality	47
5.	Rule of law	56
6.	Control of corruption	44

Source: World Bank (2009). *WGI Index.*

From 1996 to 2008, the percentile rank for India has remained more or less stable. However political stability indicator has deteriorated marginally

3. *Humane Governance Index, South Asia Regional Report, 1999.* Human Development Research Centre of the UNDP, India.

4. *http://bharatcitizen.in/corruption__humanright_in_india*

5. *Governance Matters 2009: Worldwide Governance Indicators 1996-2008. http://web.worldbank.org.* The WGI are produced by: Daniel Kaufmann, Brookings Institution, Aart Kraay, World Bank Development Economics Research Group, Massimo Mastruzzi, World Bank Institute.

over the 12 years, whereas control of corruption indicator has improved marginally. This indicates that India has not improved its governance significantly. On a scale of -2.5 to 2.5, India's average governance indicator is -0.02 again indicating its middling level of governance.[6]

India ranked 72 among 180 nations in the year 2007 in terms of corruption index, according to Transparency International (TI). TI India's *India Corruption Study 2005* found that water was one of the public services, which is ridden with corrupt practices.[7]

With these middling scores on governance would India satisfy the criteria for Grindle's definition of 'good enough' governance. It would appear from the above evidence that India does have a little above the minimum level of governance required to deliver social development. However, its governance deficits have to be judged against the criterion of whether it is good enough to trickle-down growth to the poorest of the poor? The slow trickle down especially in comparison to similar countries (see Figure 6.1) shows that India needs much better governance for implementing its trickle down policies. What is missing? Is it the lack of will or the ability of the Indian government to implement these policies. Is it a question of accountability and lack of institutions to hold the government accountable. Besides the lack of will and ability of the government and civil society to monitor the effects of its own policies, there are other reasons why government policies have not trickled down to the poor.

So What is Going Wrong in India?

For an economy which has grown at over 7 per cent over the last 15 years (1994-2009), why has poverty reduction been so slow. Compare India's poverty reduction with that of Vietnam or China.[8] India's performance seems abysmal. In fact Figure 6.1 compares India with other countries in terms of human development indicators (HDI) over a period of time. While the post-2005 high growth period is not captured by this analysis, the trend over time shows that HDI in India has been slow to move upwards. From the various *Human Development Reports* of the

---

6. Ibid.
7. *www.transparency.org*
8. See Figure 6.1.

UNDP some key indicators of India have been compared in Figure 6.1. The figure indicate very poor trickle down in India in comparison to comparator countries.

Figure 6.1

A. Life Expectancy at Birth (Years) during 2000-2005

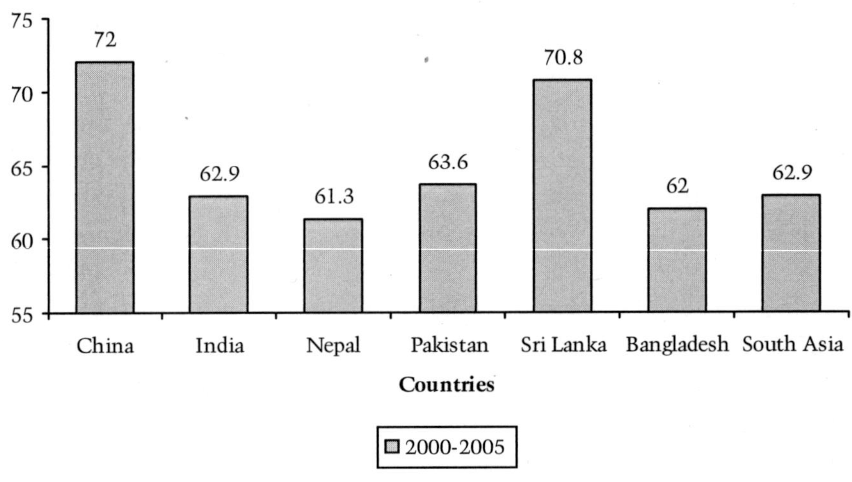

B. Under-Five Mortality Rate (Per 1,000 Live Births)

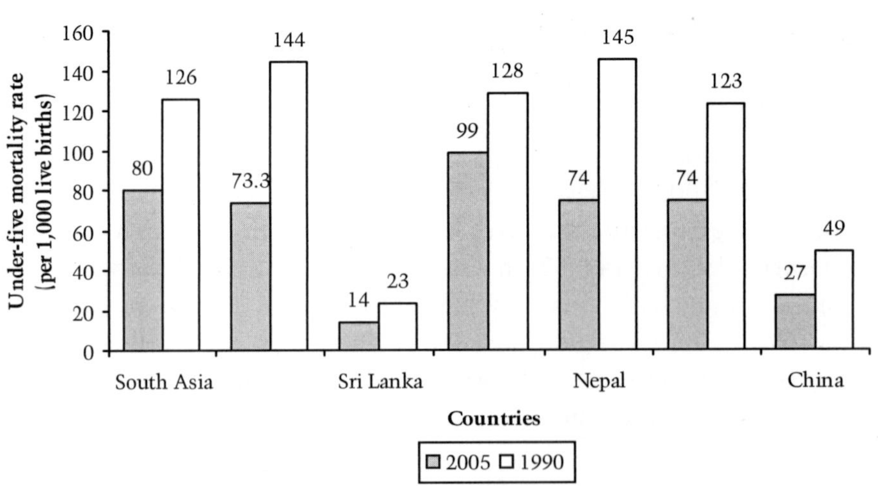

C. Infant Mortality Rate (Per 1,000 Live Births)

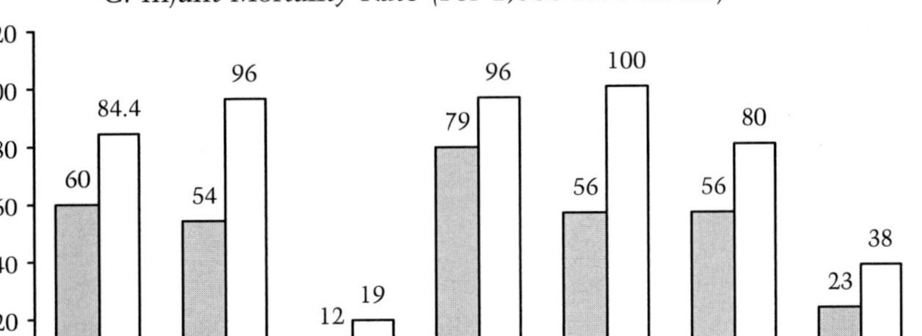

D. Maternal Mortality Rate (Per 1,00,000 Live Births) in 2005

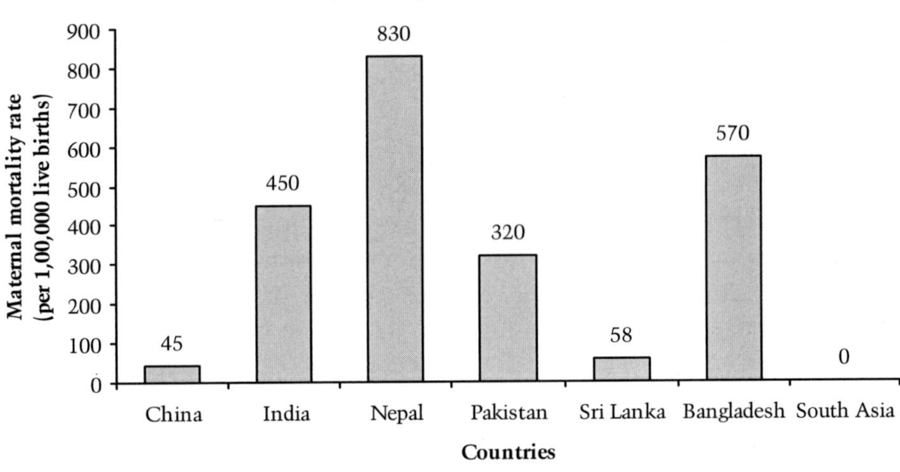

Source: Human Development Reports of UNDP. New York: Oxford University Press.

Why Government Policies have not Accelerated Trickle Down: Political and Administrative Rent-Seeking

The last few chapters have shown that while growth has trickled down to the poor, it has done so slowly and organically. There is little to suggest that government policies have accelerated the process of trickle down. A lot has been written on why growth does not trickle down. One explanation offered by political scientists is based on the fact that the vested interests and the survival instinct of the ruling classes prompts them to increase their support base. This is mainly operationalised through the administrative class by creating situations, which on the one hand, help politicians achieve their motives and two give a dominant position to them (the administrators) to wield massive administrative power. In essence, there exists a strong nexus between the rulers and the administrators and both strive to exist for each other: politicians desire to hold and consolidate their power, while administrators seek to establish their supreme administrative authority often holding even the politicians hostage. All this is exhibited through what economists term the 'rent-seeking' and 'directly unproductive profit-seeking' activities in the terminology of the 'New Political Economy'. These activities seriously hamper the growth process and especially the trickle down, by dissipating the country's resources and national income. A case study of India has estimated that the rent-seeking losses to national income amount to between 30 per cent and 40 per cent of India's gross national product (GNP) (Anand, 2010).

India has an administrative structure dominated by bureaucrats chosen on the basis of a generalist examination (rank in that early entry examination largely determines the career path of an officer no matter how well or ill-suited s/he is in the various jobs s/he is scuttled around, each for a brief sojourn), and promotions are largely seniority-based not merit or performance-based. There are no well-enforced norms and rules of work discipline, very few punishments for ineptitude or malfeasance, and there are strong disincentives to take bold, risky decisions. Whether one likes it or not, the government will remain quite important in the Indian economy for many years to come, and it is difficult to discuss the implementation of economic reform without the necessary changes in public administration including incentive reforms, accompanied by changes in information systems, organisational structure, budgeting and accounting systems, task assignments and staffing policies. In these matters there is a lot to learn from the (successes and failures of) innovative administrative reform experiments that have been carried out in many developing countries in the last decade or so.

Lately, political parties have been using India's high GDP growth rate for advertising their economic and political performance. This GDP obsession also leads to an attitude of easy tolerance of corruption. All anti-corruption measures are viewed as obstructions to development. After all, corruption in business circles has come to be known as the grease which speeds up commerce or as it is popularly known as 'speed money'. Thus if you give a contract for a bridge by taking a bribe, to a contractor who uses substandard material, the collapse of the bridge after five years doesn't reduce GDP.

But there is an even more important reason why GDP growth cannot be an indicator of development, particularly the well-being of common citizens in the country. Growth in India has been achieved fastest in the sector which is least material and most virtual. There are natural limits to land and water availability for agricultural growth. There are virtually no limits to the growth of the virtual industries like the financial markets industry, which is the most rapidly growing industry currently in India. Thus a 10 per cent spurt in the stock market which can be achieved by mutual fund operators within a week, increases the market capitalisation and hence the virtual wealth of citizens by several percentage points. Similarly, many other high-end service industries like IT and insurance could also grow rapidly, thus fuelling rapid GDP growth. But the common people in the country can neither get jobs in these industries, nor do they have any use for these services. While there are some inevitable multiplier effects from even these industries (as shown in Chapter 1) their trickle-down effects would by their very nature be limited and is unlikely to touch poverty rates. Nevertheless as shown in the earlier chapters sustaining growth is the most important recipe for trickling down growth.

Liberals are skeptical about the usefulness of more spending by the government on education and health as long as spending consists of a mere intensification of existing programmes. This is because there is now ample evidence that existing programmes work pretty badly, as is borne out by evidence of absenteeism by health/education workers, the poor learning accomplishments associated with Sarva Shiksha Abhiyaan (SSA), and other such programmes.[9] Many liberals would support a view that more government spending would help—or is essential for obtaining—better health and education outcomes, as long as fundamental surgery is made to

9. *Annual Status of Education Report (ASER), 2009.* Published by Pratham. *http://asercentre.org*

the way in which programmes work—e.g., shifting from teachers as civil servants to vouchers.

However before judging the merits of any of these arguments, it is necessary to make an objective evaluation of governance issues in delivery of social services. To do this it is first of all necessary to examine the legal framework for the delivery of public services. This forms the first ring in the chain of economic governance.

The Legal Framework for Poverty Alleviation and Greater Accountability

The evolution of democracy in India, its impact on inequality and poverty has been rather complex. In the history of western democracies, extension of franchise has been associated with welfare measures for the poor. Democracy has clearly brought about a kind of social revolution in India. There is, however, a major disjunct between politics and economics in India. Hence, economic reform and reform of the ongoing political and administrative processes has been slow.

The major political and administrative reform of the 1990s consisted of devolution of power to the local governments or village level *panchayats*. This was known as the policy of decentralisation. However decentralisation was visualised as a means of delivery of welfare services, and *panchayats* have had limited and varied degree of success in implementing welfare services. This is because the quality of leadership in *panchayats* has been varied and corruption amongst them is also rampant.[10]

From the perspective of economic development at the grassroot level so as to emancipate and empower the poorer and marginal sections of the society, India has enacted the following laws:

a. Right to Information Act, 2005 for ensuring transparency and accountability at governance level.[11]

10. "Empowering Panchayats for Actual Devolution of Power", Information on this scheme can be obtained from *http://www.mynews.in/News/Empowering_Panchayats_for_actual_devolution_of_power*

11. Information on this Act can be obtained from *http://righttoinformation.gov.in*

b. Right to Compulsory and Basic Education by implementation of Sarva Shiksha Abhiyan (SSA) and Mid-Day Meal (MDM) schemes. This became a full-fledged Act in 2009.[12]

c. Right to Food by proper running of the public distribution system (PDS) and the Integrated Child Development Scheme (ICDS).[13]

d. Right to Employment by enacting the National Rural Employment Guarantee Act (NREGA).[14]

e. Right to Self-governance by empowering the process of decentralisation and strengthening of the panchayati raj institutions (PRIs) and urban local bodies (ULBs).[15]

f. Right to Health by effective implementation of National Rural Health Mission (NRHM).[16]

While these Acts would appear to provide an adequate legal basis for poverty reduction and good governance it is critically important to examine the implementation of these Acts. Another critical question is whether there is an adequate framework of resources of various kinds in India to implement these Acts.

The Right to Information Act, 2005 was essential to check corruption and ensure transparency in the implementation of various development-related schemes and programmes that are directly or indirectly intended to reduce poverty, ensure employment and expand livelihood opportunities. However, matters related to India's internal security and defence cannot be brought within the purview of this Act. There is some ambiguity on whether the administrative decisions of the Chief Justice of India are exempt from the RTI Act.[17] The Department of Personnel and Training

---

12. Information on the Act and schemes can be obtained from *http://www.education.nic.in/ssa*

13. Information on these schemes can be obtained at *http://wcd.nic.in/icds*

14. Information under this scheme is available at *http://nrega.nic.in/netnrega*

15. "Empowering Panchayats for Actual Devolution of Power", Information on this scheme can be obtained from *http://www.mynews.in/News/Empowering_Panchayats_for_actual_devolution_of_power*

16. Information on this scheme is available at *http://www.mohfw.nic.in/nrhm.htm*

17. Debate between the NGOs and the Government of India as reported in *The Hindu*, November 9, 2009.

(DoPT) is the nodal agency for the implementation of RTI Act. Even 'file notings' can be disclosed to the general public under this Act. The RTI Act is useful to ensure freedom of expression, too. However, it is largely NGOs and media which have used the RTI so far. Cases of common citizens accessing the RTI are few and far between. Essentially widespread recourse to the RTI to hold the government accountable for public delivery of social services can only take place through improvements in the education and awareness of the general public.

The Right to Compulsory and Basic Education became a full-fledged Act in 2009. Free and compulsory education to children belonging to the age group 0-14 years, including those below six years of age is provided under this Act. This scheme is implemented with the mid-day meal which has proved critical in reducing dropout rates especially among girl students, reducing the number of out-of-school children, providing employment to women cooks who would serve meal to students, increasing cohesiveness among students who would be eating together (via MDM scheme) despite coming from diverse backgrounds, and preventing the curse of child labour when their poor parents do not have to worry about the cost of sending their children for school education. The SSA is seen as a positive intervention to change the fabric of Indian education. Yet there are hurdles that include: lack of infrastructure facilities in schools, lagging state of professionalism among teachers, lack of training, opportunities and incentives for good teachers, discrimination against students coming from weaker sex and oppressed communities, redundant course content etc. It is difficult to implement the SSA and the MDM schemes effectively in such a big and diverse country like India unless there is cooperation coming from the government and public at large. The SSA has been criticised from the perspective of quality education too.

India had to enact its own Right to Food despite having a PDS. According to the National Family Health Survey (NFHS-3), more than a third (36%) of women have a body mass index below 18.5, indicating a high prevalence of nutritional deficiency.[18] The anaemia situation has worsened over time for Indian women.[19] Indian women suffer from gender-based

18. *http://www.nfhsindia.org/nfhs3.html*

19. Ibid.

norms and discrimination, which adversely affect their nutritional status. The importance of ICDS scheme to combat malnutrition and undernutrition among women and children cannot be undermined. The PDS, which was a major institution to ensure food, nutrition and livelihood security, has eroded overtime due to corruption, inefficiency, adoption of wrong policy choices etc. At the international level, although India has become self-sufficient in food production, yet a large section of its population remains unfed. Due to early weaning, children in the 0-6 years of age-group suffer from wasting and stunting. Leakages from ration shops owing to differences between administered and market prices can be tackled by RTI activism. However, the lackadaisical attitude of the officialdom may not help India to reduce hunger by half by the year 2015, which is one of the Millennium Development Goals (MDGs).

The United Progressive Alliance (UPA) government, which started with the National Rural Employment Guarantee Act (NREGA) by implementing it initially in 200 districts, faced criticisms that included: leakages and corruption in the scheme, a large chunk of the expenses being siphoned off for meeting material cost instead of labour cost, lack of co-ordination among Centre and states for regular release of funds, presence of corrupt actors at the village level etc. India had seen failure of food-for-work programmes in the past too before the enactment of the NREGA. It was earlier thought that by providing 100 days of work to a person (one each from a single household), during the lean seasons (i.e., between *rabi* and *kharif*), the livelihood security of those who are willing to do manual labour can be ensured. It was speculated that the NREGA would help in stopping distress migration of labouring communities during lean seasons. The NREGA was supposed to solve the problem of unemployment amidst income-poor groups. However, in many states of India, the labourers are not getting employment under NREGA despite demanding it, presently. Minimum wages are often not paid to the labourers. Non-payment of unemployment compensation has become a regular feature of this scheme. In many parts of India, there are complaints of non-issuance of job cards. NREGA envisaged that rural infrastructure such as water bodies, schools, roads etc., could be constructed and maintained by employing the toiling labouring classes, which would raise their purchasing power. This, in turn, would lead to creation of 'effective demand' in rural India. However reports show that this did not happen.

The Right to Self-governance was essential to escape from bureaucratic controls and shackles, whereby villages would have more autonomy and power in decision-making than before. The creation of proper rules and institutions for further decentralisation came into being in the early 1990s in the form of 73rd and 74th amendments to the Constitution of India. In fact, decentralisation was a result of the decay of centralised planning system that existed during the Nehruvian era. Empowering the PRIs and ULBs is considered essential for proper implementation of government funded programmes and schemes so that villagers and elected *panchayat* members have the right to cross-check the official documents, which used to be under the control of local administrative officers earlier. Strengthening of PRIs and ULBs was envisaged to help in release of people's dissenting voices. The state in that case would then be leaning more towards listening to short creative stories rather than meta and grand narratives. Giving power to the local and elected bodies is now seen as a major policy instrument for ensuring grassroot democracy. The rise of regional political parties and the evolution of political and fiscal decentralisation are now essential features of Indian democracy. But it does not mean that decentralisation has been all the way a positive experience. The elected members of the local bodies turned out to be corrupt individuals in many cases. Women's and oppressed classes' representation in the elected local bodies have not been upto the mark. Many *panchayats* in India practiced caste-based ostracism, and some even directly got involved into honour killings, particularly from the North Indian belt.

The National Rural Health Mission (NRHM) is another flagship programme of the UPA government to assure right to health for the Indian citizens. After liberalisation of the Indian economy, one could observe privatisation of health service delivery, which used to be costly and hence excluded the poor. The accountability of the private sector to their clients has been low. According to the Report of the Independent Commission on Development and Health in India (ICDHI), there exist regional disparities in outcome indicators for health.[20] India does not have enough doctors to cater the need of its rural population. Medical colleges are unevenly spread

20. See *http://www.vhai.org/ceo/current_focus.php*

throughout India, which affect access to health care. Public health security is lacking in India. Out-of-pocket expenses are too high, which adversely affect the poor. Expenditure on provision of public health is meagre. There is a need to think whether there can be alternative affordable mechanisms for delivery of good quality health services for the public at large. The National Health Policy (NHP) 2002 in principle 'welcomes the participation of the private sector in all areas of health activities'—primary, secondary or tertiary. This stand contradicts the basic goal of NHP-1983, which aimed at providing 'universal, comprehensive primary health care services, relevant to actual needs and priorities of the community'. Although health insurance schemes have cropped up in recent times, yet majority of the population have little or no access to such schemes. The condition of public hospitals and health care centres is abysmal. Prevalence of lifestyle diseases is on the rise. Despite the Government of India's commitment in providing 'Health to All' as mentioned in the Articles 21 and 47 of the Indian Constitution, it has been alleged that increased private expenditure as compared to the public expenditure has adversely affected the poorer section's access to basic health services.[21]

The first question to be asked for the poor implementation of these Acts is whether funding for social services delivery is adequate. This issue has been examined in the next section using the figures available from the 2010/11 financial revenue and expenditure budget of the Government of India.

Is Funding for Social Services Delivery Adequate?

Several studies point to the inadequacy of government spending on social services in India.[22] According to the author's estimates, the total expenditure on public services accounts for no more than 6 per cent of the GDP and over 10 per cent of the total expenditure of the Government of India in 2009-10.[23]

---

21. *http://eindia2007.blogspot.com/2009/02/towards-good-governance-in-india_15.html*
22. See articles at *http://www.labourfile.or*
23. *http://www.indiabudget.nic.in*

The total budget outlay in education as a proportion of GDP has increased only marginally from 3.88 per cent in 2009-10 to 4.5 per cent in 2010-11, far from the 6 per cent allocation recommended in the Kothari Commission 44 years ago.[24] The enactment of the Right to Education Act 2009 guarantees that education is now free and compulsory at the elementary stage. However, it is not so in government schools as parents still incur expenses on books, stationary and private coaching among other miscellaneous expenses. The National Sample Survey (NSS) 64th round in 2008 mentions the per capita out-of-pocket expenditure for a government school education by an average parent to be Rs 1,243 (US $30) for the elementary level and Rs 2,597 (US $60) for the secondary/higher secondary level.[25] So while the Union government continues to inject money into SSA year after year, issues of implementation, service delivery and poor financial processes have marred its progress.

Health expenditure accounts for one per cent of GDP and private sector controls the reins of health care service delivery. The Union government's expenditure on health has increased marginally from 2.1 per cent in 2009-10 to 2.3 per cent in 2010-11.[26] As a proportion of GDP, the combined expenditure of the Centre and states on health, which was around 1.02 per cent in 2008-09, increased to 1.06 per cent in 2009-10.[27] Another major programme—the Janani Suraksha Yojana (JSY) which was started as a major intervention under the reproductive and child health (RCH) programme, has benefitted 8.4 million women in 2008-09. With the objective of reducing maternal and neonatal mortality in the country, JSY promotes institutional delivery among pregnant women from poor households. However, the total number of women giving birth each year is estimated to be around 26 million and hence the coverage of JSY is still very limited.[28] In many cases private facilities have filled the gap. It is estimated that hospital assisted births now cover over 80 per cent of the women in India, so by natural deduction most of the hospital assisted births are in the private sector hospitals.

---

24. Ibid.

25. Data obtained from the NSS, 64th round to be found at *http://www.indiabudget.nic.in*

26. *http://www.indiabudget.nic.in*

27. Calculated from data obtained from *http://www.indiabudget.nic.in*

28. *http://www.observerindia.com*

After stagnating at 5.5 per cent of total Union government expenditure, the total allocation on women as per the gender budgeting statement has increased to 6.1 per cent in 2010. There has been a 50 per cent increase in plan allocation for the Ministry of Women and Child Development. What remains disconcerting is that disbursements for several important schemes under the ministry, when added for the last four years, do not reach even 50 per cent of the proposed allocations for the Eleventh Five Year Plan period.[29]

India has one of the poorest records on hunger and food security in the world. It ranks 65th among 84 countries in the Global Hunger Index.[30] The picture assumes graver overtones when seen in conjunction with spiralling food prices. The Rashtriya Krishi Vikas Yojana (RKVY) launched in 2007 aims to incentivise states to increase the share of investment in agriculture.

Targetted PDS like the Antyodaya Anna Yojana (AAY) aims at providing subsidised food grains to the poorest of the poor families. But the allocation on food subsidy as percentage of GDP during 1990-91 to 2009-10 period hovers around less than one per cent and is on a decline since 2003-04.[31] Similarly, expenditure on food subsidy as a proportion of combined total expenditure of Centre and states taken together remained between 2.5 to 3.5 per cent.[32]

In comparison to social services, nine per cent of the GDP allocation in 2010 went to physical infrastructure.[33] Its stated resolve to cross the 'double digit growth barrier', the *Union Budget 2010-11* has gradually shifted the focus from 'inclusive growth' to economic growth. This shows that the government believes that growth will trickle down and places little reliance on its social delivery mechanisms to accelerate the process of trickle down.

How can we evaluate whether the budget allocations to social services is adequate? One measure of its adequacy is the outcome in terms of social indicators. India ranks at an embarrassing 134th position (out of 182

29. Ibid.
30. *http://www.ifpri.org/publication/2009-global-hunger-index*
31. *http://www.indiabudget.nic.in*
32. Ibid.
33. Ibid.

countries) on the Human Development Index (HDI)—and seems to be maintaining it (UNDP, 2009). Whatever India could achieve during the last five years in terms of human and social development is inadequate. However, in a large country such as India, it is expected that overall indicators would be slow to move. Do we indeed have pockets of excellence and what is the analysis available to us for the evaluation of social programmes in India. Often it is not just a question of overall budget allocation but of better governance and management. It would be instructive to analyse some of the third party evaluations of government programmes to obtain some decisive insights into areas of governance deficit in the Indian economy.

Third Party Evaluations of the Various Government Programmes in India

Few studies have made a comprehensive assessment of all or most public services in India. There are even fewer studies on the state of public services in the different states of India based on user feedback gathered through a stratified random sample survey of households. In the developed countries, there are some examples of governments seeking user feedback on their services and programmes (Paul *et al.*, 2004). In developing countries, however, there are hardly any examples of governments adopting this approach. The few initiatives in developing countries have come from civil society organisations such as the Public Affairs centre (PAC) that pioneered the 'report cards' on urban services (Goetz and Gaventa, 2001; Paul, 2002). PAC has used its report cards not only to create public awareness, but also to advocate policy and governance reforms. In recent years, several studies of social sector expenditure have been undertaken in India to assess impacts and outcomes (Dev and Mooij, 2002; Shariff and Ghosh, 2002). One survey which dates back to 2004 has been based on user feedback on five public services in India (Paul *et al.*, 2004). The five services included are drinking water, health facilities, road transport, PDS of food grains and primary school education. While this study dates back to the early part of this decade, inter-state differences in accessing public services has not changed much.

According to this survey, drinking water is accessible to 55 per cent of Indian households within a distance of 100 metres from home (Paul *et al.*, 2004). A quarter of all households depend on unprotected sources of drinking water. One-fourth of the users of public sources of water have reported frequent breakdowns of supply. Access to reliable drinking water supply is thus a problem for a significant proportion of households (Paul *et al.*, 2004). Public health facilities are accessible to over 40 per cent of the households within a distance of one kilometre. The presence of private health facilities makes up for this limited access to some extent. The presence of doctors at public health facilities (a measure of quality and supervision) leaves much to be desired. One-third of the patients did not find a doctor present during their visits (Paul *et al.*, 2004). Absence of paved roads in their village, was reported by nearly 60 per cent of all households. Both public and private buses are available in many states, though in some states there is a domination of either government or private bus transport (Paul *et al.*, 2004). Government buses are rated quite low on punctuality and frequency. PDS of food grains has wide coverage across the country, with over 80 per cent of the households owning ration cards and 72 per cent using fair price shops at least once every two months. But only one-fourth of the cardholders reported regular availability of food grains in the shops. Display of prices was reported by less than 50 per cent. While the reach of the PDS network is wide, its effectiveness is greatly hurt by the high degree of unreliability and non-transparency associated with the service (Paul *et al.*, 2004). Government owned or supported primary schools are available to nearly 80 per cent of the households within one kilometre of their homes. Awareness about the mid-day meal programme is high among households and most are beneficiaries of the scheme. *Anganwadis* (child crèche scheme for poor households) are accessible to over two-thirds of the eligible households, but only 30 per cent are regular users of the service (Paul *et al.*, 2004). A major reason for low use is the time and cost of transporting children back and forth to avail of the service. Even when people give high marks for access to a service, they signal that reliability and public satisfaction leave much to be desired. Nearly three-fourths of households consider PDS unreliable and their full satisfaction rating for this important service is indeed low. One-third of people attest to the irregular availability of doctors in public health care facilities. Other services do not fare much better (Paul *et al.*, 2004).

Of the 16 major states, the better performers are the southern and western states of Tamil Nadu, Maharashtra, Karnataka, Gujarat, Andhra Pradesh and Kerala. At the other end of the spectrum are Assam, West Bengal, Orissa, Rajasthan and Bihar. In between are the remaining states, Haryana, Himachal Pradesh, Punjab, Madhya Pradesh and Uttar Pradesh. While many factors have contributed to the positioning of the states in the three categories, the distinguishing feature of the first set is that, by and large these states have relatively high ratings in terms of both access and reliability in all services. The opposite is true for four out of five of the states in the bottom category. The middle set includes states that for the most part are high on one attribute (i.e., access) but low on the other (i.e., reliability) (Paul *et al.*, 2004).

With respect to the striking inter-state disparities discussed above, it is well known that per capita expenditure on the social sector is lower in the bottom five states than in the top six. Whether this means that resource constraints are behind their poor record in the five services is not clear. If access and use of services are lower in these states, the funds they require will also be smaller. The question is whether their ability to expand and improve services has been limited by their inability to mobilise the needed resources. One possibility is that resources are available, but that the ability and will to plan and utilise them properly leave much to be desired. It is also possible that increased financial allocations have been made to the bottom five states, but diversion of resources to meet other priorities or leakages has made it difficult to use them productively. Where the state is ineffective or non-responsive, civil society efforts could have played a role to demand better performance and accountability. In the better performing states, there is much greater civil society involvement in service provision and increasing evidence of alternative models of service delivery that have an influence on the responsiveness of public service providers. It is possible that people's ability to articulate 'voice' of this type is also absent in the weaker states. If it is this kind of support and technical assistance that weaker states need in addition to funds, ways must be found to generate strategies to meet those needs.

Whether public services are reaching the poor and other disadvantaged groups is a matter of great concern to most policymakers. Here again, one sees a mixed picture. Primary education and drinking water are two services that have done reasonably well in terms of access for the poor. The poor are worse off in terms of access with respect to the other three services. Despite the barriers to access, a larger proportion of the poor use most of the services rather than other households, the singular exception being public transport. In terms of reliability and satisfaction, the poor give lower ratings to almost all the services across the country compared to non-poor households (Paul *et al.*, 2004).

Village size also makes a difference when it comes to access to services. Residents of the larger villages (A and B class) invariably report greater ease of access to all the five services. Drinking water shows the least disparity in terms of access. Use patterns, on the other hand, are more similar, which means that the poor walk long distances to avail of the services. Clearly, longer distances mean that those living in the smaller villages and the poor incur additional costs that hurt their ability to earn a livelihood. Even more striking is the finding that the poor in the top six states are better served than even the non-poor in the bottom states in the five areas! (Paul *et al.*, 2004).

Third party surveys including the author's own surveys also confirm the story above.[34] The results of some of these surveys are summarised below.

Nutrition Programmes

Despite impressive economic growth, India remains home to one-third of the world's undernourished children. From 1980-2005 real GDP per capita in India grew by 3.95 per cent per year, yet between 1992-2006, the percentage of underweight infants under three in India only fell from 52 to 46 per cent (Haddad and Zeitlyn, 2009). Economists argue that this problem reflects a failure in governance—it is difficult to hold nutrition service providers accountable, nutrition practices exclude large groups of individuals and benefits often don't reach those who need them. They point

34. See Annexure A-6.1 for details of survey.

to the fact that although the Indian government's national Integrated Child Development Services (ICDS) plan has committed a four-fold increase of approx $250 million since 2008 to tackle malnutrition, this money will be wasted unless it is better targetted. This programme was implemented through the *anganwadi* scheme among other schemes. This scheme has been evaluated by the author below.

Author Survey of the *Anganwadi* Scheme

This survey was conducted in the districts of Kishangarh and Ajmer to make it consistent with the NREGA survey (see below). The state of Rajasthan has by and large enjoyed better governance than the rest. Thus if an evaluation of schemes implemented by Rajasthan shows governance deficits, the other states would be much worse off.

The survey showed that large families did not avail of the *Anganwadi* scheme perhaps because the elder siblings looked after the younger ones when their mothers were out for work. It could also be attributed to the fact that a large number of the older children were out for work or had migrated. Generally government schemes were the source of information of the *anganwadi* scheme. The *gram panchayat* or local governance institutions were only minimally important in obtaining information on the schemes. Generally the families availing the scheme were happy with it as expressed by the satisfaction over the quality and quantity of food or the behaviour of local teachers.

The average time saved by mothers varied between six and eight hours from availing of the *Anganwadi* scheme. This time saved was used mostly (60%) in either household chores or in family schemes. Further data provided in the Annexure A-6.2 shows the overall satisfaction with the *Anganwadi* scheme. However, a small percentage of large families avail of the scheme so the overall satisfaction is reflected by a relatively small percentage of the eligible population.

Table 6.2

Families Availing Anganwadi Scheme

Family Strength	*Yes*	*No*
2	0	2
3	19	4
4	27	15
5	14	34
6	6	23
7	2	23
8	1	12

Table 6.3

Ambience of the Anganwadi Centres

Hygenic	74.3%
Unhygenic	25.7%

Table 6.4

Source of Information: Anganwadi Scheme

Fellow villagers	27.7%
Government initiatives	41.6%
NGO workers	10.9%
Sarpanch	19.8%

The relatively limited coverage of the scheme even in the state of Rajasthan suggests that other states would be much worse off. There is an urgent need to improve the coverage of backward areas and of large families in the scheme.

The *Anganwadi* scheme not excepted, it is suggested (Haddad and Zeitlyn, 2009) that a failure of nutrition governance is responsible for the shocking state of malnutrition in the country:

- millions of citizens are unable to hold government officials to account for delivering the nutrition services they need;
- practices frequently exclude large groups of individuals—including lower castes, women and girls—from accessing quality services;

- the benefits of economic growth have not trickled down to the poor, whilst the wealthy are increasingly using private services.

Specific recommendations (Haddad and Zeitlyn, 2009) include:

- enabling communities to anonymously rate and publish the local provision of nutrition services;
- creating new mechanisms that enable different Government departments to work together to deliver food, care and health in combinations that work;
- giving the Comptroller General and Auditor Office a bigger role in monitoring Government action on nutrition;
- improving engagement by historically-excluded groups with nutrition programmes, in particular involving women from these groups in designing better outreach programmes;
- introducing simpler but more regular monitoring of nutrition status so that civil society and the media can hold the Government and non-state actors to account;
- developing new ways of thinking and conducting research on how to improve nutrition—so that it is not just seen as a technical exercise, but also as an exercise in politics, governance and power.

National Rural Employment Guarantee Act (NREGA)

Studies on the evaluation of the NREGA are intended to assess the impact on income-earning levels of each household, expenditure on food and non-food items, household and cultivable assets creation by the beneficiaries. Studies also capture the impact of the scheme to arrest out-migration, views and feedback of the beneficiaries on various facets of implementation.

A study carried out in 20 districts targetted 300 beneficiaries from each district.[35] The data pertains to the year 2006-07 during which period this scheme was launched in 200 districts in the first phase. By way of open-ended questionnaires, data on several variables were collected from these beneficiaries who are part of the NREG scheme. The study showed

35. Institute of Applied Manpower Research. *All India Report on Evaluation of NREGA, http://planningcommission.gov.in/reports/genrep/rep_NREGA.pdf*

that female-headed household (HH) participation in the works is very encouraging ranging from 12 to 52 per cent.[36] Most beneficiaries got their job cards through *gram sabha* (GS) meetings and the rest by steps taken by *gram panchayat* (GP). Majority of the rural households agreed that there was a transparent mechanism followed for issue of job cards. Enrollment and registration under the scheme was an open-ended one, however, 15 per cent of the respondents thought otherwise. Migrant families could not register for job card.

Eighty per cent of the HHs did not get the work within the stipulated 15 days time of demand for work in writing, neither were they paid any unemployment allowance. All locally available communication modes were utilised to spread awareness and information about the scheme. Only a small fraction of HHs could utilise more than 35 days of work. The reason for non-utilisation of maximum permissible 100 days was late implementation of the scheme. NREG scheme stipulates at least one-third of the wage allocation i.e., person-days to women beneficiaries. It was found that only in 42 per cent households, women could share 1/3rd of the allocated person-days (wage days). In 22 per cent of the households, women could not utilise more than one-third of the utilised person-days in the household. In most of the work sites, facilities like a shed to shelter from the sun, drinking water etc., were provided. Fourteen per cent of the HHs did not agree that the names of workers, number of days and the amount was read out at the work site as stipulated in the guidelines of the Act. It was found that more than half of the beneficiaries were agricultural and unskilled workers. The survey revealed that the number of families spending less on food had come down drastically where as there was an increase in the number of families who were spending more on food and non-food items.[37]

Only two per cent of the HHs opened bank accounts among the surveyed beneficiaries. More than half of the HHs revealed that they purchased livestock like sheep/goat etc., during the year. Four-fifths of the HHs did not have any outstanding loan. However, in the western region, nearly 60 per cent of the HHs had an outstanding loan either from bank or

36. Ibid.

37. Ibid.

local moneylender. 3.3 per cent of the beneficiaries bought a bicycle for the first time, 1.5 per cent of the beneficiaries did buy electric fans, or other appliances, 3.2 per cent of the HHs purchased steel utensils etc., with the income generated from the scheme.

One-fourth of the families surveyed opined that there is migration from their respective village to towns/cities in search of job. Almost 50 per cent of the HHs in western region expressed that migration is taking place from their villages. In the northeastern region, in the district of North Lakhimpur, everyone agreed that there is migration from their villages. There is migration taking places from districts such as South Garo Hills (Meghalaya), Medak (AP), and Dahod (Gujarat) in addition to almost all the districts from the eastern region. In some of these districts, the out-migration is to the extent of 40 per cent. Only 40 per cent agreed that the *panchayat* was taking appropriate steps to create wage employment. In the eastern region 46 per cent did not express any confidence in their respective village *panchayats* about their efforts of checking out-migration.[38] So in general, at the early stages of the scheme it had little effect on out-migration.

A report of the CAG shows that the government is aware of these problems and has taken corrective action.[39] The Act was extended to the entire country and provided employment to 29.3 million households generating 10.93 million person-days of employment and reaching out to the marginalised group as STs/SCs and women who constituted 54 per cent and 49 per cent of the NREGA workforce respectively. Nearly two million works have been undertaken during 2008-09, of which 46 per cent related to water conservation.[40]

In 2007-08, more than 68 per cent of funds utilised were in the form of wages paid to the labourers. In 2008-09, 71 per cent of the funds had been utilised in the form of wages.[41]

38. Ibid.
39. CAG reports on NREGA for 2008 and 2009 can be downloaded from *http://icrindia.org/pdf/CAG_Draft_Report_NREGA_II.pdf.* These are the reports used here.
40. Ibid.
41. Ibid.

Minimum wages have shown remarkable upward trend after the implementation of NREGA. It had risen in Maharashtra (from Rs 47 to Rs 72), Uttar Pradesh (from Rs 58 to Rs 100), Bihar (from Rs 68 to Rs 81), Karnataka (from Rs 62 to Rs 74), West Bengal (from Rs 64 to Rs 75), Madhya Pradesh (from Rs 58 to Rs 85), Himachal Pradesh (from Rs 65 to Rs 75), Nagaland (from Rs 66 to Rs 100), Jammu & Kashmir (from Rs 45 to Rs 70), and Chhattisgarh (from Rs 58 to Rs 72.23). However, whether this wage increase was related to the overall levels of inflation in the country, to rising agricultural prices or to NREGA is difficult to judge.[42]

Another survey of NREGA conducted in 2008 involved nearly 40 per cent of India's population and 62 per cent of the expenditure in 2007-08 on this scheme. It covered nearly 100 randomly selected work sites spread over six states and about 1,000 workers. Eighty-one per cent of the workers lived in *kucha* houses, 61 per cent were illiterate and 72 per cent had no electricity. Thus, they covered the poorest households. This survey showed that only 13 per cent of the respondents had secured 100 days of work as mandated by the Act in the preceding year. Of this the lowest was in Chhattisgarh (1%), Bihar (2%), UP (3 per cent) and Jharkhand (7%). Rajasthan had the highest employment with 35 per cent securing 100 days of work. The all-India average number of days secured under NREGA was 16 with considerable inter-state variation. This could be hardly enough to dent poverty in India. Only half of the sample workers were aware of their entitlement to 100 days of work. However, half the respondents also feel that NREGA had staved off hunger (69%) or avoided migration (59%), helped them to repay debt (32%) or avoided hazardous work (35%). A majority of the workers (57%) used the money to buy medicines or treat illness (Drèze and Khera, 2009).

However, reports of rampant corruption under NREGA have also been received. Master rolls were fudged, while wages of the fictitious workers were siphoned off by middlemen or officials. Even bank accounts were opened under fictitious names and money was transferred to the accounts of middlemen with the concurrence of the bank manager. However, it is difficult to judge whether direct payment or payment through bank accounts is more corrupt.

42. Ibid.

Author Survey of NREGA

As surveys had shown that the Rajasthan NREGA scheme had been most successful, the author conducted a survey spread over a couple of months in Rajasthan in 2009.[43] The results of Kishangarh and Ajmer are summarised below. Of the people surveyed who availed of the scheme, roughly 71 per cent were men and 29 per cent women.

While the scheme was available at several locations, about 40 per cent of the people surveyed did not avail of the scheme. While the reasons for not doing so were not clearly expressed, several pointed to the inadequacy of the coverage of the schemes. Some also expressed the view that better incomes were available to them elsewhere such as construction sites or stone mines.

Figure 6.2

Income Level versus Percentage of People Availing NREGA

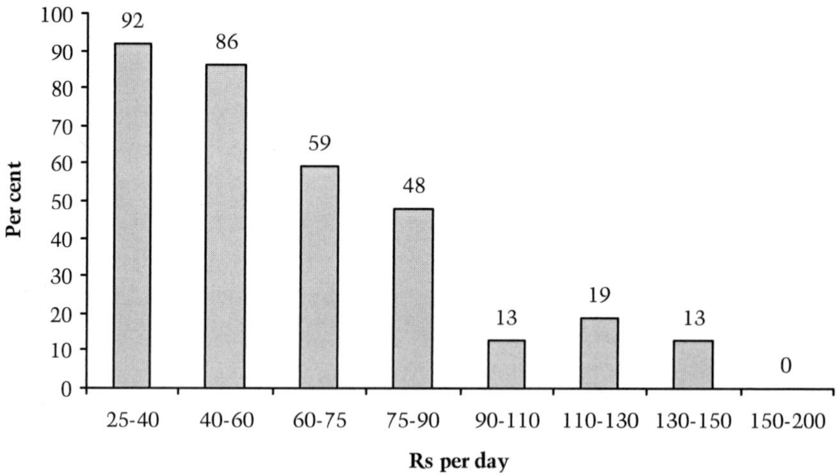

The income levels of those who availed the scheme was in general much lower than NREGA wages. The income levels of people indicated on the x-axis was in terms of rupees per day.

43. For details of the survey see Annexure A-6.3.

A little over half of the people surveyed were either happy with NREGA or found it satisfactory. Only 7 per cent considered it a bad scheme.

Figure 6.3

Working Conditions

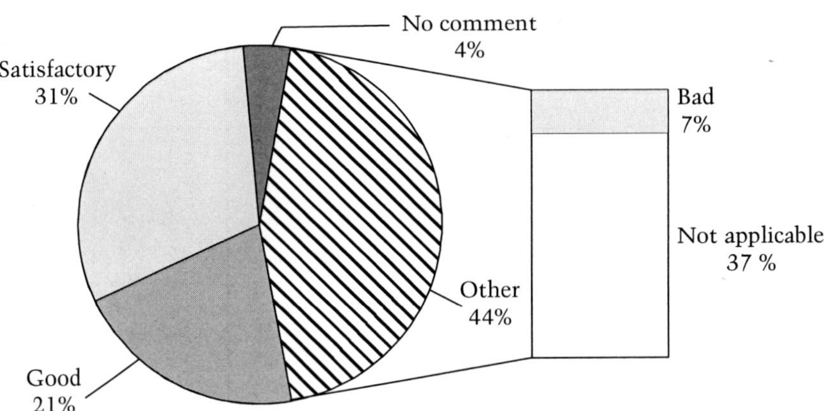

Over half of the participants did not have any problems in getting a job card, while 34 per cent of the participants did not consider it of relevance. Only a small percentage considered it a problem to get a job card. In fact a great majority expressed the view that it was easier to get a job card after one job card had already been obtained.

A large percentage of the people surveyed expressed satisfaction with the NREGA and did not face problems in drawing money. While the overall level of satisfaction with the scheme was high, at the level of details several cracks appeared. First of all the much touted state of Rajasthan has clearly seen a lot of economic development in the recent past to suggest that Central schemes are implemented with less corruption than in other states. This is shown by the fact that nearly 40 per cent of the people surveyed did not avail of the scheme. Second, alternative employment schemes at relatively high wages were already available in Rajasthan. Third, proximity to Delhi resulted in better awareness of such schemes and private investment in Rajasthan has been relatively high than in other states. The important question to ask is whether the experience with

NREGA can be replicated in other states. An important issue in this context would be the improvement in governance in the poorer states such as Bihar.

Figure 6.4

Problems Faced in Getting Job Card

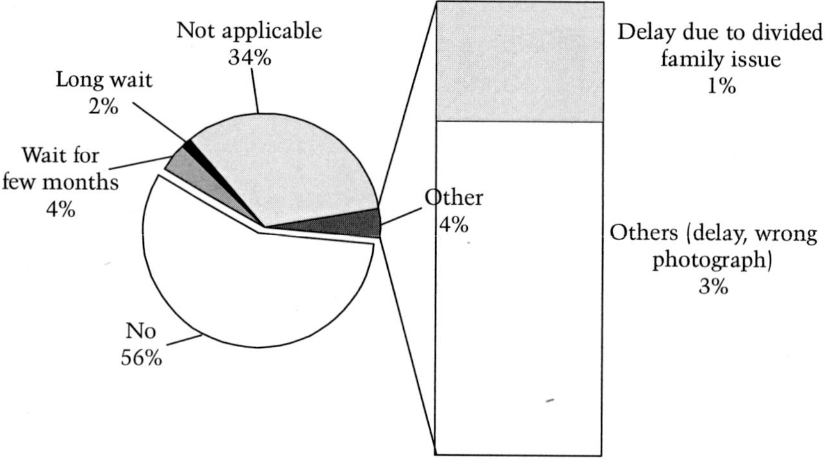

Key findings of the National Tribunal on NREGA suggest that:[44]

1. Factual information about the programme appears lacking, not only among the people but also among those who are responsible for implementation.
2. There are tremendous hurdles faced at the first stage of registration and acquiring of the job card itself. Proofs of identity and fees have been demanded for registration. There is also reluctance on behalf of NREGA workers to accept applications for work even after the individual is registered.
3. Women-headed households and joint families are at a distinct disadvantage in accessing the benefits of the scheme. The provision of work to one person of the household has been

44. For full details on the outcomes of the deliberations and surveys of the National Tribunal on NREGA see *http://www.elbag.org,* Outcomes of the National Tribunal on National Rural Employment Guarantee Act, India, Wada Na Todo Abhiyan, which literally means 'Do not break your promises'.

interpreted to mean that it is applicable only to the male head of the household.

4. Even after the procurement of a receipt for the application for work—work has not been made available in many instances, and there are few reported cases where an individual has actually received the unemployment allowance.
5. There appears to be a lack of transparency in the allocation of works. In several instances, no reasonable explanation has been given for the selective distribution of works to certain hamlets within the village, or specific individuals. Dalits, women, minority groups and persons with disabilities bear the brunt of this selective process of allocation.
6. Systems for measurement of work are inadequate and disparate. There is no distinction between skilled and unskilled work, and the same wage is provided for both.
7. Facilities for shade, water, first aid and crèche are not being provided at the work site.

Figure 6.5

Problems Faced in Getting Job after Having Job Card

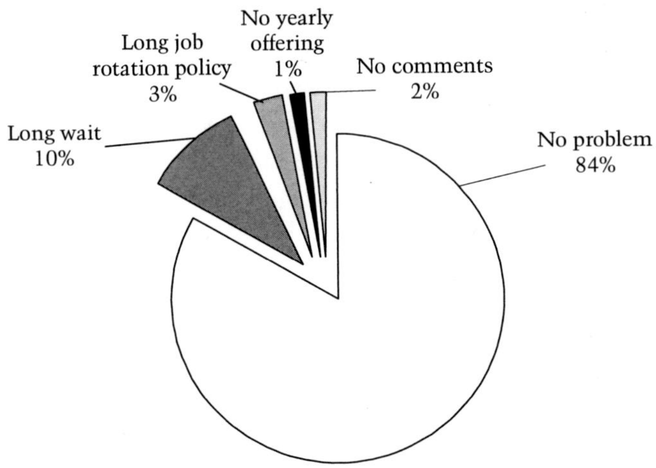

Sarva Shiksha Abhiyan (SSA)

The SSA was a scheme of the government to provide education to all. Reports of the outcome of these programmes are not very encouraging. Teacher's attendance, maintenance of hand pump, health service providers were all very low. This was because teachers were not accountable to the local citizens whose children were studying in the school. Instead they were accountable to distant supervisors who may be staying very far from the school (United Nations *et al.*, 2007).

UNESCO's *Global Monitoring Report 2009* is a severe indictment of the Indian government's commitment to education. India's public investment in education is 3.3 per cent of its gross national product, lower than sub-Saharan Africa's median. But India would achieve a net enrollment rate of over 97 per cent by 2015 (UNESCO, 2009).

India is one of 17 countries in the world with the greatest number of out-of-school children. UNESCO's *Education For All (EFA) Global Monitoring Report 2009*, released recently, says enrollment in secondary education in India increased from 39 per cent in 1999 to 43 per cent in 2006. Around 7.2 million Indian children are still out of school (UNESCO, 2009).

On the positive side, the report says India is on track to achieving its enrollment targets for elementary education, which will be cut to just 600,000 in 2015. Since 2001, the government's flagship elementary education programme, the SSA, has helped to bring some 20 million children into school, most of whom are first-generation learners. The gender gap has reduced and more children are transitioning from primary to upper primary school. Many of India's states are now either approaching universal primary enrollment or have already achieved it. According to the Government, less than 5 million children between the ages of 6 and 14 now remain out of school. The programme is now focussing on bringing the hardest-to-reach children into primary school, raising access to upper primary education and improving retention and learning outcomes (UNESCO, 2009).

According to the 2001 national Census, India has a literacy rate of 65 per cent. UNESCO's annual report suggests a further strengthening of policy commitments towards quality education (UNESCO, 2009).

The report highlights, among other things, the need to ensure that children have basic literacy and numeric skills. This has been an area of concern for India. Fewer than half of the children in Grade 3 can read simple text; only 58 per cent can subtract or divide (UNESCO, 2009).

Teacher absenteeism is another area of concern. The report finds that contrary to popular perception, absenteeism among teachers plagues both private and government schools. It suggests greater commitment to reducing inequalities and sustained political leadership to reach education targets.

A look at the figures in year 2008, shows that 98 per cent of India's habitation has primary schooling facility,[45] while 90 per cent of Indians have upper primary schooling facility. For every five primary schools there are two secondary schools. Also in certain primary schools, the current infrastructure is being upgraded to provide secondary school education at the sites of primary school education. Over the years the government has taken many steps to improve the education system through various innovative steps, like public-private partnerships, NGO's involvement, pure private initiatives in the school education system etc. Still the national average dropout rate between standard I to X is 62.69 per cent.[46] This is a matter of grave concern because out of every 10 enrollments, six individuals (majority) are not able to finish their schooling.

Poor quality government schools are important factors in the growth of private players. In India, contract teachers (para-teachers) have been used to increase the number of teachers in remote rural schools.

'As they are often less qualified and more inexperienced than civil service teachers (trained teachers), the situation raises concerns about providing teaching of equal quality to all areas' (UNESCO Report, 2009).

UNESCO identified a range of policies to remedy extreme inequality, including the removal of school fees for basic education, increased public investment and incentives for girls, whilst warning against decentralisation

45. *http://www.education.nic.in*

46. Dongaonkar (2006), *http://www.iau-aiu.net/conference*

which often widens inequalities by reinforcing financing gaps between rich and poor regions (UNESCO, 2009).

Achieving Gender Parity

Reports on the outcomes for women in relation to the National Common Minimum Programme and its three flagship initiatives, namely the National Rural Employment Guarantee Act (NREGA), the National Rural Health Mission (NRHM) and the Sarva Shiksha Abhiyan (SSA) draw attention to the need for additional efforts to be made to ensure that women are able to benefit from and participate in the national programmes for livelihood, health and education (Wada Na Todo Abhiyan, 2007).

Amarjeet Kaur of the All India Trade Union Congress (AITUC) points out that although 96 per cent of working women in India belong to the informal sector, the country still lacks social security legislation that can ensure fair wages and safe working conditions for millions of women (Wada Na Todo Abhiyan, 2007).

Annie Raja of the National Federation of Indian Women (NFIW) notes that despite the provision for 33 per cent preference for women workers in NREGA, field audits show that women are prevented from taking up work through the scheme, and paid lower wages for their work (Wada Na Todo Abhiyan, 2007).

Abhijit Das of the Centre for Health & Social Justice (CHSJ) and Jashodhara Dasgupta of Sahayog adjudge that for the NRHM to achieve its intended objective, the explicit recognition of gender disparity as a determinant of health status and access to health care is imperative (Wada Na Todo Abhiyan, 2007).

Malini Ghose of Nirantar draws attention to the adverse impact of privatisation of education on women and girls, particularly from socially disadvantaged sections, and strongly recommends that the state should arrest its withdrawal from the education sector and the formal education system should be strengthened not downsized (Wada Na Todo Abhiyan, 2007).

Problems in Monitoring Government Programmes

Tracking the delivery of public service delivery is a difficult exercise. First of all, outcome measures such as a decline in poverty rate, or increase in literacy rates, or decrease in infant mortality and the like are long-term in nature and may be influenced by a multiplicity of factors. Poverty reduction may occur over time, but it does not necessarily mean that anti-poverty programmes have been efficiently managed and delivered. Health services will certainly have an impact on the levels of infant mortality and the average life span of the population. But the latter are also influenced by factors such as general economic conditions, increased public awareness, growing role of non-governmental initiatives and communications, etc. These are not all factors within the control of the health ministry or its service providers. A second limitation of this approach is that the findings come too late to help the government make mid-course corrections to its strategy and to manage its operations more effectively in the short- or medium-term.

In theory, governments could easily fill this monitoring gap. Yet all evidence points to a poor track record on their part to monitor public service delivery and its effectiveness. Planning new projects and spending public funds are often higher priority for governments than monitoring performance and outcomes. There are several reasons behind this phenomenon. There are some services that are difficult to monitor. For example, how a doctor treats his/her patient is not easy for a superior authority to monitor. A more important problem is that the kind of systems and practices needed to perform the monitoring function are seldom put in place by governments. Even when systems are in place, collusion between service providers and their superiors (e.g., between bureaucrats and politicians) may make them toothless. One would have expected political leaders to highlight the issues pertaining to services at least at the time of elections. But such issues are seldom on the agenda in elections, perhaps, in part, because of the ignorance of the people and their inability to articulate their concerns. In the absence of external pressure by an informed public, it is unlikely that the government's monitoring of services will improve (Paul, 2002).

Conventional technocratic answers for improving service delivery or a call to allocate more financial resources may not be an adequate response to this problem. The range of reforms required may cover a wide spectrum

—from political leadership and administrative structures and incentives to service-specific changes including alternative delivery options.

Learning from Successful Examples of Social Service Delivery

The possibility of drawing lessons from success cases rather than the large legacy of failure has also been the subject of much debate in India. This may also help in specifying the type of reforms required. New information about household level health and fertility through NFHS-3 (National Family and Household Survey) suggests that health outcomes in India may be improving. In terms of methodology, NFHS is the best household survey in India—it's the gold standard against which all surveys compare themselves. The first survey was conducted in 1992-93, the second in 1998-99 and the third in 2005-06 (Gupta *et al.*, 2006). The quick summary is: that public health service delivery was terrible, but the health and fertility outcomes got tremendously better.

The percentage of infants dying before they attain the age of one has dropped significantly in the last seven years in all five states surveyed. These include Punjab, Gujarat, Orissa, Maharashtra and Chhattisgarh. It has reduced in Punjab by 26 per cent, in Gujarat by 21 per cent, in Orissa by 20 per cent. When compared to the data from NFHS-1 carried out in 1992-1993, Orissa, one of the poorest states in India in terms of per capita income, has witnessed a decline in infant mortality by 40 per cent.

For many years, the sense in India was that Kerala and Tamil Nadu had achieved replacement-level fertility (two children per woman) but fertility in the rest of the country remained stubbornly high. The NFHS findings indicate that over the past 13 years, significant progress in fertility has taken place in all five states. Punjab and Maharashtra have achieved replacement fertility. Women in Orissa, Chhattisgarh and Gujarat now average 2.5 children each. The Indian average fertility rate according to the 2011 Census was 2.6, which is 0.3 points above replacement rates.

Preliminary evidence as shown above indicates that the quality of public health services has been worsening. As NFHS data shows, immunisation, which is largely done by the government, has worsened in Gujarat, Punjab and Maharashtra in recent years. This information is in conformity with the data from the report on Reproductive and Child Health Programme of the World Bank which found that out of 274 districts in the country, child immunisation declined in 197 districts (Gupta *et al.*, 2006).

Similarly, indicators of maternal health from the NFHS data show that while antenatal care is now universal in all five states, only 55-75 per cent of women are getting the recommended three antenatal visits. Moreover, the report on Reproductive and Child Health Programme found that the increase in in-hospital childbirth is caused by a rise in in-hospital births in private hospitals. There has been a decline in in-hospital births in public hospitals. The data on antenatal care and assisted deliveries showed that the percentage of deliveries assisted by health workers went up from 39.6 per cent in 1998-99 to 47.5 in 2002-03, the percentage of women delivering in public health facilities declined from 24 per cent to 18.5 per cent. The increase took place in deliveries in the private sector, where they rose steeply from 9.4 per cent to 21.5 per cent.[47]

Moreover, women in richer states were seen to be using public health facilities less and turning to private health. In Andhra Pradesh, the percentage of women delivering in public institutions declined by 9.8 per cent, in Kerala by 28.9 per cent, in Karnataka by 10.2 per cent, in Maharashtra by 9.1 per cent and in Tamil Nadu by 15.3 per cent. Further, the number of women who received postnatal care by public health workers (ANM) through home visits within two weeks of delivery also declined from 14.1 per cent to 12.7 per cent. The Planning Commission's mid-term appraisal of the Tenth Plan observed that when people first seek treatment, an estimated 70-85 per cent visit a private sector provider for their health care needs.[48]

This result flies in the face of the two pet hypotheses cited above. If we believe that the lot of poor people is not improving, then this evidence is inconsistent with this position, because it suggests that poor people were a lot better off in 2005-06 when compared with 1998-99. If you believe that government spending and/or programme design is important, then this evidence is inconsistent with this position: the NFHS (and other sources of

47. *http://ajayshahblog.blogspot.com/2006/12/trickle-down-economics.html*

48. Ibid.

evidence) show that the government system did badly, but that people got healthier and had fewer kids anyway.

When people get richer, they buy better food, have better sanitation and cleanliness, more knowledge (e.g. education within the family), and services of private doctors/hospitals. India has been experiencing powerful economic growth, which is trickling down to poor people. So even though the public health system is doing badly, health outcomes have improved, amongst poor people. These could be termed the trickle-down effects of economic growth.

The orthodox view of public policy in India equates 'the health of the public' with the spending on and the design of 'public health programmes', and assumes that poor people are not sharing in economic growth. NFHS-3 suggests that if you completely froze the spending on the Ministry of Health in nominal terms, and just had high GDP growth, you would most likely continue to get strong improvements in health outcomes.

Such an understanding—where health outcomes are not equated to the public health system—is consistent with the history of health in Europe, where a great deal of improvements in health took place owing to rising incomes feeding into nutrition, cleanliness and private purchases of health services. Such an understanding is also consistent with analysis of NFHS-1 and NFHS-2, where the basic story which emerges is that the presence of a primary health centre does little for health (Dass, 2000).

Governance Indicators and Poverty Alleviation: A Business-based Approach

Following this argument, some argue that donors and governments should provide loans at low interest rates directly to businesses that are prepared to invest in rural areas. Instead of trying to create entrepreneurs out of poorly educated adults, the emphasis ought to be in generating sustaining jobs in large numbers (George, 2006).

India's rural population is increasing by over 9 million annually according to the 2011 Census. Urban prosperity will not trickle down fast enough to reduce rural poverty. Government-run projects are not capable of adding 600 million sustainable jobs. NGOs can at best lower the misery faced by the poor, but not much more. Only the private sector can produce the kind of vibrant economic activity that will generate sufficient employment and higher income for the rural population.

Handouts will not solve poverty. The poor want jobs and not benevolence. A market-based approach to poverty reduction will result in income and wealth creation, and lay the groundwork for the next generation to avail of a wider range of opportunities with enhanced resources.

Business has been the greatest beneficiary of globalisation. The rapid expansion of trade and cross-border capital flows made possible through the globalisation have created unparalleled opportunities for growth and financing of business. Globalisation cannot work properly if the poor are not made part of it. They need to be reassured that globalisation can benefit them equally. The biggest business challenge of today is to bring the poor into the market economy. It should be in the self-interest of corporations to do that as a matter of top priority. Business has to realise that sharpening of the inequalities as a consequence of globalisation is the greatest threat to the security and sustainability of their businesses (Mehra, 2005).

Secondly, for the first time in human history business has the power and technology to make a difference in human lives. It has a social cause to make profits instead of the invisible hand of Adam Smith.

Thirdly and more importantly, businesses have to realise that throughout history businesses have expanded and multiplied only by reaching what C.K. Prahalad, the noted management guru called, 'the bottom of the pyramid.' (Prahalad, 2009). Both Microsoft and mobile telephony that spawned some of the 21st century's most successful businesses have proved the point. Microsoft succeeded because it aimed to reach every home. IBM failed because the vision of its founder Thomas Watson was 'there was to be a world market of just five computers.' Reliance Infocomm, a mobile phone operator in India received one million applications in the first 10 days when it offered a mobile phone for $10. India today has more mobile phones than landlines.

The success stories of Gramin Bank in Bangladesh, Casas Bahia in Brazil, Cemax in Mexico and ICICI Bank and Nirma in India show how accessing the poor markets have transformed both these businesses and the poor constituencies they served. ICICI Bank has developed a new model of relationship with its customers. It has no direct contact with its half a million rural clients. It monitors their loans which are as little as six dollars with instalments of 20 cents each month through self-help groups formed by rural women. Cardiac care and cataract operations are reaching new heights of process innovation in India. A cataract operation in Aravind Eye Hospital costs barely $50 including hospitalisation costs. Forty per cent of the patients are treated free. Yet, the hospital is debt free and has a return on capital of 120 to 130 per cent (Prahalad, 2009).

Another revolution has been brought by Unilever subsidiary in India, Hindustan Lever. They have created a distribution network of some 30,000 women called 'Shakti Ammas' to distribute their products in remote villages as direct-to consumer initiative targetted at individuals at the bottom of the pyramid. Training these women in entrepreneurial skills will have a cascading effect on the rural economy. Scaling up this model worldwide can have phenomenal results in alleviating poverty and bringing the poor into the market economy (Prahalad, 2009).

What should be done to Stimulate the Private Sector to Share in the Delivery of Public Services

So what is stopping businesses from becoming a part of the poverty alleviation drive of India. There are complex answers to this simple question. Is it a simple case of passing the buck, i.e., business considers that it is largely the government's role to alleviate poverty, whereas what it does is more in the nature of philanthropy and by no means a substitute for government delivery of public services. If the government has become ineffective in the delivery of public services, should not business step in and take a role in its own self-interest, i.e., that of generating consumers, an effective and productive labour force, and services which have intimate linkages with the economy. The interesting question is why is this not happening in a large enough scale to make a visible dent to poverty in India? The answer is in the lack of accountability in public service delivery. Lack of accountability applies to both the public and the private sector. The polity of India has to hold the government and the private sector responsible for public delivery of services and there has to be an objective evaluation of the money spent and the services delivered.

Some insights into these issues can be found through an evaluation of the innovations made in service delivery in the last 20 years. A World Bank study has examined successful cases of public service delivery and has narrowed the range of reforms which could foster and multiply such examples (World Bank, 2006). The study identifies six categories of reforms to improve service delivery. These are: (1) fostering competition, (2) simplifying transactions, (3) restructuring agency processes, (4) decentralising management, (5) building political support for programme delivery, and (6) strengthening accountability mechanisms.

Private players can complement government's delivery of social services. This was observed in all the five services as shown above (Paul *et al.*, 2004). However, for private players to act efficiently, it is necessary for the government to create a level playing field and effective conditions of competition. The manifold increase in teledensity is a working example of how the government successfully levelled the playing field between its own operators and that of the private sector.[49] Mobile telephone services are now available even to the poor in India. While it may not be easy to extend this example to other sectors, it is nevertheless a telling success story in India. There may be some scope for its extension to the education sector where standards of service provision and monitoring can be laid down by a regulatory authority and both government and private service providers can compete for provision of the service.

Another important experiment of the government was simplifying access to government services. Telling examples in this field have been the simplification of the system of payment of income taxes leading to a manifold increase in the collection of income tax, as well as reservation of rail and flight tickets over the internet. Extension of this service to the maintenance of land records, paying house and land taxes and other forms of e-Seva can reduce corruption to a large extent (World Bank, 2006). Experiments with the use of internet for these purposes and digitising databases on the poor in India are currently under way. The widespread use of internet for the delivery of social services may reduce corruption though not eliminate it. In this context the role of the private sector in the development of databases will be of crucial importance.

49. See Chapter 4.

Changing agency processes and decentralisation are based on the involvement of the local community and end users of services which is crucial to the delivery of public services. A good example of such a system was the Education Guarantee Scheme (EGS) of Madhya Pradesh in 1997 (World Bank, 2006). The EGS scheme ensured that if the local polity or the *panchayat* forwarded a list of at least 40 children without access to a school within walking distance, the state would ensure a functioning school within 90 days. Under the programme, communities were expected to contribute physical space for a school, choose a teacher and supplement resources. The government bore the costs of teachers' salaries, provided teaching and learning materials as well as seed money for infrastructure, and took responsibility for teachers' training. Parent-Teacher Associations (PTAs) were charged with monitoring the functioning of EGS schools and reported to village education committees. In a short period of three years from July 1997 to July 2000, the number of EGS schools rose to 26,571 (42 per cent of them in tribal areas), catering to some 1.2 million children of Madhya Pradesh (World Bank, 2006).

Madhya Pradesh's Rogi Kalyan Samiti (RKS) turned district hospitals into independent societies, which not only managed hospitals, but had the power to levy user fees, solicit private donations, use vacant hospital land to generate more revenue, and outsource cleaning and other functions. RKS societies consisted of all important players locally including the collector, MLAs and NGOs. User fees collected by RKS societies were directed towards funding maintenance and the cost of purchasing new equipment for the state's often dilapidated hospitals. The RKS model was popular with doctors and staff because it made available equipment that might not otherwise be affordable given the high proportion of the budget spent on salaries. By earmarking user fees for maintenance and equipment, RKS societies helped improve the productivity of salary expenditures by topping them off with necessary non-salary spending. The poor were exempted from paying user fees on the basis of self-identification, rather than any formal criteria. The Central government's National Rural Health Mission identified the RKS model for replication across the country (World Bank, 2006).

Examples of improvement of accountability are few and far between. Madhya Pradesh also introduced a more decentralised system of teacher management to improve accountability. The state's unionised regular teachers were declared a 'dying' cadre and no further recruitment was permitted to the cadre: regular teachers were recruited by the state government and could be transferred across districts. *Panchayats* had no role in hiring them and could not remove them in the event of non-performance or poor attendance. A new category of teachers, Shiksha Karmis (SKs), in 1996 at the primary school level were to be recruited by block or *janpad panchayats* (JPs) for a probationary period of three years. If after three years, the JP was not satisfied with teacher's performance, it could simply decline to confirm the teacher in the post; alternatively, the JP had the power to put off confirmation by extending probation for another two years and revisit the decision later (Ramachandran, 2003; Sharma, 2001). During probation, SKs could be removed by JPs for dereliction of duty with one month's notice. *Panchayats*, according to a government order issued in 1999, were also given the power to withhold salary payments for non-attendance for all primary school teachers. Preliminary results from ongoing research in Andhra Pradesh suggest that even providing small monetary bonus payments (with an average annual bonus of around 3 per cent of annual pay) to teachers on the basis of the average improvement in students' performance on independently administered tests led to large gains in students' learning outcomes. This programme was over 10 times more cost-effective in improving learning than simply spending along existing patterns. It was also popular with teachers with over 85 per cent of them being in favour of the idea of bonus payments on the basis of performance (Muralidharan and Sundararaman, 2009).

Another method of improving effectiveness of service delivery is to modify the contractual structure of employment to make job renewal subject to satisfactory performance as measured by both administrators and the community that is being served. A good example is the use of contract teachers who are hired locally at the village level. Again, research shows that contract teachers are significantly less likely to be absent (15 per cent compared to 25 per cent) and are much more likely to be engaging in teaching activity even though they are paid only Rs 1,000 (US $25) a month as opposed to an average of Rs 7,500 (US $190) a month for government-employed teachers. The research also shows that providing schools with extra teachers on contract is a highly cost-effective way of improving learning outcomes. The key features of this arrangement are that the teachers belong to the same local communities that they are serving, and that the renewal of their contract is subject to satisfactory performance (World Bank, 2006).

One response to the poor quality of public schools and clinics was the increasing prevalence of private schools and clinics even in backward parts of the country. A key feature of private providers is the much higher level of accountability of their employees. For example, data shows that absent teachers in private schools were 175 times more likely to have action taken against them than absent teachers in government schools, though their salary levels were much lower (Muralidharan and Sundararaman, 2009). However, in terms of education outcomes a recent ASER report has shown that there is little to choose between private and public schools (ASER, 2009). Moreover, the problem from the point of view of social justice is that these facilities are only available to those who can afford to pay for them, which puts them out of the reach of the poor.

A promising way of addressing this problem is for the government to directly provide health and education grants or vouchers to the poor, which in turn would be redeemable at any recognised school or clinic (that would be subject to some basic regulation). The attractiveness of such a scheme is that it harnesses the power of incentives and competition to ensure efficient production that is sensitive to what the users want while avoiding the biggest weakness of the market—which is that it only caters to those with purchasing power. Such a scheme would be indifferent to whether the provider was public or private, but would ensure that providers only get compensated if their service is demanded by users. However, mechanisms will have to be devised for avoiding corruption in the distribution of these vouchers and ensuring that it reaches only the poor and not the non-poor. Moreover, private service delivery will have to multiply manifold in scale and be accessible to the poor in rural areas. If the distribution of vouchers is just and reaches the poor, an effective demand for these services would be created in rural areas forcing the private sector to create facilities in these areas.

Tying the compensation of service providers to the satisfaction of users (as revealed by their use of the facility) can be a very effective way of improving the quality of basic services. Such a scheme can also be a highly effective way of targetting government support, since the amount of the grant can be calibrated to an index of backwardness and funds can be effectively targetted to the neediest segments of society.

The importance of political leadership in delivering inclusive growth cannot be overstressed in a country like India. Even poor states such as Bihar, Orissa and Madhya Pradesh have seen bouts of good performance on both growth and inclusion front through dedicated political leadership. In fact, political leadership at the state level is of crucial importance in delivering inclusive growth. Bihar's economic growth is higher than that of most states because of the dedicated leadership of its chief minister over the last four years, 2006-2010. Similarly, despite its abject poverty, Madhya Pradesh has great strides in the delivery of public services as shown above.

In conclusion, it is clear that improving the quality of health and education services for all Indians is a critical component of ensuring 'inclusive growth'. While budgetary increases for health and education are definitely welcome, their effect will be magnified if accompanied by measures to improve the effectiveness of spending. In particular, the lack of both accountability and performance incentives for government employees in health and education (as manifested by high rates of absence) is an enormous hurdle for effective service delivery.

Conclusions

India has made some strides in the area of good governance. There have been successful innovations in service delivery as shown above. Media, NGOs and international agencies have created a new level of awareness and sensitivity to the epidemic evil of corruption. Free press in India does serve to report some of the heinous corruption cases.[50] Several reform initiatives in the wake of globalisation and emerging communication technologies, particularly e-Seva initiatives as shown above have also helped to improve governance. The rule of law is recognised as a major governance issue by governments. Police and judicial reforms have

50. "President Patil Cautions against Corruption", August 14, 2009. *http://www.expressindia.com/latest-new*

received new impetus. Core reforms in economic, political and administrative arenas have also been introduced in the form of civil service, education, social sector, public-private partnership and gender reforms. India is putting more emphasis on training of civil servants to enhance their efficiency and effectiveness. The Indian state of Kerala also presents a good example of community and state partnership in the effective implementation of poverty alleviation programmes at the local government level (Mohindra *et al.*, 2008).

India has realised that its immense human capital would be wasted as a result of women not fully participating in the economic, political and administrative arena (See Chapter 4). Gender empowerment is an important component of economic, political and administrative reforms in India. Philanthropy, self-help, self-development and common pool resources have long been recognised as traditional and religious values in India (See Chapter 5). As was pointed out earlier, good governance could channel philanthropic impulses to the social sector in a coherent and organised manner (See Chapter 5).

However there are several constraints to good governance in India as was shown above. Primarily weak institutional norms for the efficient and effective management for public service delivery is responsible for the slow trickle down of Indian economic growth. Improving accountability to beneficiaries in private and civil society organisations is vital for ensuring that growth trickles down to the poor. A management system with internal accountability in government, the private sector and civil society organisations constitutes the basics of any good governance agenda. Unless these organisations have strong control systems, they cannot contribute effectively to good governance.

Due to massive inequalities in society and a small but growing middle class, both bureaucracy and democracy strengthened traditional elites and created new elites. Inequalities in society are also reflected in the market and civil society. Elitism exists not only in the public sector but is also seen in the realm of non-state actors. So what is the way out? Internal and external accountability in conjunction with sound competition policy and strong regulation across the board through efficient and effective management systems and transparency in decision-making is the answer.

Capacity for good governance is an issue not only for the state; the private sector and civil society suffer with the same problem.

In view of the above, the concept of humane governance coupled with good enough governance as discussed earlier has direct relevance to India (Grindle, 2004). Thus, good governance is good political, good economic and good civic governance which promotes human development. The rule of law, provision of basic services and poverty reduction with the participation of the private sector and civil society should be taken on priority basis. However, government still has to play a major and leading role in human development.

Implementation of policies is a major problem in India. It is less related to capacity but more to political will at institutional and organisational levels. Effective implementation begins from the formulation and design stage of policy, programme, or project; if it is based on wrong theories or concepts poor implementation is the obvious result. It also becomes a problem if the implementation strategy is not built in the planning of a project or policy. It is important that Indian states should learn from each other by sharing successes and failures in order to improve implementation.

The importance of e-governance for speedy, efficient and transparent delivery of services at the doorsteps of citizens has grown over time. Computerisation of government offices has become part of e-governance. Booking of railway tickets has become easier due to e-governance. Social and public auditing of muster rolls in development-related schemes and programmes has become an empowering practice in some parts of the country. However, these schemes are all too inadequate and need to multiply manifold if they are to impact poverty.

As long as significant poverty exists in India, and disparity between the rich and the poor widens, private sector would need to make a contribution to solving the problem. A dialogue must begin between and among business leaders on devising rules for business conduct in deprived communities. The model must consider how poor people can be brought into the mainstream of consumers with sufficient purchasing power within a reasonable time period. Distribution of health and education vouchers should be considered seriously by the Government of India.

To sum up, the process of reform must continue in India in an effective framework of good governance. India has to find dynamic ways of public-private partnerships in the delivery of social services. It has to undertake massive administrative and political reform to ensure high growth rates and inclusive growth. Inclusive growth is not automatic but small incremental changes and building on success cases of administrative and political reform may be the way forward.

References

Anand, Vinod (2010). *Trickle-down versus Trickle-up. http://www.merinews.com/article*

Court, J. (2001). "Assessing and Analyzing Governance in India: Evidence from a New Survey", World Governance Assessment Project, *Working Paper* No. 1.

Dass, Purvi (2000). *Global Democratic Governance: Role of Global Civil Society Organisations. http://www.civicus.org/pg/world-democracy-day/1127-global-democratic-governance--role-of-global-civil-society-organisations*

Dev, S. Mahendra and Jos Mooij (2002). "Social Sector Expenditures in the 1990's: Analysis of Central and State Budgets", *Economic and Political Weekly* 31(9): 853-66. March 2.

Dongaonkar, D. (2006). "Missing Links in Education System in India". Obtained through the internet: *http://www.dise.in*

Drèze, Jean and Reetika Khera (2009). "The Battle for Employment Guarantee", *Frontline* 26(01). January 03-16. Publishers of The Hindu, India.

Easton, D. (1965). *A Systems Analysis of Political Life.* New York: Wiley.

George, Abraham M. (2006). *Rural India Needs Corporate Investment: A New Approach to Poverty Reduction.* December 29. *http://www.tgfworld.org/Rural_India_Needs_Corporate_Investment.htm*

Grindle, M. (2004). "Good Enough Governance: Poverty Reduction and Reform in Developing Countries", *Governance: An International Journal of Policy Administration and Institutions* 17(4): 525-48.

Goetz, A.M. and J. Gaventa (2001). "Bringing Citizen Voice and Client Focus into Service Delivery", *IDS Working Paper* 138. Brighton: Institute of Development Studies.

Gupta, Kamla, Sulabha Parasuraman, P. Arokiasamy, S.K. Singh and H. Lhungdim (2006). "Preliminary Findings from the Third National Family Health Survey", *Economic and Political Weekly*, October 21.

Haddad, L. and S. Zeitlyn (2009). *Lifting the Curse: Overcoming Persistent Undernutrition in India. http://www.ids.ac.uk*

Himanshu (2010). *Should we Worry about Inequality? http://www.livemint.com/2010*

Human Development Centre (1999). *Human Development Report*. New York: Oxford University Press.

Hyden, G. and J. Court (2002). "World Governance Survey", *Discussion Paper* 1. Tokyo: United Nations University.

Hyden, Goran, Julius Court and Ken Mease (2003). "Government and Governance in 16 Developing Countries", *World Governance Survey Discussion Paper* 6. July. London: Overseas Development Institute. *http://www.odi.org.uk/resources/download*

Jabeen, Nasira (2007). "Good or Good Enough Governance in South Asia: Constraints and Possibilities", *Inaugural Address* as Professor to the Prince Claus Chair in *Development and Equity 2006-07.* April 2. Netherlands: Utrecht University. *http://www.princeclauschair.nl*

Kauffman, Daniel, Aart Kraay and Pablo Zoido-Lobaton (1999). "Governance Matters", *World Bank Policy Research Working Paper Series* No. 2196. *http://ideas.repec.org/p/wbk/wbrwps*

Kaufmann, Daniel and Aart Kraay (2007). "Governance Matters VI: Governance Indicators for 1996-2006", *World Bank Policy Research Working Paper* No. 4280. The Brookings Institution, World Bank-Development Research Group (DECRG), Massimo Mastruzzi, World Bank Institute. July.

Mehra, Madhav (2005). "Taking Corporate Governance Beyond the Boardroom", Keynote address at *ICSA International: Making Poverty Alleviation a Business Issue.*

Mohindra, K.S., Slim Haddad and D. Narayana (2008). "Can Microcredit Help Improve the Health of Poor Women? Some Findings from a Cross-sectional Study in Kerala, India", *International Journal for Equity and Health* 7: 2. Published on line at *http://www.ncbi.nlm.nih.gov/pmc/articles*

Muralidharan, K. and V. Sundararaman (2009). "Teacher Performance Pay: Experimental Evidence from India", *NBER Working Paper* No.15323. September. *http://www.nber.org/papers/w15323.pdf*

Paul, Samuel (2002). *Holding the State to Account: Citizen Monitoring in Action.* Bangalore: Books for Change.

Paul, Samuel, Suresh Balakrishnan, K. Gopakumar, Sita Sekhar and M. Vivekananda (2004). "State of India's Public Services: Benchmarks for the States", *Economic and Political Weekly* 39(9): 920-933, February 28–March 5.

Prahalad, C.K. (2009). *The Fortune at the Bottom of the Pyramid: Eradicating Poverty through Profits.* Wharton, USA: Wharton School Publishing.

Ramachandran, Vimala (2003). *Lok Jumbish: Rajasthan People's Movement for Education for All.* New Delhi: The World Bank, SASHD.

Reddy, Y.V. (2003). "Towards Globalization in the Financial Sector in India", Inaugural Address by Dr Y V Reddy, Governor of the Reserve Bank of India, at the *Twenty-Fifth Bank Economists' Conference-2003.* Mumbai. December 11. *http://www.bis.org/review*

Shariff, Abusaleh and Prabir Ghosh (2002). "State-Adjusted Public Expenditure on Social Sector and Poverty Alleviation Programmes", *Economic and Political Weekly* 38(8), February 23.

Sharma, Amita (2000). *Improving Primary Teacher Provision through Better Management: A Study of Madhya Pradesh.* (Unpublished manuscript, 2000).

UNCTAD (2009). *World Investment Report, 2009.* Geneva, Switzerland: United Nations Conference on Trade and Development.

UNDP (1997). *Re-conceptualizing Governance.* New York: UNDP. pp.2-3.

———. (2009). *Human Development Report, 2009.* New York: Oxford University Press.

UNESCO (2009). *EFA Global Monitoring Report, 2009: Overcoming Inequality: Why Governance Matters*. Oxford, U.K.: Oxford University Press. *http://unesdoc.unesco.org*

United Nations ESCAP, ADB and UNDP (2007). *The Millenium Development Goals: Progress in Asia and the Pacific, Asia Pacific.* MDG study series.

Walton, Michael (Forthcoming). "The Political Economy of India's Malnutrition Puzzle", *Institute of Development Studies Bulletin.*

Wada Na Todo Abhiyan (2007). *Gender & Governance: Review of the Women's Agenda in the National Common Minimum Programme*. March. Delhi. *http://www.wadanatodo.net/images/160407/GenderNCMP_Eng.pdf*

World Bank (1992). *Governance and Development.* Washington D.C.: The World Bank.

————. (1999). *World Development Report 1999-2000.* New York: Oxford University Press. pp.258-59.

————. (2006). *Reforming Public Services in India: Drawing Lessons from Success Stories.* Prepared by the Poverty Reduction and Economic Management Sector Unit, South Asia, Report No. 35041-IN. Published by the World Bank.

Annexure A-6.1

Common Questions

- Name of the family head:
- Occupation:
- Working members in the family:
- Annual income:
- Number of children in family:
- Which all schemes are being availed by the family?
  1) ASHA
  2) Anganwadi
  3) NREGA
  4) Smart Card
- Which scheme is the best scheme according to you and why?
- Which scheme is most easily available?
- Have you faced any difficulty in obtaining any schemes?

NREGA

- How many people from your family have been given employment under this scheme?
- What is the monthly wage you get?
- What all documents need to be submitted?
- How many months it took you to get the job after the application were filled?
- Are you getting all the promised things?

Anganwadi

- Total number of kids at home?
- Do you know about Anganwadi?
- What do you know about Anaganwadi and where did you hear about it?
- How many kids are sent to Anganwadi?
- If none of the kids not sent, then why?
- Are they properly managed?
- Is the food quality available?
- How much food is available and how much is allocated by the government in value terms?
- Is the place neat and clean?Are your children happy going there?
- Do you get free time by sending your children to Anganwadi?
- What do you do in this free time?
- Are you getting all the promised benefits?

ASHA

- Does your family avail the ASHA scheme?
- What benefits are given to you in the scheme?
- Are the medicines free of cost?
- If not then how much do you have to pay?

- How do you pay?
- Are the vaccinations free of cost?
- If not how much do you pay?
- What was promised to you for the scheme?
- Are you getting all the promised things?
- Which medicines and vaccinations are not available?
- Are the services available at time of emergency?
- How many dispensaries are there?
- How many doctors are there?
- How may support staff people are there?
- Is the place neat and clean?
- Are you getting all the promised benefits?

Smart Card

- How many days it took to obtain the Smart Card?
- What all papers you have to submit for obtaining the Smart Card?
- What was your annual saving before availing the Smart Card?
- What is your annual saving after availing the Smart Card?
- Have you purchased new durables after coming of Smart Card?
- Have you started using new items after the Smart Card?
- If yes, which all items?
- Is it easy to debit the Smart Card?

Annexure A-6.2

Anganwadi Scheme
(Rajasthan: Kishangarh + Ajmer)

Figure 1

Families Availing Anganwadi Scheme

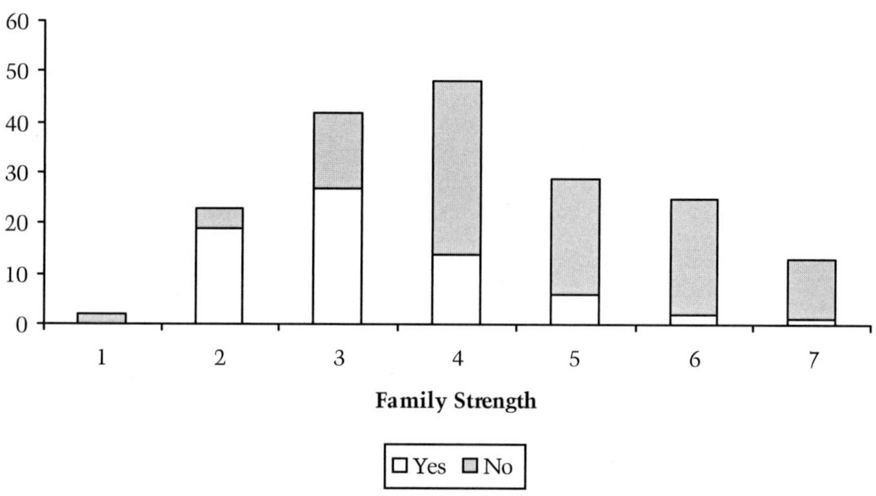

Figure 2

Source of Information: Anganwadi Scheme

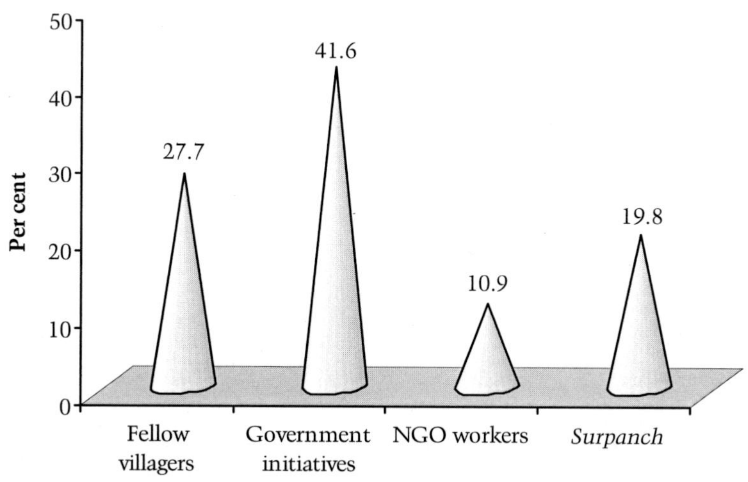

Figure 3

Average Time Saved by Mothers for Availing Anganwadi Scheme

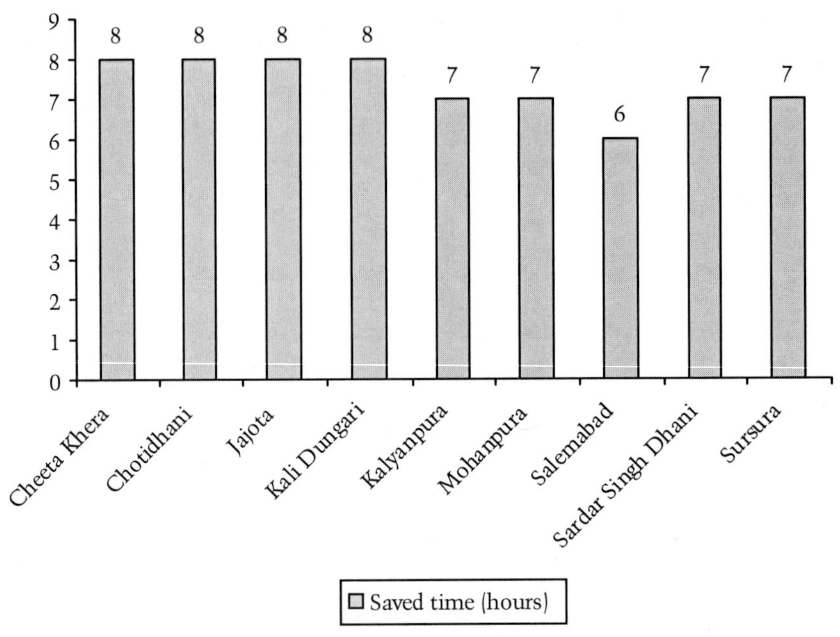

Figure 4

Activities Performed Utilising the Saved Time

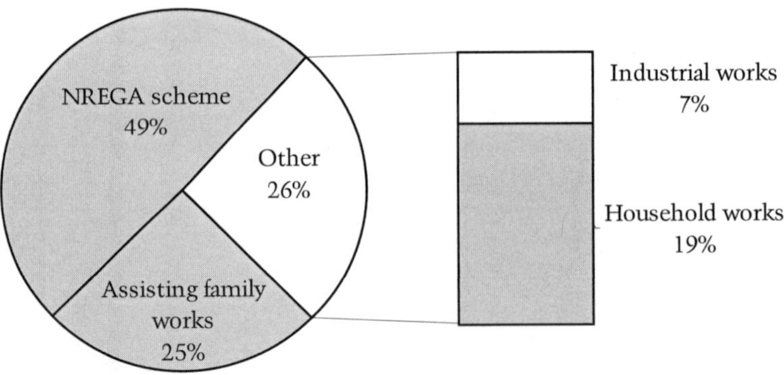

Figure 5

Average Daily Income Earned by Mothers through the Activities Performed

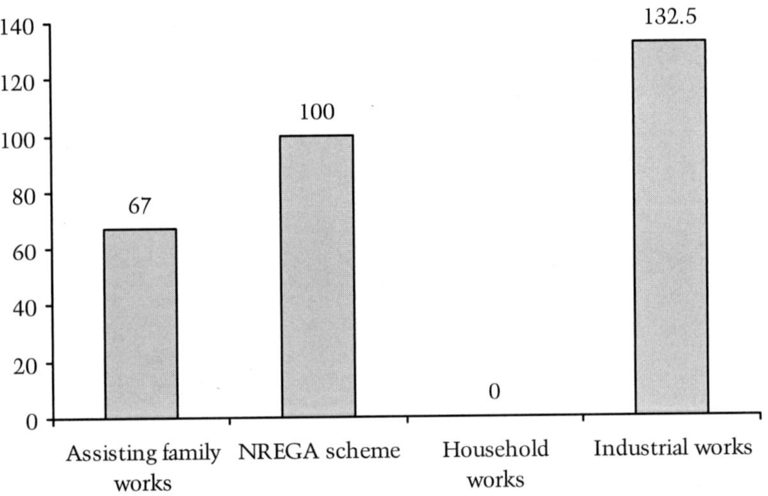

Figure 6

Ambience of the Anganwadi Centres

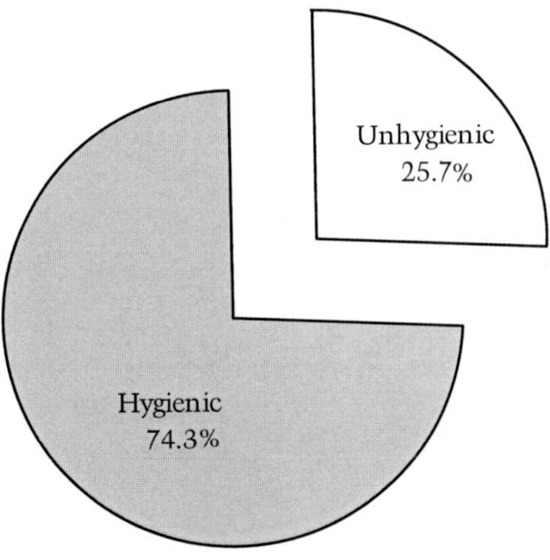

Figure 7

Quality of Food Served

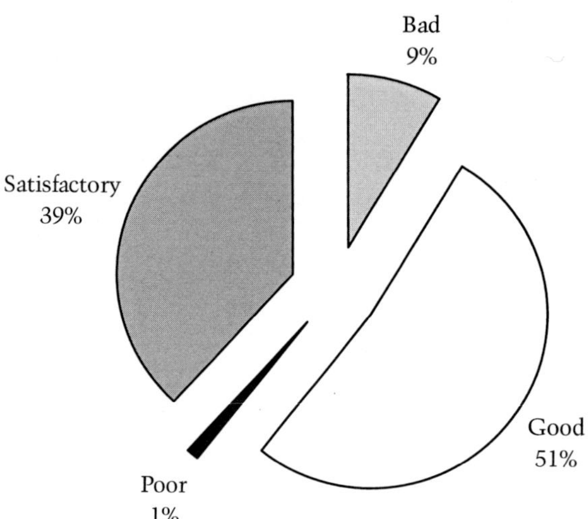

Figure 8

Type of Food Served to Children

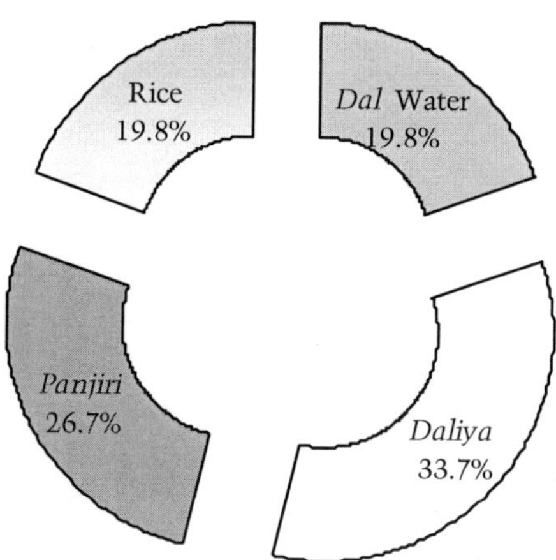

Figure 9

Is Food Served to Children Sufficient for them?

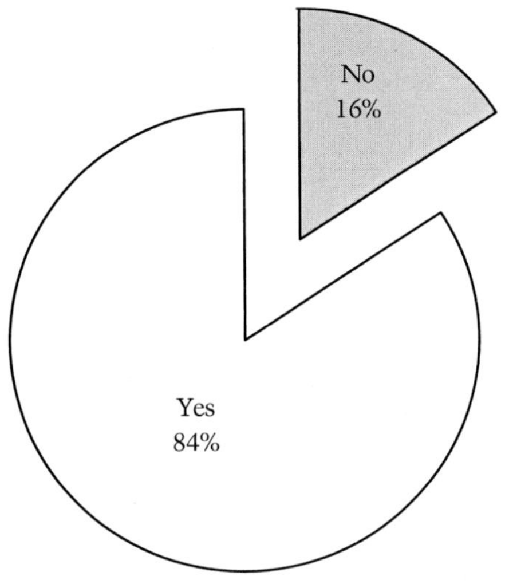

Figure 10

Staff Behaviour towards Children

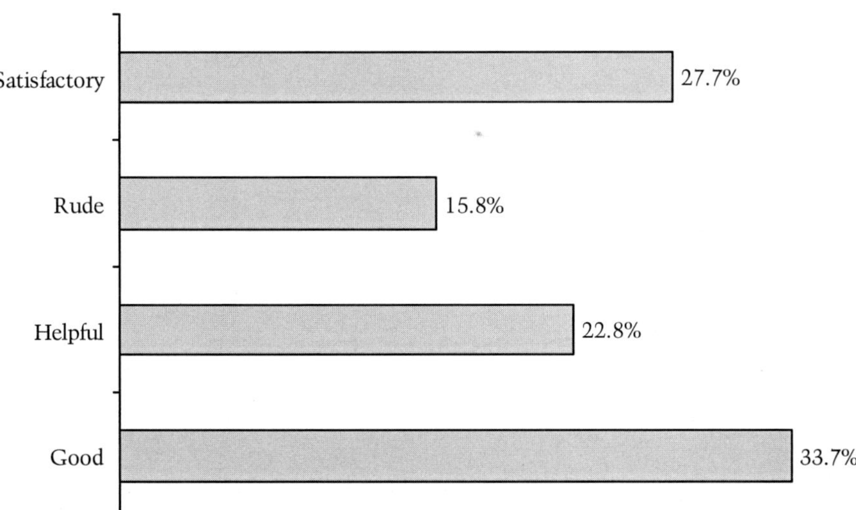

Table 1

Break-up of Eligible Children Not Availing Anganwadi Scheme

Number of Children in Family Aged under 6 Years	*Total Number of Families*	*Break-up*	
0	59	Families that send no child	0
		Families that send one child	0
		Families that send two children	0
		Families that send three children	0
1	63	Families that send no child	17
		Families that send one child	46
		Families that send two children	0
		Families that send three children	0
2	46	Families that send no child	4
		Families that send one child	22
		Families that send two children	20
		Families that send three children	0
3	12	Families that send no child	0
		Families that send one child	3
		Families that send two children	5
		Families that send three children	4

Figure 11

Problems Faced in Availing Anganwadi Scheme

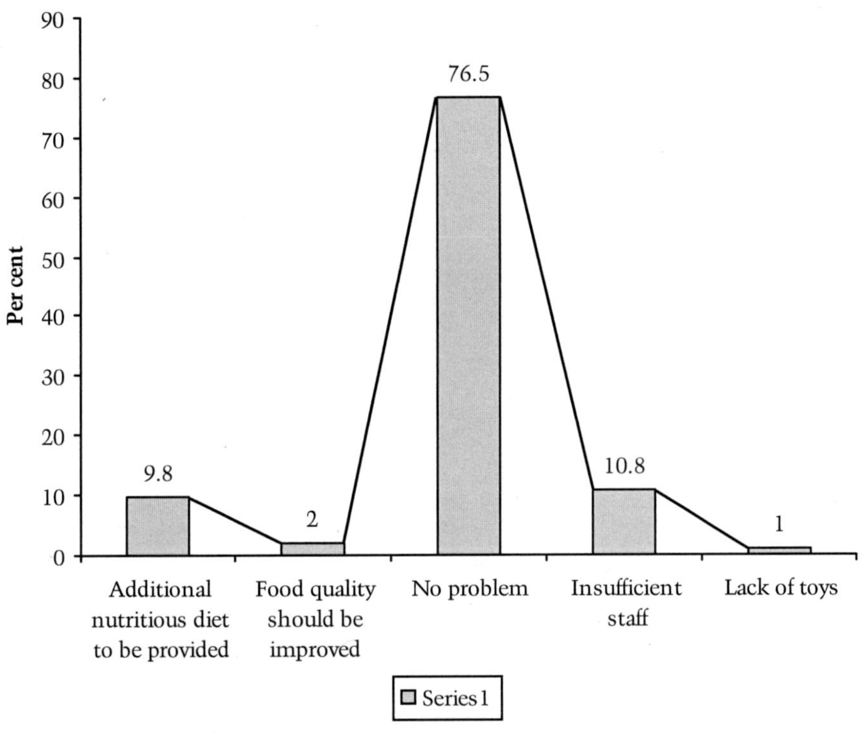

Annexure A-6.3

NREGA Scheme
(Rajasthan: Kishangarh + Ajmer)

Figure 1

Gender Distribution

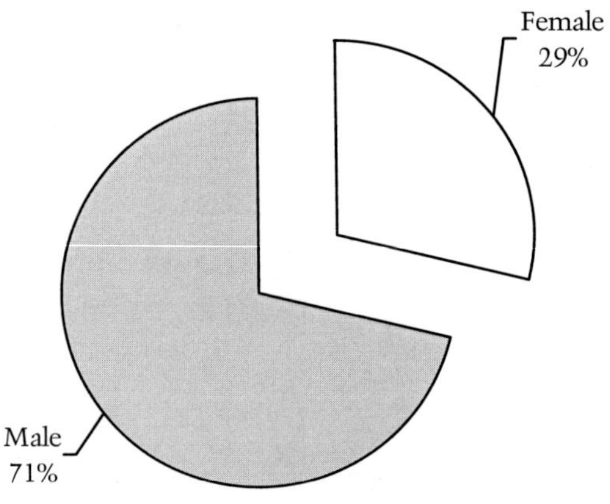

Figure 2

Marital Status

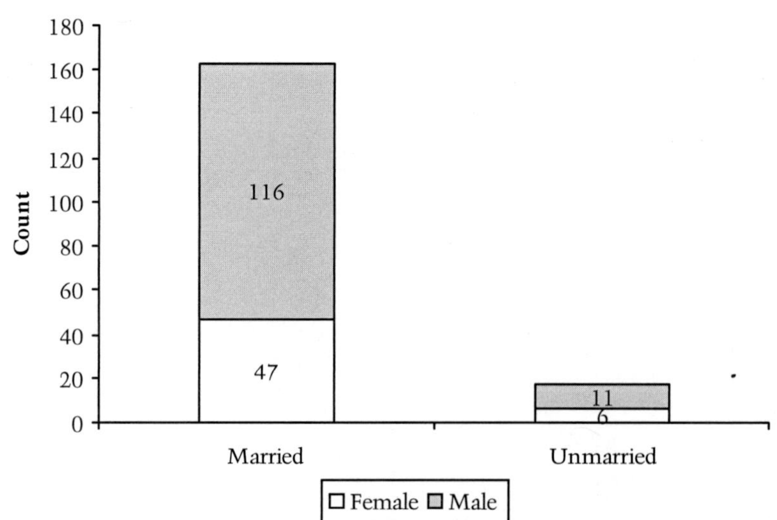

Figure 3

Family Strength

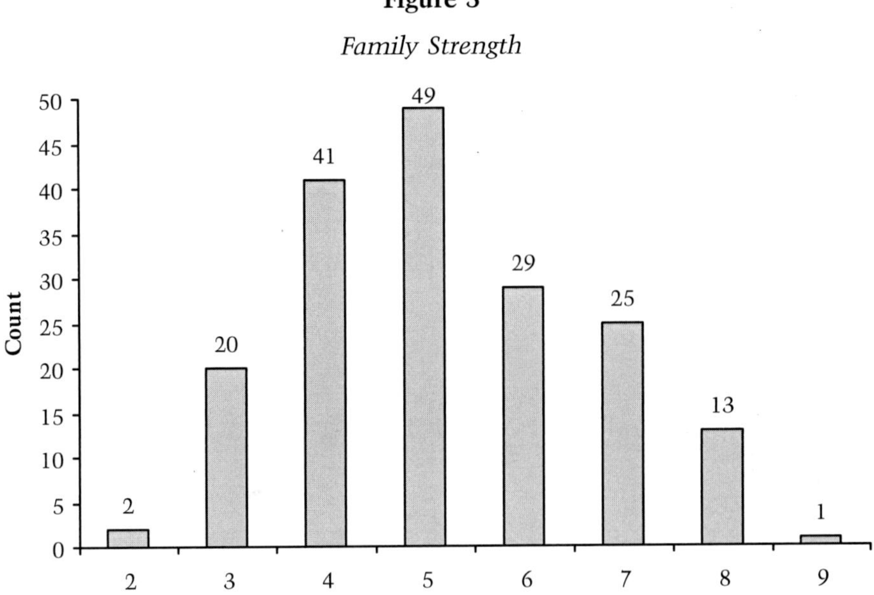

Figure 4

Scheme Availed at Different Location

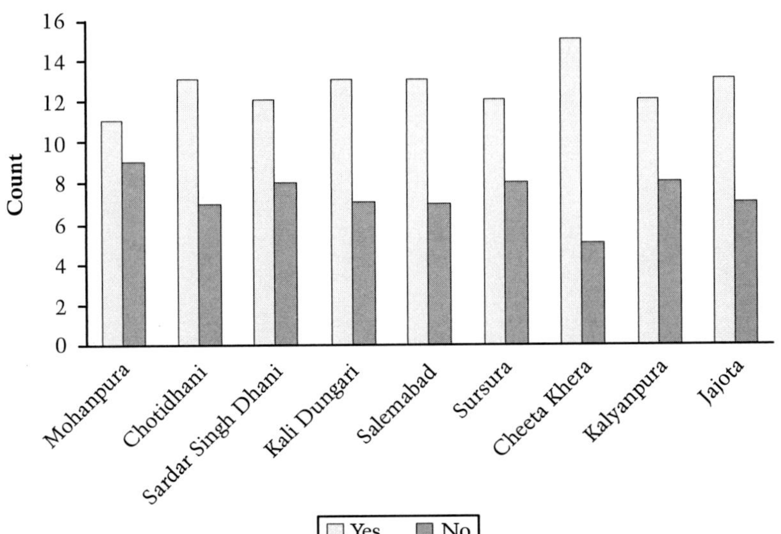

Figure 5

Family Strength versus People Availing Scheme

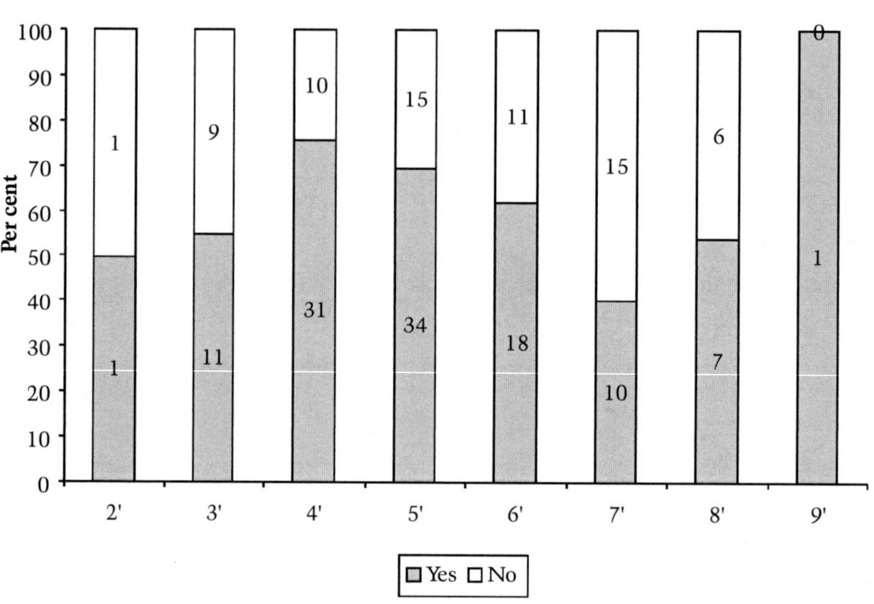

Figure 6

Income Level versus Percentage of People Availing

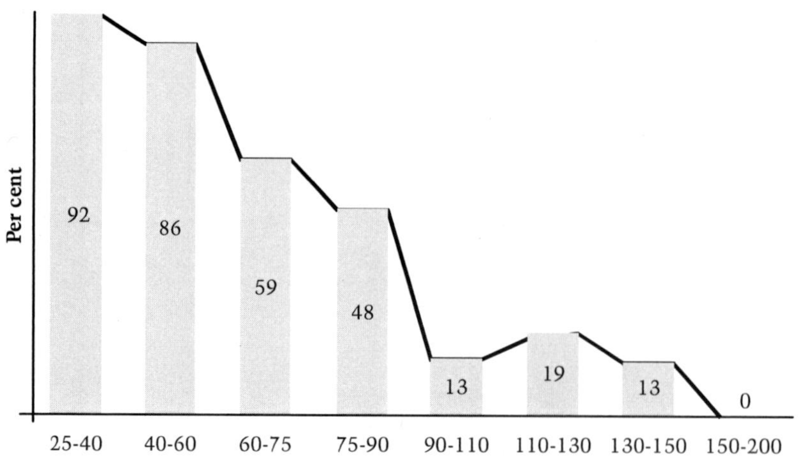

Figure 7

Income Distribution versus Marital Status

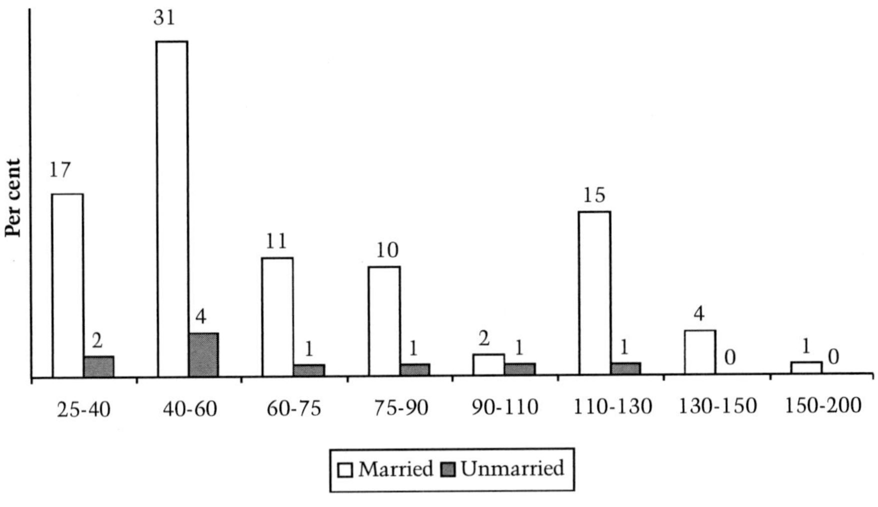

Figure 8

Working Conditions

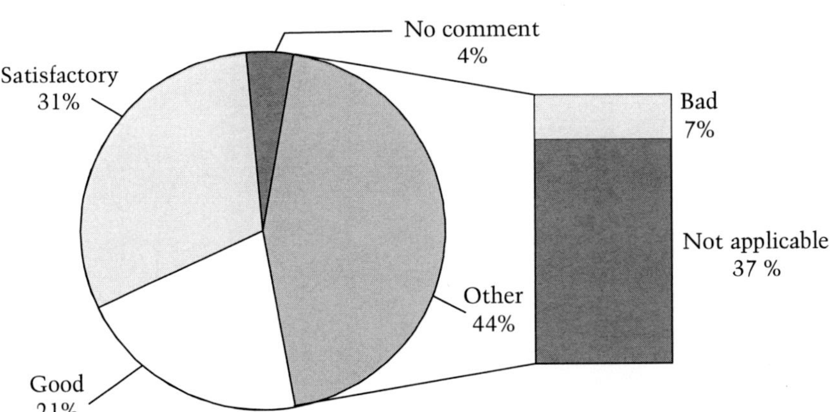

Figure 9

Problem Faced in Getting Job Card

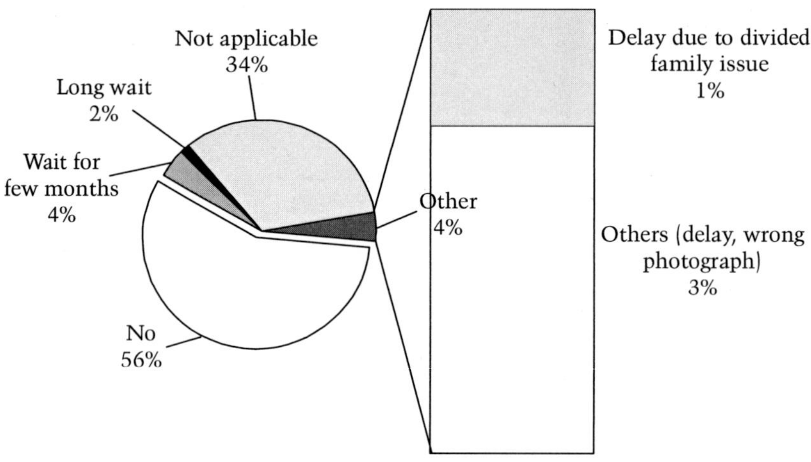

Figure 10

Problem Faced in Getting Job after Job Card

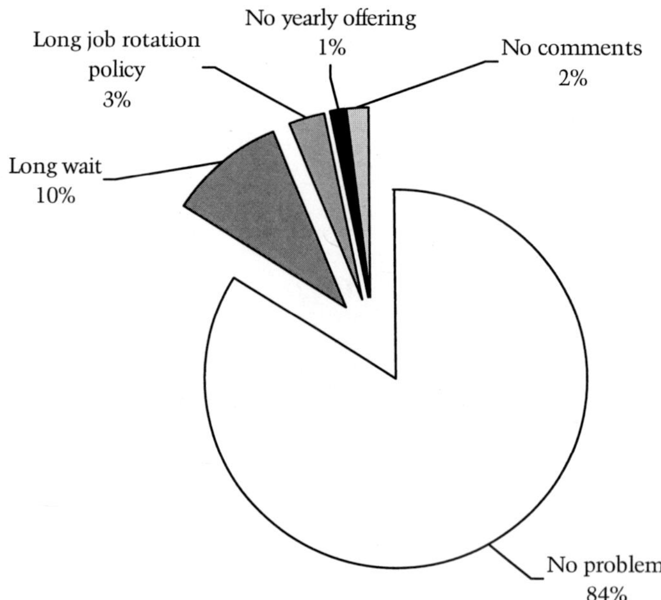

Figure 11

Problem Faced while Drawing Money

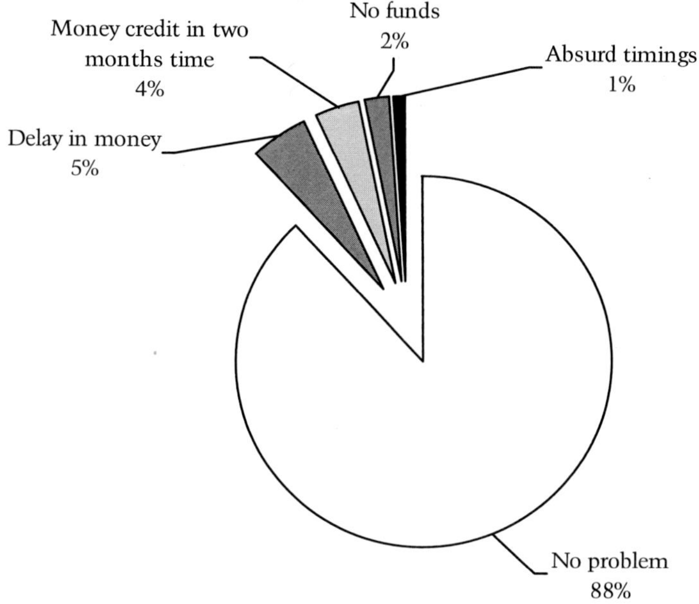

Figure 12

Problem Faced with NREGA Scheme

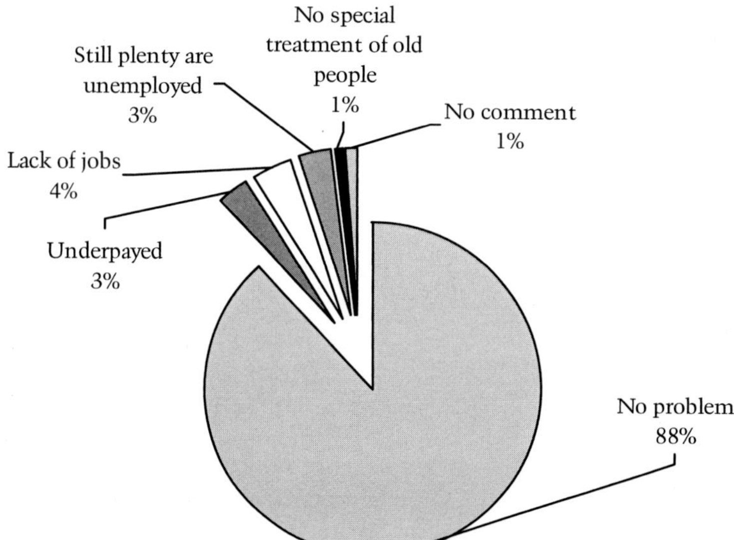

7 Conclusions

This book has established that high rates of growth in India have trickled down in various ways to the poor. Whether this trickle down has been or will be sufficient to get India out of poverty in the foreseeable future is another question. Several commentators especially in India question the trickle down hypothesis (Mazumdar, 2010). The World Bank's estimate of poverty for India has been revised upwards several times. The World Bank estimates India's poverty at 23.6 per cent in 2015. One of the few papers which have argued that India's poverty reduction has been even more impressive than China's is by Chandy and Gertz (2011) of the Brookings Institution in Massachusetts, USA. They argue that on account of India and China's poverty reduction, the MDG goals have already been achieved in 2007 and would half further by 2015. They estimate India's poverty at 7 per cent in 2015. These differing views can in part be attributed to changing definition or method of measurement of poverty. The measurement of poverty is fraught with difficulties as the definition, the recall period and the benchmarks are constantly being revised upwards. This is justified in some senses as with high rates of growth, poverty definitions today should include besides a minimum calorific consumption, also issues such as ability to spend on health and education.

While the different estimates of poverty show different levels of poverty, they all agree that poverty has decreased. This book has tried to establish the trickle down hypothesis through different approaches instead of just looking at the headcount ratio. However while the book argues that poverty has reduced because of high growth rates, it is still stark and glaring inequalities are evident in several sections of society. The emergence of issues such as environmental problems and social tension are beyond the scope of this book, but these are the inevitable fallouts of inequalities in economies such as India. This is because the high rates of growth benefit mainly the rich and the educated while leaving the poor majority far behind. Another issue that the book has not tackled are the macroeconomic aspects such as exchange rates and inflation which could affect poverty adversely. Inflation, particularly food inflation, would have a negative effect on poverty. Inflation in food prices in India particularly after 2008 has become a serious problem.

How Growth can Trickle Down

With all these caveats, the book has tried to go behind the numbers to get an idea of the agents and processes of trickle down that the high growth rates in India have generated. The natural starting point for the India story is to focus on how this growth period was different from others and what were the main drivers of growth. The book begins with an examination of the information technology and telecommunications sector which has seen growth rates upward of 20 per cent for nearly two decades. A back of the envelop calculation shows that their contribution to growth rates was nearly 2-3 per cent of the average 6 per cent growth rate over the last 20 years. This shows that they accounted for nearly one-third to half of the total growth of the Indian economy. The ICT and mobile sector accounts for over 10 per cent of India's GDP and over 30 per cent of India's exports. However the employment potential of this sector is limited, thus the spread effects of a large part of India's growth has been limited. Directly this sector employs less than 0.33 per cent of the labour force, though indirectly it employs over 1 per cent of the labour force. Most of the employment is, however, in the formal private sector. Mobile telephony employs a slightly higher number of over 2 per cent, but all in all employment in this sector is miniscule in comparison to its share of GDP or exports. Given the limited employment both directly and indirectly of the sector, the trickle down effects of necessity would be somewhat limited looking at the numbers.

However, what the IT and telecommunications sector has done indirectly is to change the perceptions of Indians about themselves. The use of ICT while relatively limited at present could become a significant agent of trickle down if it were to become a general purpose technology for the Indian economy. Similarly while mobiles have improved India's connectivity drastically, there is only anecdotal evidence to suggest that it is used to improve productivity. While IT is largely export oriented, a growing share is now being directed to domestic needs. Mobiles are almost exclusively domestically oriented. The multiplier effects of both are high as they employ young people with a high marginal propensity to consume. When both start being used widely for improving the productivity of the economy, its trickle down will accelerate.

To fully realise the potential of ICT and mobile telephony, educational improvements to support not only this sector but also other related sectors (telecom, internet, data processing, etc.) will be required. In short, the e-readiness of states should be improved to assimilate ICT induced improvements in governance which in turn would have a large impact on poverty alleviation. In some sense, improving the e-readiness of states would also help to reduce inter-state disparities and the development of mid-sized towns which is the focus of Chapter 2 on inter-state migration.

While the growth points of India have been focussed on some sectors, they have also been centred geographically. Thus, the states in the south and west of India have grown much more rapidly than those in the east. There is some indication that the states in the east are catching up but by and large there are huge disparities in the growth rates. One way of trickling down the growth from higher growth states to lower growth states is through inter-state migration. The important contribution of migration to poverty alleviation has been recognised in this book. Migration permits the use of flexible labour policies which would help accelerate growth. But there is a need to build on the human skills of migrants so that their remuneration and opportunities increase over time. There is a need to support migrants by improving their access to renumerative work, schooling, health care, training, safe working conditions and adequate housing. The Union Government of India should put in place policies that do not discourage migration and at the same time discourage regional factionalism.

Given that India is a land-scarce country, economic development would involve several forms of urbanisation. As shown in Chapter 2, this would improve productivity and reduce poverty. It is important to note that in India, there is a continuum in terms of population density from remote villages to the large urban centres. The conventional dichotomy of rural *versus* urban areas still seems to dominate development thinking and poverty research and may be less applicable to India. This continuum has to be utilised to improve infrastructure and build mid-sized towns. There is a need to decentralise infrastructure and activities with a view to create new centres of growth that will be able to absorb the rural population influx. Overall while some argue that providing rural employment may have stemmed migration, evidence on this issue is mixed at best. The best policy for dealing with inter-state migration is to improve infrastructure so that strains on overcrowded cities are alleviated. This policy is particularly important as there are indications that rural-urban migration is now acquiring a permanent characteristic and is becoming less seasonal in nature.

How Growth can Trickle Up

While a lot has been made of trickling down growth, in India growth has also trickled up from its vast informal sector. Growth has created opportunities for the informal sector which is reflected through an increase in their employment, wages and reduction in poverty. The most important factor which has led to a decline in poverty through this sector has been through the asset accumulation of this sector. It is important that while markets determine wages and employment, government should be cognisant of the need to devise policy instruments which will develop the capacity of this sector to build assets. Informal sector assets do not merely comprise physical assets but also human capacity development. The book shows that informal sector asset building and incomes are particularly sensitive to easy access to transport facilities and to infrastructure. Government policy should thus focus on infrastructure building. This would also tackle in part the problem of inter-state migration and gender inequity which is also discussed in the book.

The book shows that these interventions would only lead to higher incomes and higher asset formation in the informal sector if and when the rates of growth of the economy are high. So the first and foremost requirement to ensure that growth trickles down is to maintain a high rate of growth in the Indian economy. Along with high growth rates it is necessary to find mechanisms to link formal and informal mechanisms for skill generation and infrastructure provision. This implies that there should be some symmetry between the two sectors in terms of skill generation, access to information on markets, technical know-how and credit. The informal sector can itself be used as a vehicle for the delivery of these services and innovative vocational education mechanisms have to be found to meld formal schooling with on the job training. The Swiss system of education is one example given in the book for such training. It is important to get children trained in some vocations from the age of 12 onwards. This could be combined with some formal schooling, otherwise India is losing its youth to crime, illiteracy and social conflict. Training can take place in the informal sector itself with incremental improvements in productivity and innovation. An overall improvement in infrastructure and organisation can create an enabling environment for credit and improve access to markets. It is important to understand that an overall improvement in the economy in terms of infrastructure, training and credit would have far greater effects on the informal sector than specific policies which target the sector. Both are needed but meshing the micro and macro policies are critical in poverty alleviation through this sector.

The need to meld micro initiatives with overall macro improvements in education and infrastructure would also help improve gender disparities. The book has explored the links between gender equality and economic growth in India. The simple scatter plots presented in this book hint at a positive relationship, as do (somewhat) more sophisticated panel regressions. Yet there is abundant reason to be sceptical of these results: one should never take simple correlations very seriously, and panel regressions are plagued by a number of shortcomings especially the difficulty of establishing causality.

With regard to the macro-level links between gender equality and poverty reduction, the macro correlations are stronger than those for gender equality and growth and more robust to different measures of gender equality. Here, not surprisingly given the easier applicability of the concept of poverty at the micro (household) level, there is more micro research buttressing this link. Ample evidence suggests that greater gender equality in resources such as education, health and access to employment (economic resources) can reduce the likelihood of a household being poor.

While female labour force participation has increased with growth, this increase has been concentrated at higher education levels. This suggests that as economic opportunities increase, educated women are more likely to enter the work force. The policy variable that has emerged as crucially important from the analysis in the book is education. Education is seen to affect both health and access to economic resources.

For policy purposes, two factors stand out in the case of India. One that high growth rates will lead to better gender indicators and reduce gender inequality. Hence, it is first of all crucially important to maintain high rates of economic growth. To accelerate the trickle down effects of growth on poverty, education and particularly vocational education of women should be targetted by government policy. This would also be in keeping with the cultural context of India where women may often prefer home-based employment. Hence, focussing on improving skills and education through the Swiss system of schooling as outlined above is an option that should be explored.

How can Trickle Down and Trickle Up be Assisted

The book has clearly identified the need for two kinds of policies—the first relates to the building of key physical infrastructure and the second to human and social development. The responsibility for building both lies with both the government and the NGOs. The book explores the role of philanthropy in delivering social services. While at this moment the government spends roughly 8.3 per cent of the GDP on the social sector, private philanthropy accounts for less than 1 per cent of the GDP. However, the delivery of public services such as education was in general found to be more effective from the private than the public sector. The differences were, however, not very high.

Nearly 20 per cent of the children aged between 8-14 years attend a private school, or a non-profit organisation. The percentage of children attending philanthropic schools are much higher, closer to 50 per cent in the Northeast, Punjab, Haryana and Kerala. In other states it is closer to 15 per cent, and is the lowest in West Bengal at 3 per cent. The quality of education obtained in philanthropic schools is generally considered better than government schools.

The private sector plays a major role and accounts for about 80 per cent of all primary health care and 40 per cent of tertiary medical care. However, because of lack of a nationwide system of registering either practitioners or institutions providing health care in the private and voluntary sectors, it is difficult to accurately assess the impact and extent of services.

Although many look to the government to improve infrastructure and implement health care, many more turn to provide free clinics and emergency medical treatment. There are believed to be over 7,000 non-profit initiatives providing health care services—from implementing government programmes to providing basic health care or else specific care for diseases like leprosy and cancer. This excludes a host of rural-based voluntary organisations for whom conducting health awareness programmes is a common activity. The corporate sector has opened a number of charitable hospitals like the Escorts Heart Institute and Research Centre in New Delhi, Lupin Human Welfare and Research Foundation which runs an effective TB programme and Tata Memorial Hospital, a premier cancer hospital in Mumbai. Many religious institutions and *mutts* too have started hospitals, mostly incorporated as not-for-profit organisations. Majority of these institutions have a dual policy of collecting high fees from those who could afford and providing concessions or free medicines to the economically weaker groups.

The potential to promote more—and more strategic—social investment in India is tremendous. Perhaps more than most other countries, India is ready and fertile for the infusion of private funds into development initiatives. The Government of India, more than ever before, is ready for partnership and has, in fact, opened up key social sectors to third-sector investment. The challenge before the voluntary sector is to evolve mechanisms and strategies for domestic philanthropy and social investment. Communication and fundraising are two sides of a coin. How effectively the sector positions itself to attract private investment is the challenge for this century. There are fairly diverse philanthropic organisations that address social ills and are competent to champion philanthropic giving. These organisations will, however, need to look keenly at addressing issues of mistrust, accountability, transparency and governance—critical in hampering partnership and investments for development.

On the part of the government too, there are several constraints to good governance in India. Primarily weak institutional norms for the efficient and effective management for public service delivery is responsible for the slow trickle down of Indian economic growth. Improving accountability to beneficiaries in private and civil society organisations is vital for ensuring that growth trickles down to the poor. A management system with internal accountability in government, the private sector and civil society organisations constitutes the basics of any good governance agenda. Unless these organisations have strong control systems, they cannot contribute effectively to good governance.

As long as significant poverty exists in India, and disparity between the rich and the poor widens, private sector especially philanthropy would need to make a contribution to solving the problem. A dialogue must begin between and among business leaders on devising rules for business conduct in deprived communities. The model must consider how poor people can be brought into the mainstream of consumers with sufficient purchasing power within a reasonable time period. Distribution of health and education vouchers should be considered seriously by the Government of India.

To sum up, the process of reform must continue in India in an effective framework of good governance. India has to find dynamic ways of public-private partnerships in the delivery of social services. It has to undertake massive administrative and political reforms to ensure high growth rates and inclusive growth. Inclusive growth is not automatic but small incremental changes and building on success cases of administrative and political reform may be the way forward.

References

Chandy, Laurence and Geoffrey Gertz (2011). "Poverty in Numbers: The Changing State of Global Poverty from 2005 to 2015", *Global Views, Policy Brief* 2011/1. Brookings: Global Economy and Development.

Mazumdar, Surajit (2010). "On the Sustainability of India's Non-Inclusive Growth", *Working Paper* 2010/12. New Delhi: Institute for Studies in Industrial Development.